A WRITER'S WORLD

A Writer's World

Travels 1950–2000

JAN MORRIS

faber and faber

First published in 2003
by Faber and Faber Limited
3 Queen Square London WC1N 3AU

Typeset by Faber and Faber Limited
Printed in England by Mackays of Chatham plc,
Chatham, Kent

All pictures reproduced by kind permission of
Magnum Photos:

1950s – Egypt, Cairo
         © Henry Carter-Bresson / Magnum Photos
1960s – Moscow, Saint-Basile
         © Burt Glinn / Magnum Photos
1970s – India, Delhi
         © John Vink / Magnum Photos
1980s – Germany, Berlin
         © Guy Le Querrec / Magnum Photos
1990s – Australia, Sydney
         © Trent Parke / Magnum Photos

Also, thanks to Sickle Moon Books for
permission to reproduce the essay on
Oman (p.40) and Viking Press for the
essay on Romania (p.411).

A CIP record for this book
is available from the British Library

ISBN 0–571–21524–6

10 9 8 7 6 5 4 3 2 1

To the Honour of Wales
Er Anrhydedd Cymru

Contents

The 1970s

The 1980s

The 1990s

Prologue: Is that the Truth?

A Writer's World samples a half-century, peripatetically. It selects its subjects as it goes along. Its title may perhaps imply a more considered and objective work, the sort of memoir in which a philosophically minded novelist might reflect upon his times, or a retired columnist from a quality broadsheet. Do not be deceived. This portfolio of my reports and essays is something much less measured and inclusive. It does indeed mirror the progress of the world during five decades, but in a much showier way. It is more in the nature of an exhibition or a performance, and is at least as much about the writer as it is about the world. It begins with a bit of a bang, and if it ends more modestly, well, fifty years of a writing and wandering life would make most people a little quieter in the end. Even the thrush sings with careless rapture only when the day is young.

The book covers the second half of the twentieth century, from the 1950s to the 1990s, from the aftermath of the Second World War to the end of the millennium. I am tempted to say, of course, as is the custom, that this was a fateful segment of history, but it was probably no more fateful than any other. In fact the spirit of my half-century was perhaps happier than most, and more optimistic. It was the period of the Cold War, it is true, when the capitalist and communist segments of humanity were locked in implacable suspicion, and there were many other public anxieties too. Minor armed conflicts frequently occurred. The prospect of nuclear extermination obsessed some people, the inexorable spread of the drug culture disturbed many more. The environment was becoming cruelly polluted. The cursed plague of Aids appeared. Poverty and even famine was endemic in some parts of the world, and globalization began to set in – which meant, in effect, the ever-increasing Americanization of the planet. The movement of peoples around the globe, which had become so much easier, raised generally unforeseen problems, and the growth of the world's population cast shadows over susceptibly prophetic temperaments.

But if it all sounds frightful, there was much to make up for the fear and misery. For example there was the retreat of the European empires from their vast dominions around the world. This was not always beneficial in the particular, and the process was marred by many conflicts, but in the general it was a wholesome recognition that no nation had the right to claim sovereignty over another. The United Nations, though all too frequently impotent, was at least a token of intended fraternity. Organized religion was losing its more primitive grip upon the peoples of the West, while in the East Islam seemed on the whole a noble force for order, and for many Buddhism was the true light of the world. Communism, the God That Fails, was finally discredited in the course of my half-century, and the squabbling states of Europe appeared to be moving towards unity at last. Ecological degradation led to much greater interest in the state of nature. If half the world's population was as poor as ever, the other half was unprecedentedly prosperous. And mankind's first penetration of space seemed to foreshadow, at least in the early years, wonderful fulfilments to come.

In general, in large parts of the world, people were more tolerant, kinder, more generous than they had been before the Second World War. I seldom felt threatened, wherever I wandered, and was hardly ever robbed. We still thought – I did, at least – that on the whole mankind was in hopeful progress, fitfully moving towards a happier denouement, however unlikely it sometimes seemed. Traces of Victorian optimism lingered, I suppose, and it was possible still to believe in Teilhard de Chardin's theory of in-furling, a process by which, almost imperceptibly, all the races were moving towards some ultimate reconciliation.

These were my own responses, anyway, my own conceptions of my own zeitgeist. This is how I felt about my world. I was twenty-four years old at the start of the 1950s, seventy-four at the end of the 1990s, so the passage of the globe described in this book is the passage of a life, too, from the twilight of adolescence to the dawn of senility. All its judgements, unreliable enough in any case, are coloured by the grand change of life from youth to old age – in some ways such a majestic progress for all of us, but in others weakened by finicky shifts in ways of thought and changes of mind. Few of us are consistent in our opinions and values for fifty years, and we are affected not only by experience and maturation, but by moods, fickle tastes, boredom and personal circumstance.

I was not often profoundly involved in the matters this book describes. I am by nature an outsider, by profession an onlooker, by inclination a loner, and I have spent my life looking at things and happenings, and observing their effect upon my own particular sensibility. It has not generally been an introspective life, but in one respect self-examination did obsess me. Since childhood I had been irrationally convinced that I had been born into the wrong body, and should really be a woman. Coping with this mystery, during the four years I spent in the British Army, and the ten in which I worked as a foreign correspondent, did require a degree of introspection, not to say deception: when I finally solved the conundrum by completing what is vulgarly known as a sex change, becoming Jan instead of James, I felt a sense of liberation which some critics have claimed to find apparent in my writing (if you would be amused to judge for yourselves, the final metamorphosis occurs on page 209). Such a theatrical episode does not often provide a centrepiece for reflective collections, and it does not really provide one here, either, because it was always overshadowed for me by a constancy of love and personal happiness which was far more influential upon my style than any simple change of sex.

Anyway, as fledgling and as veteran, as man and as woman, as journalist and as aspirant littérateur, throughout my half-century I peregrinated the world and wrote about it. I began as a reporter, having been persuaded (chiefly by American examples) that journalism was a proper avenue into literature. I joined *The Times* of London from Oxford, and almost immediately began my vagrant life, presently gravitating to what was then the *Manchester Guardian*. These two characterful newspapers, then at the height of their fame, prestige and varied idiosyncrasy, not only allowed me to treat the writing of news dispatches more or less as the writing of essays, but also gave me a grandstand view of events, which disgracefully boosted my ego. In no time at all I was pontificating about humanity's problems, and advising states and nations how to solve them. As Max Beerbohm said of himself and Oxford, it was *The Times* and the *Guardian* that made me insufferable, and I am grateful to them still.

If I was an aspirant littérateur, I was also an aspirant anarchist. I have disliked Authority always, though sometimes seduced by its resplendence. When I was writing for newspapers this prejudice sometimes invigorated and sometimes inhibited my journalism, but by the middle of the 1960s I had freed myself from all employers anyway, and wandered on my own. I had become precociously soured by the great world, and no longer wanted my writing to be pegged to the day's news. For the rest of the century I was engaged chiefly in writing books, enabling the process by selling travel essays to magazines, mostly American, to keep my family from destitution. I had worked for only two newspapers, but during the last four decades of the century I wrote for dozens of magazines in the English language, and produced some thirty-five books of my own.

Start to finish, adolescent reportage to ageing attempts at literature, I travelled through all the inhabited continents in the course of my half-century, observing some of the historical events of the time, describing most of the world's great cities, sampling many of its cultures, feeling in my bones some of its epochal changes and recording always its influences upon myself. I had a marvellous time of it, and I hope that, however nonsensical my judgements or distasteful my self-indulgences, at least some of my life's delight will have infected my prose.

This, then, is the substance of my performance. The pieces in this book all concern travel to one end or another. They appear almost as they did when they were first printed, however immaturely they read now, except for cuts here and there when they get boring, or take up too much room. I have added elucidatory comments sometimes, and allowed myself a modicum of literary rather than reportorial afterthought (for example I think I used to overdo the use of the semi-colon, and I have grown to dislike my youthful practice of calling a city 'she', like a ship). I have dropped passages of straight description which seem to me superfluous now that all readers of books have been everywhere themselves. Sometimes the writing is less politically correct than would be demanded now, and sometimes my attitudes of long ago are embarrassing. If the chronology is occasionally hazy, that is partly because history wilfully declines to organize itself by decades, partly because my memory has grown hazy too, but chiefly because I have never attached much importance to dates. I have included very little about my own country, Wales, but believe me, between the lines of almost every piece in the book something of Cymru lurks and smiles, like a Green Man on a misericord.

As a reflection of the world's half-century the selection may often be misleading or naïve, but that is beside its real point. I was writing about the world, certainly, but it was *my* world – as I put it myself in another context: 'Is that the truth? Is that how it was? It is *my* truth. If it is not invariably true in the fact, it is true in the imagination.'

The 1950s

This was the first of the postwar decades, when the world was still getting its breath back after the cataclysm of the Second World War. In a Europe half shattered by the conflict Soviet forces still dominated the eastern part of the continent, and American armies were stationed throughout the west, while both powers sent their first satellites into space. A defeated Japan was steadily regaining some national assurance under the compulsory tutelage of the United States; communist China was emerging as a potential rival to the Soviet Union. Elsewhere events were dominated by the protracted abdication of the British Empire, for so long a principal arbiter of the world's affairs. India and Pakistan were flexing their muscles in their first heady years of national independence, and in the Middle East Arabs and Israelis, released from British restraint, brooded over each other's futures.

It was a euphoric decade in many ways, though, and not least for the British, who basked in the glory of recent victory, however impoverished it had left them, and still thought of themselves as uniquely privileged among nations. I was particularly preoccupied during these years with the steady withdrawal of their power and influence from around the world, and I spent the decade reporting for their two most distinguished newspapers: first The Times of London, which considered itself the greatest newspaper on earth, and later the Manchester Guardian, which considered itself the most enlightened.

1

Everest 1953

*My professional life really began with an imperial exploit. On 29 May 1953
Mount Everest, Chomolungma, the supreme mountain of the world, was
climbed for the first time by Sir John Hunt's British expedition, including
two New Zealanders, a famous Sherpa mountaineer from the Everest
foothill country and a team of Sherpa high-altitude porters. I went with
them on behalf of* The Times, *as the only reporter with the expedition, and
the experience provided me with my one great scoop (as we called it in
those days). The ascent was the last such achievement of the British
Empire, and it was capped by the circumstance that my report of it was
published in London on 2 June 1953, the very morning of the coronation of
Queen Elizabeth II – the start, as it was fondly thought then, of a new
Elizabethan age.*

*On the afternoon of 30 May I was with Hunt and most of the climbers
some 22,000 feet up in the Western Cwm, awaiting the return of the New
Zealander Edmund Hillary and the Sherpa Tenzing Norkay from their
attempt upon the summit. We didn't yet know whether they had got there.*

'There they are!'

I rushed to the door of the tent, and there emerging from a little gully, not
more than 500 yards away, were four worn figures in windproof clothing.
As a man we leapt out of the camp and up the slope, our boots sinking and
skidding in the soft snow, Hunt wearing big dark snow-goggles, Gregory
with the bobble on the top of his cap jiggling as he ran, Bourdillon with
braces outside his shirt, Evans with the rim of his hat turned up in front like
an American stevedore's. Wildly we ran and slithered up the snow, and the
Sherpas, emerging excitedly from their tents, ran after us.

I could not see the returning climbers very clearly, for the exertion of
running had steamed up my goggles, so that I looked ahead through a
thick mist. Down they tramped, mechanically, and up we raced, trembling
with expectation. Soon I couldn't see a thing for the steam, so I pushed up

the goggles from my eyes; and just as I recovered from the sudden dazzle of the snow I caught sight of George Lowe, leading the party down
the hill. He was raising his arm and waving as he walked! It was thumbs
up! Everest was climbed! Hillary brandished his ice axe in weary triumph;
Tenzing slipped suddenly sideways, recovered and shot us a brilliant
white smile; and they were among us, back from the summit, with men
pumping their hands and embracing them, laughing, smiling, crying,
taking photographs, laughing again, crying again, till the noise and
delight of it all rang down the Cwm and set the Sherpas, following us up
the hill, laughing in anticipation.

As Tenzing approached them they stepped forward, one by one, to
congratulate him. He received them like a modest prince. Some bent their
heads forward, as if in prayer. Some shook hands lightly and delicately, the
fingers scarcely touching. One veteran, his black twisted pig-tail flowing
behind him, bowed gravely to touch Tenzing's hand with his forehead.

We moved into the big dome tent and sat around the summit party
throwing questions at them, still laughing, still unable to believe the truth.
Everest was climbed, and those two mortal men in front of us, sitting on
old boxes, had stood upon its summit, the highest place on earth! And
nobody knew but us! The day was still dazzlingly bright – the snow so
white, the sky so blue; and the air was still so vibrant with excitement;
and the news, however much we expected it, was still somehow such a
wonderful surprise – shock waves of that moment must still linger there in
the Western Cwm, so potent were they, and so gloriously charged with
pleasure.

*International competition for the news was intense, so I scuttled down the
mountain that same evening, and by skulldug means sent my first report of
the ascent off to London. When two days later I followed it away from
Everest with my Sherpa helpers, I did not know whether I had secured my
scoop, or whether the news had been intercepted and the story filched by
some competitor even more unscrupulous than I was myself.*

It was the evening of 1 June. The air was cool and scented. Pine trees were
all about us again, and lush foliage, and the roar of the swollen Dudh Khosi
rang in our ears. On the west bank of the river there was a Sherpa hamlet
called Benkar. There, as the dusk settled about us, we halted for the night.
In the small square clearing among the houses Sonam set up my tent, and

I erected the aerial of my radio receiver. The Sherpas, in their usual way, marched boldly into the houses round about and established themselves among the straw, fires and potatoes of the upstairs rooms. Soon there was a smell of roasting and the fragrance of tea. As I sat outside my tent meditating, with only a few urchins standing impassively in front of me, Sonam emerged with a huge plate of scrawny chicken, a mug of *chang* (a sort of alcoholic porridge), tea, chocolate and chupattis.

How far had my news gone? I wondered as I ate. Was it already winging its way to England from Katmandu, or was it still plodding over the Himalayan foothills? Would tomorrow, 2 June, be both Coronation and Everest Day? Or would the ascent fall upon London later, like a last splendid chime of the Abbey bells? There was no way of knowing; I was alone in a void; the chicken was tough, the urchins unnerving. I went to bed.

But the morning broke fair. Lazily, as the sunshine crept up my sleeping-bag, I reached a hand out of my mummied wrappings towards the knob of the wireless. A moment of fumbling; a few crackles and hisses; and then the voice of an Englishman.

Everest had been climbed, he said. Queen Elizabeth had been given the news on the eve of her coronation. The crowds waiting in the wet London streets had cheered and danced to hear of it. After thirty years of endeavour, spanning a generation, the top of the earth had been reached and one of the greatest of adventures accomplished. This news of Coronation Everest (said that good man in London) had been first announced in a copyright dispatch in *The Times*.

I jumped out of my bed, spilling the bedclothes about me, tearing open the tent flap, leaping into the open in my filthy shirt, my broken boots, my torn trousers. My face was thickly bearded, my skin cracked with sun and cold, my voice hoarse. But I shouted to the Sherpas, whose bleary eyes were appearing from the neighbouring windows:

'Chomolungma finished! Everest done with! All OK!'

'OK, sahib,' the Sherpas shouted back. 'Breakfast now?'

It has often been suggested that The Times *delayed publication of the news of the ascent in order to make it coincide with the Coronation. What a canard! We had no long-distance radios on Everest, and I nearly killed myself slithering down the mountain to get the news home in time. To safeguard my scoop I put the message in a code. I had devised it simply for a final announcement of success, and this is how it read: SNOW CONDITIONS BAD (= summit reached) ADVANCED BASE ABANDONED (= Hillary) AWAITING IMPROVE-MENT (= Tenzing) ALL WELL (= nobody hurt).*

My dispatch reached the paper safely, although it didn't make the front page because it was another thirteen years before news stories were printed on the front page of The Times. *Nor was it exclusive for long, because the editor magnanimously decided to print it in the first edition of the night's paper, thus allowing all others to copy it. Stories were published anonymously in those days, so I got no by-line, and it was three years before I was able to publish a book about the adventure:* Coronation Everest.

When we returned to London from Nepal we were invited to a celebratory dinner at Lancaster House, the government's official place of entertainment. I found myself sitting next to the major-domo of the occasion, a delightful elderly courtier of old-school charm, while opposite me sat Tenzing Norkay, away from Asia for the first time in his life. The old gentleman turned to me half-way through the meal and told me that the claret we were drinking was the very last of its particularly good vintage from the cellars of Lancaster House, and possibly the last anywhere in the world. He hoped I was enjoying it. I was much impressed, and looked across the table to Tenzing, who most certainly was. He had probably never tasted wine before, and he was radiant with the pride and pleasure of the occasion – a supremely stylish and exotic figure. The lackeys respectfully filled and re-filled his glass, and presently my neighbour turned to me once more. 'Oh, Mr Morris,' he said in his silvery Edwardian cadence, 'how very good it is to see that Mr Tenzing knows a decent claret when he has one.'

2

A Benign Republic: USA

After Everest I went to the United States for the first time, on a year's Commonwealth Fellowship. America was still in a condition of benign exhilaration, rich and confident after its victories in the Second World War, but as unaccustomed to foreign visitors as we were unfamiliar with it. I travelled the entire country, sending dispatches to The Times *throughout, and when it came to writing a report for my patrons I presented them with my first book,* Coast to Coast. *Its opening chapter, about Manhattan, was in effect the first essay I ever wrote about a city.*

Manhattan

Suddenly in the distance there stand the skyscrapers, shimmering in the sun, like monuments in a more antique land. A little drunk from the sight, you drive breathlessly into the great tunnel beneath the Hudson River. You must not drive faster than thirty-five miles an hour in the tunnel, nor slower than thirty, so that you progress like something in an assembly line, soullessly; but when you emerge into the daylight, then a miracle occurs, a sort of daily renaissance, a flowering of the spirit. The cars and trucks and buses, no longer confined in channels, suddenly spring away in all directions with a burst of engines and black clouds of exhaust. At once, instead of discipline, there is a profusion of enterprise. There are policemen shouting and gesticulating irritably, men pushing racks of summer frocks, trains rumbling along railway lines, great liners blowing their sirens, dowdy dark-haired women with shopping bags and men hurling imprecations out of taxi windows, shops with improbable Polish names and huge racks of strange newspapers; bold colours and noises and indefinable smells, skinny cats and very old dustcarts and bus drivers with patient weary faces. Almost before you know it, the mystique of Manhattan is all around you.

* * *

Everyone has read of the magical glitter of this place, but until you have been here it is difficult to conceive of a city so sparkling that at any time Mr Fred Astaire might quite reasonably come dancing his urbane way down Fifth Avenue. It is a marvellously exuberant city, even when the bitter winds of the fall howl through its canyons. The taxi-drivers talk long and fluently, about pogroms in old Russia, about Ireland in its bad days, about the Naples their fathers came from. The waiters urge you to eat more, you look so thin. The girl in the drug store asks pertly but very politely if she may borrow the comic section of your newspaper. On the skating rink at Rockefeller Center there is always something pleasant to see: pretty girls showing off their pirouettes, children staggering about in helpless paroxysms, an eccentric sailing by with a look of profoundest contempt upon his face, an elderly lady in tweeds excitedly arm-in-arm with an instructor.

Boundless vivacity and verve are the inspiration of this city. In its mid-town streets, away from slums and dingy suburbs, you are in a world of spirited movement and colour. The best of the new buildings are glass eyries, gay as cream cakes. One structure on Park Avenue has a garden for its ground floor and a slab of green glass for its superstructure. A bank on Fifth Avenue has creepers growing from its ceiling, and the passer-by, looking through its huge plate-glass windows, can see the black round door of its strongroom. Outside a nearby typewriter shop a real typewriter is mounted on a pedestal, for anyone to try. Once when I passed at two in the morning an old man with a ragged beard was typing with hectic concentration, as if he had just run down from the garret with a thrilling new formula or a message from the outer galaxies.

The traffic swirls through New York like a rather slobby mixture running through a cake-mould. Some seventy-five years ago an observer described New York traffic as being 'everywhere close-spread, thick-tangled (yet no collisions, no trouble) with masses of bright colour, action and tasty toilets'. The description is not so far from the mark today, and the colours especially are still bright and agreeable. The women are not afraid of colour in their clothes, the shop windows are gorgeous, the cars are painted with a peacock dazzle. From upstairs the streets of Manhattan are alive with shifting colours.

Sometimes, as you push your way through the brisk crowds ('*Pardon me, I hope I haven't snagged your nylons*') there will be a scream of sirens and a little procession of official cars will rush by, pushing the traffic out of its way, crashing the lights with complacent impunity, on its way to the Waldorf or City Hall. The motor-cycle policemen, hunched on their machines, look merciless but are probably very kind to old ladies. The reception committee, in dark coats and Homburgs, is excessively official. In the recesses of the grandest car can be seen the distinguished visitor, opera singer or statesman or bronzed explorer, shamefully delighted at being able to ignore the traffic rules.

There is a row of hansom cabs at the corner of Central Park, each with its coal heater (if it is winter), each tended by an elderly gentleman in a top hat, the horses a little thin, the wheels a little wobbly. Lovers find them convenient for bumpy dalliances in the park. If you wander down to the waterside on either side of the island you may stand in the shadow of an ocean liner, or watch a tug (with a high curved bridge, a nonchalant skipper and an air of Yankee insolence) steaming under the black girders of Brooklyn Bridge. Outside Grand Central Station, through a grille beneath your feet, you may see the gleaming metal of a Chicago express down in the bowels; you could live permanently in Grand Central without ever seeing a train, for they are all secreted below in carpeted dungeons.

The stores of Manhattan bulge with the good things of the earth, with a splendour that outclasses those perfumed Oriental marts of fable. 'Ask for anything you like,' says the old waiter at the Waldorf-Astoria with pardonable bombast, 'and if we haven't got it we'll send down the road for it.' Furs in the windows shine with an icy distinction. Dresses are magnificent from Paris, or pleasantly easy-going in the American manner. There are shoes for every conceivable size; books for the most esoteric taste; pictures and treasures summoned from every age and every continent; foods of exotic delight; little dogs of unlikely breed; refrigerators already stocked with edibles; haughty Rolls-Royces; toys of dizzy ingenuity; endless and enchanting fripperies; anything, indeed, that fancy can demand or money buy. It is a storehouse of legendary wonder, such as only our age could stock. What a prize it would be for some looting army of barbarians, slashing their way through its silks and satins, ravishing its debutantes, gorging themselves in its superb French restaurants!

Yet so obvious and dramatic are the extremes of New York that you still see many beggars about its streets. They stand diffidently on the sidewalks, decently dressed but coatless, asking civilly for help before they leave the bright lights and go home for the night to their doss-houses. They are ambassadors from another Manhattan: the countless gloomy streets where Negroes and Puerto Ricans, Poles and poor Italians live in unhappy neighbourhood, fighting their old battles and despising one another. A suggestion of ill-temper, resentment or disgruntlement often sours the tastes of New York, and it is an unpleasant thing to see the current crime register in a Harlem police station. Page succeeds page in terrible succession, thronged with stabbings and rapes, robberies and assaults, acts of lunatic spite or repellent perversion. 'Well,' you say as casually as you can, a little shaken by this vast superfluity of Sunday journalism, 'Well, and how many weeks of crime do these pages represent?' The police sergeant smiles tolerantly. 'That's today's register,' he says.

America is the land acquisitive, and few Americans abandon the search for wealth, or lose their admiration for those who find it. Unassimilated New Yorkers, the millions of un-Americans in this city, however poor or desolate they seem, however disappointed in their dreams, still loyally respect the American idea – the chance for every man to achieve opulence. Sometimes the sentiment has great pathos. An old man I once met in a cheap coffee-shop near the East River boasted gently, without arrogance, of the fabulous wealth of New York, for all the world as if its coffers were his, and all its luxuries, instead of a grey bed-sitting room and a coat with frayed sleeves. He said: 'Why, the garbage thrown away in this city every morning – *every morning* – would feed the whole of Europe for a week.' He said it without envy and with a genuine pride of possession, and a number of dusty demolition men sitting near by nodded their heads in proud and wondering agreement.

All the same, it is sometimes difficult to keep one's social conscience in order among the discrepancies of Manhattan. The gulf between rich and poor is so particularly poignant in this capital of opportunity. There is fun and vigour and stimulation in New York's symphony of capitalism – the blazing neon lights, the huge bright office blocks, the fine stores and friendly shop assistants – and yet there is something distasteful about a pleasure-drome so firmly based upon personal advantage. Everywhere there are nagging signs that the life of the place is inspired by a self-interest not scrupulously enlightened. 'Learn to take care of others', says a poster urging women to become nurses, 'and you will know how to take care of yourself'. 'The life you save may be your own', says a road-safety advertisement. 'Let us know if you can't keep this reservation', you are told on the railway ticket, 'it may be required by a friend or a business associate of yours'. Faced with such constant reminders, the foreign visitor begins to doubt the altruism even of his benefactors. Is the party really to give him pleasure, or is the host to gain some obscure credit from it? The surprise present is very welcome, but what does its giver expect in return? Soon he is tempted to believe that any perversion of will or mind, any ideological wandering, any crankiness, any jingoism is preferable to so constant an obsession with the advancement of self.

But there, Manhattan is a haven for the ambitious, and you must not expect its bustling rivalries to be too saintly. Indeed you may as well admit that the whole place is built on greed, in one degree or another; even the city churches, grotesquely Gothic or Anglican beyond belief, have their thrusting social aspirations. What is wonderful is that so much that is good and beautiful has sprung from such second-rate motives. There are palaces of great pictures in New York, and millions go each year to see them. Each week a whole page of the *New York Times* is filled with concert announcements. There are incomparable museums, a lively theatre, great publishing houses, a famous university. The *Times* itself ('All the News that's Fit to Print') is a splendid civic ornament, sometimes mistaken, often dull, but never bitter, cheap or malicious.

And the city itself, with its sharp edges and fiery colours, is a thing of beauty; especially seen from above, with Central Park startlingly green among the skyscrapers, with the tall towers of Wall Street hazy in the distance, with the two waterways blue and sunny and the long line of an Atlantic liner slipping away to sea. It is a majestic sight, with no Wordsworth at hand to honour it, only a man with a loudspeaker or a fifty-cent guide book.

So leaving Manhattan is like retreating from a snow summit. The very air seems to relax about you. The electric atmosphere softens, the noise stills, the colours blur and fade, the pressure eases, the traffic thins. Soon you are out of the city's spell, pausing only to look behind, over the tenements and marshes, to see the lights of the skyscrapers riding the night.

Of course Manhattan greatly changed in the course of the century, from its cab drivers to its crime rate, but the responses it sparked in me in 1953 did not much alter, and I have been there every single year since.

The South

My first experiences of the American South left me less buoyant. I happened to be in Atlanta the day after the Supreme Court in Washington declared, in the seminal Brown v. Board of Education *decision, that racial segregation in state schools was illegal.*

* * *

When the decision was announced all the simmering discontent of the white Southerners boiled over in bitter words. I spent the day listening to angry men and women. The abuse they used was at once so theatrical and so repetitive that I could scarcely believe it had not been plucked wholesale from some common phrase-book of prejudice. I joined a conversation, in a coffee-shop, with the manager of the place and a man who told me he was a senior officer of the police. They spent some minutes reminiscing about race riots of the past, talking comfortably of 'niggers' baited and beaten in the streets, and of one especially, hounded by the mob, who had thrown himself into the doorway of that very coffee-shop, only to be pushed back on to the pavement. 'The only place for a nigger,' said the manager with finality, 'is at the back door, with his hat in his hand.'

Other, gentler Atlantans, as horrified as anyone by these expressions of brutality, advocated other ways of sustaining white supremacy. Drugged by the sentimentality of the Old South, they would say, like sanctimonious jailers: 'Leave the matter to us. We understand the Negroes, and they understand and respect us. After all, we've lived together for a long time. We know them through and through, and believe me, their minds are different from ours. Leave it all to us. *The South takes care of its own.*' If I were a Southern Negro, I think I would prefer, on the whole, the loud-mouthed to the soft-spoken.

As to the country Negroes, they seem identical still with those pictures in old prints of the slave-owning times; still toiling half-naked in the fields, still addicted to colour and gaudy ornaments, still full of song, still ignorant and unorganized; a people of bondage, infinitely pitiful. Few of them appear to think deeply about their social status, but they reflect it often enough in a sad apathy. I talked once with a Negro farmer in Alabama, and asked him if things were getting any better for the coloured people. 'Things ain't gettin' no better, suh,' he said, 'and things ain't gettin' no worse. They jess stay the same. Things can't ever get no better for the coloured people, not so long as we stay down here.'

The nature of the region itself contributes to the oppressive quality of the South. It is, generally speaking, a wide, dry, dusty, spiritless country; sometimes hauntingly beautiful, but usually melancholy; lacking robustness, good cheer, freshness, animation; a singularly un-Dickensian country. As you drive through South Carolina (for example) on a summer day the endless cotton fields engulf you. Here and there are shabby villages, dusty and derelict, with patched wooden buildings and rusting advertisements, and with a few dispirited people, white and black, gathered around the stores. Outside the unpainted houses of the poor whites there are often decrepit cars, and washing machines stand among the cluttered objects on the verandas. Sometimes there is a little white church with a crooked steeple. There are frequent swamps, dark and mildewy, with gloomy trees standing in water. The plantation mansions are sometimes magnificent, but often in depressingly bad repair.

I called at one such house for a talk with its owner, and found it no more than a sad echo of a munificent past. Three generations ago the Parker plantation embraced some 10,000 acres, and was one of the great estates of the region. Now it is whittled down to about 150 acres, of cotton, tobacco, sweet potatoes and corn. The drive up to the house is a narrow one between pine trees, unpaved; a cloud of dust rose up behind us as we drove along it. Near the road there were a couple of small wooden shacks, one of them inhabited, for there was a string of washing outside it, the other filled to the eaves with straw; and far at the end of the drive stood the big house, crumbling and classical. It had a wide and splendid porch, with four pillars. Mrs Parker thought that only Washington or Thomas Jefferson could really do justice to it, but I felt myself better qualified to sit there when I noticed that its broad steps were rickety, that the frame of its front door was sagging, and that high in its roof there was a dormant wasps' nest. Inside, the house was agreeably untidy; in the hall, which ran clean through the building front to back, there was an elderly harmonium, with a large hymn book propped on its music stand.

The planter, fresh from a tussle with his tractor, had greasy hands and wore a toupee and an open-necked shirt. But like most Southern gentlemen he had a talent for hospitality, and soon we were sitting on the balustrade of the porch, sipping long cool drinks and looking out through the pines. He told me that he ran the plantation almost single-handedly, with only a single full-time employee. His children go to the local public school and his wife does the housework. The five cabins on the estate are let to Negro families whose men work elsewhere, and 'The Street', the double row of uniform cottages where the slaves used to live, is empty and tumble-down.

While we were talking on the porch a great cloud of dust approached us from the drive, and there emerged in stately motion two large mules. They were pulling a kind of sledge, a cross between a bobsleigh and

13

Cleopatra's barge, and sitting on it, very old and wrinkled, very dignified, was a Negro in a straw hat. Round the corner he came in imperial state, the mules panting, the sledge creaking, the dust billowing all round us; and as he passed the porch he raised his hat by its crown and called: 'G'd evening, boss, sir; g'd evening, Missus Parker.' 'Good evening, Uncle Henry,' they replied.

Chicago

I travelled to Chicago on the Twentieth Century Limited *from New York, and remembered the nineteenth-century English visitor who was told, as he rode his train into the city: 'Sir, Chicago ain't no sissy town.' This impertinent piece about the Chicago of 1953 was the first of several – I was to write a new essay about the city in each subsequent decade of the century.*

On my first evening I was taken down to the waterfront to see the lights of the city. Behind us Lake Michigan was a dark and wonderful void, speckled with the lights of steamers bringing iron ore from Duluth or newsprint from Canada. Until you have been to Chicago – crossing half a continent to reach it – it is difficult to realize that it is virtually a seaside city. It has its sea-storms and its rolling waves, its sunny bathing beaches, its docks; you can board a ship for Europe in Chicago, and see the flags of many nations at its quays. So wide is the lake, and so oceanic in aspect, that more than once I have been compelled to walk down to its edge and reassure myself that it really contains fresh water, not salt.

So, with this queer land-locked sea behind us, we looked that evening at the city lights. A glittering row of big buildings extends mile upon mile along the lake, brilliantly lit – some of its skyscrapers clean and clear-cut, some surmounted by innumerable pinnacles, turrets and spires, so that the generally functional effect is tempered by a few touches of the baroque. Beside this magnificent row there sweeps the great highway, following the line of the lake, and along it scurries a constant swift stream of lights, with scarcely a pause and scarcely a hesitation, except when some poor unacclimatized woman stalls her engine or loses her way, and is deafened by a blast of protest behind; then the line of lights wavers for a brief moment, until with a roar of engines and a spinning of wheels the traffic diverts itself and races away, leaving the poor lost soul behind, biting her lower lip and having a terrible time with the gears.

For in many ways Chicago is still a heartless city. The incompetent will meet few courtesies in these streets; the flustered will be offered no cooling counsel; it is necessary in life to get places, and to get there fast. Between the buildings that stand like rows of hefty sentinels above the lake, you may see numbers of narrow canyons leading covertly into shadier places behind. The façade of Chicago is supported by no depth of splendour; hidden by its two or three streets of dazzle is a jungle of slums and drab suburbs, a hodge-podge of races and morals.

In the daylight, indeed, the bright glamour even of the business district is not quite so irresistible, if only because of the din and the congestion. This must surely be the noisiest place on earth. The cars roar, the elevated railway rumbles, the policemen blow their strange two-toned whistles, like sea birds lost in a metropolis, the hooters shriek, the horns hoot; the typists, on their way back from coffee, swap their gossip at the tops of their tinny voices. Across the crowded intersections scurry the shoppers, like showers of sheep, while the policemen wave them irritably on and the cars wait to be unleashed. The tempo of Chicago is terrible, and the over-crowding desperate. Just as each new plan to improve the life of the Egyptian peasant is overtaken and swamped by the inexorable march of the birth-rate, so in Chicago every new parking place is obliterated, every freeway blackened, by the constantly growing flood of cars. Each morning the highways into the city are thick with unwearying cars, pounding along head to tail, pouring in by every channel, racing and blaring and roaring their way along, until you think it will be impossible to cram one more car in, so bulging and swelling is the place, so thickly cluttered its streets, so strangled the movement of its traffic. It is good business in Chicago to knock down offices and turn them into parking lots. And it is decidedly unwise for the nervous or over-considerate driver to venture into the turmoil of these streets, for in this respect, as in others, Chicago still ain't no sissy town.

Crime and corruption are still powerful influences here. The Syndicate, the shadowy central office of vice, is still busy, and is said to have its agents in both local political parties. There have been many hundreds of unsolved murders since the days of Al Capone, but most citizens prefer to let such matters slide. People have too much to lose to meddle. The big man may lose a contract, the little man the dubious cooperation of his local police chief or petty boss. Extortion, on many levels, is still a common-place in Chicago. Everyone knows that a five-dollar bill slipped to your examiner may well help you along with your driving test. Everyone knows

15

too, if only by reading the papers, that murders are still terribly frequent; but when I once talked to a senior Chicago police officer on the subject, he adroitly ducked away to the twin topics (for they seem to go arm-in-arm) of traffic congestion and prostitution.

All this sordid unhealthiness would be less intrusive if the city itself were spacious and wholesome of appearance. But despite the illusory grandeur of its lake-front, Chicago is a festering place. From the windows of the elevated railway, which clangs its elderly way through the city with rather the detached hauteur of a Bath chair, you can look down upon its disagreeable hinterland. The different sectors of slumland each have their national character – Italian, Chinese, Puerto Rican, Lithuanian – but externally they merge and mingle in a desolate expanse of depression. Here is a brown brick building, crumbling at its corners, its windows cracked or shattered, its door crooked on its hinges, a Negro woman in frayed and messy blouse leaning from an upstairs window with a comb in her hand. Here an old Italian with long moustaches squats on the steps of a rickety wooden tenement, its weatherboards a grubby white, its balcony railings sagging and broken. Slums are slums anywhere in the world, and there are probably areas just as blighted in Paris or Glasgow; but here the misery of it all is given added poignancy by the circumstances of the citizenry, people of a score of races who came to America to be rich, and have stayed on to live like unpampered animals.

Such a climate of existence has inevitably eaten away like a corrosive at the old blithe and regardless self-confidence of Chicago. Not so long ago Chicagoans were convinced that their city would soon be the greatest and most famous on earth, outranking New York, London and Paris, the centre of a new world, the boss city of the universe. During the period of its fabulous nineteenth-century growth, when millionaires were two a penny and the treasures of the continent were being summoned to Chicago, it was not unnatural for such an eager and unsophisticated community to suppose that the centre of territorial gravity was fast shifting to the Middle West. In a sense, I suppose it has; the railway tracks, the sprawling stock-yards, the factories of Chicago and its sister cities are the sinews of the United States, and so of half the world. But the blindest lover of Chicago would not claim for the place the status of a universal metropolis. Too much of the old grand assertiveness has been lost. Nobody pretends that Chicago has overtaken New York; instead there is a provincial acceptance of inferiority, a resignation, coupled with a mild regret for the old days of brag and beef. For one reason and another, the

16

stream of events generally passes Chicago by. Even the Chicago theatre, once a lively institution, has fallen into dull days, making do with the second run of Broadway productions and a few mildewed and monotonous burlesques. Despite the tumult and the pressure, Chicago sometimes feels like a backwater.

The impression is only partly accurate, for there are many wonderful and exciting things in Chicago. There are magnificent art galleries and splendid libraries. There is a plethora of universities. There is an excellent symphony orchestra. The huge marshalling yards lounge over the countryside, littered with trains. The bridges over the Chicago River open with a fascinating and relentless ease to let the great freighters through. The *Chicago Tribune*, which calls itself the World's Greatest Newspaper, is certainly among the sprightliest. It was for Chicago that Frank Lloyd Wright conceived his last marvellous effrontery, a skyscraper a mile high. It was in a Chicago squash court that Enrico Fermi and his associates achieved the first nuclear chain reaction.

But such driving activity no longer represents the spiritual temper of the city. Chicagoans are still pursued by the demon of progress, and haunted by the vision of possible failure, so that the pressure of their existence is relentless; but the strain of it all, and the persistent rottenness of the place, have blunted some of their old intensity and lavishness of purpose. They have accepted their station in life, no longer swaggering through the years with the endearing braggadocio of their tradition, but more resigned, more passive, even (perhaps) a little disillusioned. Chicago is certainly not a has-been; but it could be described as a might-have-been.

Elsewhere in my book I called the Chicago Tribune *the most inanely prejudiced paper in America, and marvelled that its employees could reconcile themselves to its pervasive malice. 'For this newspaper', retorted the* Tribune *in its review of the book, 'James Morris, 28, has moderate praise, mingled with paternal admonition.'*

Chicago was the first American city I spent any time in. Hardly had I arrived there than I was invited by kindly citizens to stay with them in their house in one of the suburbs. I gratefully accepted, and at once found myself embraced in a ceaseless sequence of cocktail parties, receptions, lavish dinners and lakeside picnics. If this was the United States, I thought in my naïveté, it was certainly a great place, where the martinis flowed like water and hospitality never flagged. Only gradually did I realize that Lake Forest in 1953 was not simply the richest and grandest suburb in Chicago, but probably in the entire republic – if not the world!

The Rocket

Here is a last image from the United States of 1954 which captured my imagination then, and has never relinquished its grip – the image of the great American train.

It was the railroads that made the West, and for me it is still the great trains, rushing by with their huge freights, or streaming past a level-crossing with a flash of white napkins and silver, that best represent the flavour of the place. We lodged one night at a small, cheap, cigar-stained hotel at a typical Western railway town, within sight of the lines, and within sound of the hoarse and throaty voices of the railway porters. During the afternoon the friendly landlord said to me: 'If you like trains, don't miss the *Rocky Mountain Rocket*. The *Rocket* comes through here every evening 8.19 on the minute, and if you like railroads, as I say, it's a sight to see.' At 8.17 or so we crossed the road to the station. There was a little crowd waiting for the *Rocket* – a few travellers, with their bags and buttonholes, a few friends and a motley collection of sightseers like ourselves, some with children, some with shopping bags, some lounging about chewing and occasionally expectorating.

It was dusk, and the lights were coming on. Before long we heard a deep roar far in the distance, and the blast of a whistle, and then the clanging of a bell. Down the line we could see the beam of a powerful light. The travellers gathered their luggage, the children skipped, the loungers chewed the faster, a few extra passers-by dropped into the station; and suddenly the *Rocket* was with us, four huge shining diesel units, big as houses, with the engineer leaning grandly out of his window; and a string of flashing coaches, all steel and aluminium; and a glimpse of padded sleepers; and black porters jumping from the high coaches and grabbing the bags; and travellers looking indolently out of diner windows, sipping their coffee; and a chink of light, here and there, as somebody moved a window-blind. The diesels roared, the conductors jumped aboard, the doors shut noiselessly, and off the great train went, like a long silver ship, cool, clean, glittering and powerful. Soon it would be out of the plains, and climbing into the Colorado mountains.

3

Kingdom of Troubles: The Middle East

After my year in America I became The Times *correspondent in the Middle East, at a time when that region was, as usual, a hotbed of trouble, inflamed by the establishment of the State of Israel in Palestine seven years before, by the rivalries of oil, by Soviet scheming and by the lingering influence and presence of the British Empire. I later evoked the experience in a book,* The Market of Seleukia. *My bailiwick embraced the whole region, and my base was Cairo, a city which I had known under British control, and under King Farouk, but which was now, after a military coup in 1952, the independent republican capital of President Gamal Abdel Nasser.*

Egypt

Rolling grandly northward out of the African interior, at last the noble River Nile splits into the several streams of its Egyptian delta, and creates a region so rich, so old, so deep-rooted in constancy, that there is something almost obscene to its fecundity. At the head of this country, at the point where the river divides, there stands the city of Cairo. It is the capital of Egypt, the largest city in Africa, the metropolis of the Arab world, the intellectual centre of Islam, and for more than a millennium it has been one of the great places of the earth.

Nothing ever quite dies in Cairo, for the air is marvellously clear and dry, and the temper of the country astringently preservative. If you stand upon the Mokattam Hills, the bare-back ridge that commands the place, you can see the pyramids of Giza upon its outskirts. From here they look faintly pink and translucent, like alabaster pyramids. They stand upon the very edge of the desert, where the sands are abruptly disciplined by the passage of the river, and they look fearfully old, terribly mysterious and rather frightening. Years ago the traveller would find these monuments lonely and brooding in the sand, with a Sphinx to keep them company and an attendant priesthood of unscrupulous dragomen. Today the city has expanded upstream, and digested a little irrigated desert too, until a line of villas, night clubs, hotels and golf courses links the capital with the Pharaohs, and the pyramids have acquired a distinctly suburban flavour. They are to Cairo what the Tivoli Gardens are, perhaps, to Copenhagen.

Another layer of the city's life is darkly medieval, straight-descended from the times when the Arab conquerors, storming in from their Eastern deserts, seized Egypt in the name of Islam. Look westward from your eyrie on the hill, and you will see a mottled section of the city, brownish and confused, from which there seems to exude (if you are of an imaginative turn) a vapour of age, spice and squalor. This is the Cairo of the Middle Ages. A forest of incomparable minarets springs out of the crumbled hodge-podge of its streets: one with a spiral staircase, one with a bulbous top, some single, some double, some like pepper-pots, some like hollyhocks, some elegantly simple, some assertively ornate, some phallic, some demure, rising from the huddle of houses around them like so many variegated airshafts from an underground chamber. There is said to be a mosque for every day of the Cairo year, and around them there lingers, miraculously pickled, the spirit of mediaeval Islam, just emerging from the chaos of animism and pagan superstition. Among these narrow lanes and tottering houses the Evil Eye is still potent, and a hundred taboos and incantations restrict the course of daily life.

At one of the great gates in the city wall you may still see dirty scraps of linen and paper pinned there in supplication to some misty saint of pre-history, and when there is a festival at a mosque, and the squeaky swings are erected for the children, and an endless crowd clamours through the night around the tomb of the local holy man, then all the gallery of medieval characters emerges into the street in the lamplight – the half-mad dervish, tattered and daemonic; the savage emaciated beggar, with long nails and gleaming eyes; the circumciser, preparing his instruments delicately at a trestle table; the saintly imam, bland and courteous; the comfortable merchant, distributing sweetmeats and largesse; the clowns and peddlers and pickpockets, and many a small company of women, identically dressed in coarse-grained black, squatting in circles at street corners, gossiping loudly or idly rapping tambourines.

Two or three minutes in a wild-driven bus will whisk you from this enclave to the boulevards of modern Cairo, the power-house of the

Middle East. Westernized Cairo was born in 1798, when Napoleon arrived in Egypt with his team of savants, and it has developed since under a series of foreign influences and interferences. Today, truly independent at last, it is a city so sophisticated and well equipped that all the other Arab capitals pale into provincialism. The Republic of Egypt is the self-appointed leader of the Arab world, and there is no denying the dynamism and assurance of its capital. A company of tall new buildings has burgeoned beside the river: two great hotels, all glass plate and high tariffs; a tower with a revolving restaurant on top; vast new official offices, immaculate outside, raggle-taggle within; expensive apartment blocks and sprawling housing estates. A splendid new corniche runs along the waterfront, from one side of the city to the other. A spanking new bridge spans the river. It is not a stylish city, contemporary Cairo, and its sense of dignity comes almost entirely from its river and its past, but it has undeniable punch and power.

It is the very opposite of a backwater. It is a fermenting city, often bombastic, always on the move. Fielding tells the story of a blind man, asked to convey his impression of the colour red, who replied that it had always seemed to him 'somewhat like the sound of a trumpet'. Cairo is not silvery: but something similarly blatant and penetrating is the image that should be summoned for you, when it leaps into the headlines again. Something is always happening here. It may be some great economist flying patiently in, or a statesman flying philosophically out, or a new démarche from Moscow, or a British economic mission, or a fulmination against Israel, or a reconciliation with Iraq, or the arrival of a Russian dam-builder, or a meeting of the Arab League – a threat, a parade, or simply the President of Egypt sweeping by, with a roar of his convoying motor cycles and a scream of sirens, in his big black bullet-proof car.

It is a blazing place. It blazes with heat. It blazes with a confrontation of opposites, the clash of the modern and the traditional. Above all it blazes with the glare of contemporary history. Pause on a bridge in Cairo, amid the blare of the traffic and the shove of the citizenry, and you can almost hear the balance of the powers shifting about you, as the black, brown and yellow peoples come storming into their own. In Cairo is distilled the essence of the Afro-Asian risorgimento. It is fertile in ideas and bold ambitions – often undistinguished, sometimes positively childish, but always intensely vigorous, brassy, combative and opportunist. Its corporate tastes run to the belly-dancer, the dirty story, overeating, hearty badinage. It loves fireworks and big-bosomed singers. Its newspapers are clever. Its cartoonists are brilliantly mordant. Its radio programmes, laced with propaganda, shriek from every coffee-house. It is a city with an incipient fever, always swelling towards the moment when the sweat will break out at last.

All the material amenities of Western life are available in Cairo, but it never feels remotely like a Western city. It welcomes you kindly, and guides you helpfully across the streets, and engages you in cordial conversation – only to do something distinctly queer at the end of the lane. Sometimes these things are frightening (when a mob streams down the back streets, or the great tanks rumble by). Sometimes they are very charming (when you share a bowl of beans with a jolly family in a park). Sometimes they are baffling (when you wake in the morning to learn of some totally unpredictable about-face of national policies). Sometimes they are marvellously encouraging (when some young upstart politician expresses a truth so clear, so clean, so free of inherited trammels that all our horny conjectures seem out of date). The particular forces of history and conflict that have moulded our Western societies have had little share in the making of Cairo. It is a city sui generis, sustained by all the hopes, strengths, weaknesses and grievances of an emergent world.

It is not really a rich city, any more than Egypt is a rich country. It is, though, a capital of formidable character and natural power. It stands there at the head of its teeming delta like a watchtower at the gate of a lush garden, and around it the world seems to lie supine, so that when this old city stretches its arms, its elongated shadow spreads across Asia and Africa and along the Mediterranean shores like the image of a genie. It is unlike any other city on the face of the earth: just as the greatheart Nile, passing proud but placid through the hubbub of the capital, marches down to the sea with a sad deep majesty all its own, as of a man who has watched the cavalcade of life pass by, and wonders what all the fuss is about.

Gamal Abdel Nasser's revolutionary regime, although I admired it in many ways, was frankly autocratic, and I often had occasion to write about its techniques, both in the city and in the countryside.

If you leave your car for long in the village street of Bai-el-'Arab you are likely to find things scribbled in the dust on the windscreen: a funny face perhaps, a name or two, an obscure witticism, and 'Long Live Gamal Abdel Nasser!' There is probably not a village in the Egyptian Republic where you can escape the impact of al-Gumhuria – the regime led by Colonel Nasser which, in the eyes of its supporters, is now dragging Egypt by the heels from its misery. This does not mean that Bai-el-'Arab looks or feels very different because of the junta's ruthless reforms. It remains largely inviolate, like a thousand others, all but untouched by the material progress of a century or more, still deep in poverty and ignorance.

Its intricate jumble of mud huts lies off the main road in the delta country north of Cairo. From its dusty courtyards, across the fields, you may see the great white sails of the Nile boats sweeping by. Near by, blindfold oxen tramp endlessly round their water-wheels, and men with their clothes rolled up to the thigh pump water into irrigation canals with archaic instruments. The fields of cotton, wheat and beans are dazzlingly bright. The narrow roads are lined with trees. Only an occasional car passes by with an alarming blast of its horn.

Both Muslims and Copts live in this small community, and it is easy to enter their houses, for they are friendly and hospitable. As you drink their coffee you may see for yourself how the *fellah*, the Egyptian peasant, lives: in squalor indescribable, sharing his mud floor with dogs, goats, chickens, turkeys and sometimes cattle, with a hard bed to lie on, and an open fire to cook by, and a litter of junk and tin cans, the whole enveloped in a pall of dust. Dirt and want dominate the lives of these people, but their society is not without grace. Their courtesy is instinctive, and here and there you will find traces of aesthetic yearnings; a door-knocker made curiously in the shape of a hand, some childish colourful wood-carving, an ornamental tray or a trinket of beaten brass.

A convoy of cars recently arrived in this village bringing a high dignitary of the regime, Major Magdi Hassanein, and a number of important visitors. They were welcomed with ceremony, for the purpose of the dignitary's visit was to choose suitable *fellahin* from Bai-el-'Arab for resettlement in Liberation Province, an enormous agricultural area which is being reclaimed by irrigation in the western desert. A good house, new clothes and secure communal living were among the prizes for selection, and the response was ecstatic. In a field beside the road a marquee of large carpets was erected, and a band struck up a reedy melody, all third-tones and off-beats. Caparisoned Arab horses performed their celebrated dance – the *haute école* of rural Egypt. Slogans of enthusiasm were shouted, and the women shrilled the queer high-pitched whistle they reserve for weddings and such festivities.

23

Liberation Province, like many other projects of the regime, is a courageous and imaginative conception, but if this government is in many ways
reasonable, it is also despotic. The Press is muzzled; laws of profound
effect are issued suddenly and unpredictably; foreign issues are shamelessly exploited for purely political ends; opponents of the regime are
removed without ceremony. So at a whisper from the cheer-leaders at
Bai-el-'Arab there is a roar of approval and a chorus of 'Long Live Major
Magdi Hassanein!'

Inside the school some of the candidates for Liberation Province are
lined up for visitors to see, like material for some new master race. 'They
must all be under 30, and literate, and of good appearance. See how
intelligent they look! They will wear a fine new gabardine uniform in
Liberation Province. They will be examined by psychologists to see if
they are suitable. Come and see them taking their written examination.'

There they sit at a wooden table, these new Egyptians, each in a spotless white *galabiya*, each fingering a newly sharpened pencil, each with
a virgin question sheet in front of him. 'They will start in a moment. It is
a very stringent test. Watch them prepare for it! No, no, certainly they
have not been chosen already. They are about to begin. Wait!' But here
the candidates rise as one man, with a look of ineffable piety upon their
faces, and bawl a few more 'Long Lives!' before resuming their academic
duties.

So despotism applies itself to the humanities, and it may be that an iron
hand is necessary for the rebuilding of Egypt, together with regular infusions
of compulsory pride and loyalty. On balance, despite the scepticism of the
financiers, the odium of the intellectuals, the misgivings of the liberals, the
fears of the Jewish minority and the growing alienation of the Arab world,
al-Gumhuria seems to be good for Egypt. But who can foresee whether
the thrusting young men of the junta, with their examinations and their
big battalions, will be able to last the course; or whether they will be outlived, like so many before them, by the flies, the mud houses and the old
tin cans?

*On the other side of Cairo is the oasis of Kharga, on the west bank of the Nile,
a group of small desert villages which has been traditionally a place of
exile. Nestorius, who was of the opinion that the Virgin Mary could not
really be called the Mother of God, was banished there after propounding
this revolutionary doctrine in the fifth century, and so, it is said, was*

Athanasius of the Creed. Under President Nasser it was a place of incarceration for political opponents, mostly members of the fundamentalist Muslim Brotherhood, one of several detention camps into which it was very easy for a man to disappear without warning or appeal. I went there for The Times *hoping to meet some of the prisoners.*

It is the perfect place for exile. It lies in a wide declivity in the western desert, about 140 miles west of the Nile, overlooked by burning bluffs and surrounded on every side by waterless sands. So unfriendly is the desert, so brooding of appearance, that it feels as though at any moment the sands may reach some momentous decision, and engulf the whole oasis, palm groves, villages, detention camp and all. A rough road, once the route of slave caravans from the Sudan, runs away north-east to the Nile; but the easiest way to get to Kharga is to take a diesel rail-car from a place on the river called Nag Hamadi. This endearing little vehicle (the locals say its father was a steam train, its mother a bus) starts very early in the morning and arrives in the shallow bowl of the oasis just as the terrible heat of the sun is at its most blistering. The passenger thus disembarks feeling rather as though he too has been fostering schisms.

I spent a couple of days learning something of Kharga's curious character. It had a hushed, swathed quality to it, I thought, well befitting a collection of small villages of so bleak a position and so ominous a reputation. The sand of the desert, moving restlessly and irresistibly with the prevailing winds, was in fact marching upon the place inch by inch through the years. Some of the outlying settlements had already been swamped. Some had built great protective walls around themselves. In one small hamlet a single householder was left in possession, and he too was preparing to leave, for a brutal yellow sand-dune was poised above his shack. 'The sand has its needs,' he said philosophically. 'We must allow the sand its rights.' Everywhere there were broken walls, shattered houses and discredited barricades, all half-buried in the dunes.

The detention camp was several miles away in the desert, and nobody seemed very keen to take me there, so I settled down in the main village of the oasis hoping to find some friendly guard or prisoner at large, but content enough to drink my coffee in the rambling main square of the place. Its manner was deadened but soothing; its people, mostly Berbers, listless but friendly. Many of the narrow streets were roofed with wood and earth, to dissuade the wild Beduin marauders of old from riding pell-mell down them on horseback. Along these shady paths

25

the people moved with padded footsteps, carrying baskets decorated with odd little tufts of wool, and at night lanterns swung down side streets and over the open fronts of stores (with piles of beans, big glass pots of spices, and silent shopkeepers lounging against shutters). Hardly a woman was to be seen in this town of rigid tradition; only one cringing soul, embalmed in black, did I meet scurrying from the square in the shadow of a wall. The weather was excessively hot, and the hours of Kharga passed heavily.

On market day, though, the place was transformed, and then I found a trail to my prisoners. The main street was lined with butchers' stalls, piled high with white fatty camel-meat which the butchers, after a few brusque strokes with the chopper, tore between their bloody hands with a noise of rending flesh and muscles. Piles of this horrible stuff, I noticed, were being loaded into a small truck, guarded by a couple of policemen, and when I asked where it was going they said: 'To the prisoners.' Oho, I said, might I come too? Certainly not, they said. They were political prisoners, and obviously no foreigner could talk to them – what would the Governor say? However, somebody added with the suspicion of a wink, I might be interested instead to visit the hospital of Kharga, just over there, turn right at the square, and very interesting I would find it. So I went along that morning, and a young and agreeable doctor showed me round the place. In one ward we found a number of grumpy and scrofulous patients lying on palliasses on the floor. 'What's this?' said I. 'Not enough beds, then?' 'Oh, we have enough normally,' said the doctor casually, 'but just at the moment we've got a ward full of prisoners from the camp. Care to meet them?'

And there they were, those successors of Athanasius, propounders of very different faiths: some of them communists, some Muslim Brethren. They looked a murderous lot, all the more sinister because of the bandages and plasters which covered their eyes or supported their limbs. We talked of this and that, of the past and the future, of the conditions of their detention and their hopes of release. Every morning, I learnt, they were given a lecture of indoctrination by a representative of the regime, but something in their eyes told me they were far from brainwashed. Two grey-haired police guards watched us from the veranda as we talked; and now and then a savage old reprobate lying on a bed in the corner intervened with some caustic witticism, delivered in the most cultured of English accents and with the bite of an educated and incisive mind.

Thus Nestorius might have spoken, I thought, during *his* exile at Kharga.

* * *

26

Something about the detainees' injuries, too, told me of the camp's reformatory methods, but since I had to go on living and working in President Nasser's Egypt I felt it wiser to let readers of The Times *glimpse that between the lines.*

Lebanon

In the 1950s Beirut, the capital of the Lebanese Republic, was the delight of the Arab world, largely apolitical, still Frenchified after years of French mandatory rule, beautiful of setting and kindly of temperament – the very antithesis of the dangerous city of terrorism and religious bigotry that it was later to become. I went up there from Egypt whenever I could find a professional excuse.

Beirut is the impossible city, in several senses of the adjective. It is impossible in the enchantment of its setting, where the Lebanese mountains meet the Mediterranean. It is impossible in its headiness of character, its irresponsible gaiety, its humid prevarications. It is impossible economically, incorrigibly prospering under a system condemned by many serious theorists as utterly unworkable. Just as the bumble bee is aerodynamically incapable of flying, so Beirut, by all the rules and precedents, has no right to exist.

Yet there it stands, with a toss of curls and a flounce of skirts, a Carmen among the cities. It is the last of the Middle Eastern fleshpots, and lives its life with an intensity and a frivolity almost forgotten in our earnest generation. It is to Beirut that all the divinities of this haunted seaboard, the fauns and dryads and money-gods, orgiastically descend. It is a tireless pleasure-drome. It is a junction of intrigue and speculation. It is a university city of old distinction. It is a harbour, a brothel, an observatory on the edge of the Arab deserts. Its origins are ancient but it burgeons with brash modernity, and it lounges upon its delectable shore, half-way between the Israelis and the Syrians, in a posture that no such city, at such a latitude, at such a moment of history, has any reasonable excuse for assuming. To the stern student of affairs Beirut is a phenomenon beguiling perhaps, but quite, quite impossible.

Beirut stands on no great river, commands no industrious hinterland, and all through the centuries it has been chiefly significant as a gateway and a conduit, the threshold of Damascus and the outlet of Syria. It has been a halting place or transit camp, through which successive civilizations have briefly tramped, leaving a stele here, a carving there, a legend in a library or a pillbox on a beach.

A stele, a pillbox – nothing more substantial has been left behind by the conquerors, for the texture of Beirut is flaky and unretentive. Earthquakes and fires have destroyed much of its heritage, but mostly it is the character of the place that makes this a city without a visible past. It is always contemporary, shifting and tacking to the winds of circumstance. It is the capital of a state that is half Christian, half Muslim, and it remains poised between the Eastern way and the Western, between the Francophile and the Afro-Asian, between the suave hotels that line the waterfront and the tumbled oriental villages spilled on the hillside above. It is not one of your schizophrenic cities, though: on the contrary, it has triumphantly exploited its own dichotomies, and become the smoothest and most seductive of entrepreneurs. Everything is grist to this mill: a crate of steel bolts, a letter of credit, a poem, a navigational system, a cocktail, a tone of voice, a power press, a soup – Beirut accepts them all, processes them if necessary, and passes them on at a profit.

It lives by standing in the middle, and by the itchiest of itchy palms. There is almost nothing this city will not undertake. It will pass your wheat inland to Damascus, or ship your oil westward to Hamburg. It will paint your upperworks, translate your thesis, introduce you to the Sheikh of Araby, accommodate you in pampered splendour in an air-conditioned suite beside the water. It will perform your atonal music at an open-air festival, or feed you with unreliable statistics about political controversies in Zagazig. It will, without a flicker of surprise, convert your Norwegian travellers' cheques into Indian rupees and Maria Theresa dollars. It has nothing of its own, no resources of iron or coal, no factories to speak of, no big battalions, but it will do almost anything you ask of it, providing you pay properly.

No, that's unfair – it is not all for cash. Beirut is also an entrepôt of ideas, linking the bazaars with Cambridge and the Sorbonne. Whether a man comes from Peking or Pittsburgh, he will soon find some corner of this liberal place where, lapped in eroticism or deep in the discussion of philosophical concepts, he is sure to feel at home. There is a tang in the Beirut air, bitter-sweet but easy-going, that survives nowhere else on earth: for it is compounded of an old alliance between east and west, washed in the humanism of the ancients and bathed in the incomparable Mediterranean sunshine. It is the spirit that created old Alexandria, and it makes Beirut, for every lover of the classical mode, for everyone of generous instinct, a city of nostalgic regret.

Regret always, for Beirut is a prodigy of the second class – a sideline city. It stands on the rim of the Arab world, peering inside with a wry and sceptical detachment, and its conscience is rudimentary.

This undeniably makes for fun. All the Middle East makes for Beirut. Here you may see the political exiles, talking dark and interminable subterfuge, or the resplendent hawk-nosed sheikhs, in all the gilded refulgence of the Arab patrimony, fingering their beads and indulging in flamboyant bickering. Here are the silken ladies of Syria, svelte and doe-eyed, and here are the waterside harlots, curled but smouldering, Semite with a touch of baroque. There are many poets in Beirut, and artists of visionary tendencies, shaggy existentialists in frayed sandals, dilettantes by the score, spies by the portfolio. Sometimes you may see Druse tribesmen in the city, out of the eastern hills, ferociously hirsute and gloriously swaggering. Sometimes the fleet puts in (British, American, French or Greek) and the waterfront bars are loud with ribaldry. And when one of the perennial Middle Eastern crises erupts into the headlines, then the imperturbable hotels of Beirut are crammed again with foreign correspondents, the hall porters brush up their jargon and sniff around for tittle-tattle, and the whole city seems transformed into one sensitive, quivering antenna.

But in Beirut you are seldom in the heart of things. The firemen are always visiting, the crisis is usually somewhere else. It feels a transitory place, like an exceedingly corrupt and sophisticated girls' school. Such a way of life, you feel, cannot be permanent: it is all too fickle, too fast, too make-believe and never-never. It is Alexandria without the philosophers, without the Pharaohs, perhaps even without Cleopatra (for age does distinctly wither the *grandes dames* of Beirut, waddling with poodles and sunglasses from salon to couturier). For all its age and history Beirut feels a rootless city – salacious but not earthy, virile but infertile. A breath of wind, it seems, a shift of fortune, and all this bright-painted fabric would be whisked away into oblivion.

Such is the nature of the place. Beirut is the small capital of an infinitesimal republic, and its events do not often feel crucial. Give it time, Beirut always whispers, don't fuss, wait and see, have a drink. You can usually find a blind eye here, a hole in the corner, the back of a hand, the underneath of a counter. This is not an earnest city. Proper Victorians would have hated it. Harvard economists or British civil servants, examining its improbable methods, its flibberty-gibbet charm, its blatancy and its blarney – men of sombre purpose, deposited one scented evening in Beirut, would probably pronounce it irredeemable.

But who would redeem such a place, in a world of false redemptions? Club-women and bluestockings infest our age, but the frank and lovely libertine still makes the heart lift. Such a heedless delight, such a glint in a blithe eye, is the gift of Beirut. This is a city without much soul, but with allure immeasurable, and above all it is graced by a celestial beauty of setting: beauty of a classic and timeless kind, a blue and wine-dark kind, with bewitchment such as you dream about in long damp northern evenings, as you pine for a beaker of the warm south. The city of Beirut often feels second-rate, but the setting of Beirut is superlative. At this point on the Levantine coast the mountains of Lebanon stand in magnificent parallel beside the sea, so close that the citizens of Beirut may, if the wild whim takes them, ski in the morning and swim in the afternoon. It is the presence of these fine hills, all around the city, that elevates Beirut from the entertaining to the sublime, and provides, in its contrast between the ephemeral and the eternal, a marvellous foil to the bubbling frivolity of the metropolis.

Imagine a terrace table beside the sea in Beirut, during the brief moment of the Mediterranean twilight, when the shops are raising their shutters for the evening's business, and your restaurant rustles with the first silks and sibilances of the night. There are prawns on your table, perhaps, or red mullet from Sidon, fruit from the lush Bekaa valley, a gay white wine of Lebanon or some haughty vintage out of France. Around the bay the city rumbles, hoots and chatters: there is a clink of metal from some unseen smithy, a suggestion of spice and raw fish on the breeze, the echo of a blaring radio beyond the promenade, a distant clanging of trams – all the hot, heavy, breathless symptoms of an expiring Levantine day, like a sigh in the sunset. Below you the last of the water-skiers scuds home in a flurry of spray, showing off to the girls on the beach. Out at sea a tall elderly schooner loiters, like a ghost in the half-light, and beyond the breakwater, perhaps, an Italian liner steals out for Greece with a soft tread of her turbines and a flutter of her flags. Sometimes an airliner labours in from the sea, blinking its red lights as it lands beyond the cedar groves, and sometimes a razzle-dazzle sports car, top-heavy with blondes and young muscle-men, screams and skids along the corniche towards the night clubs. All along the shore the tall white buildings stand, concrete and rectilinear, with their parasols and their lighted balconies, their dim-lit bars and their muffled music.

Now, before the night comes, while the evening is still purple and hazy, while the velvet twilight lasts – now you may taste the impossible beauty of Beirut: for rising in strides above the capital, in serried terraces, above the skyscrapers, above the last suburbs, above the olive groves, above the foothill villages, above the winding Damascus road – there, lording it above sea and city, stand the mountains, 'afloat in heaven's pool'. A sheen of snow hovers about their high ridges, and their tawny slopes tumble away through scree and field and olive grove to the Mediterranean below. Beneath their serenity Beirut festers and celebrates: and even as you watch, sipping your wine or toying with your fish, the lights go on like star clusters in the villages of the hills, higher and higher up the slopes, until at last the dark falls, the end of the sunset fades, and away above Beirut only the snow of the summits remains like a dim corona in the night.

Beirut was an all-too-favourite place of recreation for the Western Press corps in the Middle East, and one of my American colleagues in Cairo happened to have escaped up there for a few days of hedonism when a great news story broke in Egypt. Legend says that he was handed a message from his newspaper while sunning himself on the beach with a long cool drink. 'King Farouk has abdicated', it said. 'What are your plans?'

Jordan

The Times sent me, in 1955, to cover the wedding in Amman of King Hussein of Jordan and his Egyptian bride. The Hashemite monarchy there owed its existence to the British Empire, which had sponsored its creation after the First World War, and until 1946 it had been, as Transjordan, a British mandatory territory – a sort of imperial protectorate. This occasion was almost the last demonstration of the hybrid sense of ceremony which had been born out of Turco-Arab tradition by British imperialism.

The King received his wedding guests standing beneath a portrait of his father the unbalanced King Talal, and beside him stood a royal cousin – King Feisal II of Iraq. How small and helpless and nice they looked, those two little kings, both of them youths, both small and stocky, with their somehow ill-fitting dark suits and their hands not quite at ease – Hussein, not long from Sandhurst, standing roughly to attention, Feisal, a little more experienced, with his legs apart and his hands clasped in front of him. Kings they were, but kings in a troubled and republican world.

The really significant moment of that lavish day (for the capital was alive with parades and demonstrations from dawn to fireworks time) was the assembly, later that evening, at which the King officially met his Queen. In the past this would have been held behind the curtained doors of the harem, and the innumerable ladies of the household would not for a moment have been exposed unveiled to the gaze of the world at large. This time, though the affair was still predominantly female, some men were allowed to attend it; and the ladies, far from being veiled, appeared bewitchingly, or at least compellingly, uninhibited.

I stood in a corner of the room while the assembly prepared itself for the arrival of the royal couple. Circassians in long black cloaks, astrakhan hats, high boots and cluttered accoutrements guarded the entrance to the hall, as the eunuchs would have stood sentry in an earlier age. At the head of the stairs were two bold lancers in scarlet tunics and white breeches. But the body of the room was a mass of women. They were dressed magnificently, a glitter of satins and brocades and furs, a mosaic of lipsticks and mascara, a tinkling kaleidoscope of earrings, a flurry of sequined handbags. Chanel and Dior thickened the air. When the Queen Mother of Jordan arrived a sibilant Arabic whisper rippled through the hall; for the first time she was appearing in public with no veil above her sumptuous silk gown.

All the same, I could not help feeling that we were close in spirit, if not in textile, to the huddled jealousies and schoolgirl pleasures of the harem. How often and how brazenly did those women of the court eye each other's couture and coiffure! How heavily accentuated were the outlines of their eyes, like eyes seen through diaphanous curtains in forbidden corridors of the Seraglio! How scratchy and talon-like were the fingernails, how pinkly fleshy the figures, and how passive and doll-like those emancipated ladies looked, in serried and perfumed phalanx, as if some lascivious Sultan was about to pass through their ranks, picking a beauty here and a beauty there with a lordly gesture of his forefinger!

But it was only little King Hussein who entered the room, with his calm, intelligent, literary wife. The illusion vanished in a trice, and as the court ladies smoothed their skirts and pressed the wrinkles from the wrists of their gloves, a cameraman in a crumpled jacket suddenly pressed his way past the Circassian guards and said just one more, ladies, please, give us a nice smile now.

Despite these formalities, Jordan in the 1950s was in an endemic condition of incipient revolution – like much of the Arab world as a whole. For a different glimpse of the national preoccupations I attended the trial, in Amman too, of five political subversives.

A revolution is an awesome thing and we think of it, as often as not, in grand abstractions. We talk spaciously, like astronomers, of the turmoil that is now sweeping across the Arab world and only occasionally, in sharp passing moments of enlightenment, do we collate the great political design with the poor little human conscience, struggling there beneath the manifestos. One such flash of illumination occurred this morning in the officers' mess of the Jordanian Army training regiment on a hill outside Amman.

The mess was white with tablecloths, as though lunch were about to be served, and the silver baubles of the regimental collection gleamed from their glass cabinets handsomely. The neon lighting was bright in spite of the sunshine. There were pictures of armoured cars on the walls, and a faint tangy fragrance emanated from the dwarf pines outside the window. The trial was taking place of five Jordanians accused of conspiracy and the possession and illegal use of explosives, the penalty demanded being death: and here, as in some fierce silhouette, you could see the images of revolution clear and cruel.

On one side of the court sat the accused. There were two placid, shabbily dressed Jordanians in *kuffiyahs*, sitting silent and composed, as though they were in church. There was a fattish, puffy-faced man with a towel over his head, clearly so harshly used by his interrogators that he was near death already: great blue weals scarred his hands, his movements were agonizingly slow, suffering stared from his watery eyes, and sometimes with a gesture of despair he heeled over and laid his head on his neighbour's lap. And at the end of the row sat a pair of lovers, he tall and bearded, she slim and wide-eyed, the very epitome of revolutionary and Byronic romance. The young man was cheerful and smiling, in a blue open-necked shirt: the girl was pale but proud, her great black eyes anxious and unsettled, in a dress with orange stripes and a white bangle, and a fragile gold crucifix round her neck.

33

On the other side of the room sat authority in the form of a military court, stern and khaki-coloured, and shuffling its papers portentously. The defence lawyers sat in double-breasted suits at one table. The prosecutor, a scared and ineffectual subaltern, sat at another. Two rather pudgy majors formed the ancillaries of the bench, and the president was a brigadier, red-tabbed and beribboned, of fine commanding presence and assurance: his face was large and craggy, like a face from the desert, his voice was very loud and rather rasping, and he glared at the court from deep-set eyes above a clipped and bristly moustache.

So they sat there, the accusers, the accused, and the judges: and all around them jostled the audience, idly lounging or half-heartedly enjoying themselves. There were troops of soldiers, apparently off-duty, sitting in the courtroom or crowding about the open door. There was a handful of eager attentive civilians. Policemen sat stoutly in their spiked helmets, vacant but willing, like country coppers on bicycles in pre-war English comedies. A few foreign pressmen doodled on their pads ('You might do an atmosphere piece on it, old boy, but you can't call it hard news, except for the girl angle'). A policewoman with bobbed black hair, gold earrings and a forage cap, sat incongruously among all the men, her face heavily powdered. There was a sense of muted and unhilarious recreation to the scene, such as you might experience in a suburban cinema during a fairly dreary second feature.

In fact, though, this little courtroom was alive with terrible emotions, with fears and loyalties and defiances, and all the conflicts of human judgement that are the basis of revolutions. The touching young lovers were facing death and had (if the charges against them are true) been perfectly prepared to blow any number of strangers to oblivion to further the cause of nationalism. Sweet was their obvious affection, and pretty the girl's dress, and delicate her crucifix, but they were living close to savage things. The nervous young prosecutor, fiddling with his tie and smiling ingratiatingly at the brigadier, was relying upon alleged confessions obtained by methods of remorseless violence; perhaps he was only thinking of his promotion, poor chap, but if he looked across the room he could see the great blue weals still, as that crippled prisoner painfully moved an arm to pull the towel closer around his head.

The brigadier, presiding so forcefully over the hearing, knew that he might well be writing his own death sentence too; the forces he was judging are much more powerful, much more irresistible than the strength of his own authority, and if ever at last revolution reaches

34

Amman itself he will doubtless suffer the penalties of loyalty. They were all anxious people, every one, judges and prisoners and prosecutors and jailers and all, caught cruelly in the whirlpool of change.

And what of the audience, metaphorically sucking its thumbs on its kitchen chairs? It represented that bog of apathy in which the human conscience, perceptive or misguided, sparkles like a diamond. It sat in the middle of great emotions; a tortured man on one side, a pair of star-crossed lovers on another, and you could almost hear its unspoken communal plea, above the harsh pronouncements of the president: 'Pass me my work basket, will you, dear, and I'll get on with my knitting while you men have a good old talk. What I always say is, you can't change human nature, can you?'

I never heard what became of the accused, but revolution never erupted in Jordan anyway.

Jerusalem

In the late 1940s I had soldiered in the British mandated territory of Palestine, but the British had withdrawn from the country in 1948, leaving its Arab and Jewish inhabitants to fight for its possession. Jerusalem, sacred to both parties, seemed an insoluble obstacle to an agreement between them. In 1955, when I wrote this report for The Times, *the walled Old City of Jerusalem was in Jordanian hands, considered part of Jordan and garrisoned by soldiers of Jordan's British-founded Arab Legion, while the modern parts of the city were held by the Israelis.*

Old Jerusalem is golden still, especially seen from the Mount of Olives or through the gnarled trees of Gethsemane on a late summer evening. It is still the holiest of holy places, still a magnificent Islamic city, still a fortress. Its buildings, scarred in the recent fighting, stand mellow and serene; through its tortuous streets move the pilgrims and priests, Beduin, bootblacks, coffee-sellers and gowned merchants of its tradition; upon its ramparts, guarding the embattled frontier with Israel, soldiers of the Arab Legion stand guard in pink-checked *kuffiyahs* and battledress.

It would be alien to its tradition for Jerusalem to be peaceful. Deaths and battles, armies and sieges, bloodshed and privation are the normalities of the city. Among its sparse hills the place certainly lies in a wonderful silence, calm and cool, with the first chinks of lights appearing and the call to evening prayer ringing from the mosque on the Hill of Ascension. But an implacable frontier divides the Old City from most of its modern suburbs, and the blaze of lights on the western ridge marks the centre of New Jerusalem, in the hands of the Jews and as inaccessible to the Arabs as Bhutan. An enemy is literally at the gates.

The spirit of Jerusalem has withdrawn from the grand new suburbs, now mostly in Israel, into the walled city where it belongs. The streets are crowded, prosperous and clean. Big American cars are driven precariously up ramps along stepped alleyways, for many rich Arab retailers, driven from New Jerusalem, have set up shop within the walls. They will tell you, as you drink their spiced coffee, of the enormous emporia, the vast estates, the bursting bank balances they invariably seem to have left behind – a myth of vanished opulence, a sort of gilt-edged Atlantis of the soul. Sadly such unfortunates will take you to the top of their buildings for a view into No Man's Land. There it runs, a strip of depressed and littered soil, cluttered with derelict buildings, coils of wire, piles of miscellaneous rubbish. Into a few tumble-down buildings near the Arab line a few poor house-hunters have surreptitiously seeped; in the middle an Israeli housewife, oblivious of international asperities, has hung her washing; and on the very edge, close to the walls of the Old City, a small Jewish army post sits boldly behind sandbags on top of a ruined terrace.

It is another world across that frontier, bland and barred, as if some totally foreign and aloof civilization has implanted itself there. The Arabs can only look across and wonder, but they live in the second holiest city of Islam, and their own world survives. The glorious Dome of the Rock was damaged in the fighting, but surrounded by its wide courtyards, its arches and stairways and old walls, it is still of a shimmering splendour, and the peasants still stand reverent and awestruck before it.

Christians too, as they wander the sacred sites, may feel their philosophies secure. The Franciscan pilgrims make their way as always along the Via Dolorosa, the brown-robed monks, the American women in their cotton frocks, the family of Italians kneeling on the hard cobblestones beside the Stations of the Cross. In the Church of the Holy Sepulchre, split, shuttered, disfigured and profaned by ancient schisms and rivalries, the Latins process each evening: cultured voices and Gregorian chants, a visiting English priest, a stream of pilgrims carrying lighted tapers. A few moments later come the Greeks, their music harsh and discordant, their aged bishop so enshrouded in his vestments that only his spectacles and a few white hairs can be glimpsed beneath his hood in the half-light. An old woman lays down her stick and raises her hands in worship in the subterranean chapel of the Armenians; a tall Abyssinian monk stands, lost in meditation, silent among the pillars; in the little Coptic chapel behind the Sepulchre a moon-faced kitchen clock ticks tinnily upon the altar.

So the piety of Old Jerusalem survives, and countless sects of Islam and Christendom still thrive among its walls. But this city is never at ease, and in its southern section, inside the Dung Gate, there is a wide expanse of ruin, flattened houses and crumbling courtyards, inhabited only by unhappy scabrous refugees begging *bakitesh*. The Jews have left their quarter of Jerusalem, and their houses are laid waste. The Wailing Wall is deserted, with never a crumpled paper inserted between Herod's gigantic stones, and cabbages grow in the Jewish cemetery above the Vale of Kedron.

In 1967 the Israelis were to seize the whole of Jerusalem, and since then – well, you know the rest.

Iran

Persia, as Iran was generally called then, was still governed by the Shah-in-Shah, King of Kings, successor to the dynasties of the Qajars, the Afsharids, the Safayids and the Ilkhans. The Times was chiefly interested in the affairs of the huge Anglo-Iranian oil refinery at Abadan, in the south, but I preferred to potter around the Shah's cities of the interior, because I greatly relished the peculiar tang of their ancient civilization, not yet coarsened in the world's reputation by Iranian fanaticisms to come.

Persia makes its own rules. There never was such a tortuous, inside-out, back-to-front way of thinking as the Persian way; never such a fascinating, will-o'-the-wisp, unpredictable community of people; nowhere buildings so inexpressibly lovely, nowhere a landscape more peculiar than the wide Iranian plain, sometimes bleak beyond description, sometimes warm and multi-coloured, often queerly criss-crossed with the big round craters that

37

mark the passage of underground water channels. Ask a Persian which is his right ear, and he will put his left hand behind his head and point it out from behind.

Life in Persia is largely governed by a sense of humour, and depends for its continuity upon a series of non sequiturs, so that affairs there progress bumpily but soothingly, like an opiate with grit in it. It has long been so, for through centuries of despotism the Persian has erected around himself an indefinable screen of humour, slipperiness and oddity, a smoke-screen or camouflage, a false trail, a tear gas, behind which he can dive when trouble approaches him, to the bewildered chagrin of his tormentors. All this old tang and quiddity of Persia is best sniffed or experienced in the bazaars of Isfahan. Of all the splendid bazaars of the Middle East I enjoy these most. They are winding and rambling and mysterious, lit by shafts of sunshine streaming through the roof, full of fabrics and carpets and jewellery and vegetables, with exotic turbaned figures wandering through them, and a constant pushing and tumbling and shouting and bargaining; the whole conducted in a series of vaulted corridors of faintly ecclesiastical character. Women get short shrift in this Islamic mart, and are pushed out of the way with donkeys or sworn at mercilessly, and sometimes the vivid gusto of the place evolves into the macabre or the eerie.

I was once walking through the bazaars when a young man fell off his bicycle; a package wrapped in newspaper, fastened to the carrier rack, came undone, and there rolled on to the pavement the complete head of a horned sheep, its eyes glassy, a thin trickle of blood oozing from its neck. Obscurely disturbing, too, is the antique camel mill which works in a kind of dungeon near the entrance to the bazaars. You enter it down a flight of worn steps, and find yourself standing in a windowless subterranean cavern. In the middle of this awful place two aged camels, their eyes padded, lope round and round a grinding mill in the half-light, with a smell of dung, hair, straw and burning wood, and the flicker of a flame from a distant corner where three old camel-men in rags are cooking themselves a meal.

In such a place you can clearly hear the beat of the Persian heart – old, shuttered, wily, erratic. There is an edgy feeling to the crowds that shuffle and barge through these draughty arcades, and in the Persian's eye, though he has a gaudy streak of the buffoon to his make-up, there is always a look of deep and calculating introspection. You never feel remote from the desert in Isfahan; you are never divorced from Islam; there are many reminders that the city stands on the brink of wild, unworldly territories, inhabited by roaming bands of tribesmen and coloured by many a lingering taboo and superstition. This is the home of the Zoroastrians and the great Persian mystics, and the nurturing-place of the fragile Persian poets of antiquity. To this day, up more than one winding and rickety staircase in the bazaars, amid the dust and the sweet smoke of the hubble-bubbles, you will find the miniaturists still at work, squatting cross-legged on their benches with their pupils around them.

Isfahan is both bitter and perfumed: and if you are ever lulled into sentimentality by the charm of it all, there will soon come swaggering by some figure of glorious insouciance in turban, cloak, fur hat, sheepskin boots, cummerbund, limpid gown or tight-belted jerkin, the very personification of the perennial Persia. His astringent image haunts the scene, and breathes a spiced breath upon most of its activities.

Tehran, the Shah's capital, was in those days hardly less rich in piquancy. If I illustrate the trait with a comic anecdote, it is not because the trait itself was comic, but because Persian characteristics were so often served up soufflé style – their flavour fluffed about in humour, but none the less strong and subtle beneath.

It is said of the great Reza Shah that he was once making an inspection tour down his new trans-Iranian railway when a preceding locomotive was derailed and capsized beside the track. The railway workers did not want His Imperial Majesty to see this evidence of their ineptitude. Desperately they worked to put the engine on the track again, or at least on its wheels, as the royal train sped down the line towards them. But they failed to move it an inch, and only just in time hit upon a spaciously Persian solution. They buried it.

Persia's ambiance is pungent and defensive – as distinctive a national flavour, perhaps, as any on earth – and the foreigner is easily absorbed by it. In the vaults of the Central Bank of Persia, in Tehran, are kept the Crown Jewels, an astonishing collection of gems and objets d'art which provide backing for the national currency. They have been assembled over several royal generations, and are rich in spoils of war, begemmed weapons, enormously expensive baubles and gifts from other kingly dynasties. Kept in a huge underground strongroom seething with plain-clothes men, the collection has become a great tourist attraction.

I was down there one crowded weekday morning, among the blue-rinsed coiffures and jangling charm bracelets of my fellow marvellers, when I came across an agreeable case of brooches and little jewelled watches – more to my scale, I thought, than the colossal diamonds and tiered crowns that set the general tone of the exhibition. I stooped to examine these ornaments more closely, and as I did so the treasure-house suddenly reverberated with the ear-splitting blast of an alarm hooter. Everyone froze. Not a word was spoken. Not a pixie-charm tinkled. We waited aghast for the sound of splintered glass, gunshots, handcuffs or explosions. The hooter went on hooting. For a moment nothing else happened: then a smart young woman in green walked with composure across the room. She avoided the case containing the Gika of Nadir Shah, with its diamond ornaments of bayonets and gun-barrels around a monumental emerald. She ignored the sceptre presented to Reza Shah by the people of Azerbaijan, with its gold lions rampant around a jewelled globe. She took no notice of the Sea of Light, sibling to the Koh-i-Noor, inherited from the first Mogul emperor of India by way of the treasury of the Qajar tribe. Instead she walked calmly, with a loud clicking of her heels, directly across the vault to me.

'May I please ask you', she said with an amiable smile, 'to remove your elbow from that metal bar around the jewel-case?' I moved my arm. The hooter stopped. She thanked me. I kicked the last sand over the buried railway-engine, and the glory of Persia proceeded.

Oman

In the winter of 1955 the Sultan of Muscat and Oman, a faithful client of the British Empire, decided with London's encouragement to establish his authority over the disputed interior of his country, the Omani part, which he had never visited and where it was hoped there might be oil. It would entail a royal journey across the south-east corner of Arabia that had never been made before, starting from Salalah on the Arabian Sea, where the Sultan had his southern palace. I went along with the Sultan as representative of The Times, the only European among the Beduin guides and Nubian slaves of the enterprise – for Muscat and Oman then was one of the most shuttered states on earth, and slavery as an institution still existed. I later wrote a book about our journey, called Sultan in Oman.

In the courtyard of the palace there stood a stubby, powerful American truck, piled high with baggage, and beside it the Sultan stopped and unfolded the map. I stood over him, taller by a foot or more, and examined his face while he pointed out the route to me. He was only 44, but the voluminous dignity of his robes, his stately bearing, his heavy turban and his luxuriant beard all combined to make him look much older. His eyes were large, dark, long-lashed and very serious. His mouth, though kindly and humorous, looked to me capable of an occasional sneer, and often seemed to act independently of the rest of his features. It was an antique, melancholy face, such as you might see in old pictures of the East, as profoundly enigmatic, I thought, as the Pyramids.

The driver of the truck stood trembling beside its door, and the Sultan climbed in athletically. I watched him hitch up his robe, adjust his sword, arrange his papers and settle himself in the front seat. With deliberate care he put on a pair of sunglasses, and the driver jumped in and started the engine.

'Now, Mr Morris,' said the Sultan. 'If you are ready I think we might start. It will be an interesting journey, I think. I hope you will be comfortable, and if there is anything at all you want, please let my people know.'

I bowed; he smiled; the retainers clanked their rifles; and I walked from the inner courtyard into the big yard outside. There stood our convoy, ready for the journey. There were six more American trucks, all identical, piled almost to overturning with stores and bags. Each carried its complement of strong Negro slaves, wearing blue jerseys like sailors of the Royal Navy or skippers of *Skylarks* at faraway piers. In one vehicle five small goats, doomed but stoical, stood with their heads just showing above its sides, their ears waggling vigorously. In the front seats of others a strange assortment of dignitaries was sitting, and I had a smudged glimpse of beards, turbans, rifles, daggers and bright eyes as I hastened across the yard. There was a champagne feeling in the air.

The Sultan was evidently a man of punctuality. The engines were already racing, the slaves were clinging precariously to the mountains of stores. 'Here, Sahib! This way!' said two smiling Negroes, running across the yard to meet me. 'Your bags are in. Welcome!' And practically frog-marching me across the yard they guided me to my truck, its door already open, its driver grinning at me from inside. I jumped into my seat; the slaves climbed agilely up behind; and at that very instant there was a loud insistent blare of the Sultan's horn. The trucks leapt away like dogs from the leash, manoeuvring for position. Exhaust smoke billowed about the palace. We were off! The slaves struck up a loud unison *fatha*, invoking blessings on our mission. The household retainers lining the several courtyards bowed low and very humbly, and some of the men prostrated themselves. The keepers of the portals swung open the gates with a crash. The bystanders waved their sticks and shouted loyal greetings. Slave-girls, after preliminary reconnaissance, ran giggling into their houses with flying draperies. With a tremendous roaring of engines we rushed through the town and into the plain, and even the old camels, labouring around their wells, looked up for a bleary moment to watch us pass.

First went a truck flying the red flag of Muscat. Beside its driver sat our Beduin guide, a small withered man with an avaricious look about him. Next rode the Sultan, his big turban bobbing up and down with the bumps of the track. In the third truck sat an elderly functionary with a long white beard; in the fourth were two splendid desert sheikhs, crowded together over the gearbox, with their rifles protruding from the window; in the fifth was a very old *qadi* of saintly bearing; and the rest of us followed behind, at tremendous speed, jolting wildly over the plain like raiders hot on the heels of an enemy. The flag flapped bravely. The big slaves laughed at each other and clutched their weapons. The little goats huddled together for company. It was a gloriously exhilarating start.

'Where are we going?' inquired my driver.

We were going to the Sultan's capital, Muscat on the Persian Gulf, and all went well. The Sultan humiliated various dissidents of the remote and mountainous interior, satisfied himself about oil rights and arrived at his capital in triumph (although fourteen years later he was to be deposed by his own son, and the country was renamed simply Oman). His slaves, by the way, seemed to me more like privileged servants than chattels, and the British, as semi-suzerains of the sultanate, tried to dissuade me from calling them slaves at all. 'I have spoken to Morris,' wrote one Foreign Office official to his superiors in London, 'and have, I hope, convinced him of when a slave is not a slave.' As to my book about the journey, it has remained banned in Oman from that day to this. I don't know why.

The Suez Affair

In 1956 Gamal Abdel Nasser nationalized the French-managed Suez Canal, and in response the Israelis, in collusion with the British and French, launched a lightning invasion of the Egyptian Sinai peninsula, brilliantly capturing it. Anglo-French forces then seized the canal itself, ostensibly to separate the Israelis from the Egyptians. This almost surreal enterprise in fact signalled the end of European colonial interference in the Middle East, and was a seminal moment in the collapse of British imperial confidence.

By then I had migrated from The Times *to the* Guardian, *which sent me to Sinai to observe the Israeli Army in the field at the moment of its ambiguous victory – for nobody knew what was going to happen next, whether the Russians would intervene, or the Americans, or the United Nations, or whether a third world war was hatching.*

A rainbow appeared this afternoon, though nobody seemed to notice it but me. All around me as I stood at the road junction the soldiers of the Israeli Army were hitch-hiking home from battle, and they hailed their passing lorries, swapped their war stories, compared their souvenirs, whistled their tunes without a glance at that poor pale phenomenon above them. Perhaps they were right. Great forces are swirling around Israel nowadays. In all its ten years of dangerous living Israel was perhaps never so precarious as this.

Still, it is always nice to see an army going home, especially when it is so young and confident and full of conviction as this. The Israeli Army still has some of the free-and-easiness of an irregular force, and the soldiers around me, from nearly every country under the sun, shared a peculiar defiant panache that I have never experienced before. They were not only fighting soldiers, but unwavering zealots.

Their views admitted no argument, their claims no query; and if ever I felt moved to remonstration there was always a young man with a clear eye to remind me that the Israelis, if ever they *should* lose a battle, have nowhere else in the world to go. How can you argue, however impartial you are, however divided your sympathies on Palestine, with a people whose only alternatives are victory or extinction?

Many and enthralling were those soldiers' stories. They told of a blond German officer captured with the Egyptians who had the insignia of the SS tattooed on his arm; of Russian orders issued to Egyptian tank crews; of underground tunnels packed with weapons. They spoke of vast quantities of captured ammunition, and of Egyptian commandos wearing pyjamas over their uniforms. They spoke harshly, as soldiers have since the beginning of war, and they unanimously agreed that not on any account would Israel withdraw from Sinai just because Britain or Russia or the United Nations happened to say so. Such was their mood, and such was mine, that I preferred on the whole not to debate the point.

Trucks came and went, soldiers climbed aboard and waved goodbye. It rained, and I prepared to move on. Just then the rainbow came. 'Look, a rainbow,' I said to a bearded and taciturn sergeant not long from Romania, and added sentimentally, 'An omen of peace!' But that unusual NCO needed no handkerchief to disperse his emotions. 'It is not a reasonable analogy to the present situation,' he replied, shifting his Sten gun on his shoulder. 'God showed Noah the rainbow as a promise of no more floods in the future. When He merely wished to signify that Noah could now leave the ark, He dispatched a small bird, carrying a piece of tree in its snout.'

At the end of the campaign I sat with an Israeli officer watching an apparently endless convoy of captured Egyptian armoured vehicles rumbling by on their way northwards into Israel. I asked him what they would do if the United Nations ordered the tanks to be returned to the Egyptians. 'Tanks?' he replied. 'What tanks?'

I went on from Sinai to Port Said in Egypt, the northern outlet of the Suez Canal and a place I had known for years, to see how it was after the British had bombed and occupied it.

There is an air of berserk unreality to the Suez adventure, so it is not surprising to find Port Said bathed in a sense of fantasy. There is a nightmare feeling to the city today, a suggestion that we shall all wake up one welcome morning and wash the memory away with the morning tea.

War falls easily enough upon sprawling capitals among the darkling plains, where ideologies clash and there are statues of dictators to topple from their pedestals. Port Said used to feel infinitely distant from such affairs. It was something different and apart, a place with a single purpose in life, neatly deposited upon the map like a town on a model railway: and until a few weeks ago it had a certain pungent sparkle to it, so that it was fun to watch the tankers pounding by as you drank your coffee among the dowdy blue crêpe dresses of the Simon Artz department store.

It still looks familiar, when you fly into it from Cyprus on an RAF aircraft. Soon, you may feel, the touts will be at your heels as always, and the gharries will be clip-clopping down the faded boulevards, and among the back streets, in rambling tenements and houses of peeling flotsam, the purveyors of sin will be preparing their debaucheries. But no, even before your aircraft lands you can sense the heavy despondency that now pervades the town.

The streets below are nearly empty. No impudent bum-boats hurry about the harbour. No teeming crowds wander through the Arab quarter. Off-shore half a dozen warships lie watchfully brooding, and over the town there seems to hang an unhealthy hush. It is as though some blighting epidemic has fallen upon Port Said, chasing the householders behind their doors, and leaving only uneasy scavengers at large.

Soon, as in a daze, you are entering the town. A squadron of Centurion tanks sprawls among churned mud in its outskirts. The big buildings along the waterfront are spattered with shell-fire. Part of the Arab quarter lies devastated, and a faint smell of death lingers in the streets, but it is not the tragedy of war that strikes you most forcibly as your bus rolls towards the Canal. It is the dreamlike quality of the experience. Something has happened in Port Said that shatters any previously held conception of the laws of probability. The British Army has seized it by force.

There are Union Jacks everywhere, familiar uniforms, officers driving requisitioned Citroëns. Courteous British sailors stand sentry upon the quayside, and there are war correspondents, and pompous army captains, and splendid ample petty officers, and people you were at school with, and a bustling jumble of British jokes and epithets. For a time none of it seems real. You shake your brain about like a drunk trying to disperse his liquor, until you look out across the harbour entrance and see the cluttered masts and funnels of sunken ships. Alas, it is no hallucination.

The shopping streets are dampened and depressed. The tourist stores are shuttered. Only a few merchants sit listlessly on kitchen chairs outside their premises. Here and there a shop has been mildly looted, and there is a litter of broken glass upon its floor and a few satin-padded boxes, empty of dubious emeralds or spurious antiques. In the Casino Palace Hotel, now a field hospital, you may search in vain for the courtly tarbooshed manager whose presence used to link that establishment indissolubly with the Edwardian era. Staff officers move importantly about the domed offices of the Suez Canal Company. Lounging soldiers lean from the windows of the shipping offices.

Here and there an Egyptian hawker accosts you. He peers around him before he offers you his wares, for somebody may accuse him of collab-oration, and he brings his prices down far, far more easily than he used to. Outside the coffee shops a few men sit at empty tables, looking blank. They answer your inquiries with an air of moody resignation, with shruggings of shoulders and raised eyebrows, and manage to tell you very little. Port Said is scared, not of the British Army, still a homely

45

force, but of the menacing powers of resentment and revenge that seethe behind the town's façade.

What a queer, contorted, significant mess has overcome the activities of this poor town! Motives have become hazily confused, moralities are topsy-turvy. The liberal finds himself allied with autocracy, the reactionary with the forces of progress. The decline of empires, the rise of the new Asia, the clash of east and west – all these portentous movements are suddenly illustrated with a peculiar clarity among these shabby urban streets. One can imagine such things easily enough in some war-scarred cockpit of Europe, but how anomalous they seem in Port Said, of all places, where the boatmen used to cheat you over the Turkish delight, and the young seamen tried to look experienced as they lounged towards the brothels, and pale colonial children on liner decks sat cross-legged and enthralled around the gully-gully men!

'Elephant and Castle!' say the soldiers, as the bus pulls in, but there is a false ring to the witticism. It has no heart in it, and springs from no roots of cheerful certainty: just as there feels no depth of truth or purpose to the present predicament of Port Said.

All three powers were soon obliged by international disapproval to withdraw from Egyptian territory. The Suez Canal has remained under Egyptian administration ever since, and all its European pilots were withdrawn. I asked a Royal Navy captain if this would create problems. Not at all, he said. All one had to do anyway was order one's helmsman: 'Steer down the middle'.

Baghdad

In 1958 a revolution put an end to the Hashemite monarchy in Iraq, for forty years a client state of the British Empire. The young King Feisal II and his uncle the Crown Prince Abdulillah were both murdered, and so was Nuri es-Said Pasha, the strong man of the regime and the best-known statesman of the Arab world. I had met all three in easier times, and I got to Baghdad a couple of days after their deaths.

In the broiling sun I walked through an open gateway and said goodbye to the old Iraq. 'Nuri es-Said is dead,' my driver informed me, performing some gestures of disembowelment. 'Now we will look at his house, which was also his fortress.' It is an ugly brick building with a garden running down to the Tigris, and its façade is chipped with machine-gun bullets. By the time the crowd reached the house on the day of the revolution Nuri had slipped away across the river, and now the place is a desolation, a charnel heap, littered with papers and broken furniture and dirt. A small boy sells soft drinks outside the front door, and a constant bustling curious crowd churns through its corridors, picking at the wreckage or peering into the broken shower-baths.

Relics of hideous poignancy lie everywhere about the house, and the crowd pokes its way into everything, breaking bits of wood off the wardrobes and ripping the last locks from the bedroom doors. Here is a packet of 'denture fixature'. Here is a race card. Half of an old helmet, such as the Turkish Army used to wear, is squashed beneath a box. Scraps of books swirl around the floors: a page on Allenby's strategy, a thesis on Roman law, an article on railway engines, a fragment of a thriller – *'Bellay bent forward and looked at the instruments. Sir James leaned across him and asked 'Did we send an emergency signal, captain?'*

A safe has been broken open, and a small crowd is shaking it backwards and forwards in the hope that a few treasures may have been left behind by early comers. A couple of young men are examining a broken cupboard with a commercial air, like rag and bone men inspecting an old suit. A sentry with a rifle stands guard at the back door, and as you approach he gives you a smile that is almost domestic: 'Welcome,' he says, bowing slightly, as if to give you the run of the garden.

So strong is the lingering presence of old Nuri, so all-powerful has he been through decades of Iraq's history, that it is hard to imagine his remains dismembered in ignominy across the Tigris. His house is wrecked and filthy and stripped of its grandeurs, and when he was dead, so I am told, they drove a car backwards and forwards across his body, 'for he was a man of great corruption'. But as you stand at the top of the garden it feels oddly as though the house has merely been thrown open to the public in aid of some charitable fund; as though the old grandee himself, to avoid the pressure of the mechanic crowds, has locked himself upstairs with a cigar and a pile of papers.

So I looked suddenly back into the hall of the house, as I passed the boy selling soft drinks, half-expecting to see his stocky figure lumbering down the staircase, or catch a glimpse of his cynical, leathery face high in some garret window; but only a happy family party came laughing and chattering into the hall, and from upstairs there came a noise of thudding and thumping, and a shouting of small boys and scampering footsteps, and all the sounds of holiday.

Israel

Nearly a decade after its foundation the Republic of Israel was at once a marvel, an affront and a perpetual anxiety – surrounded by Arab states formally dedicated to its extinction and surviving by a combination of guts, arrogance, charitable contributions and plain chutzpah.

Civis occidentalis sum, and so I do not feel altogether abroad in Tel Aviv. The air is Asian, the sun oriental, the buildings are white and the trees tropical, the beer of the sidewalk cafés possesses a curiously chemical quality, far removed from the vegetable grandeurs of European ale: but if you feel yourself to be a Western man, you will always be half at home in this, the principal city of the Jewish State.

Jerusalem is the official capital of Israel, and Haifa up the coast is a more serene and elegant city, but in the streets of Tel Aviv are enshrined, once and for all, the formidable efforts of the Zionists to achieve a homeland of their own. Here, better than anywhere else in the world, you may consider what it means to be a Jew, ponder the tragic significance of this astonishing people, and wonder whether this smallish seaside town, half resort, half business centre, will ever be a great city in a great nation, or whether the heart of Jewry lies elsewhere still. There was to the energies of Zionism, before the Israeli State became a fact, a mystical, biblical, tribal force, like the shifting of a season or some enormous celestial truth: but Tel Aviv is one of the deflations of history, for today it feels an essentially provincial, hopefully prosaic town, where the nice young women promenade down Allenby Road with their babies, and the conversation at the next table is generally concerned not with dark fundamentals of truth and cruelty, but only the cost of cucumbers or why little Moshe can't spell.

Tel Aviv, indeed, wants to be an ordinary town, and to any Western visitor nowadays it seems half familiar from the start. The climate is a dream, and all along the city's waterfront run heavenly golden sands, with the long slow swell of the Mediterranean curling up to the esplanades: but though the setting is exotic, this is almost a European city, inhabited by people who, though handsomely bronzed by the perpetual sun, are almost

Europeans. You hear English, German, Polish or Yiddish almost as often as you hear Hebrew, and time and again you will see someone walking down the street who seems at first sight to be somebody you know, a publisher in Paris or a musician in London, but who turns out to be familiar only because he is a Jew and a man of the West. Just as America was once called, by the poet Philip Bailey, the 'half-brother of the world', so Tel Aviv is distantly related, through the blood-brotherhood of Jewry, to all the greater cities of the West.

It still feels a city of the thirties, as do those London suburbs where the refugees from Hitler's Europe chiefly settled. There is little to show of the British who were its rulers between the wars – a street name here, a police station somewhere else: but its architecture smacks heavily of watered Bauhaus, its undistinguished squares, trim and symmetrical, look like town-planning designs in architectural reviews before the Second World War, and even its sea-front, though it has its glittering new hotels and raucous coffee bars, mostly retains a demure but determined period flavour. Tel Aviv was founded in 1910, but it was really born after Hitler came to power: the refugees who came then stamped it with the mark of their times, and beneath its housewifely exterior you may still detect, if you think long and hard enough about it, some of the art or sadness of fugitives, and the nostalgia of exiles.

Tel Aviv wants to be an everyday city, but can never quite achieve it, for Israel is not an everyday state. It has mellowed since its most defiant days of resentment, lost some of the chips upon its shoulders, but it still lives by the slogan of Ein Brera – 'No Alternative' – and is still precariously isolated among a ring of enemies. Moreover, every now and then the Israelis are halted in their tracks by a declamation out of the past, a reminder from State or history that they are no ordinary people, but a nation still apart, a nation of awful suffering genius, beyond the normal processes of the time. They are still confronted by a unique dilemma, apparent sure enough to the thoughtful stranger in the country: either they can abandon their Jewishness, their separateness, and become ordinary healthy citizens of a second Lebanon, or they can deliberately preserve their sense of persecution, superiority and detachment, and attach their new State to the dark and splendid centuries of the Jewish past. They can contract out of genius, if they please, and live as a small but gifted Levantine republic: or they can remain within the prison-palace of their magnificent heritage, and make this place not simply a city of the Israelis, but a city of the Jews.

In Tel Aviv you may feel that they have already made their choice, for there is nothing very gilded or terrible about this city, and here all feels plump and satisfied. Watch them closely as they saunter down to the beach, so tall and fit and laughing, with their gay sun-hats and brief shorts, their picnics and their plump babies – watch them with a detached Gentile eye, and you will see that Tel Aviv is already moulding, as Crevecoeur said of America long ago, a new kind of man. A generation is maturing that was born in Israel, and never knew the horrors of the ghettos or the lesser humiliations of Jewishness: and it is both the triumph and the tragedy of Tel Aviv that though its younger citizens are unmistakably Israeli, they do not feel like Jews.

Is this a worthy function for such a city, born out of the genius of such a people? Many Jews think not, and for myself I cannot suppose that Tel Aviv properly represents the Jewish future, faithfully though it may reflect the prospects of the Jewish State. Such an end to a supreme story does not ring true to history, to prophecy, to art, or to Judaism itself. The longer I spend among the cosy comforts of Tel Aviv, the more it seems to me that the Jews are, in a towering and inexplicable sense, some kind of Chosen People. So often, if you pursue a human activity to its source or its conclusion you end up among the Jews. They will never be quite the same as us, however happily humdrum they manage to make this city, and will perhaps never be restful, serene or ordinary for long. They are a nation doomed but exalted, lapped perpetually in the divine twilight.

Tel Aviv will fructify, I have no doubt, and play a worthy part in the affairs of the lesser states: but the only proper conclusion to the tale of the Jews is the victory of the selfless over the selfish – and sure enough, in the heart of that conception too every Christian finds a Jew.

I was once sitting beside the Mandelbaum Gate in the new part of Jerusalem, held by the Israelis, with Randolph Churchill, wayward son of the great Winston, who was then also working as a newspaper correspondent. Randolph, having perhaps taken one too many glasses of Israeli red wine, sat meditatively surveying the scene until in a loud but dreamy tone of voice he made the following statement to nobody in particular: 'Mandelbaum, Mandelbaum! If my name wasn't Churchill I would like to be called Mandelbaum.'

4

South African White and Black

In 1957 the Guardian *sent me for some months to the Union of South Africa. It was still a Dominion of the British Crown, but since 1948 the Afrikaner Nationalist Party had been in power and was gradually implementing its policy of apartheid – forcible racial separation.*

In the Drill Hall at Johannesburg 156 opponents of the regime, brought from all over the country, were being tried for high treason, compounded by communist affiliations. I covered the trial for the newspaper and made use of my reports in a book, South African Winter.

This was one of the oddest and nastiest of African phenomena, and it had an obscurely aboriginal flavour to it, as of recalcitrant chieftains dragged before their paramount ruler, or slaves examined *en masse* before their absorption by cannibal kings in Dahomey. The Drill Hall had been built in the old days of British South Africa, and it had a low veranda and lots of notice boards, and a varnished brown orderly-room air. In this place the accused assembled each morning in attitudes of bored or truculent resignation. There was a suggestion of punch-balls and puttees to the big dun-coloured hall, a sort of leathery, gym-shoe smell, and a large notice above one door proclaimed incongruously: 'Escape Door: Not Locked'. The light was rather dim those cold winter mornings, and beside the entrance a policeman sat at a deal table holding his thriller to the sunshine, the better to find some excitement in life.

This is one place in South Africa where racial segregation is tacitly abandoned. The audience is separated, to be sure, into the usual white sheep and black goats, but the accused are herded together hugger-mugger in their wire pen. Some are white, some are brown, some are proudly black. One or two read newspapers, some write letters, a few usually seem to be asleep. One man wears a green, yellow and black blazer. A tall elegant Jew sorts his colour slides with detachment; a young African girl, in a green beret and black-and-white flowered skirt, spreads her papers around her on the bench and works upon a thesis. Here a merry little Indian giggles with his neighbours, and here a lean bearded black man, inexpressibly sinister of appearance, stares coldly at the ceiling like an upturned idol. Every shade of leftist opinion is represented here, sometimes in awkward proximity. The handsome black giant with the silver hair and the benign smile is Chief Luthuli, a great man of the Zulu people and the most remarkable black leader in the Union. There are lawyers and clergymen and students and taxi-drivers and writers and wives and political activists: all are enemies, from one motive or another, of apartheid; all are opponents of the Nationalist Government, and all are, in theory anyway, candidates for the gallows.

South Africa is an odd amalgam of tyranny and liberty, about equally compounded, and to this strange hearing there is an unexpected element of old-school fairness. The magistrate is scrupulous, the police treat their prisoners kindly, there is something faintly academic or even recreational about the hearings. The Crown's evidence, presented by semi-literate plain-clothes detectives, is sometimes downright comic; one Presbyterian clergyman of communist leanings, for example, is alleged to have been received by the Pope in audience 'at his church in Moscow'. The defence lawyers are often witty. When the court adjourns for its tea break, at eleven each morning, there is usually quite a cheerful atmosphere to the scene. Thermos flasks emerge from baskets. An eager African hawks group photographs headed 'Treason Trial, 1956', in which all this assembly sits in smiling rows giving the thumbs-up sign – the salute of African nationalism. The Presbyterian parson shows his neighbour the manuscript of next Sunday's sermon, already stamped with the cachet of the Special Branch censorship. The defence lawyers, who have volunteered their services, stroll among their clients or chat with Crown counsel (as they are still laughably called). A couple of reporters doodle at their table, and one or two Africans from the audience talk to their friends through the mesh of the wire. The unacclimatized visitor, fresh from the logicalities of Europe or America, feels his head whirl as he talks to a Zulu chief, a taxi-driver's wife from Durban, a rich Marxist lawyer, an Afrikaner police officer, and a schoolgirl from the audience in the gymslip and long black stockings of an almost forgotten England. Lear and Carroll would often feel at home, at tea break in the Drill Hall.

* * *

A sad daily postscript to the charade of the trial was provided outside the Drill Hall in the evening, when the stores had closed and the factory hands were hastening out into the night.

Now all the poor black workers of Johannesburg, forbidden to live within the precincts of the city, rush for the buses that will take them to their locations, to the slums or sprawling estates of the Western Areas. Each evening as dusk falls, and as the bitter night wind begins to whistle through the buildings, a vast tattered queue moves in raggety parade towards the bus depot. It encircles the entire square outside the Drill Hall, so that the tail of the queue meets its own head, and all those thousands of Africans shuffle their slow way in double file towards their shabby buses. It is the longest, and saddest, and coldest queue I have ever seen. The bus service is frequent enough, and the black people do not usually have to shiver in the cold for too long: but there is an air of unutterable degradation to the scene, so heartless and machine-like is the progress of the queue, as the white folk hasten off in their cars to Hillbrow and Parktown, and the lights glitter in windows of the department stores, and these poor lost souls are crammed into their buses and packed off to their distant ill-lit townships. Many of them are half-starving. Most of them live in fear of robbery and violence when they step off the buses into the dark streets of the locations. Half of them spend almost all their leisure hours travelling between the city and the far-flung patches of high veldt in which they are, by law, forced to live. They reach their homes long after dark at night, and they start for work again while the morning is still only a suggestion. You can hardly watch such a scene, and ponder its implications, and collate it with that dotty trial in the Drill Hall behind you, without the stirring of some crusading instinct, some Byronic impulse, or at least a stab of pity.

But when you get back to your hotel again, and are drowning the memory in a Riesling from the Cape, perhaps you will hear some tinny twangs of music from the street outside: and there beneath the arcades of President Street some solitary black man will be lounging by, in a tattered brown hat and blue dungarees, plucking away at a guitar as he walks, humming a high-toned melody and expressing in his every gesture, in the very swing of his shoulders, the spirit of carefree indolence.

The worst repressions of apartheid were not yet in force, the judiciary was still relatively independent, and after four years of hearings all 156 of the accused at the Treason Trial were acquitted. The gulf between blacks and whites in the country, however, already seemed to be unbridgeable. In Port Elizabeth one day I visited Christopher Gell, an implacable white opponent of the regime, immediately after meeting members of a black sect whose leader claimed to be the Voice at Midnight that gave warning to the foolish virgins of the Bible.

Few Europeans stand astride the racial divide. Only a handful can without self-consciousness share the confidences of educated, politically minded blacks, so sooner or later nearly every foreign inquirer finds his way to Christopher Gell. He probably knows more than anyone about the strengths and weaknesses of African defiance. His articles appear all over the world, and within South Africa his name is almost legendary. To his stuffier Port Elizabeth neighbours he is a fanatic and a freak. To many Africans he is magic. To the reporters and commentators of the world, he is a unique source of guidance and information. To the Nationalists he is anathema. His telephones are tapped, his visitors observed, his mocking trenchant opinions no doubt preserved in the vaults of Afrikanerdom. He is one of the symbolic figures of the South African tragedy, exerting from this dull provincial port a peculiar and incalculable influence upon the national affairs. And all this is the more interesting because, as it happens, Gell is crippled by poliomyelitis and lives in an iron lung.

He is an English-born South African of a truly inspiring force of character. I disagree with much of what he says; I find him often intolerant and sometimes unfair; but I have never met a man I would more willingly follow into the inferno. His father was a British naval officer, and Gell himself is a former member of the Indian Civil Service. He talks in the racy, sometimes expletive idiom of the English gentleman, and nobody could accuse him for a moment of any fuddy-duddy muddle-headed liberalism. He knows exactly where he stands, and so does everyone else. 'Don't ring off!' he says, when you telephone and introduce yourself. 'Wait till I put my telephone down and then listen, and you'll hear a kind of click when these stiffs stop tapping the line. Ready? OK, I'll ring off now – you listen!' And sure enough, when his laughing voice has gone and you have waited for a moment or two, you may fancy you hear a muffled embarrassed click, as some unseen censor, his ears burning, adds an entry to the Gell dossier.

In such a gay spirit Gell cocks a perpetual snook at the authorities and contributes manfully to his chosen cause, the emancipation of the African. A well-trodden path leads to his little house (where his remarkable young wife supports them both with a physiotherapy practice). Here the African politicians come, and the editors of the local newspapers, innumerable visiting investigators, a stream of people interested in the African risorgimento and anxious to meet this strange Byronic figure. Gell receives them in his lung or in his bed (he can leave the machine for three hours every day). He is very tall, painfully cadaverous, immensely vivacious. He wears glasses and has one of his arms suspended above him in a kind of sling. Books and elaborate filing cabinets line the room. There is a painting of the battle cruiser *Hood*, one of his father's ships, and the table beside the bed is littered with proofs and pamphlets and letters and open books. Sometimes an African servant wanders in with coffee, carrying a baby slung to her back: Gell treats her with affectionate unsentimentality. Often the telephone rings and Gell, making a grimace at you, launches himself into a torrential farrago of opinion and prejudice and argument, until the voice of the man at the other end sounds breathless and dispirited, and Gell's face is wickedly aglow, and the conversation ends in an intellectual annihilation.

Then, like a swivelling gun or a fire-hose, he turns to you. 'Now then, let me put you straight about these bloody Nats . . .' He talks with tremendous energy, animated, witty, outrageous, caustic, irrepressible, interspersing his diatribes with devastating confidences, pausing sometimes to scribble a name down for you or dash off a letter of introduction, swearing, laughing, quoting Schweitzer, in a most extraordinary flood of stimulation and conviction. Slowly, though, his damaged physique runs down. His breathing becomes heavier and more difficult, his conversation more gasping and spasmodic, his face more strained with effort, and the gusto drains from his body before your eyes, like the symbolisms of a Gothic painting: until at last his wife comes cheerfully in and moves him back to his iron lung. He will still be talking as you leave him, and his anxious humorous eyes will be following you in the little mirror above his head. 'Of *course* we're intolerant,' he says as you go. 'We have to be. We'd never get anywhere with these stiffs if we weren't!' Some people believe Christopher Gell to be a saint. Certainly his presence at Port Elizabeth gives it, to my mind, a strong lead over the Voice at Midnight in the immortality stakes.

5

Confusions in Paradise: The Caribbean

In the later years of the decade I went to the Caribbean for the Guardian. *The region was in some confusion, in this first period of post-imperialism, and I reported on as many aspects of it as I could, and used some of the resultant essays in a collection called* Cities.

Trinidad

Trinidad was the most cosmopolitan of the British West Indian colonies, with a large Asian population and a particular fizz to go with it. In those days its capital, Port of Spain, was great fun to visit.

If you walk across the Savannah in the dying heat of evening, you may sometimes hear the strains of unaccompanied music, and know that young Mr Morgan is practising his violin. The Savannah is a wide green common on the northern side of Port of Spain, in Trinidad, where the tropical hills come sidling down to the sea, and around its perimeter there stands a company of legendary Trinidadian mansions. One is gorgeously Gothic, one exotically Moorish, one predominantly blue: but the most stylish of them all is No. 25 Maraval Road, where Mr Morgan lives. It is a big white house surrounded with balconies, like an eccentric gunboat on the China Station, and it is encrusted with every kind of ornament, towers and turrets and filigree and wrought iron and balustrades and flagstaffs and weathercocks and all possible fractions of elaboration.

In the Moorish house there lives an archbishop, in the Gothic castle an old plantation family, but it is characteristic of Trinidad that among the inhabitants of No. 25 should be young Mr Morgan, who came from England only a few years ago and who loves to play his violin in a cool vaulted upstairs chamber. Port of Spain is a city of endless tumbling variety, mingled races, haphazard collusions, surprises and incongruities;

gilded with the histories of the Western world, with a past of piracy, slavery and war, and a present ranging from razzle-dazzle politics to the British Council. Mr Morgan may sound an improbable figure, up there with his music-stand, but he is only an agreeable chip in a gaudy and multitudinous mosaic.

As you wander on through the Savannah, with his music faintly in your ears, you may sense some of the gusto and exuberance of this heterogeneous society. This is the piazza of Trinidad. In the empty grandstand of the racecourse a big Negro in a straw hat sprawls across the seats in indolent splendour, but below him on the grass all is movement, bustle and vivacity. Wherever you look, from the hills to the city, they are playing cricket. To be sure, they are playing the game all over the island, in numberless unmapped clearings in the bush, overhung by lugubrious banana trees or gorgeous flamboyants: but this is the very heart of Trinidadian cricket, where the game is played today with more dash and delight than anywhere else on earth. There may be thirty or forty games going on, all at the same time. The thud of the balls echoes like muffled fireworks across the green, and wherever you look there are the crouching fielding figures, stylish black batsmen, a game suddenly collapsing in hilarity or the poised theatrical expectancy, all white eyes and arms, that follows the magical cry of '*Howzat!*'

Some of these sportsmen are grand and mannered, with spotless whites and rolled wickets, but they trail away through immeasurable gradations of clubmanship to the raggety small boys on the edge of the field, with an old bit of wood for a bat, and a stone for a ball, and the wicket-keeper peering with breathless excitement over a petrol can. Whatever the style, the game is pursued with panache. Balls, stones and fieldsmen hurl themselves indiscriminately across your path. Wild cries of scorn or enthusiasm punctuate your progress. 'Him's out! Him's out!' shout the small boys in delight, and the young man with the pipe murmurs, 'Pretty, very pretty shot.' Many a culture or tradition contributes to the texture of Port of Spain, and one of the strongest is that tough old umbilical, cricket.

Not all the cricketers are black. Many of these citizens are Indian by origin, and many are a melange in themselves, part European, part African, with a touch of Chinese and a Hindu grandparent on the mother's side. Racial rivalries are still potent, especially between brown and black, and sometimes you may catch a hint of them on the Savannah. An Indian father, for example, shoos away a small black boy anxious to play kites with his son. 'Go away, sonny,' he says crossly, 'this is a private game we are

57

playing, you see, we do not want other people coming and playing here.' The black boy gazes stubbornly into the middle distance. He is wearing an old army forage cap, much too big for him. 'I'se not playing with you anyway,' he says. 'I'se playing here all by myself. This ain't no private garden. I'se just flying my kite right here where I belong.' And you can see a spasm of annoyance cross that Hindu's smooth face, a spasm that runs through the society of Trinidad, and gives an extra vicious animation to the politics of the city.

There are white people on the Savannah, too. The girls playing hockey on the south side, watched by an audience ranging from the maternal to the frankly salacious, well represent the shades of allure once conceived by a local competition promoter: 'Miss Ebony and Miss Mahogany, Miss Satinwood and Miss Allspice, Miss Sandalwood, Miss Golden Apple, Miss Jasmine, Miss Pomegranate, Miss Lotus and Miss Appleblossom.' Here and there a weathered white West Indian plays long-stop or lounges in the grass, and sometimes you may even see an elderly imperial couple, in khaki shorts and linen skirt, exercising themselves doggedly across the green. Beside the botanical gardens the Governor-General's house still looks exceedingly British, but there seems no public resentment against so diffident a pigment as mine, and the loiterers will grin at you pleasantly as you pursue your watchful navigations between the pitches.

Often they will do more than merely grin, for the Trinidadian is a great talker. He may want to talk about religion. 'You have to understand that we are Sunnis; it's all a matter of orthodoxy, we do not agree about the succession, you see.' Or: 'My friend, I come here not to play games but to meditate. I come to think, to try to understand, you get me?' Or they want to talk politics. 'It's all a matter of race, man. This man's a dictator, that's quite clear. He's got no experience. A man like Bertie, he's got politics in his blood. That's the truth, man.' Or: 'Where do you belong? England? I've got two brothers and an aunt and a cousin in Birmingham. They live 102 Middens Lane, Birmingham 2. Sure, they like it fine, making plenty money!' Or here, as everywhere in the Western world, you may hear the time-honoured cry of the taxi-man, leaning across the railings beside the road. 'You want a car, sir? I take you all round the island, Pitch Lake, Benedictine Monastery, Airport, Calypso, Limbo Dance, Night Clubs? Here's my card, sir! That's my name, Cuthbert B. Harrison!'

And finally, a climax to your wanderings, you may find yourself embroiled in the counter-marchings of an embryo steel band, twenty boys in home-made uniforms beating on cans and tin plates and chanting rhythmically. On their sailor jackets the words 'Brass Boys' are hazily embroidered, and they prance there in the evening sunshine like black leprechauns, banging away at their plates, singing their boisterous but monotonous ditty, round and round in a vigorous, long-legged barefoot circle. The cricketers play their ancient game; the kites stream above the Savannah; an English lady waits patiently for her dog beside the race track; the Negro in the grandstand stirs, tilts his hat over his eyes and goes to sleep again; and in the middle of it all this noisy rite exuberates, the shining lithe legs kick to its clattering rhythms, and the white teeth flash in the sunshine.

Port of Spain is a tolerant, cosmopolitan, relatively well-educated city; but one sometimes feels that for all the stroke-play and the intelligence the real essence of the place is contained in these raw and raucous celebrations. Certainly there are moments when the music of Mr Morgan's violin, still riding the breeze uncertainly, seems the melody of a retreating world, just as the intoxicating turrets and baubles of his house are memorials to a Trinidad of long ago.

Barbados

'Barbados is behind you', this minute colony had encouragingly telegrammed the British Government at the start of the Second World War, and two decades later it was still unmistakably loyal of style.

It was a coral-island Easter in St John's, Barbados, today, an Easter set in a silver sea, with the long line of the Atlantic surf breaking benignly on the beach beneath the church, and the fields of tall sugar cane ruffling gently in the sunshine. But as I sat in the churchyard after service this morning, what I thought was how small and interrelated a world this is, how many ghosts and traditions we share, how strong are the links that bind us willy-nilly, whether it be a Kentish drizzle that freshens our Easter flowers or a warm trade wind off the Caribbean.

The parishioners who came to the service were nearly all black people, sugar-workers and their families from the estates that divide this old island like a chequer-board, but few of them were really strangers to me. Their white muslins and their wide straw hats once graced the English social fabric, and when they sat down expectantly for the sermon the rustle of their petticoats and the crackling of their starch filtered through to me across the pages of many an Edwardian memoir. I knew which hymns they would sing with gusto, for I had heard these same tentative starts and communal diapasons at many a grumbling British Army church parade. The verger in his black cassock I had often met before, pointing out the ravages of death-watch beetles in the shires. And when the piano struck up its preliminary chord I knew from her air of proud command which of these old friends would be the one who always comes in half a beat before the beginning of the verse.

And if I shut my eyes and listened to the responses, why, the voices were those that Parson Adams used to lead in prayer in the brave days of Tom Jonesian England. The people of Barbados have the oldest, home-liest, quaintest, most rustic and evocative of accents, with a rich West Country burr and a thin sliver of Irish on top of it, like cream. 'There's your pew yonder,' the verger will say, handing you your prayer-book, and instantly you are back in the eighteenth century, with the rattle of a carriage outside the door and the bonnets of the squire's ladies nodding above the mahogany. 'Amen, Amen,' murmured the congregation rev-erently as Mr Simmon's excellent sermon ended this morning, and it was like the country clatter of hobnail boots on the stone-flagged floor of a dairy.

Barbados is not paradise unalloyed, but in such a rural district as this, well away from the clubs and the big hotels, you may well feel yourself in some lingering old Arcadia, or in that pleasant mythical land devised by Professor Tolkien as the habitat of his hobbits. It seems to be inhabited only by kind and courteous people. They are admittedly busy demanding higher wages from the estates, but they still speak nicely of 'Mistress Spreadbury up at the dwelling-house', and they welcome you to their wooden homes with immediate stout hospitality. Wherever you look on the map of their district there are reassuring folk-story sorts of names – Moonshine Hall and Gun Hill, Windsor and Cattlewash and Locust Hall, and Bickden, down along of Easy Hall, yonder by Joe's Ride.

So after service this morning, as the church bells rang out in celebration, as I basked in the sunshine and hummed the hymn tunes, I thought that no island is really an island, and that the brawny black bell-ringer whose face grinned at me from the tower above was pealing for us all. The flowers in that churchyard were exotic enough, and all around my horizon the brick chimneys of the sugar factories, buried among their fields, looked gaunt and unfamiliar. But the tombs of the Kerrs, the Carters, the Toppins and the Sealeys dreamed beside me in the shade, and I swear I could have heard Squadron Sergeant-Major Harris leading the hallelujahs in the church. (He always liked a good old hymn. Cleared his lungs, he said.)

Cuba

Cuba had recently emancipated itself from what had been in effect a long, corrupt and invasive overlordship of the United States. I had been there in the days of the Mafia-linked dictator Fulgencio Batista, and certainly did not admire that crooked and oppressive regime, but I got a nasty shock, all the same, when the Guardian *sent me back to see what the island felt like under the charismatic left-wing guerilla Fidel Castro.*

If I am dreaming, pinch me and wake me up; but if I am awake already, then arriving in Cuba these days is one of the queerest nightmares of our insomniac world. Here we are in a gay and sunny island, not a hundred miles from Miami, peopled by friendly musical Latins, set in a luscious holiday sea, with all the joys of the American way to tempt us and half the pleasures of Spain to tickle our desires. Dear old bumbling Uncle Sam lives just across the way, and the *New York Times* lies plump upon the news-stands. Yet pick up a Cuban paper and here is a fellow in a deplorable beard spouting horrible death to the Yankees, here is a trade delegation just arriving from communist China, here is an American talking quite seriously about invading the place, and here is some lunatic explaining that Cuba's first line of defence is the Soviet Union's armoury of rockets. And Miami, that archetypal welter of hot dogs and women's clubs, is scarcely out of sight from your bedroom window!

Your first arrival is ordinary and pleasant enough. The Cubans still give you a most hospitable welcome, and this must be one of the easiest states on earth for a foreigner to enter. A Calypso band plays deafeningly while you stagger through the Customs. A raggle-taggle mob of smiling citizens, all brown faces and polychromatic cotton, leans festively over the barrier. And when you drive away to the city through the night all is as you expect it – the indefatigable cicadas fiddling merrily in the grass, the blinding advertisements and neon lights, the drive-ins and the spruce gas stations, the parade of cars streaming down the great dual highway in the dark. It feels like a tropical monument of the American way – as brashly American as Puerto Rico, say, and not much less so than Miami itself.

But when you wake up in the morning, with the brilliant white spread of Havana beneath your window, the blue bay ineluctably calm, and the rumble of the traffic along the splendid waterfront, then the dream takes over. Queer, queer things are happening here. This sugar and bikini state ('the inviting island next door', as the New York tourist brochures say) has lurched so far from the American ideal that people can seriously talk of it as a potential Russian satellite, like Czechoslovakia or Hungary. The city streets are almost indistinguishable from the boulevards of Miami or Tampa – the same kind of shop, the same kind of building, the same makes of cars, the same smells, sights, and sounds, tinged as southern Florida is with the sting of the tropics and a late flourish of Spain. Yet already, you will discover, there are to this island some first niggling reminders of People's Democracies. There are Russian ships in port, bringing Black Sea oil to the nationalized refineries. There are Chinese communists about, and the papers are full of Mr Khrushchev's paternal interest. There is a cartoon in one of the dailies, showing the United States spurned by a pious and unanimous world, that might have come direct from the pages of *Krokodil*. The city is heavy with banners and slogans, and only last night, so the grapevine says, a couple of Americans were arrested upstairs in my hotel.

To the simple newcomer, though, it is the hints and innuendoes that seem more ominously uncanny. The Havana Hilton hotel, for example, looks as fabulously vulgar as ever – vast and glittering and quintessentially capitalist. Yet it is already, like the plush old hostelries of Warsaw and Leningrad, a state enterprise. It is renamed the Havana Libre, its American umbilical has long been cut, and in the unemptied ashtrays and the echoing restaurants you may glimpse, as in a crystal mirror, the drab image of public management. Tucked away in the newspapers (still, in format and funnies, as American as blue jeans) are dark droppings of new philosophies. The Foreign Ministry announces that the former Ambassador in Bonn, who resigned this week, is a traitor. All citizens whose homes have been 'requisitioned or confiscated' are told that in future their affairs will be handled by the War Victims Aid Department. Captain Antonio Jimenez has returned from his commercial mission to Czechoslovakia, Poland, Russia and East Germany, announcing that he has obtained there equipment for thirty new Cuban industries. The Cuban Sports Commission wants to participate in the chess tournament at Leipzig. Three factories making toothpaste, soap, nail polish, and hair lotion have been seized by the militia 'at the request of the Workers' Union'. Forty-eight lawyers have been dishonourably expelled from the Havana Bar Association by the Revolutionary Committee which took control last week. The university students' federation demands that the university council and deans of all faculties – 'the landowners' culture' – resign to make way for reforms.

Not, you may say, very immediately alarming. No wild crowds are storming through Havana this morning, no hairy fanatics are foaming on the balconies, nobody so far seems discourteous or revengeful. But if you want to understand how queer it feels, try to understand that, in externals anyway, this might almost be American territory. It is dollar country. It is as though a near-communist regime had seized control in Washington itself, and were toppling the loftiest members of the American system, from the great oil companies to the flashy hotels. It is like experiencing some catastrophic shift of circumstance – a virulently fought divorce, or even a change of sex – a harsh, grinding, infinitely disturbing procession, reversal and renunciation.

Some nightmares are like that. They place you in a fairly familiar situation and then subject you to some unimaginable ordeal. It feels almost incredible to me that this old Catholic island, linked by a thick mesh of intercourse and interest with its neighbour across the water, could really be joining the communist block, as so many of the pundits have it. It is like some awful hallucination even to read conjectures about a Russian military base in Cuba. But there we are. That's the way people are talking in Havana today. If I am dreaming it all, please wake me quick.

Nearly half a century later, when the Soviet Union had disappeared and 'dear old bumbling Uncle Sam' no longer seemed so benevolent a presence in the world, Fidel Castro was still in power in Cuba. Once, in Havana, I interviewed Ernesto Guevara, then president of the national bank. Thirty years later, long after Ernesto had matured into Che and had become a world-celebrated icon of the youth culture, I gave a lift in England to a hitch-hiker whose T-shirt bore a familiar picture of him – by then one of the best-known photographs on earth. 'I bet I'm the only person you've ever got a lift from,' I remarked, 'who actually met Che Guevara.' 'Oh yeah,' was the reply. 'Who was Che Guevara?'

6

Europe: After the War was Over

Towards the end of the 1950s in Europe I wrote brief pieces for the Guardian *about three European capitals, approaching them in different moods and with different techniques. I also recorded distant and disparate contacts with the two most admired wartime leaders of Europe, still alive but already subsumed into legend.*

Berlin

I meandered meditatively and rather morosely around the former German capital. The infamous Berlin Wall had not yet gone up, but the city was divided between Western and Soviet zones of occupation, and was still largely in ruins.

Berlin is the centre city of Europe – some might say of the world – and its heart is the stark, scarred archway called the Brandenburger Tor: not because it stands upon the last great frontier of the West, but because, poised as it thus is between two overwhelming alien philosophies, it remains quintessentially German. It is a harsh and often hated monument, but at least it feels real.

For although Berlin is an exciting and an ominous place, divided as it is both by masonry and by method, yet for me it feels chiefly like a queer stage-city. In the east it reads its communist lines, in the west its libertarian, to a thump of dogmas or a tinkle of profit: but in neither role does it feel quite natural. Not so long ago its subject territories extended from the Atlantic to the Caucasus, and it had a brutal ideology of its own. Today it has become a kind of nightmare fair, where the two halves of the world meet to set up their pavilions. There is an emptiness and a pretence to its spirit, as though the meaning of the place had been forcibly ripped out twenty years ago, and only replaced by slogans and sealing-wax.

It is fashionable to say that Berlin is no longer neurotic, but I cannot agree. It feels to me a terribly mixed-up metropolis, tortured by old anxieties or inhibitions, and understandably shot through with fear. That the Berliners have guts, diligence and realism nobody can deny. They have an almost Cockney gaiety to them, an almost chirpy bonhomie, and they seem on the face of things undismayed by their ferocious ups and downs of fortune. But beneath their genial public veneer, I suspect, they cherish darker layers of emotion: cynicism, self-disgust, shattered pride, morbid resolution. Some people say the difference between East Berlin and West Berlin is the difference between light and shade. To me, though the transition from one to the other is shattering to endure, nevertheless they both feel at once dark and floodlit, like the scene of an accident.

Berlin is the capital of a lost empire, and its imperial past lies like a helmeted skeleton in its cupboard. It forms on one side the capital of the Democratic Republic of East Germany, on the other a province of the Federal German Republic: but the Germanness of it survives by sufferance, by suggestion, by retrospection. In the eastern sector the placards and the exhortations, the state shops and the slit-eyed arrogance of Lenin-allee bring to the purlieus of the old Unter den Linden an oily whiff of Asia. In the west all the gallimaufry of the American world prances and preens itself: neon signs, juke boxes, *Time*, apartments by Corbusier, hotel rooms by Conrad Hilton, paperbacks, pony-tails, dry martinis and Brigitte Bardot. The old Germany lives on underground, surfacing sometimes in a splendid opera, a Schiller play, a melody or a neo-Nazi.

On the one side the East Berliners find themselves remoulded, month by month, year by year, crisis by crisis, into a new kind of people – brainwashed, as it were, *en masse* and by force of habit. On the other, the West Berliners have become walking symbols: inhabitants of a city that has no economic meaning, no geographical sense, no certainties and no security, but which is kept alive like some doomed and cadaverous magnate, just to spite the beneficiaries. Few Berliners seem to suppose that their city will ever again be the capital of a free united Germany. The East Berliners live for the hour, or the Party meeting after work. The West Berliners accept what a paradoxical fortune offers them, and move blithely enough through life, like fish in a glittering goldfish bowl.

It remains, though, a single city, and there is no disguising its traumatic quality, its mingled sense of ignominy, defiance, futility and pathos. Bitterly mordant are the comments of the Berliners when they show you around their boulevards. Their jokes are coarse and often cruel, their allusions streaked with self-mockery. Caustically they tell you that each side of the Brandenburger Tor calls itself democratic – the east with a capital D, the west with a small one. Wryly they observe that the Perpetual Flame of Freedom uses an awful lot of gas. Almost apologetically they point to Tempelhof, still the most astonishing of the world's airports, as 'the one good job that Hitler did'. They sound resigned but secretly resentful. They know what you are thinking.

For the fact is that their city remains, to this day, a constant and terrible reproach against all that Germany has meant to the twentieth century. The Liberty Bell, no less than the gigantic Russian war memorial, is a reminder that in our times German values have been rotten values. Berlin, east and west, is a city built upon the ruins of Germany, watered with German tears, haunted by the shades of a million lost young men, a million lost illusions, the ghost of a dead and discredited patriotism. It is the most melancholy of cities. It has lost its soul, and is still acquiring replacements.

And for myself, I find its neuroses ever apparent: in the almost obsessive pride, for example, that Berliners have in their zoo, deposited in the very middle of the city and famous for its shackled elephants; in the passion for flowers that bloom so eerily in this most warlike and fearful of capitals; in the bizarre assurance of the nightlife – the placid composure with which, for instance, comfortable burghers and their homely wives accept their beers from a man dressed up as a waitress; in the flashy extravagance of the western sectors and the dulled apathy of the east; in the inevitable, ever-growing alienation of one side from the other; in the absolute stunned silence with which the cinema audience files out from the ghastly film *Mein Kampf*, an appalling laceration of German pride and self-respect.

So it is I say that Berlin's heart is the Brandenburger Tor, with its great Quadriga restored but hardly regnant upon the top of it. Around that symbol of old pomp the real Berlin still stands: the gaping Reichstag, the ruined Wilhelmstrasse, the shells of broken cathedrals and shattered palaces, Goering's offices and Hitler's bunker, the tumbled halls of the Third Reich, the grave of a lost empire. Anything may happen to Berlin in the second half of our century; but whoever rules it, until the shades of that dreadful capital are exorcized at last, until the very memory of it dims, all the brilliance and bluster of the new city will be sham, and its spirit will never be easy.

Paris

In Paris, physically unscathed by the war, I tracked the progress through the city of an imaginary Englishman, evidently some years older than I was myself. Like many Britons he obviously resented France's ability to surmount shameful memories of a war which they themselves had fought so epically.

Gingerly the middle-aged Englishman, tilting his trilby, emerges out of the Gare du Nord into the streets of Paris. He has a couple of hours to spend before he rejoins his train at the Gare de Lyon, but he views the prospect with no wild abandon, for deep inside him, however hard he tries, however polite his French or cosmopolitan his past, deep inside him there stirs, like a rustle of bones in a dark cavern, an old English antipathy to the place. It stems from centuries of bloodshed and rivalry; from the bitterness of tragic alliance; from the puritan strain that still runs through the English character, and long ago stigmatized this incomparable capital as ante-room of Purgatory; from envy, and a sense of provincial origins; from the robust self-assertion of sea-going islanders, and the blinkered vision of history. Americans adore Paris, hasten there to write their novels or paint their violent abstracts, love her in the springtime, hire her same old taxi-cabs, set themselves up with slinky blondes in desperately expensive garrets. The middle-aged English approach, however, is altogether more wary and restrained, and the visitor looks sharply right and left, tucking his wallet more securely into his pocket, as he walks briskly through the maniacal taxis and settles at the corner café for what, he thinks with a wry smile, the French comically call a cup of tea. He knows he is in the wrong. He knows he ought to have coffee. But there is something about Paris that inflames his insularity, and makes the Channel behind his back feel very deep, wide and important.

It is partly the confounded foreignness of the place. To this Englishman nowhere in the world is more irrevocably abroad than Paris, which is a good deal nearer London than Newcastle is. If it felt a little closer before the war, four years incommunicado sealed it once and for all as a city beyond the divide. Danger and ignominy have hardened its arteries of pride, and spared as it is the burden of a common language it remains

67

today, in a world of fading frontiers, overwhelmingly and magnificently French. It is the fulcrum of Europe, but it is emblazoned with all the splendours of old-school patriotism. It shelters, as always, a vast foreign community, but its guests are clothed in the fabric of France. Hardly anybody in the Paris streets seems to speak English. Hardly anybody looks Americanized, or Anglicized, or Italianized, let alone Germanized. Paris is French all through, from *pissoir* to Academy, and the middle-aged Englishman, with all his inherited instincts of patronage, feels himself at an unfair disadvantage. Like the poet before him, he loves Humanity with a love that's pure and pringlish, but he feels an obscure resentment towards the French, who never will be English.

Then, says he to himself, Paris is so damned pompous. A Mall or two is all right in its way, of course, and comes in useful for royal processions or emergency car parks: but a whole city drawn geometrically, in circles, arcs and right angles, offends the English taste for studied informality. Paris has, it is perfectly true, its vast rambling filigree of back streets, climbing over Montparnasse and through the warrens of Montmartre, but as the Englishman pays his bill and sets off through the city, he feels himself to be transiting endless acres of formality. The Champs-Elysées goes on and on. The Place de l'Etoile goes round and round. It feels a mile from one corner of the Place de la Concorde to another, and retreating through the Tuileries from the gorgeous severity of the Louvre is like retiring backwards, with frequent obsequious bows, down the interminable audience chamber of some royal presence. The very river of Paris feels artificial, like a long water-folly in an elaborate belvedere, and the Eiffel Tower looks as though it has been placed there by a divine landscape gardener, as a lesser practitioner might erect a wicker pagoda behind the rose-beds. All this upsets our Chestertonian, who, reflecting that Britannia needs no boulevards, no spaces wide and gay, feels it somehow irritating that the French should need them either.

He supposes, as he broods down the Rue de Rivoli, that it's all part of the Frenchman's *cleverness*. Everyone knows the Parisians are as clever as so many monkeys, and in this city nothing feels simple or unsophisticated. Everything is scented. Even the crusty door-keepers inspect you with a knowing air, and the fat market ladies of Les Halles do not look like proper working women at all, but rather like enormous eccentric dowagers slumming it for fun, or honouring some cracked family conviction. The worldly Parisiennes are not only unattainably elegant, but also dauntingly well read, and have a maddening habit of being good with horses, too. The suave young men are rubbed smooth as almonds with the unguent of *savoir faire*. The students at the Sorbonne blaze with politics and weird philosophical speculation, but never seem to ladder a stocking. Even the dustmen sip modish drinks, like Pernod, and eat fancy cheeses, like Camembert or Brie, and smoke strong tart cigarettes, and generally behave with an urbanity that seems to the middle-aged Englishman just a little presumptuous. He stifles the thought at once, of course, for he is a liberal sort of fellow: but it is there, it is there, as it was when the heads rolled.

He distrusts them, too. Yes, he does. He cannot restrain the sensation that he has fallen among thieves. There is something sly and underhand to the careful indolence of the little shops, those lovely clothes tossed into the windows like nightdresses in a bottom drawer, that calculated clutter of exquisite frivolities, that scalpel juxtaposition of the gay cheap and the ruinously extravagant. There is something very suspicious about the sullen brusqueness of the taxi-driver, as though he is swiftly summing his customer up with a view to disembowelling him. There is something horribly ingratiating to the waiter's smile, as though he is secretly chuckling over false additions. Nothing feels quite straightforward to the middle-aged Englishman: and what's more, he tells himself, as though this really were the last straw – 'what's more, I wouldn't be surprised if these blighters *actually cheat each other*!'

For long ago, far back in his origins, he was taught to look twice at a Frenchman's credentials, and in his own lifetime, he feels, the Parisian record has scarcely been impeccable. Philip Sidney could write of 'that sweet enemy, France', but later the feeling wore off. Who knows, the Englishman asks himself with a sniff, whether the French will be any better next time? Who knows when the next coup will occur? Who has not seen the gendarmes, in the land of Fraternity, bashing the poor students with batons, or spraying them with tear-gas? What about this fellow de Gaulle, and Laval, and Fashoda, and Old Bony, and the burning of Rye, and Agincourt? Who (says the middle-aged Englishman to himself, getting quite hot under his collar, which is made of the same heavy Sea Island cotton that his father always had) – who, says he bitterly, are the Parisians to talk?

And so at the end of his brief stay, disturbed but undeniably stimulated by his visit, he makes his way once more towards the station – a little apprehensively, for he feels pretty certain that they gave him the wrong departure time, and anyway he has never been very adept with the 24-hour clock. He is, you see, a man of habit, and he is also middle-aged. He is expressing all the prejudices of an imperial generation, reared to grandeur, fostered on the last fragments of splendid isolation. He can just remember, dimly in childhood, an England that was still the world's arbiter, grandly correcting imbalances of power, here crossly checking a potentate, there patting a suitable revolutionary kindly on the head. He does not realize how fast they are draining his beloved Channel. He is not, I think, a married man, but if he had children of his own he would know that every thought that crossed his mind in Paris stamped him a child of his age. His is the last generation into whose silly old eye, when the white English cliffs appear at last above the blurred horizon, a hot atavistic tear embarrassingly insists upon rising. He is well the right side of fifty still, but he is almost the last of the islanders.

We should not blame him, or scoff at his ideas. His way was singularly successful in its time, and honourable too, and enabled the English, entrenched behind their moat, to evolve a national genius that has enriched, astonished and amused us all. The cycle of history has turned, though, and one of the excitements of our time is the thought that the old European comity is awakening again, recalling its estranged children, stretching itself like Rip Van Winkle and massaging its mighty muscles. Never again, I prophesy, will an English generation step so cautiously into Paris, with so many prickly reservations. Who could long be jealous of such a place? Even our friend in the trilby, startled to find his train at the right platform at the advertised time, has to admit, grudgingly, that the Parisians seem to be making some progress at last.

London

I had lived abroad for most of my adult life, and was somewhat of a stranger in my own capital. As a consequence I spent a happy morning wandering about a icty with which I was innocently infatuated.

The day was very early when I began my morning's affair with London, and I started, as determined lovers should, with a nourishing English breakfast, the most potent of aphrodisiacs. The first watery sunshine was glimmering as I walked into the streets of Covent Garden, and the noble façade of the Opera House stood there above the vegetable-wagons pale and romantic. The alleys were stodgy with lorries, and the pavements were bustling with porters, and a fine old lady in black strode by with a tray of cabbages on her head. In the shade of a classical portico some union propagandist had pinned a notice suggesting several disagreeable methods of dealing with strike-breakers. Hanging, it observed, was too good for such vermin.

There was a public house around the corner. Licensed for the porters of the market, it was the one pub in London where you could get beer at that time of the morning, so I sat down to a brown ale, three smoking golden sausages, and a slice of toast – a princely breakfast. Two extremely stout men shared my table and swapped an incessant flow of badinage. Their Cockney was proud and undiluted, and every now and then one of them winked blearily at me, to put me at my ease. I put lots of mustard on my sausages and tried hard to enjoy the ale. London is a rich and saucy city, for all its espresso-bar veneer, and its heart still thrives on beer and bangers and such old stalwarts of the palate.

Presently the sun, like a timid tippler, appeared through the glass of the saloon bar door: so I said goodbye to those two portly jokers and made my way east to Billingsgate. London Bridge was almost empty when I arrived there, and as I climbed down the gloomy staircase to the fish market my footsteps echoed desolately away beneath the bridge: but when I emerged from the tunnel into Lower Thames Street there before me was all the blast and colour and virility of Billingsgate, against one of the most glorious city settings on earth.

Away to the east stood the bastions of the Tower, like misty cardboard replicas; and behind me there arose the mountainous hump of Cannon Street Station, grandly cavernous; and beside me, hunched against an office block, there stood the fine old church of Magnus Martyr, with its 'inexplicable splendour of Ionian white and gold'; and to my left a mesh-work of city lanes, Fish Street and Pudding Lane, Botolph Lane and St. Mary at Hill, clambered up the slope around the Monument; and every-where there were the fish-men, in their white coats and queer leather hats, barging and pushing their way from the refrigerator trucks to the market, splashed with mud and gusto and fishy liquids. There was grandeur, and humour, and vivacity, and brutality to this compelling scene: and in the middle of it all stood the City policemen, like holy men, writing things down in little black notebooks.

Across the river on Bankside no such noble turmoil animated the wharves. A hush lay over the alleyways and warehouses, and only a few early dockers were coughing and talking throatily on the barges moored alongside. As I wandered, though, I could feel the rising animation of the place as the city woke to the day; and soon there approached me down an empty lane a figure whose eager stride and sharp decisive footfalls were the very epitome of morning purpose. It was dressed all in black, and as it advanced down the shadowy canyon of the warehouses I saw that its legs were sheathed in gaiters. I stopped in my tracks, overcome by this pungent confrontation of the commercial, the medieval, and the ecclesiastical. 'Magnificent!' said I. 'Well, er, yes,' said the clergyman, 'it always is lovely at this time of the morning, and if you go a little farther you'll see the new house they've just built for me next to Christopher Wren's, thus enabling me to be the first Provost of Southwark to live on the spot since my cathedral was founded some, let me see, yes, some *one thousand, three hundred* years ago: Good morning!' – and the Provost strode off to his cathedral.

But even London's chain of associations is sometimes broken, and when one of the old landmarks is destroyed, replaced or made redundant, then you may feel the melancholy of the place, and realize how heavily it leans upon the grandeurs of the past. You may sense this nostalgia beside the forgotten India Office, or outside an Admiralty that is no longer the world's final arbiter, or beside Buckingham Palace, where Queen Victoria gazes bleakly across an empire that has vanished: or you may do as I did that morning, cross by Blackfriars Bridge, meander down an awakening Fleet Street, turn into Kingsway, and pause for a moment to watch them pulling down the old Stoll Theatre, all too soon to be one with St James's and the Tivoli.

A ramp leads you down through the gaunt skeletonic walls to the great pit of the theatre beneath; and there you can stand in reverie, like a sentimental singer in a Hollywood musical, gazing at the sad hulk of the building above you, with the dark wooden panelling of the box office still sedately in place among the ruins, and all the grabs and cranes and shovels burrowing desperately into the stalls. You can scarcely find a more evocative symbol of London than one of the celebrated Edwardian theatres, so long flushed with grace and gaiety, now being systematically bashed into oblivion.

By now the day had burst, so I took a bus to Harley Street: for there on any weekday morning, parked in lordly comity, you may inspect the best selection of Rolls-Royces in the world. The oldest of these cars is an orange coupé from the twenties, unashamedly antique; the newest is the 1958 model, a car fit for royal surgeons; and between these haughty extremes there runs the whole range of Rollses, an irresistible London assembly. There are upright pre-war Rollses, inclining slightly backward, as though they are uncomfortably laced; and there are faintly sporty Rollses, belonging to dashing cynical psychiatrists; and there are uncompromising heavy-weight Phantoms, black and awful, into which the dread specialist stoops himself with a soft word to his chauffeur and a sigh of responsibility. To taste some of the ingrained hierarchies and pretensions of London, take a walk down Harley Street and inspect these splendid machines, the finest instruments ever devised for going one better than the Joneses.

I drove to Sotheby's next, by way of Wipers and the Somme, for my taxi-driver had some lurid tales to tell of the First World War, of drunken attacks and incipient mutinies, and the unhappy shortcomings of the French – 'I wouldn't trust them no more than I would these Yanks – and there's an uneducated lot for you!' It was glass they were selling that morning, and smooth as Swedish crystal was the elegant young auction-eer who presided. There were the canny, hard-bitten dealers, huddled around the table beneath the desk; and there were the Americans, sitting in baffled attitudes on sofas around the perimeters; and one or two girls in the highest and brightest and shortest of fashions sat cross-legged on occasional chairs; and the suave auctioneer, observing the inexplicable flickerings and noddings around him, suavely sold each piece and suavely banged his desk.

And so to luncheon (as the auctioneer might say). In a little side street called St Martin's Court, beside the stage door of Wyndham's, is to be found Sheekey's, one of the great fish restaurants of Europe. Here you may buy the Londoner's fish, halibut and turbot and stewed eel, and you may eat radishes with your cheese, and wash them down with white wine. Every kind of person frequents Sheekey's, and when I investigated the people who were sharing my table I discovered one to be a refugee from Bavaria, now a successful manufacturer; and one to be a designer of shoes; and the third told me modestly, eyeing my stewed eels with distaste, that he was a member of a vocal group called the Keynotes and was also engaged in the production of jingles for commercial television. I drank to his harmonies, and congratulated the Bavarian on his fortune, and com-plained about the price of shoes, and thought to myself, as my morning slid to a replete, if not greasy, conclusion: 'London! A hodge-podge, a kaleidoscope, a secret cupboard, a regular old stewed eel of a city!'

There is one deliberate falsehood in this piece about the London of the 1950s. I could have had beer for breakfast at that pub in Covent Garden, and metaphysically, so to speak, I did. But the morning was very young, the sausages were fat, the coffee was steaming invitingly, and I said to myself as I peered wanly across the bar, no, I said, here's one time where Art is more beautiful than Truth. It is the only lie in A Writer's World.

Two Grandees

Two old European heroes of the Second World War still entered the news in the last decades of the 1950s. Charles de Gaulle, the charismatic leader of the Free French during the war, was still a formidable president of France. In 1958 he was facing not only a protracted colonial war in the French colony of Algeria, but also a military revolution there supported by the hundreds of thousands of French settlers, the colons, *who feared he was going to sell them out to the indigenous Arabs. When he flew into Algiers that May he could expect a mixed reception.*

Tonight was the moment of catharsis for the Algerian revolution, the moment when all the inflamed emotions of the past few weeks burst into something dangerously approaching madness. Pumped full of slogans, drunk with militarism, blind with patriotism, at once triumphant and embittered, anxious and hopeful, the *colons* of Algiers gathered once again in the forum on the hill. When they sang their patriotic songs the music was the loudest and deepest and most frightening I have ever heard, and it was carried away like thunder across the harbour and out to sea. They were honest emotions that were expressed as well as vicious ones, kindly as well as intolerant; but by and large, to an old-fashioned democratic observer brought up on bearskins and blanco, the forum at Algiers this evening stank unpleasantly of jack-boots and gun-metal. Into this hideous setting, instinct with force and chauvinism, sustained by 300,000 cheering, shouting, singing, clamouring *colons*, General de Gaulle entered with an air of almost innocent integrity.

He seemed as welcome and incongruous as a bishop among gangsters. His face is rather pudgy these days, and when he spreads his arms in his victory sign, it looks an effort. But his voice had a ring of honesty to it, and he seemed to look at us, all 300,000 of us, straight in the eye. He said that all the people of Algeria, whatever their race or creed, must be French citizens with equal rights and duties. They must be given the means to live a decent life, he said, and there must be a reconciliation between the French people of North Africa and the Muslims, whose rebel forces had put up a brave fight and must be brought back within the French fold.

Bursts of cheers and chanted slogans interrupted his speech, and repeated cries of '*l'Algérie Française*'; and you could feel the sensitive mass reaction of this complex-ridden crowd as he moved from subject to subject, from the Republican institutions to the future of Algeria, from integration to reconciliation. For there *must* be reconciliation between the peoples, he said again, and bracing himself behind his microphone while the crowd waited, he thumped his chest, surveyed the arena before him and proclaimed magnificently: 'I, de Gaulle, open the door!'

The colons were left confused by this speech. What door had he in mind? 'Je vous ai compris,' he grandly told them before he flew away again, comforting many of them with the thought that he would never abandon a French Algeria, but he had really understood them all too well. He knew they had no intention of integrating with the Arabs, and within two years he saw to it that l'Algérie Française was Française no longer.

In the same year Winston Churchill, the most charismatic of all the war leaders, was living in retirement – as Prime Minister of Great Britain he had lost his last election in 1952. By 1958 he was very ill, and seemed about to die at the villa where he was staying in the south of France. Like much of the world's Press, I was rushed there by the Guardian *to be in at the end, but found myself more preoccupied by my colleagues than I was by the statesman's impending demise (which didn't in fact happen for another seven years).*

Through the marbled magnificence of the Hôtel de Paris in Monte Carlo a thickened American voice exploded this evening. 'Look, you lousy two-timing son of a bitch,' it said, not without dignity, 'I may be a goddam reporter but I'm a human being too, see, and this isn't Marilyn Monroe we're waiting for, it's Churchill, see, Churchill! So I get mad!'

We always get mad on our big competitive assignments, but only rarely do we admit to humanity. When that angry American thumped the bar this evening, in the pursuance of some obscure and ephemeral grievance, he was expressing a historical truth. Waiting for Churchill, as he says, is something different, and to the long vigil at Roquebrune, maintained all day and half the night by a jostling international Press corps, there has been a suppressed undertone of something precariously approaching sentiment.

75

Today's communiqué on the patient's health announced that his temperature was normal and that his progress continued to be satisfactory; but 'you never know if you can believe these lousy doctors', we all said, and only a few confident and self-disciplined reporters flew away this evening from the hardships of a Monaco expense account.

For the rest, the selfless vigilance is maintained. The watch begins early. 'To the villa!' the taxi-cab drivers are told, and up to the Villa la Pausa, high above Monaco, streams the morning caravan. A private road leads up to the house, and by midday it is blocked with cars and vans. A gaudy yellow saloon is emblazoned 'Europe No. 1'. A covey of cameramen sits on a wall dangling its legs. A tall BBC commentator, wearing a very British blazer, stands in incongruous dignity among the miscellaneous ill-shaven photographers of the Paris weeklies. The gate is guarded by two sedate French policemen, and all is calm and quiet.

A pleasant dusty path runs around the ground of the Villa la Pausa, and along it there wanders a sporadic procession of photographers, elaborate with telephoto lenses. Somebody has littered the path with the torn pages of a vividly salacious magazine, and a few determined continentals squat in the sunshine earnestly trying to piece them together again. Around the corner a solitary cameraman stands like a statue at the garden wall: from this place he once caught a glimpse of Lady Churchill, far in the garden below, and he hasn't budged since.

The best vantage point of all is on the seaward side of the house. From here you can see part of the villa clearly enough, from its shuttered upstairs windows to its closed out-house door. The trees are cool and shady, and a little knot of reporters is passing the time by throwing stones at a tin can. 'You can't see much from here!' says an elderly English gentleman, passing laboriously up the hill. 'Ha, ha, no,' say the reporters politely, and add, *sotto voce*, 'You're all right, Jack, you've got your bread buttered already.'

So have they, for the moment anyway. Perhaps they will drive down to Menton for their lunch, or pass an hour or two in some agreeable little bar before gathering at the Hôtel de Paris for the afternoon communiqué. Mr Montague-Browne, Sir Winston's secretary, delivers it coolly and precisely, and deftly declines to elaborate. No, he can't explain the medical terms more exactly. No, he's very sorry, but Sir Winston is a guest at the villa, and it would be impolite to talk in more detail of the ménage. Yes, he quite understands the difficulties of the Press. No, he much regrets he cannot say what book Sir Winston is reading today. 'We're thick-skinned up at the villa,' says Mr Montague-Browne endearingly, as he escapes through the squashy armchairs and disappears in a cloud of unanswered questions.

Then the Press corps, only mildly simmering with its occupational disgruntlements, dispatches its cables and settles down for the evening. As always, our pleasures are spattered with shop talk. They say the *Daily So-and-so* tried to get hold of the villa housemaid. Lord what's his name himself, one hears, has told his reporters to lay off. 'What about *Paris-Presse*, hey? That guy overheard Winston talking in his sleep!' A few hardy or nervous practitioners take a cab up to the villa after dinner, to peer staunchly through the darkness in the general direction of the statesman. A few have inconvenient deadlines to meet on the other side of the earth. The rest obey the conventions of the place, and presently plunge unerringly into the variegated salons of its pleasure domes. And up on the mountainside, the subject, object and predicate of all these constructions, old Sir Winston lies in bed.

The messages are pouring in from the four corners of the world, but he lies there in seclusion, the last of the giants, reading his newspapers and confounding his pleurisies. Some of my colleagues depict him demanding brandy, puffing cigars, writing his own health bulletins, reading Somerset Maugham, calling for splendid enormous meals. For myself, when I was up the mountain this evening I thought I heard a sound from the Villa la Pausa, above the sweetness of the birds and the distant sawing of a woodman. It came from an upstairs window of the house, and it sounded to me uncommonly like a chuckle: a rich, quixotic, irrepressible, ageless Harrovian chuckle.

'How come you heard that and nobody else? You got influence some place? Hey, garçon, two dries.'

7

Orientalisms: The Far East

I spent much of 1959 in the Far East, writing for the Guardian, *making some television films for the BBC, and preparing material for a book,* The Road to Huddersfield, *which I was improbably to write for the World Bank in Washington DC. It was before the astonishing economic explosion in Asia that was later to change the world.*

Japan

Fourteen years had passed since the first nuclear bomb ever dropped upon a city had been dropped on Hiroshima, but the city was still in a state of shock and obsession.

Poised in the estuary of the Ota River, where a covey of islands meanders into the mists of the Inland Sea, lies the city of Hiroshima. It is a seaport, an industrial town, an old military base, a market centre: but to this day it lives and breathes and talks and thinks the atomic bomb that exploded over it on 6 August 1945. The city has long been rebuilt, and a new population has flooded in to replace the victims of the holocaust: but for all the bright new buildings and the broad boulevards, no Pompeii is more surely frozen in its attitude of disaster, and no Mont Pelée more permanently scarred. From the hillside above the city you can see how horribly plump and passive a target Hiroshima was. It lies compactly in a funnel among the hills, where the Ota flows pleasantly into the sea. Because it is built on a group of islands, it is criss-crossed by channels of water, and in its very centre is the T-shaped bridge that was the bomb-aimer's objective. Today it has all been reconstructed. The usual straggly houses of urban Japan run away to the sea, and in the business district there stands a group of tall buildings such as you may often see, an earnest of commerce and hospitality, silhouetted upon the American horizon. A ship or two stands offshore. Traffic flows fairly thickly down the streets. Loudly striped advertising balloons loiter above the City Hall, and a homely hum of activity hangs on the soft damp air. It all looks normal enough from the hillside – even beautiful, with the city lying there so new and shining, and the deep blue of the high ground behind, and the placid island-speckled expanse of sea sweeping away to Miyajima and the Pacific.

A few days in Hiroshima, though, and you begin to feel oppressed by the hideous abnormality of the place. The soul was ripped out of this city and though the taxi-cabs may scurry about you, and the street-cars clang, and the neon lights blaze merrily enough, and the girls in kimonos bow you seductively into the night clubs, yet it somehow feels an empty city still. There is something obscurely pallid and muffled about it, for all the world as though the tall new buildings are not there at all, and the islands of the Ota delta are still blackened and smoking. Assured indeed must be the visitor who has not, just for a fleeting foolish moment, wondered if the stones of Hiroshima were still radioactive, or eyed the running water thoughtfully.

This inescapable presence of dread is partly artificial. The horror of the atomic explosion has been deliberately cherished in Hiroshima, and the memory is purposefully sustained. In the centre of the town you are trapped within this tragic and morbid cage. Outside the windows of your grand new hotel stands the Peace Memorial Museum, partly an exhibition of nuclear science, most compellingly a chamber of horrors, dominated by a huge circular model of the devastated Hiroshima, and ornamented with terrible photographs. From the cultural centre across the way there emerge at hourly intervals the saccharine harmonies of adagio hymn tunes, played with lush vibrato on a recorded carillon. There are shrines all about you, the Children's Memorial and the inter-denominational shrine, and the celebrated Shadow on the steps of the bank, and the noble epitaph on the central memorial: 'Rest in peace, for the error shall not be repeated.' You must be pathologically callous or world-weary beyond cure to remain unmoved by the reminders of Hiroshima: but staying in the city today, nevertheless, is like spending a nightmare weekend in one of Evelyn Waugh's California cemeteries, where the dignities of death were honoured with such sickly and cosmetic fulsomeness.

One could stomach it the more easily if this were a catastrophe of long ago, but there are many people in Hiroshima still directly suffering from the effects of the atomic explosion. There are unfortunates so hideously disfigured that they seldom emerge from their houses. There are the

79

patients still, to this very day, in hospital. There are the sufferers from leukaemia. There are the mothers whose children, in the womb at the time of the attack, were born with terrible handicaps and distortions. And there are those who experienced the thing, but were not injured by it, and who now seem like hollow men, haunted and devitalized, with something sucked out of them – 'always tired', as one man said to me, 'I seem to have been tired ever since.' Most pitiable of all, there are those many young people who are afraid of the genetic effects of the bomb. Cruelly cynical has been the exploitation of this foreboding, by Press and by politicians; wild and heartless have been the rumours of two-headed babies and strangely endowed goldfish, and a kind of eerie stockade has been erected about the young people of the place. Men look for their brides elsewhere. Girls try to hide their origins. Cruel reporters sniff about for horrors.

Yet one finds only kindness and common sense from the average citizen. The girl with the hideously disfigured face looks you straight and sweetly in the eye. The Man with the Bomb Story tells it with about the same wry relish as his opposite numbers in Bristol or Berlin. Except on the level of the newspapers and the museums, Hiroshima appears to harbour astonishingly little recrimination. So the skull-like emptiness of Hiroshima seems to be something organic, as though through all the reviving human activity some grim nuclear influences still permeate. I cannot describe the feeling of this place: but it is as though some indefinable essential element has been withdrawn from the ambiance – not colour, nor smell, nor sound, but something else, something which gives meaning and warmth to a city, like salt with your victuals, or eyes in a beautiful face.

Kyoto gave me very different feelings. It is true that when I was there I witnessed live on television, as I sat idly in my hotel lounge, the assassination of the Japanese politician Inejiro Asanuma, but I apparently thought the experience irrelevant to this essay.

Kyoto means Capital City. For a thousand years this famous place, encouched in mountains upon the Kamo River, was the capital of Japan and the emblem of Japanese civilization, and even today it remains to the Japanese something special among their cities, far more than just an elderly provincial metropolis in the central hills. It reigns still as the supreme repository of their ancient traditions, their culture and their custom, their religion and their high-flown patriotism, their golden heritage and their resilient pride. To ninety million Japanese it is the very soul and melody of Nippon.

To the foreigner, though, bouncing in by bus from Osaka, it seems at first sight something less than lovely: for though its setting is magnificent and its pose perennially imperial, yet the face it shows to the world is sadly coarsened. The frenzy of the new Japan has fallen upon Kyoto, cramming its streets with wild-driven traffic, tainting its old wisdom with doubt and disillusion. Kyoto was spared the worst tragedies of war, but it shares with the rest of Japan a sense of causes lost and ideals soured, of warped emotions and passions suppressed. The shape of this town was decreed by the Emperor Kammu eleven centuries ago, but Kyoto has long since lost its symmetry and pattern, and seems to lie there, as your bus lurches through the faceless streets, floundering and inelegant, a city of lost style.

Both views are right: the impassioned Japanese, the disappointed alien. Kyoto as a whole is a plain place, shabby and shanty-like, but like other of the world's great cities it is a place of reticent enchantment, a private place, a place behind walls, a place whose beauties you must search out, and whose meanings, like the exquisite subtleties of the Japanese tea ceremony, lie hidden beneath layers of innuendo. Kyoto is the most conservative of Japanese cities, still half living in its gilded hey-day, when its monarchs and shoguns luxuriated in cultivated splendour, and the four great sects of Japanese Buddhism settled beneath its hills in ritual and meditation. The patricians of Kyoto are aloof and lofty still. The ultimate treasures of the place are jealously guarded. The tourists may click their shutters, the traffic may rage, the radios deafen: but away beyond the tawdry façade, even beyond the temples and the incomparable gardens, the spirit of this deep city lies unruffled, like a carp in a sacred pool.

Temporal consequence abandoned Kyoto a century ago, when the emperors left it, yet for all its faded majesty it feels unmistakably a great city still, a city of lingering power and paramountcy, and sometimes even of menace. All that is most deep-rooted in the Japanese character persists in this introvert community: some of it enchanting, some of it hideous, some of it alarming, some of it delicate and fastidious beyond compare, some of it (to Western minds) perfectly inexplicable. In Kyoto you may observe, still extant and vigorous, an advanced and elaborate form of society that has no real contact with the ways of the West. It has its department stores and its television studios, of course, its airline offices and its air-conditioned hotels, yet it remains at heart among the most oriental of cities, looking at the world like some heavy-lidded potentate peering across the fun-fairs from a high window of his castle.

A myriad shrines, temples and mansions powerfully fortify this sense of hidden strength and exclusivity. They are scattered across the city like gems in mud, unexpectedly at the ends of culs-de-sac, magnificently among pine groves on hillocks, splendidly in flamboyant courtyards. In Kyoto there are nearly two thousand Buddhist temples, Shinto shrines and palaces of importance, giving to every corner of the metropolis oblique suggestions of sanctity, delicacy and wisdom. Some are vast and portentous, their steep cypress-bark roofs (fuzzy with moss) rising high in grandeur above the houses, their ceremonial gongs gigantic beneath their wooden shelters, their spotless passages meandering interminably through gilded screens, painted ante-rooms, gardens of infinite sophistication, tea-houses of faultless proportion. Some are no bigger than garden chalets, flickering small shrines of contemplation, reclining in rotting silence beneath high garden walls, or balanced beside rushing rivulets. Some are the empty palaces of the emperors and the shoguns, soaked in grandeur and symbolism: their wonderful gardens representative of the ocean, or the Inland Sea, or peace, or Paradise, or a fleet of treasure-ships, or the cosmos, their chambers rich with painted tigers, bamboo groves, sea-birds, turtles. Some are the great prayer-houses of monks and holy men, mysterious with candles and slow movement, the tinkle of bells, the fluttering of sacred papers, the fragrance of incense, the murmured incantations that will bring the Jodo brethren, in their after-life, infallibly to the Western Paradise. Some are the storehouses of mighty treasures, like the thousand images of the goddess Kannon in the Temple of Sanju-sangendo – a fabulous phalanx of glistening golden figures, silent, many-armed, sad-eyed, accusatory, each one stuffed with Buddhist scripts, rank upon rank, eye upon eye, attended by the Gods of Thunder and Wind, the Spirit of Merciful Maternity, the Spirit of Devotion, the Spirit of Exorcism. Some are airy gems of lucidity, like the little golden pavilion called Kinkakuji, which was once burnt down by a mad monk, but now stands again featherweight above its lake, with one room reserved for poetry-reading and incense parties, and a rustle of conifers all around. Some are shrines of awful solemnity, poised upon high places, approached by tall breathtaking steps, with pagodas lonely among the larches and mountain streams rushing by below. The great buildings of Kyoto are inexhaustible and inescapable. It would take weeks only to glimpse them all, and because they are distributed through every ward and every suburb, they give the city dignity in depth, and clamp its drab sprawling fabric powerfully together.

The quiddities and idiosyncrasies of the Japanese tradition, surviving here more potently than anywhere else, contribute no less to the intensity of Kyoto. This is a knobbly, enigmatic kind of entity, a city for initiates, streaked with eccentricity, rich in grace-notes. Jammed beneath the eaves of one great temple you may see an old umbrella, dropped there aeons ago by a divine personage, and preserved there for ever as a sign of holy favour. In another you may admire a painting of Fujiyama whose perspective falls into accuracy only if you kneel before the canvas. In a third you may hear the floor-boards, squeaking beneath your tread, 'emitting a sound' (as the guide-book says) 'resembling the song of a Japanese bush warbler'. You may walk the soft paths of a garden clothed entirely in moss, a padded shadowy retreat for contemplatives; you may hear the hollow rhythmic clatter of a deer-scarer, a hinged wooden tube animated by the passing water of a stream; or you may wonder at the great chains hanging down the rooftops of the Imperial Palace – placed there for the convenience of fire-fighters, but 'also forming', says the guide hopefully, 'a kind of ornament'. If you are specially privileged you may even catch sight of the slightly improper medieval picture which, wrapped in innumerable silks and stored in impenetrable caskets, is regarded as so precious a possession that only twenty people are allowed to view it each year.

The rice-paper windows of the Kyoto palaces are often pierced by children's fingers or the beaks of inquisitive birds, but they are mended characteristically: over each hole a small piece of paper is meticulously glued, cut by eager fingers into entrancing flower patterns, every petal of perfect symmetry.

Everyday life in Kyoto is patched with similar fastidious grace. Of all the big Japanese cities, this remains nearest to the water-colour Japan, the Japan of the print-makers and the flower-makers. The main streets are dreadfully banal, but beyond them are alleys of seduction. Here the butterfly kimono, the white stocking, the cloven boot and the flowered kerchief may be seen down any back street, and the fringes of the city are full of brawny country folk, brown as goblins and wreathed in grins. Often you will hear, as you pass beneath some towering wall, the shrill whistling of strange flutes, or the pad of a Japanese drum. Possibly you will encounter, on the grassy sunlit verge of the river, a wandering monk in a grey robe and a bulbous basket-work hat, begging his way to immortality. All around the city, on the high mountain skyline, the pine trees stand in willow-pattern silhouette, and sometimes you may catch the local students, in their peaked caps and drab serge uniforms, entreating a Shinto shrine for good marks in their examinations.

Kyoto is also *par excellence* the home of the geishas, where those talented performers (part artists, part courtesans) are trained to an apogee of perfection, to perform their elaborate dances deliciously in many a lacquered salon, and bring contentment to many a paunchy protector. Half close your eyes one evening among the narrow streets of the geisha quarter, and you might almost be back in feudal Kyoto, before the razzle-dazzle West arrived. The lanes are gay with tea-houses and restaurants, dainty screens masking their entrances, soft slippers paraded invitingly at their doors. Hundreds of globular lanterns light the district, bathing it in orange radiance, and high above your head there floats an advertiser's balloon, flaunting illuminated letters on its tail. Now and then between the houses you may glimpse the Kamo River, wide and gurgling, with a glitter of lights and gaiety on the opposite bank, and the dim moonlit hump of the hills beyond. Two or three young men go rolling noisily pleasure-bound; and suddenly there emerges from some unexpected alley a vision of the legendary Japan – a geisha in all her plastered glory, moving fast and purposeful towards an assignation. Immensely tall is her mound of hair, jet black and shiny; her face is vivid with white and scarlet; her costume is gorgeous with silks, sashes, the gaudiest of clashing colours and the floridest of patterns; and as she hastens awkwardly down the street, embellished from head to foot with paint and brocade, she seems less like a living woman than some fabulous toy, some last masterpiece by Fabergé, enamelled like a queenly trinket, animated by the ultimate refinements of clockwork.

For Kyoto is still a capital, despite the rebuffs of history: within these old walls, behind these dainty shutters, up these temple stairs, hidden in these perfumed gardens, along these green river boulevards, in the silence of these tea-houses and honoured libraries, high on the mountains or lost among the moss, infused into the very texture of Kyoto is the essence, the fragrance, the pith of Japan.

All this is true, and it is the continuity of Kyoto life that gives this place its sense of power. No less real, though, are those corroded aspects of modern Kyoto that affront the foreign visitor like a juke box in an abbey; and it is the harsh juxtaposition of the near-sublime and the almost unbearable that gives the city its sting, and its bitter after-taste.

Kyoto does not leave every visitor soothed or elevated: there is something disturbing to its quality, some hint of the morbid or the unhealthy. In some ways it is a dead city, rotting among its mementoes, but in others it is, like the rest of Japan, pulsing and proliferating with hybrid life, part ordered familiar past, part groping present. It is not serene, no longer Heian-kyo, the City of Peace. Hardly anywhere in Kyoto is ever empty, except the cloistered family gardens or the remoter forest glades. Down every street the citizenry pulses with a babel of horns and a gallimaufry of styles, from the immaculate *obi* to the jeans and sweaters of rip-roaring adolescence. Through every brooding temple the Japanese tourists noisily pour – schoolchildren by the multitude, festooned in satchels and luncheon bags, honeymooners ceaselessly photographing each other, businessmen gravely bowing one another out of the sight-seeing bus. At every holy portal the souvenir-sellers raucously greet you, brandishing their postcards or dangling their toy birds, and the mendicant ex-soldiers, in parade-ground travesty, salute you with a hook hand or stand their wooden legs to attention. The trains, those unavoidable essentials of the Japanese scene, rumble through the night beside the river, and the taxis career maniacally among the rattling trams. Sometimes you may see a bride in kimono, but just as often you will see her in a hired Paris copy, with her bridegroom pin-striped and wing-collared, and her father displaying the unmistakable satisfaction of a man who is going to charge it all on his expense account. They play baseball in the shadow of Kyoto's shrines. They practise athletics around the wall of the Imperial Palace. In Kyoto today you can never be quite sure whether some picturesque bauble is an object of Shinto veneration or an advertising notion. It is a two-faced city: one head a phoenix, one a jackdaw.

Is it a ferocious city, too? Do there linger yet, among these symbols and sanctities, some old savageries of the Japanese spirit? Does a sword glint sometimes, up on the hill? Perhaps. Kyoto, for all its enclaves of perfection, feels a troubled place. Even the most fulsome of tourists may sometimes sense, as they pass from temple calm to highway frenzy, some buried malaise in the flavour of this great city. Kyoto is the soul of Japan, a microcosm of the inner nation. You may taste all the fascination of this astonishing country as you wander among Kyoto's marvels – the Sparrow Chamber or the Wild Geese Chamber, the Silver Pavilion or the Hall of a Thousand Mats, the paintings of the Thirty-Six Famous Poets, the Veranda of the Archery Contest, the immortal garden of Ryuanji: but you may feel obscurely ill at ease in the Hall of the Imperial

Visits, and all too likely the blare of a loudspeaker or the vicious hooting of a taxi horn will drown the sound resembling the song of a Japanese bush warbler.

Hong Kong

I had never been to Hong Kong before. It was still a British Crown Colony then, but I was struck less by its Britishness than by its Chineseness, which inspired me into some wildly imaginative statistics.

More people live in Hong Kong than in all the rest of the world put together, and they make more noise than a million electric drills, and they work like automation, and their babies are beyond computation, and their machinery chitter-chatters away for twenty-five hours every day, and in their markets they sell every fish that was ever caught, and every shrimp that ever wriggled, and every crab that ever pinched, and their excellent shirts cost fourpence-ha'penny apiece, and there are five million Chinese for every European in the city, each one of them more energetic than a power station: and all these unbelievable paradoxes of prolixity and profusion are a lesson in the impermanence of power and the mutability of history.

Just over a hundred years ago the British seized Hong Kong from an addled China, and were conceded sovereignty over it 'in perpetuity'. The island was almost uninhabited, but they made of it a tremendous port and a gunboat station supreme, where British merchants could command the China trade beneath the guns of the Royal Navy. Hong Kong became one of the greatest of free ports and entrepôts, and a brilliant symbol of European superiority. Here the techniques of the Western world were applied to the corrupt and ramshackle structure of China. The merchant princes lived in splendour on the eminence of the Peak, while across the hills in China the impotent Asians squabbled and cheated each other and carved the ivory ornaments that would one day look so pretty upon the mantelpiece in Epsom.

Today the British are still in Hong Kong, and the rich merchants roll down from the Peak each morning in their big black ponderous limousines. The great banks and merchant houses are still magnificently bustling, the company flags fly bravely beside the Union Jack. But you cannot spend a day in Hong Kong without realizing that it lives by the courtesy, and at the mercy, of the new China. Times have changed with an imperial vengeance. The

86

long grey warships that still lie in the harbour (successors to *Aphis* and *Mantis* and the elegant old river gunboats) no longer fool anybody, least of all the hard-headed British. Hong Kong is indefensible, militarily and economically, and it lives half on trust and half on cynicism.

Consider its geographical situation. If you stand on a high place on Hong Kong Island you can see virtually the whole of the Colony. Below you is Hong Kong itself, for ever England, and beyond it is the glorious sweep of the harbour, crammed with the steamers and junks and ferry-boats and launches of free enterprise, never silent, never motionless, one of the great mercantile waterways of the world. But in the middle distance are the mountains of China proper, and most of the land in between – the New Territories, the essential hinterland of Hong Kong – does not belong to Britain, but is only held on a lease that expires towards the end of this century (if international leases have any meaning by then). Not only is China ominously close. In its own back yard British Hong Kong has only the precarious rights of tenancy.

Or move, for another view, to an economic vantage point. At West Point on Hong Kong Island there is a wharf where the junks arrive from Pearl River and Canton, in communist China. It makes no bones about its affili-ations. In the tumble-down eating-house, where the labourers stoically consume their rice and villainous fish, a huge poster proclaims the indus-trial potential of communist China, and the tugboat outside carries on its superstructure a series of slogans about people's rights and imperialist aggression and that kind of thing. Somewhere in an attic above your head a lonely but determined flautist plays a communist propaganda melody, and the ducks that are offloaded in their thousands from the rickety junks, crammed in huge wicker baskets and carried by relays of cheerful and courteous coolies – even the ducks are brain-washed Khaki Campbells. Without this traffic from China, without its ducks and hens and vegetables, Hong Kong probably could not long survive. The communists know that when the lease of that hinterland expires in 1997, Hong Kong will be theirs for the plucking: but they also know that if need be they could squeeze it into submission long before then. All the cards are theirs. They can take the place by force, if they are willing to risk a world war. They can starve it out. Or they can simply wait for another few decades, a mere flicker of time among the Chinese centuries.

The British are not doing badly in Hong Kong, and are performing some good for the world, too, but the moral of this colony's situation is a daunting one. The communist Chinese tolerate its independence partly because they have bigger things to think about, and partly because they don't want to arouse new issues needlessly; partly because they need bargaining counters, and partly because they themselves find the economic services of Hong Kong useful. The capitalists of Hong Kong thrive because they do not believe the communists will move before 1998, at the earliest, thus leaving them time to make a quick new fortune or embellish an old one. The simple people get what benefit they can from good government and economic opportunity, and try not to think about the future.

But above all these several attitudes, the place is haunted by a sense of the hugeness and fertility and brute strength of Asia. Not so long ago a writer could observe that England had cut a notch in China as a woodsman cuts a tree – 'to mark it for felling at a convenient opportunity'. In Hong Kong today, with six hundred million Chinese over there across the hills, and with the whole place a tumult of Asian energy and noise, and constantly threatened by Asian power, and riddled with Asian ideologies – here in Hong Kong you cannot help wondering how ambitious a woodsman China will be when it reaches the summit of its power, and how many of us old elms it is going to notch for firewood.

In the central market of Hong Kong the edible frogs are tied together in bundles while they are still alive, a string of straw binding them around their stomachs. They thus present a multi-limbed symmetrical appearance, and one pair of little legs is constantly jumping to the left, and another pair kicking out to the right, in a very erratic and unpredictable conflict of impulses. This, though clearly uncomfortable for the poor frogs, is not altogether unfunny to watch: and when I saw it for the first time, my goodness, said I to myself, how are we to compete with this extraordinary people, when even their frogs have twelve legs apiece, and lunge about with such comic and irresistible vigour?

I was to return to Hong Kong many times, eventually writing a book about it, until some forty years later I witnessed the withdrawal of the British from their colony, and its return to Chinese sovereignty.

8

Venice 1959

I ended the 1950s in Venice, which I had first known when the British Army had sent me there at the end of the Second World War. This time my family and I lived in a minor palace on the Grand Canal, and I wrote a book about the city, called simply Venice. These are its opening pages.

At 45°14'N, 12°18'E, the navigator, sailing up the Adriatic coast of Italy, discovers an opening in the long low line of the shore: and turning westward, with the race of the tide, he enters a lagoon. Instantly the boisterous sting of the sea is lost. The water around him is shallow but opaque, the atmosphere curiously translucent, the colours pallid, and over the whole wide bowl of mudbank and water there hangs a suggestion of melancholy. It is like an albino lagoon.

It is encircled with illusory reflections, like mirages in the desert – wavering trees and blurred hillocks, ships without hulls, imaginary marshes: and among these hallucinations the water reclines in a kind of trance. Along the eastern reef strings of straggling fishing villages lie empty and unkempt. Away in the wastes there stand the sails of fishing boats, orange, yellow and magenta, with cabalistic signs or heraldic symbols, a rampant red horse, an all-seeing eye. The shallows are littered with intricate shambling palisades of sticks and basket-work, and among them solitary men, knee-deep in sludge and water, prod in the mud for shellfish. A motor boat chugs by with a stench of fish or oil. A woman on the shore shouts to a friend, and her voice eddies away strangely, muffled and distorted across the flats.

Silent islands lie all about, lapped in marsh and mudbank. Here is a glowering octagonal fort, here a gaunt abandoned lighthouse. A mesh of nets patterns the walls of a fishermen's islet, and a restless covey of boats nuzzles its water-gate. From the ramparts of an island barracks a listless soldier with his cap over his eyes waves half-heartedly out of his sentry-box. Two savage dogs bark and rage from a broken villa. There is a flicker of lizards on a wall. Sometimes a country smell steals across the water, of cows or hay or fertilizer: and sometimes there flutters in the wake of the boat, not an albatross, but a butterfly.

Presently this desolate place quickens, and smart white villas appear upon the reef. The hump of a great hotel protrudes above the trees, gay parasols ornament a café. A trim passenger steamer flurries southwards, loaded deep. A fishing flotilla streams workmanlike towards the open sea. To the west, beneath a smudge of mountains, there is a thin silver gleam of oil drums, and a suggestion of smoke. A yellow barge, piled high with pop bottles, springs from a landing-stage like a cheerful dove from an ark. A white yacht sidles indolently by. Three small boys have grounded their boat on a sand-bank, and are throwing slobbery mud at each other. There is a flash of oxyacetylene from a dark shed, and a barge stands on stilts outside a boatyard. A hooter sounds; a bell booms nobly; a big white sea-bird settles heavily upon a post; and thus the navigator, rounding a promontory, sees before him a city.

It is very old, and very grand, and bent-backed. Its towers survey the lagoon in crotchety splendour, some leaning one way, some another. Its skyline is elaborate with campaniles, domes, pinnacles, cranes, riggings, television aerials, crenellations, eccentric chimneys and a big red grain elevator. There are glimpses of flags and fretted rooftops, marble pillars, cavernous canals. An incessant bustle of boats passes before the quays of the place; a great white liner slips towards its port; a multitude of tottering palaces, brooding and monstrous, presses towards its waterfront like so many invalid aristocrats jostling for fresh air. It is a gnarled but gorgeous city: and as the boat approaches through the last church-crowned islands, and a jet fighter screams splendidly out of the sun, so the whole scene seems to shimmer – with pinkness, with age, with self-satisfaction, with sadness, with delight.

The navigator stows away his charts and puts on a gay straw hat: for he has reached that paragon among landfalls, Venice.

The 1960s

By the 1960s, as the memories and effects of the Second World War began to fade, the Cold War was in full blast. The Iron Curtain was clamped, as Churchill said, from Stettin on the Baltic to Adriatic Trieste, a gloomy barrier between capitalist and communist Europe. The Americans and the Russians implacably presided over their respective spheres of influence, as the old imperialists used to say, and Germany was divided between the ideologies. The sub-cultures of the hippies and the flower people flourished – they called it the Age of Aquarius, or the Permissive Age – and a new familiarity with drugs hard and soft added equivocal nuances to the scene. The 1960s ended with a Grand Slam – and a Cold War triumph for the United States – when two American astronauts became the first human beings to step upon the surface of the Moon.

I spent the decade partly writing for newspapers and magazines, partly writing my own books.

9

The Eichmann Trial

In 1961 I returned to Jerusalem, for the Guardian, *to report upon the trial of Adolf Eichmann, prime agent of the Nazi plan to exterminate Europe's Jews – the 'Final Solution'. He had been kidnapped by Israeli agents in Argentina a year before and had since been held incommunicado in Jerusalem. I interpreted the event not as a show trial exactly, but certainly as an expression of Jewish symbolism.*

At eleven o'clock on the twenty-fifth day of Nissan in the Hebrew year 5721, Adolf Eichmann the German appeared before a Jewish Court in Jerusalem charged with crimes against the Jewish people – and in that very sentence, I suspect, I am recording the whole significance of this tragic and symbolic hearing. All else is incidental – the controversy, the evidence, the implications, the sentence, the verdict. The point of the Eichmann trial is that it is happening at all, and that through its ritual the Jews have answered history back.

Eichmann slipped into court this morning, out of the mystery and legend of his imprisonment, almost unnoticed. Heaven knows the courtroom was ready for him. Its parallel strips of neon lighting gave it a pale and heartless brilliance. Its great Jewish candelabra shone gilded on the wall. There sat the five Jewish lawyers of the prosecution, grave-faced, mostly youngish men, with a saturnine bearded head prosecutor, lithe and long limbed, elegant in his skullcap at the end of the line. There sat Dr Servatius, the German defence counsel, earnest in discussion with his young assistant. There were the translators in their booths, and the girl secretaries at their tables, and the peak-capped policemen at the doors, and the gallimaufry of the press, seething and grumbling and scribbling and making half-embarrassed jokes in its seats. And there stood the bullet-proof glass box, like a big museum showcase – too big for a civet or a bird of paradise, too small for a skeletonic dinosaur – which was the focus and fulcrum of it all. Nothing had been forgotten, nothing overlooked. We only awaited the accused.

But when he came most of us were looking the other way. He slipped in silently, almost shyly, flanked by three policemen in their blue uniforms. No shudder ran around the courtroom, for hardly anybody noticed. 'There he is,' I heard a voice somewhere behind my shoulder, rather as you sometimes hear mourners pointing out rich relatives at a funeral: and, sure enough, when I looked up at that glass receptacle there he was.

He looked dignified enough, almost proud, in horn-rimmed glasses and a new dark suit bought for him yesterday for the occasion. He looked like a lawyer himself, perhaps, or perhaps a recently retired brigadier, or possibly a textile manufacturer of vaguely intellectual pursuits. When I looked at him again, though, I noticed that there was to his movements a queer stiffness or jerkiness of locomotion. He hardly looked at the courtroom – he had nobody to look for – but even in his small gestures of preparation and expectancy I thought I recognized the symptoms: somewhere inside him, behind the new dark suit and the faint suggestion of defiance, Adolf Eichmann was trembling.

Like a candidate at a viva voce he rose to his feet, as though he were holding his stomach in, when the three judges entered the court: Dr Moshe Landau, Dr Benjamin Halevi, Dr Yitzhak Raveh – European Jews all three of them, and two of them from Germany itself, whence they escaped almost at the moment when the racialists came to power. They were solemn, bare-headed and commanding, but the proceedings opened paradoxically without dignity, for at this moment the myriad attending journalists found that their portable radio sets, for simultaneous translations, did not seem to work properly, and the Eichmann hearing, this moment of Jewish destiny, began to a cacophony of clicks, muffled shakings and tappings of plastic. 'Are you Adolf Eichmann?' asked Dr Landau, the president of the court: and through the racket around us we heard him answer, via microphones and wires out of his glass insulation. 'Yes, sir,' he said, and the trial began.

Eichmann is charged on fifteen counts under the Israeli Nazi and Nazi Collaborators (Punishment) Law. It took Dr Landau more than an hour to read the indictment, with Eichmann almost motionless on his feet throughout it all. The ghastly essence of the charges is that he caused the killing of millions of Jews as head of a Gestapo department; that he was responsible for their slavery, deportation, spoliation and terrorization; and that he committed similar acts against Poles, Slovenes, Gypsies and Czechs.

As soon as these terrible accusations were pronounced (Eichmann twitching sometimes during the recitation, but mostly rigid as marble) Dr Servatius rose to his feet to present his objections to the jurisdiction of the court. He is an elderly man, slightly stooping, long practised in the defence of accused Nazis, and the burdens of his arguments were familiar to everyone in the building before he began. Dr Gideon Hausner, the attorney-general, replied at length, and as he argued on through the hours, opening and closing his law books, tucking his hands beneath his gown like an insect's legs within its shards – as he reasoned on most of our feckless minds, I suspect, began to wander. We left that courtroom to its aridities, and we surveyed the centuries of antagonism that were the preliminary hearings of this trial, the medieval ghettos and the American country clubs, the fears and the snubs and the envies and the gas chambers. We wondered if history had a pattern after all, and we put ourselves in Eichmann's enigmatic posture, and speculated if he had ever, in his most hideous nightmares, imagined himself sitting thus, immured in a big glass specimen case, with the power of Jewry everywhere around him, and keen, cold Jewish brains weaving their litigation all about.

There he sits between his policemen, unchanging, impassive, characterless but unforgettable. He never looks afraid, he never looks despairing, he never gives the impression that he may throw himself screaming against the glass walls of his cage or burst into tears, or even pluck our hearts with the agonizing old dilemmas of patriotism and loyalty.

There he sat, pursing his lips, until the president told him to stand, and he leapt nervously to his feet like a boy in the headmaster's study. Did he plead guilty or not guilty to the first count of the indictment against him (causing, *inter alia*, the killing of millions of Jews)? 'In the sense of the indictment – not guilty,' said Eichmann. Did he plead guilty or not guilty to the second count (*inter alia*, forcing millions of Jews into labour camps)? 'In the sense of the indictment – not guilty,' said Eichmann. So they went through the fifteen counts of the indictment, through all its fearful charges of murder, cruelty and extortion, and to each Eichmann replied in a flat but unquavering voice: 'In the sense of the indictment – not guilty.' Very well, then, the court seemed to say, as Eichmann sat down again, put on his earphones, and bent towards the triple mouths of his microphone. Very well, then, let history speak.

Instantly Hausner rose to his feet, and began his speech with an intensity so passionate, with a sense of history so overwhelming, with a pride so

95

harnessed but so patent, with a burning Jewishness so hunted but so hunting, that for a few seconds we seemed posed on some plane outside time or space, where the voices of all the Jews of all the centuries could speak at once and in unison.

I shall never forget the moment. For me it was as though a shutter had been opened, if only temporarily, through which we Gentiles could peer into the heart of Jewry, and out of which, if only for a century or two, the Jews themselves could speak with dignity. This was the meaning of the trial, and is perhaps the meaning of Israel, and for Dr Hausner himself it must have been a moment of tragic exaltation.

This is how he began his speech:

'When I stand before you, judges of Israel in this court, to accuse Adolf Eichmann, I do not stand alone. Here with me at this moment stand six million prosecutors . . . Never down the entire blood-stained road travelled by this people, never since the first days of its nationhood, has any man arisen who has succeeded in dealing it such grievous blows as did Hitler's iniquitous regime, and Adolf Eichmann as its executive arm for the extermination of the Jewish people. In all human history there is no other example of a man against whom it would be possible to draw up such a bill of indictment as has been read here.'

How would you feel, to have such a thing said of you, in the fifty-fifth year of your life, thousands of miles from anyone you love, in the hands of people who hate you? How would you feel to hear yourself numbered, as Eichmann did a moment later, with Genghis Khan, Attila, and Ivan the Terrible, whose barbarous crimes of blood-lust 'almost pale into insignificance when contrasted with the abominations, the murderous horrors' to be presented at your trial?

I looked at Eichmann to see how he was reacting, half-expecting to see some flicker of perverse pride crossing his face, to be counted among such fearful company. But he was sitting well back in his chair now, with his hands in his lap, blinking frequently and moving his lips, and he reminded me irresistibly of some elderly pinched housewife in a flowered pinafore, leaning back on her antimacassar and shifting her false teeth, as she listened to the railing gossip of a neighbour.

Presently, in any case, the prosecutor descended from the terrible general to the beastly particular, and proceeded to describe, in icy detail and precision, step by step and horror by horror, the rise of Nazi Germany, the importance of anti-Semitism to its gimcrack philosophies, and the familiar but always staggering techniques of the extermination camps. This was Eichmann's country. He was always a conscientious administrator, they say – a killer behind a desk is how the prosecution has described him – and this systematic documentation must have suited his style. Earnestly and attentively he sat through it all, and it was only towards the end of the morning, several hours, ten thousand words and an eternity of horrors later, that the old lady in the pinny began to fidget and sway a little in her chair, as though she were pining for a nice hot cup of tea.

The massive symbolism of the trial is momentarily in suspense, and the court has now turned to the examination, if not the dissection, of that extraordinary minor organism, Adolf Eichmann himself. The immemorial shades of anti-Semitism still haunt the courtroom, but mostly we are now concerned with Nazi Germany, surely the meanest and most squalid of all tyrannies: and what has emerged from the hearing this morning has been the uncanny confusion of values within the fraudulent faith of Nazism – the total inability it fostered to distinguish not just the right from the wrong, but the important from the trivial, the relevant from the immaterial, the murderous from (to use one of Himmler's favourite words) the inelegant.

This morning we have been hearing, in the accused's own tape-recorded evidence, about his introduction to the techniques of Jewish extermination. It was extracted from him during several months of pre-trial questioning in Israel, and when you hear it from his own lips it is not so much the appalling horror of it all that flabbergasts you, but the apparently totally unwitting incongruity. At the very beginning of this testimony there is a faint, confused suggestion of imperial power, of the rolling thunder and spaciousness that you might expect of a conquering people, but that was in the event so totally lacking from Hitler's Reich. 'Shall I begin with France?' Eichmann asked his interrogators. 'Did it begin with France at first? How it began there, or whether it was in Holland – did it begin there? . . . What happened in Thessalonika? The Aegean? How was it in Bratislava, when it first began there? When did Wislicency reach Bratislava and how was it in Romania?'

Dim echoes of St Paul, of Doughty, perhaps of Homer ran through my mind as I heard this magnificent opening: but in a matter of moments the whole style of the thing collapsed, and we were left with a recital so horrible, shameless, cracked, and incredible that it could only have sprung out of Nazi Germany. For Eichmann then went on to describe his first introduction to the idea of the 'final solution'. Heydrich told him about it, he said. 'The first moment I did not grasp his meaning because he chose his words so carefully. Later I understood and did not reply. I had nothing to say . . . of such a solution I had never thought.' Before long though he was sent to Lublin to inspect an extermination operation, at a camp near by, where the engine of a Russian submarine was to be used to asphyxiate prisoners.

'This was something terrible. I am not so strong that a thing like this should not sway me altogether. If today I see a gaping wound, I can't possibly look at it. I belong to that category of people, so that very often I am told I couldn't be a doctor . . .' The other thing that worried him, mentioned in precisely the same, rather peevish tone of voice, was the enunciation of the police officer in charge of the camp's construction. 'He had a loud voice, ordinary but uncultured. He had a very common voice and spoke a south-west German accent. Maybe,' – said Eichmann priggishly of this character, met so briefly twenty years ago on the threshold of hell – 'maybe he drank.' Similarly at Lwow, which Eichmann visited after watching them shoot Jews in a pit at Minsk ('my knees went weak'), he remembered most vividly the charming yellow railway station built in honour of the sixtieth year of Franz Josef's reign. 'I always find pleasure in that period, maybe because I heard so many nice things about it in my parents' home (the relatives of my stepmother were of a certain social standing).'

But if some of the incongruities of this testimony are trivial, one at least is fundamental: the prissy, goody-goody, obsequious quality that pervades this man's confessions. We must not, I suppose, prejudge the issue, but there is at least no doubt at all that Eichmann was a prominent and powerful Nazi, a senior officer of the SS and a man close enough to the springs of power to be entrusted with the execution of the final settlement – 'special treatment', to quote another Nazi euphemism for slaughter. Yet he talks, or tries to talk, like a misled, misunderstood Mr Everyman mixed up in nasty events he did not comprehend, and governed by the overwhelming sense of dutiful obedience he picked up at his mother's knee.

Every line of his evidence squirms, and makes the whole court squirm, and when in one mystical moment of self-abasement he observed that perhaps he ought to hang himself in public, 'to atone for these terrible things', there can be few people in the court who were not tempted to agree with him.

Eichmann was hanged, more than a year later, but not in public. He told the execution witnesses: 'I have believed in God, I have obeyed the laws of war and was loyal to my flag. We shall meet again.' For Jews everywhere his trial was a demonstration of racial revival. For me it was a last emblematical curtain call of the Second World War.

10

The Cold War

Throughout the 1960s the Cold War preoccupied me, whether I was reporting for the Guardian *or busy writing for myself, and I spent much of my time observing its phenomena and travelling on both sides of the Iron Curtain. I thought passing through the border-line from West to East was like entering a drab and disturbing dream, especially as foreign newspaper correspondents in communist countries were generally assumed to be agents on the side. I had my first taste of the conflict, though, in the USA.*

The UN

In 1960 I was in New York to report for the Guardian *on a crucial session of the General Assembly of the United Nations. The session was addressed by most of the world's principal leaders, and for the most part it degenerated into mutual recrimination – 'Think it over,' Nikita Khrushchev of the USSR warned the Western powers, 'if not today then soon, very soon, the colonial order will finally perish, and if you do not get out of the way in time you will be swept away . . . nations who oppress other nations cannot themselves be free.' But an improbable star of the show was the imperturbably conservative Harold Macmillan, Prime Minister of Great Britain.*

It was not exactly a prophet who descended upon us this morning out of Westminster, imperturbably patrician though Harold Macmillan looked as he walked, so slowly, so fastidiously, with such a gleam of smooth grey Etonian hair, towards the rostrum of the United Nations. It was though, incontestably – and in this sad assembly it makes an agreeable change – a statesman. The Prime Minister probably did not stir many wild passions, except in the most atavistic of British breasts, like mine, but at last, out of the welter of the Assembly's rhetoric, somebody has at least tried to see his opponents' point of view.

The point of Macmillan's speech was this: that at the base of the Cold War, at the heart of our anxieties, lies fear. The powers are afraid, each of the other. The West has been afraid ever since the war of communist expansion by force. The Russians are afraid, for understandable reasons of history, of yet another foreign invasion of their territory. The task of the world, said the Prime Minister, was to remove the causes of fear and thus, by progressive stages towards disarmament, to divert our resources at last towards the nations' real needs – 'to meet by public and private investment the needs of expanding and politically maturing populations'.

It was not a speech of theatrical gestures, of world-shaking propositions. It was the speech of a civilized, cultivated gentleman, honourably reflecting the aspirations of decent people everywhere, and thus bringing to this Assembly, for all the speaker's studied parliamentary detachment, a paradoxical streak of emotion. As a performance it was flawless. Macmillan began by expressing his pleasure that the new President of the Assembly should come from Ireland – 'a country with which my own has so many close ties'. I do not know whether he meant this ironically, but he allowed a long pause to follow the observation, and as this vacuum was filled by a slowly rising murmur of laughter from the Assembly so there crept into the Prime Minister's graven cheek the merest sly suspicion of the end of his tongue.

He countered with equal artistry several interventions by Mr Khrushchev, who seemed to be in his most boorish mood, sprawling and pouting in his seat, and who apparently failed to detect the genuinely conciliatory tone of the speech. Twice Khrushchev, waving his arms and half rising in his seat, shouted interventions in tumbling Russian, and the second time the Prime Minister, allowing the thick flow of Russian to die away across the delegates, observed sweetly that he would prefer to have it in translation – a retort which, though it may sound flat in a newspaper dispatch, was in fact so unexpected and so decisive that the whole Assembly laughed and clapped.

Mr Macmillan ran through his familiar range of styles, from the Churchillian to the faintly fireside, but it was a speech burdened with unavoidable handicaps. Throughout it one felt the overriding British need to satisfy American opinion and avoid any suggestion of weakness. Throughout it we felt the need, no less genuine, to convince the Russians that, though their viewpoint is often understandable, nevertheless they are not going to scare the West into submission. And always we felt this post-imperial statesman to be haunted by the embarrassments of colonialism, so that much of his talk had to be self-defensive, and some of it sounded, willy-nilly, patronizing.

Still, it was something in the nature of a triumph. It had the art of statesmanship to it, and it was greeted with warm, prolonged, but never raucous applause, only the communist delegations, obediently following their master's example, joining Mr Khrushchev in a rather sulky kind of disapproval. As for the substance of the speech, it was not, to be honest, revolutionary. It consisted partly of a defence of British and Western attitudes, partly of almost reluctant reproofs to the Russians, partly of sensible expressions of conciliation, partly of proposals for another move towards disarmament, partly of a plea for a kind of economic summit détente, in which the economic resources of the world would work in harness rather than in rivalry. But as a whole it was really an appeal for a fresh start, a chucking away of hogwash, and a return to common sense. Its real significance may turn out to be, not that it brings the squabbling giants together, but that it demonstrates to the rest of the world, even from a frankly partisan viewpoint, the stupidity of the Cold War and its hopeless essence of misunderstanding.

One of Khrushchev's interventions became famous, and made Macmillan something of a local hero in New York. At one point in the speech he took off his shoe and banged it on the table in protest, a gesture which particularly affronted Americans as an example of Soviet loutishness. After that evening's session I happened to be in the bar of the Waldorf-Astoria Hotel when Macmillan shuffled through. Everyone there, barmen and all, burst into applause, but I found myself obscurely on Khrushchev's side. It seemed to me that there had been a peasant honesty and humour to his behaviour which the Prime Minister might well have exploited: and I later learnt, as a matter of fact, that the gesture of banging one's shoe on the table to express disagreement is no more than an Old Russian Custom. In any case Macmillan's speech had not the slightest effect upon the Cold War or the course of history.

Moscow

I first flew into Moscow on a winter day soon after the death of Josef Stalin, when the Soviet Union was still a sinister enigma. This report for the Guardian *appeared in the newspaper in two parts on successive days, and I*

consciously modelled the opening part on the essay that Charles Dickens
wrote about his first visit to Venice, in 1845.

Through an ambuscade of aircraft the traveller stumbles – more aircraft, it seems, than he has ever set eyes on before, with their fierce noses and high tails shining dully in the snow, hulking and unfamiliar, like great predatory pike: but inside the stuffy, ill-lit reception hall a line of prickly porters, in brown quilt jackets and fur hats, lounges and slouches on benches, while an official in a blue cap peers myopically at documents, turning them this way and that for a better grasp of their purport, like a country policeman in a farce.

A fusty crowd of passengers, muffled in wrappings, hangs about the Customs desk: a fat, broad-faced woman in tears, her child tugging at the strap of her handbag; a sallow man in a velvet hat, arguing over a suitcase of brocades; a covey of Chinese, dignified and double-breasted; a welter of thick-set, sweaty, colourless men with badges in their lapels and elaborate medals dangling from their chests. Among them all the traveller warily passes, a shuffling, heavy-breathing porter carrying his bags behind, and into the car that waits outside; and so down the dank, snow-muffled road, through a landscape numb with cold, he is driven towards the city.

Thin flurries of snow are chased by the wind across the road. The windows of the car are thick with ice, frost and condensation. Blurred in a haze of winter, as if seen through a toper's eyes, are the places along the route. There are shambled lines of shacks and shanties, painted an ancient peeling blue, with rickety verandas and precarious porches, knee-deep in snow, invested by old outhouses, fences, dog-houses, bits of masonry. There are clusters of small houses, tightly huddled together for warmth and comfort, as if they have heard the howling of wolves. There are wide desolate acres of snow-encompassed land, cruel and grubby, supervised by brooding firs and crossed perhaps by a solitary old woman in a trailing tattered coat and a green kerchief, bundled with packages and buckets, and pushing her way like a lemming towards some unseen homestead in the wood.

Sometimes a gaunt horse hauls a sledge lop-sidedly down road, piled high with baskets and packing-cases; or a car ploughs past with a puff of oily exhaust and a whiff of crude oil; or a great rough-hewn lorry, painted a sombre green and wrapped around the bonnet with quilted fabric, rumbles darkly through the trees; and presently there appear through the misted windscreen the first tokens of the city. A suburban trolley-bus slides alongside, painted a bright blue and yellow, its windows so steamy that only a blur of head-scarves and wrinkled faces can dimly be seen, or the pink tip of a child's nose pressed against the glass. The traffic thickens, the empty countryside falls away, and soon there looms out of the fitful snowfall a monstrous parade of buildings. Huge, square and forbidding they appear, of no definable style or period, like so many vast eight-storey breeding-houses. They look shuttered and deserted, but for a bleak light here and there, and they rise sheer and stern on each side of the road, window after window, block after block, mile after mile, like enormous piles of ammunition boxes in some remote and secret dump. Only a few squat women move in and out of their vault-like doors, and the television aerials standing awry on their roofs seem sad but lovable impertinences. Immensely wide is the street that strikes through this gloomy cavalcade, and presently the rhythm of the buildings shifts, like a train crossing the points. Dreadful symmetry gives way to a jumble of old and new and indeterminate: a sagging, classical portico behind high walls; a rickety cul-de-sac of single-storey chalets, the plaster and lath peeling to show the criss-cross beneath; a bridge across a frozen river, its ornamental urns stacked with sculptured rifles, swords, trumpets and machine guns. The traveller rubs his window with his fur hat, and sees that the city has closed in upon him.

Not a drop, not a hint, not a memory of colour enlivens its frozen outskirts. All is brown and grey and stacked with snow. The stocky pedestrians of the place are swathed in greatcoats, furs and high boots, and move stuffed and bundled along pavements, their children so encased in hoods and sheep-skin that only their eyes appear like gems among the wrappings. Machines bustle everywhere, clearing away the sludge – jolly little motor-sweepers, like benign weasels, and huge clanking devices with spindly arms, like lobsters, and suction chutes, and tall frowning snow-ploughs; and among them, wearing padded jackets over white aprons, an army of rugged women sweeps, shovels, and picks, leaving an intricate meshed pattern of brushes on the pavement, and an obligato of swishing and chipping constantly on the air.

From an iron grille in the ground a plume of steam arises, and in its vapour crouches a flock of birds – half a dozen proud shabby pigeons, a few rapscallion sparrows. A line of small boys paces on skis through the trees of a garden, and an old philosopher with flaps over his ears sits defiantly on a bench reading a book, the snow like white fur upon his coat collar. Across the vast crossroads a stream of huddled figures endlessly plods, hurried along by the chivvying of whistles and the testy gestures of belted, padded, high-booted, fur-hatted policemen. The city feels at once curiously empty and claustrophobically crowded: empty because its buildings are pallid and aloof, like monuments to dead scientists; crowded because to the movements of the scurrying citizenry there is something dark and inexorable, as though nothing could ever staunch its sheer weight of numbers – as though impelled not by pleasure, industry, ambition, or even duty, but by irresistible physical instincts, like birds migrating, or small black salmon fighting their way upstream.

But now there appear, in glimpses among the office blocks, weird and spectral skyscrapers, solitary above the rooftops, ornamented strangely with spikes and pinnacles, like the pavilions of Eastern satraps; and just as the dusk begins to fall the traveller sees before him, raised upon an eminence, a huge and haunting fortress. Ancient turreted walls protect it, a wide icy river lies beneath its gates, and within it there shine clusters and globules of gold, complicated bell-towers, citadels, palaces, weathervanes, emblems of power and politics, a mound of cathedrals and barracks and florid watch-towers, an immense straggling tesselated rampart, a dome with a gigantic flag streaming arrogantly in the wind.

In the square beneath this chill marvel he steps from his car; and joining a silent queue of citizens, he passes between a pair of sentries, rigid as idols, their collars turned up around their cheeks, their boots glistening, their small eyes hard and unshifting. Slowly, meditatively, like mutes, the queue shuffles between granite portals into a bare and massive building. Officers in long grey greatcoats peer watchfully from its shadows, and only the cries of a heedless baby break the silence as the crowd, bareheaded and awe-struck, presses clumsily down the granite steps into the stomach of the edifice. Silently, silently it lumbers on, with a pulse of breathing and a swish of thick clothes and an awkward clatter of boots on stone: until at last the traveller, hemmed in willy-nilly among the pilgrims, finds himself within an inner chamber, like a dungeon. Four silent soldiers stand there with their rifles, and the endless queue winds its way around the room like a fascinated viper, button to button, breath to breath, gazing always at the crystal box that stands in the centre.

A pair of dead men are embalmed there among the bayonets, bathed in an unearthly light, waxen and preternaturally clean. One has a short beard and a high-domed head. The other's moustache is coarse and bushy, and the jacket of his pale blue form is heavy with medals. Not a word, not a sigh, not a cough escapes the crowd as it passes these cosmetic relics. An occult sense of ritual pervades the place, as in the eerie tomb-heart of a pyramid. The traveller, caught in the fustian momentum of the queue, is carried as in a dream out of the chamber up the broad steps into the evening light: and already he feels clinging to his person, trapped in the folds of his coat and turn-ups of his trousers, impregnating his hair like tobacco in a railway carriage, creeping beneath his fingernails, smarting his eyes, the odour and essence of Moscow.

Moscow in winter is hardly a dream, and not exactly a nightmare, but has more the quality of a hangover: blurred, dry-mouthed and baleful, but pierced by moments of almost painful clarity, in which words, ideas, or recollections roll about in the mind metallically, like balls on a pin-table.

It is a graceless but obsessive city, the capital of an alien Asiatic world. Among its avenues of ugly buildings, stamped with the inexpressible emptiness of Stalinist taste, the muffled multitudes shove their way with hungry gusto: not indeed mindlessly, as myth would have it, but with a special technique of ill manners, a kind of self-induced trance in which the existence of anybody else on the pavement is erased from the consciousness, as a yogi dismisses the blistered crowd around him. Nobody can push more effectively than a Muscovite: but drab and docile are the queues, all the same, that trail away from the milk counter in the central market, or wait in suffocating proximity, each man breathing stertorously down his neighbour's neck, for their hats and galoshes after the opera. No elegance or style is left twitching in the streets of Moscow. This is the metropolis of the common man, and he eats his borscht with a proud snuffle.

Through the dreary proletarian pall, though, crooked mysteries gleam. Some are the mysteries of communism: mummified philosophies and deifications, medallions of Lenin as a baby, a dead physicist lying in state upon his bier, a wilderness of pamphlets and slogans and Five-Year Plans, the shifting mosaic of strange faces that makes this an imperial city – Mongols and Kazakhs and bland Chinese, scarred Africans, wide-eyed Indians, lean men from Central Asia, with knobbly sticks and crinkled lambskin hats.

Some are the mysteries of ancient state: the spiked medieval helmets of the Kremlin Treasury, the gorgeous saddle trappings and the royal sledges, gold in piled elaborate formality, splendid silver from England, jewellery of minute ingenuity, thrones of ivory, sceptres, golden cocks, owls, pheasants, railway trains, ships in golden eggs, galleries of armour, all shining and glinting in their cases while the tourists, their feet muffled in felt overshoes, as in a mosque, pad in obedient groups behind their guide.

Some are the mysteries of religion – the religion of Leninism, which has already etherealized that eminent political scientist, or the religion of Tsarist Russia, still ornately surviving beneath its onion domes. Church service on Sunday morning is still veiled in strangeness and suffering. Outside the door an old man with a forked beard feeds a gaggle of mangy pigeons: inside a million Muscovites seem to occupy the nave, crammed so tightly that a sudden genuflection sends a ripple across the church. Far, far away the vestments of a priest sometimes flicker in the candlelight, and always drifting around the pillars and the ikons loiters a cadence of hidden choirs. Near the door the corpses of two old ladies, pale but peaceful, lie encouched in flowers. In a side chapel a bespectacled priest with long golden hair, sitting on a kitchen chair beside the altar, accepts a stream of murmured confessions and entreaties, the women pressing round him like dwarfs around a magician.

Strange are the encounters of Moscow, like incidents in a fevered fancy. A man in clumping boots and huge leather gloves will introduce himself in a champagne bar as a brigadier of communist labour, and ask after the welfare of the comrade plasterers in England. A gay girl in the Lenin Library will slip you an irreverent witticism about socialist realism. A female judge in a divorce court will burst into tears at the memory of her orphaned childhood. Two youths in slinky coats will solicit you for pound notes, fountain pens, *Life* magazine, chewing gum, nylon shirts or gramophone records. Moscow is full of innuendoes, hints of espionage, suspicions, the threat of imminent portentous confidences.

Sometimes a sense of suffocation overcomes you, and you feel yourself so far from the sea, in the heart of something so swollen and incalculable, that the blood throbs in your head and your mind sags. In the immaculate subterranean halls of the underground you may feel like this, stifled by gigantic symbolisms and frescoes of dancing milkmaids; or lost among the myriad text-books, tracts, collected works of Lenin, portraits of bemedalled demi-gods, economic treatises and inspirational posters of a bookshop; or wandering among the awful symmetries of Moscow University, Big Brother's *alma mater*, a brain factory, a production line where 25,000 students labour like so many ants in a 32-storey heap (33 reading rooms, 5,754 sleeping chambers, 80 Members of the Academy of Sciences, 20 Merited Sciences, a million books, 50,000 trees, an assembly hall with 1,500 seats and 11 floors of storage space – 'The best university in the world,' as an Intourist pamphlet puts it, 'can only be seen in Moscow').

Sometimes you may feel frightened: not simply by the suggestion of hidden microphones and secret police, or the strained isolation of the foreign residents, herded into their ghettos, or even by the sense of stark power that emanates from this dismal but impressive city; but by a profound sense of alienation, as though you belonged to some unrelated visiting species. Your conversations, however cordial, never really bridge the gulf of ideology. Your informant, kindly and hospitable, will suddenly assume a tone of quite unexpected arrogance. Behind the inquiries of the brigadier of communist labour there lurks not hostility exactly, but a sense of inescapable misunderstanding, as though at some predestined point both your languages and your conceptions will diverge, never to be reconciled. You can never get to grips with the truth in Moscow. It slithers away from you into the snow, and even its tracks are obliterated by armies of passing footfalls.

But sometimes you may, nevertheless, catch a glimpse of the very heart, the core of this city's mysteries, as the man with the hangover analyses with cheerless clarity the exact mixture of drinks that was his undoing. It may well be at the Bolshoi, when some gigantic Russian epic is being ferociously enacted, with rolls of kettle-drums and clashes of armour, a mammoth chorus open-throated, a clutch of heroes swelling in the foreground with a passage and repassage of knights, horses, serfs, a frenzy of conical helmets and chain mail, banners dramatically waving, flames issuing from a back-cloth, smoke, flashing beacons, the orchestra in a quivering *fortissimo*, the conductor wiping his sweating bald head, the enormous audience gripping its seats or craning from the high gilded balconies above the chandelier – then, in the middle of it all, you will glance across your neighbour's shoulder to the great state box in the centre: there will be sitting the most powerful man on earth, looking bored and rather glazed, a slight sad smile playing around the corners of his mouth, his wife, in a bun and brown sagging dress, demure and attentive at his elbow.

You need not wait for the last act. Go home and sleep it off.

In this same disturbing city, in 1960, the pilot of an American spy plane was put on trial before the Soviet Supreme Court. His plane had crashed from 60,000 feet over the Urals, seeming to show that Soviet anti-aircraft rocketry could reach unprecedented heights. Declining to use the poison suicide pin with which the CIA had provided him, the pilot was captured by peasants near Sverdlovsk and put on trial in Moscow. It was the last in the line of Soviet international show trials that had begun in the 1920s.

* * *

In the House of the Union in Moscow this morning the American Gary Powers, aged 31, described as a spy, was accused before the Military College of the Soviet Supreme Court of espionage against the Soviet state. He pleaded guilty.

His wife was at the back of the court, sad in black with a white Puritan collar. So were several hundred diplomatists, Kafka and George Orwell, but it was not, by and large, a morning of horror. The emotions of the Hall of Columns, the gorgeous setting of the case, ranged from bleak apprehension by way of growing cynicism to occasional moments of levity. It did not seem this morning a hectoring or a bullying court. Why should it be? It had all it wanted, and its purpose was merely to paint a tarnished lily.

Macabre enough, all the same, was the sense of eerie ritual as Powers was led into the limelight this morning. The court sat on a kind of stage against a background of opaque white curtains. In the centre were the military judge and his two assessors, generals all, immaculate in dove grey, and sitting in their tall wooden chairs like bulky Buddhas. To the left sat the prosecutor, the procurator-general of the Soviet Union, a heavy and formidable lawyer in a sombre blue uniform. The lights were blinding – chandeliers, strings of bare bulbs, floodlights – bathing the whole scene in chill brilliance and giving the members of the court a waxen cosmetic look.

Into this extraordinary scene Powers was led, punctually at ten, with an escort of two young soldiers in olive-green jackets and blue trousers. He wore a blue Russian suit a size too large for him, so that he had to hitch up its sleeves now and then, and his hair was cut in a kind of modified crew-cut – or perhaps a crew-cut overgrown. They put him in the wooden dock, like a big child's playpen beneath the floodlights. The sentries stood to attention beside it, as beside a catafalque, and presently, to the first whirr of the cameras, his trial began.

It began frighteningly. Powers was obviously frightened, and so was I. Coldly, precisely, ceremonially were the charges proclaimed, interpreted for Powers in a terrifyingly dry and academic English and instantly translated through headphones into French, German and Spanish. The witnesses for the prosecution were led self-consciously on stage – four stocky men in double-breasted blue, who signed the register at the secretary's table and shuffled awkwardly off again. The expert witnesses were summoned – 'Will the experts please come forward?' – six officers in uniform and a scientist in natty grey. Now and then the brilliant lights were shifted, when the cameramen needed a view of the expectant audience, or a long shot of

Mrs Powers. It all felt cold, preordained, hopeless, from the young man standing like a living whimper in the dock to the impassive general high in the judge's chair.

Once or twice Powers looked into the hall hopelessly out of the blaze of the camera lights, but he evidently could not see his wife. He looked to me like a lost man already, a broken, demoralized, almost obsequious prisoner, caught in a mesh like a shaky fly. Anxiously he stood up, sat down, answered the questions like a good boy. To be sure they treated him gently enough, allowing him full scope to play the capitalists' puppet, the nice, simple, up-the-garden-path all-American boy. The burden of the defence is clearly to be that Powers undertook the flight without really participating in its intentions – that he just did what he was told without reasoning, and in this instance without dying, either.

The procurator-general nevertheless got some strangely tart answers, and the morning passed in queer ups and downs of elation and despair. At the back of all our minds, though, lay the suspicion of brainwashing, of torture in dark offstage dungeons, and all the court became tense when at last the procurator-general, rolling the hours away, reached the poison pin.

'I was given it in case I was tortured and could not stand it, would rather be dead.'

'So your masters did not put much value on your life?'

'Well, they more or less left it to me. No one told me to kill myself.'

'Were you told you would be tortured?'

'I wasn't told I would be, but I expected to be.'

'And were you tortured?' asked the procurator-general.

'No,' said Captain Powers. 'I have been treated very nice.'

Last night Powers's defence counsel, Mikhail Grinev (who looks a little like an abstemious Oliver Hardy), presented all the expected arguments of mitigation. Powers was, he implied, just an ordinary American *muzhik*, exploited by a cynical capitalist state, striving only to set himself up in a modest business against all the handicaps of his heartless environment. He came from simple stock and had only the simple ambitions shared by working people the world over: flying a U-2 over Russia was, so to speak, just a temporary aberration forced upon him by the cruel pressures of a capitalist, war-mongering society.

The trial has had, though, its moments of piquant fascination, its glimpses of a queer world beyond our experience. We saw Powers, for example, in his oxygen helmet being dressed for the flight at Peshawar like a knight before battle – the maps thrust in his pocket, the secret equipment loaded in his aircraft, the rocket site pointed out on his map. We saw the misty figure of Colonel Shelton, commander of the U-2 detachment, crossing the tarmac to the aircraft before its take-off and giving Powers a piece of black cloth – an ill-explained talisman to be handed over by Powers when he safely reached Bodo. We looked with Powers out of his cockpit, somewhere over Russia, and saw the condensation trail of a Soviet aircraft far below.

We saw the country folk near Sverdlovsk standing beside their doors to watch the swinging parachute come down. We examined with the comrade experts all the extraordinary assembly of instruments, from cameras to radar bafflers, that are the tools of modern intelligence. Our vision ranged from the Pamirs to Scandinavia and even across to the America of Powers's adolescence, when he worked as a lifeguard 'because nobody would hire somebody who was going to be drafted'. And through it all we watched the immobile, impassive, faintly Mongol face of the court's president, sitting godlike and erect beneath a gigantic hammer and sickle.

The judgment, which had taken the judges four hours to prepare, seemed to take an age to deliver. Expectantly packed, from the reporters in the gallery to the off-duty stenographers peering through the curtain at the back, the whole courtroom rose for the entry of the three generals, and remained on its feet as the chairman read the judgment.

The court had concluded, he said, that Powers was a tool of the Central Intelligence Agency of the United States, 'which carries out its plans with the permission of the American Government'. His flight was deliberately designed to increase international tension and had created a threat to the general peace.

For a moment, just then, I feared the worst: that the prosecution's demand for fifteen years' imprisonment, and the pleas for mitigation from the defence counsel, were both no more than appetizers, designed to give dramatic impact to the supreme sentence. I could see Mrs Powers below me, as white as a sheet, clutching a handkerchief in her hand. Around me my colleagues from a dozen countries were poised at their pads, and in the body of the hall the television cameramen had laid their cameras upon the defendant and were only waiting to switch on. Just for a moment I thought we were awaiting a death sentence.

But then: 'The Military Collegium of the Soviet Supreme Court, proceeding from principles of Soviet humanism and taking into account Powers's

sincere repentance, sentences Francis Gary Powers to ten years' detention, three years of them to be spent in prison, for espionage against the
Soviet State.' A wave of emotion swept through the court, and in a moment
the chandeliers were shaking to applause. Powers walked out of court
steadily enough, a soldier before him, a soldier behind, and almost in a
matter of moments the brilliant lights were doused, the great Hall of
Columns was emptied of its guests, the three enigmatic judges had
withdrawn and the Powers trial was over.

I hated every minute of it. It was horrible. It was our brave new world in
microcosm, and it stank.

*I was suspicious at the time that Powers had not really been shot down, but
that his aircraft had suffered some mechanical mishap. When I voiced this
speculation during a private telephone call home, the cold voice of an
unknown censor immediately cut me off.*

*Powers was released in 1962, in return for a Soviet agent held in the
United States, and died in a helicopter crash in 1977.*

*While I was in Moscow I made the acquaintance of Guy Burgess, a
renegade British diplomat who was a Soviet agent for some years but was by
then sadly homesick for England. Whether on the instructions of the KGB, or
because of his own nostalgia, he often got in touch with visiting actors and
actresses, writers and journalists. I could not help feeling sorry for him, and
we agreed to go together one evening to the Bolshoi. We arranged to meet
outside the theatre door, and when I got there he was waiting for me on the
steps. I waved a greeting as I approached him through the crowd, and he
waved a response, but by the time I reached the door he had vanished. I
never saw him again.*

Leningrad

*The very antithesis of Moscow, then as always, was Leningrad, née St
Petersburg, ex-Petrograd. My first glimpse of it was in transit from Kiev,
when I spent a day and a night in the city between flights, and on my way
home next morning I wrote this bewitched essay for the* Guardian.

Peter the Great called it his 'window on the West', and it remains a look-out
still, watchfully Western in style and manner, a magnificent artefact of
Europe at the gateway to Asia. They have tamed Leningrad and harnessed

it, driven away its emperors, turned its palaces into museums and its academies for young ladies into political offices – coarsened its exquisite restaurants, exiled its fan-makers and its riding-masters, swamped its bookshops with dialectical materialism, desecrated its cathedrals, humbled its hierarchies, stifled its frivolities, left its great avenues peeling and pining. Yet it rides above its fate like the queen it is, and seemed to me, when I flew in out of the horny Ukraine, still a Cleopatra among cities.

Leningrad is more than just a geometrical, but actually an astronomical metropolis, for Moskovsky Prospekt, the southern entry to the place, is not only six miles long and dead straight but runs along the meridian from the Pulkovo Observatory on the southern heights. Calm, precise, and elegant seemed the city as I drove along this celestial boulevard: a thoroughbred still, balanced and proportioned, with no uncanny Mongolesque skyscrapers to mar the skyline, only a serenity of classical colonnades, baroque mansions, domes and gilded steeples. Sea-light and snow-light filtered perpetually through the structures and shone icily from the broad frozen stream of the Neva, scattered with islands, lined with impeccable architecture, and running away between the quaysides to the Gulf of Finland and points west.

Dazzled, the scales of the Ukraine still in my eyes, I wandered through all this lucidity. Across the river the sunshine gleamed miraculously upon the golden finger-spire of St Peter and St Paul, slim as a stiletto above its ramparts. In the upstairs galleries of the Hermitage, flooded in sunshine and surveying a brilliant landscape of white, gold and baroque, the great Renoirs, Gauguins, Monets and blue Matisses stood in gorgeous vivacity, to be inhaled like a fragrance or gulped like a draught of some exalting wine. Russia in winter is a dread and dreary country, clogged alike with sludge and dogma; but fly into Leningrad as I did, and your very glands will be rejuvenated.

For all its shrines of materialist revolution, its thumping industrial fringe, the atomic submarines upon its shipyards – for all these signs of the times Leningrad retains, like an ageless courtesan, many an inessential charm. I bought a batter-wrapped sausage that morning from a solemn woman in a white overall at a street-corner stand. I found a 1905 Baedeker Russia in the jumble of an old-school bookshop, inscribed in a spindly German hand in the ink of long ago. I strolled among the hidden statues of the Summer Garden, each one locked away for the winter, like a wayward nymph in a rock, inside its own little wooden house. I wondered at the profusion of fresh flowers on the tomb of Peter the Great, and I gazed from

113

the balcony of St Isaac's Cathedral upon the glinting steeple of the Admiralty, like a Buddhist stupa above the ice, and the fabulous immensities of the Winter Palace, where the Tsars lived in immeasurable splendour, and the revolutionaries stormed their way into history. In Moscow it is difficult not to feel a kind of snob; in Leningrad you are a serf in untanned thigh-boots, gaping at the carriages and climaxes of the past.

For this is a city with the gift of timelessness. Elsewhere most Russians seem so unalluring that it is a mystery to me how the reproduction of the species is maintained. Here there are still girls of a haunting and nostalgic beauty, such as you meet in the pages of the immortal novelists, and men of a natural elegance beyond class or era. Forgotten Western echoes, too, linger suggestively on. I observed two young diplomatists in my hotel, wearing heavy coats and high fur hats, whose immemorial English faces and languid long-limbed attitudes at the reception desk made them look like thrusting fur traders from Eastcheap, awaiting a concession from the Empress. I drank my morning coffee in a shop that might have sprung from imperial Vienna, and I listened to jazz so brassily honky-tonk that I might have been in some forgotten burlesque of the Loop, thirty years ago in Chicago.

Leningrad is a humorous city. The cloakroom attendant puts your hat on your head with a delightful parody of courtly excess. Even the official guides are slyly amused by the presence in the Anti-God Museum (the Museum, that is, of the History of Religion and Atheism) of a section reverently devoted to the adulation of Lenin. The young people of Leningrad, often rakishly and sometimes brazenly dressed, preserve a sense of bubbly fun: traces of taste, style and delicacy have survived the convulsion, and there are still a few citizens whose clothes fit and whose eyes are lit with a glint of gaiety.

There are modernistic trams in Leningrad – devices I had hitherto regarded as a contradiction in terms. There are polite and mercifully unobtrusive policemen. There is a mosque like something out of Isfahan, a square in which practically every building is a theatre, a house once inhabited by the inventor of the aeroplane (twenty years, I need hardly say, before the Wrights), a Wedding Palace for the white weddings now officially encouraged in Russia, a mammoth in a museum, a vase weighing nineteen tons and twenty-five Rembrandts. Even the snow-ploughs do their work with a special kind of symmetry, moving around Palace Square in lumpish ever-decreasing circles, like old-fashioned reapers, until at last they can revolve no more, and a squad of cheerful women with brooms and shovels leaps through their clouds of exhaust to remove the last central pile of snow, where the hare should be.

I went to a children's puppet theatre in the afternoon and watched its entrancing fooleries among an audience so enthusiastically disorganized that it made the end-of-term play at an English village school feel like Order in opposition to Chaos. And in the evening I saw *Die Fledermaus*, staged with a genuine rollicking panache, and so instinct with the magic of the waltz, the whirl of white skirts and the flick of tail-coats, that when I inspected the faces of the women about me, Soviet proletarians every one, I found them glazed with a true suburban enchantment.

They gave me champagne at dinner, placing a neatly folded napkin like a white cone over the bottle-top, and very late that night, with the fizz still in me, I slithered down the river bank beside the Admiralty, and crunched a path across the frozen Neva, The sky above me was a deep cold blue. The lights of the city shone dimly off the ice, like phosphorescence. The golden steeple of the Admiralty was floodlit and resplendent, like an archangel's wand in the night, and beneath the bridge I could just make out the three tall funnels of the old cruiser *Aurora*, and the speckled lights of her portholes. Leningrad lay lucent still, even at midnight, and seemed to me like an exemplar, a paradigm, an obituary of the European ideal.

Next morning a fog fell upon the city, and you could not see across the river from one side to the other.

I did not write about Leningrad again until 1999. By then it was St Petersburg once more, the new Russian capitalism was in full blast, and my German-owned hotel was extremely luxurious. I was still bewitched, all the same.

Odessa

I liked Odessa, too, still in those days the most Jewish city of the Soviet Union, although throughout my visit there I felt I was being trailed by the KGB more persistently than anywhere else in the USSR.

The most dramatic, as well as the most diligent, conductor in the world is to be seen in action at the Theatre of Opera and Ballet in Odessa. He is an elderly man, but passionate. All around him as he works peculiar things are happening. Behind, in the half-empty auditorium, a constant buzz of homely conversation underlies the score, and three ill-shaven Levantines in the second row seem to be in the throes of opium dreams, squirming and sighing in their seats. In front, the stage is alive with minor mishaps – trap-doors mysteriously closing and opening, fans being dropped, iron accessories clattering, while the cast of *La Traviata*, none apparently more than five feet high, smile resolutely across the footlights with a treasury of gold teeth.

The conductor is unperturbed. Majestically he sails through the confusions of the evening, impervious to them all, sometimes grunting emotionally, sometimes joining in an aria in a powerful baritone, throwing his fine head back, bending double, conspiratorially withdrawing, pugnaciously advancing, with infinite variations of mood and facial expression, and frequent hissed injunctions to the woodwind. Nobody in the socialist bloc fulfils a norm more devotedly, and nobody does more credit to the Hero City of Odessa. It is not often easy, in Moscow or Kiev, to respond to the simplicities of the Russian Revolution. In such great cities the deliberate vulgarity of communist life, the perpetual aura of baggy trousers, hair-cream and Saturday-night hop, is more depressing than endearing, and you begin to pine, however egalitarian your convictions, for a really snooty upper-crust restaurant, or the high-pitched gossip of debutantes. In a smaller provincial centre like Odessa, though, it is different. Here, far away from the dreadful workings of state, there still feels some faint suggestion of idealism to the People's Dictatorship, a sense of simple pride and purpose: and in such a setting it is difficult not to warm to the conscientiousness of the modern urban Russians, whether it is directed towards a mastery of English vowels or the correction of a wandering contralto.

A century ago Odessa was an urbane seaport of Francophile tendencies, raised into eminence by a French satrap of the Tsar, the Comte de Richelieu. Though long stripped of its boudoir fripperies, it retains a certain faded elegance. A fine wide boulevard runs above the harbour, and from it descend the broad steps that figured in *The Battleship Potemkin*. There is an ornate old Bourse in Odessa, and the ghost of an English Club, the shell of a Credit Lyonnais, an Opera House of lofty traditional opulence, muse-haunted and nymph-scrolled. There is even the old building of the local Duma, dishonestly identified by Intourist as 'yet another former Stock Exchange under the old system'. Wide, straight, and Parisian are the avenues of the city, and embedded in the thigh of a statue of de Richelieu is a cannonball from HMS *Tiger*, a ferocious visitor to these waters during the Crimean War.

Odessa was built by the Tsars as a southern outlet for Russia, and remains the second port of the Soviet Union. It faces south and east, and its quaysides are embellished with vast welcoming slogans in Arabic, Chinese, French and English – 'Long Live Peace and Friendship', they proclaim, 'among the Peoples of the Whole World'. A smell of tar hangs agreeably on the Odessa air, and a fine jumble of shipping lies always inside the moles: a pair of lovely three-masters manned by cadets; two or three smart Black Sea liners, running down to Georgia or Istanbul; freighters from Latakia or Alexandria; a squat Russian warship with sloping bulbous funnels. In the summer British and Greek cruising liners, flecked with the Aegean, put in here for brief inquisitive visits; in the winter a fringe of ice loiters around the harbour, and most of the ships seem to lie there supine and deserted.

The docks are shut off by high walls and policemen, and you can only peer at their quaysides from an eminence, or skulk about their gateways pretending to meet a comrade: but Odessa anyway feels unmistakably a port – a peeling, rather regretful port, a Soviet Tangiers. It is a cosmopolitan city still, full of Greeks, Jews, Armenians, Georgians, Egyptian seamen, Chinese delegations. The jolliest of old sacristans will conduct you around the decaying synagogue, lending you a white peaked cap for your head, and sallow Mediterranean faces will greet you solemnly in the Greek church. Odessa is a languid southern seaside city, snowless and sunlit, and even the pantheon of communist deities, even the Workers' Honours Boards, even the blaring loudspeaker from the Central Committee's headquarters, even the tinny new carillon, even the nagging suspicion that somebody is following you cannot altogether stifle the relaxed and easy-going nature of the town, like a soft warm breeze across the Bosporus.

Odessa is scarcely a show-place of the regime. It has busy industries, a large university and a celebrated eye hospital: but thanks to the occurrence of a soft subsoil it has none of your towering tomb-like blocks of flats, and you have only to step through an archway off almost any boulevard to find yourself back in pre-revolutionary Russia, with tumbledown apartments around a shambled courtyard, and women with buckets collecting their water from the communal outdoor tap in the middle. All feels small, friendly and unpretentious. In the new railway station, dedicated to Odessa's heroic resistance during the war, there is a large notice-board which, upon the pressure of a button, illustrates in illuminated signs the route to any western Russian city; and there is something very appealing to the pleasure this simple toy gives the concourse of people constantly consulting it, the air of wondering merriment that hangs about its buttons, like country festivity at a fairground.

There is also something paradoxically old-fashioned about Odessa. Its restaurants, though sprawling with greasy young men and loud with brassy jazz, are marvellously nineteenth century in appointment. Its public buildings still preserve, beneath their threadbare sloganry, shreds of old decorum. And if you observe a pair of young women sauntering together down the promenade, you will be struck by niggling sensations of *déjà vu*. What is so familiar about them? Where have you seen them before? And then, in a revealing flash, you have a vision of old newspapers lining attic drawers, full of the cloche hats and long coats of the thirties: and you realize that these young ladies of Odessa take you back mysteriously to your childhood, like snapshots in an album.

Just think! Odessa is the second port of Russia, the gateway of the Ukraine, the pearl of the Black Sea; yet it all boils down in my mind, such is the indivisibility of time and experience, to an indistinct memory of childhood, dormant for thirty years and revived only by a glimpse of forgotten fashions above the Potemkin Steps.

My hotel room in Odessa was stiflingly steam-heated, and I am ashamed to say that, finding its windows hermetically sealed, I took up some heavy object and broke one to let the air in. In the Soviet Union of the 1960s one was often goaded towards ill-discipline. One morning on Kharkov airport in the Ukraine (then a part of the Soviet Union) I experienced a more glorious moment of liberation. I had been hanging about there for hours, fobbed off by supercilious airline employees through delay after delay in a bitterly cold and uninviting waiting-room, until at last the patience of my Soviet fellow-passengers expired. They found a boarding-ramp, pushed it on to the tarmac, climbed up to the aircraft, and brushing aside the horrified stewardesses, plumped themselves in their seats and called for vodka. I followed in their wake rejoicing, feeling as though we had stormed all life's varied Kremlins.

Czechoslovakia

Czechoslovakia was probably the most oppressively communist country of the so-called Soviet Bloc, and when the Guardian *sent me there it was my first glimpse of the dark world of Stalinist satellites. After a time I ran away from Prague, its capital, to visit the celebrated spas of western Czechoslovakia, once the resort of well-heeled valetudinarians from all Europe. They were now showplaces of the People's Republic, which loved showing them off to their all too rare visitors from the West.*

'And this morning, Mr Morris,' said my guide briskly, rearranging a businesslike bun in her blonde hair, 'we shall visit Marianske Lazne, in the western area of our country.' My heart neither leapt nor sank, for it was numb with cold and scepticism. I was deep in disbelief. The country was Czechoslovakia. The time was the very depth and nadir of a grim central European winter. The car into whose back seat I lowered myself, with a rather frigid smile of acceptance, was a bow-legged green Skoda. But as she settled herself beside me, giving me a sweet but not altogether convincing smile, my guide added as an afterthought: 'Under the old regime, you know, they used to call it Marienbad!'

Marienbad! Instantly a bell rang in my mind, jangled but golden, cracked but still rich, oddly familiar after my peeling baroque evenings in Prague, my icy folk-customs in the High Tatra mountains, my long shuddering drives through the snow-enshrouded, fir-blackened, heartless and cheerless Czech countryside. Marienbad! It was like an echo of a golden age just to hear the name, and many a discredited vision crossed my mind, as my guide kindly explained to me the new medicinal treatments for workers' families: visions of lace and stiff white collars, of clip-clopping greys and fawning courtiers, here a plumed imperial hat, here a fluttering embroidered fan – little lap dogs, hurrying servants, coffee on spindly tables, the orchestra tuning its fiddles among the roses and the hotel manager, moustaches pomaded, hurrying to greet His Excellency. They were pictures of an age that was rightly ended, of a society justly abolished, of unfair privileges and outdated protocol; but they retained an old lavender charm in the imagination, as of faded holiday postcards.

For me they offered more, too: for through them all, through the strolling old-fashioned crowds and the string bands, there glared boldly into my mind the eyes of a particular face. One of the divinities of my personal pantheon is old 'Jacky' Fisher, British Admiral of the Fleet, creator of the *Dreadnought*, iconoclast, egocentric, flatterer, failure and humorist, who died six years before I was born, but who is still marvellously alive in my affections. This old greatheart was an habitué of Marienbad in its palmy days. There he consorted proudly with the imperial potentates, and danced blissfully with the imperial ladies, and picked the brains of foreign generals, and cocked a gay eyebrow at many a Continental beauty. Many a letter had I read in Fisher's huge-scrawled hand on the browning writing-paper of forgotten Marienbad hotels, with elaborate flowery letterheads, and engravings of the winter gardens.

So we were going to Marienbad! As we laboured through that grim landscape Fisher's wrinkled cynical face peered at me constantly through the firs. He had an extraordinary face, so oddly striking that legend had him the illegitimate son of a Ceylonese prince, so unforgettable that the Sultan of Morocco, once inspecting Fisher's Mediterranean Fleet, was asked what had struck him most, among all the gleaming lines of battleships, the great barbettes and the impeccable gun drills, and replied without a second's hesitation: 'The Admiral's face!' Never was a face so congealed with self-esteem, so glorious with gaiety, so proud, so contemptuous, so flirtatious and so compelling! I could see its heavy-lidded eye winking, all but imperceptibly, through the damp fog that lay like a shroud upon the fields.

But we were there, and driving through the fine avenues of the place towards the graceful squares and colonnades that surround the baths. Marienbad was stately still, for all its dismal communist miasma. The old hotels, now occupied chiefly by proletarian groups, were still stylish beneath their peeling paint. The covered promenade (along which the girls of a Youth Association were sauntering in frumpish crocodile) was still sadly elegant. The fountains were still delicate. The gardens were still fresh. The charming houses, all official or institutional, still possessed a faint scented allure of satin and window-boxes. It was a ghost with shreds of colour.

We looked around the place conscientiously; and inspected the free treatment in the baths; and examined institutions of one kind or another; and strolled a little forlornly along the pallid splendours of the spa; and presently found ourselves, marshalled by a huge comrade of the coarsest kind, looking at the civic museum. This queer collection of souvenirs, mostly about the bad old days of the Habsburg Empire, was housed in a small pretty villa in the centre of the town; and sometimes, as we wandered from room to room, from glass case to glass case, while the Comrade Curator leered at the Archdukes, and the guide attended intermittently to her hair – sometimes, as we looked at this sad exhibition my eye wandered through an open window, to the curve of the esplanade below. How easy it was to imagine those old grandees of the 1880s, wicked perhaps, often selfish, generally heedless, sometimes cruel, but alive with a vanished panache and glitter! How easy to see the whiskered potentates, and the willowy English peers, and the doll-like Austrian ladies, and Fisher himself, the boldest of paladins, like a laughing mandarin among the feather boas!

I tapped the curator, rather gingerly, upon the shoulder. The museum was fine, said I, but was there no one in the town who actually *remembered* those old times, when the plutocrats and warmongers battened themselves so shamelessly upon the spa? The churl thought long and deep before replying, and then told us with a grin that there was somebody, in that very house – none other than the woman who had owned the place and occupied it in greedy ease and luxury, until the advent of the People's Government. Like a huge shambling bear he led the way, down the steep staircase among the prints, until we stood again in the hall of the house, beside the entrance. This woman, explained the curator, was permitted to live in a room in the basement, in return for keeping the place clean: and opening a door he shouted hoarsely down the basement stairs. At first there was only silence. The curator bellowed again, in a harsh imperative, and presently there was a sound of movement below. A cough, a rustle, laboured footsteps up the stairs; and there emerged into the hall beside us an old woman, dressed almost in rags, wiping her hands on her skirt. Her face was blank and quite impassive. Her movements were oddly stiff, as though she had had a stroke. Her skin was dirty and her hands were rough and crooked. She looked like some spiritless old animal, a broken pit pony, a lame and useless sheepdog. 'Here she is,' said the curator, gesturing her roughly into the hall. 'Ask her what you want.'

I was embarrassed, and angry with the man, and wished I had never summoned the old lady into this cruel limelight: but my guide smiled at her with sudden unexpected kindness, and I asked her my one question. Did she happen to remember, out of all the foreign visitors to Marienbad, all the eminent men and dazzling women who must have crossed the corridors of her life – did she happen to remember Admiral Jack Fisher of the Royal Navy?

A glimmer entered her eye, and warmed, and flourished, and very nearly sparkled: and turning her head stiffly to look at me, and straightening her drab-cottoned back, she answered in a perfect, clear-cut Edwardian English. 'Ah!' she said. 'Jacky Fisher! Jacky Fisher! *What a face that man had!*'

So I shook her limp soap-coarsened hand, walked out of the museum into the cold fog, thought how lasting was the glow of a good man's fun, and ended my visit to Marianske Lazne.

Forty years later I re-told this tale in a capricious book about Admiral Fisher, a jeu d'amour *called* Fisher's Face. *A relation of the old lady read it, and wrote to tell me that the communists hadn't really treated her so harshly after all.*

Poland

Poland was the most restless and exciting of the satellite countries, but this made it all the sadder to experience. This essay may have been made the more unhappy because during my stay in Warsaw, the capital, I had made a fool of myself by illegal currency conversions, and half-expected to be plunged into a Polish gaol at any moment.

Seen across the hours from a hotel window in the depths of winter, Warsaw could only be Warsaw, for nowhere else on the face of the earth breathes quite the same fusion of atmospheres. Room 221 in the Bristol Hotel is heavily but quite cosily Victorian, with a wicker mat hung in incongruous ornamentation on one wall and a bright if unadventurous abstract on another. Outside the door two dear old pudgy housemaids sit habitually on the floor in white caps, aprons and carpet slippers, sibilantly gossiping, and down the corridor the immense glass lift, like a cage for a phoenix, slides in magnificent lurches to the foyer, its voyagers slipping a few zlotys to the operator as they leave. There is a violent smell of cooking on the landing, and downstairs you may just hear the tapping of a progressive American playwright's typewriter – he spent last evening with a group of eminent sociologists, and is busy working up his notes.

It is a fusty, old-fashioned, plush but mournful hostelry, but outside the window Warsaw is nothing if not spacious. The sky is grey, immense, and unmistakably central European. The snow lies thick and sullen on the broad streets. Down the hill only a thin winding stream of water forces a way through the frozen Vistula. The air, to a visitor from England, seems slightly perfumed with petrol and boiled potatoes, but feels nevertheless like country air, blown out of forests and endless plains and Carpathian ravines; and when you first lean from your window in the icy morning you will hear the clatter of horses' hooves and the triumphant crow of a cold but irrepressible cock. Below you then the first citizens of the morning intermittently appear: an elderly lady with a jolly black dog, a covey of merry schoolchildren, entrancing high-boned faces peering through their fur hoods like fox cubs through the bushes. Long carts full of snow go by, with a column of big lorries, and even an antique barouche trundles with creaks and squeaks towards its cab-rank; and presently Warsaw is wide awake, the sun is wanly shining, and the observer in Room 221 can watch the world of the Poles pass by.

It is not altogether a drab world, for the Poles have forced many concessions out of their communist masters. The citizenry that now pours down the pavement is not badly dressed – colourlessly, perhaps, by Western standards, but well shod and warmly coated. Sometimes a young beauty steps by almost ludicrously glamorized, slinking skilfully in the Bardot manner, in the finest nylons and the most preposterously frivolous of fur hats. Sometimes a peasant stumps down the street in thick but threadbare serge and mighty boots. Mostly the people look less arresting than workmanlike, as though they are more concerned with keeping warm and getting to the butcher's first than with turning heads or charming the boss's daughter.

The shops across the way might not win prizes in Fifth Avenue or Regent Street, but have more sparkle to them than you might expect (weary though the queue may be at the grocer's, and tiresome the shortage of meat). A surprising variety of inessential imports glitters bravely among their displays – American cigarettes, French sardines, Hawaiian pineapples, Florida fruit juice, tinned coffee from England, tea from Madras, olives from Argentina, things that look like bottled gooseberries from Bulgaria, Chinese jams (in bottles shaped like illustrious mandarins of the eighth degree). A bright parade of foreign books shines in the bookshop down the road, from a picture book of Oxford that almost breaks the homesick heart to an empirical range of American paperbacks. You can even buy French perfumes in Warsaw, if you happen to prefer them to the local product, and have an indulgent husband.

The cars that pass in increasing but still moderate profusion mostly look beetle-backed and froward, but now and then one of the smart new Russian limousines appears, not a bit socialist-realist, and sometimes an opulent Mercedes-Benz slides by, or a delicate Fiat. Agatha Christie is probably on at one of the theatres. You can read the *Manchester Guardian* at the Grand Hotel. The buses are made in France. Just down the road is the headquarters of the British and Foreign Bible Society. Nostalgic you may be for Tom Quad or Times Square, but in Warsaw there are still tenuous links with home.

And even from Room 221 you can see something of the character of the Poles, for they move with a special kind of vigour, almost jaunty, and they have strong and interesting faces. Warsaw is haunted always by sad memories, but there is nevertheless a liveliness, a jollity, a gaiety in the air that springs only from the hearts of the Poles. A gleam of wrinkled humour lightens the eye of the elderly chambermaid when she arrives, some hours after lunch, to make your bed. Polish conversation, for a visiting Briton anyway, is infinitely easy, entertaining and somehow familiar. Sometimes in the street below a rip-roaring jovial drunk will stagger through the snow, bawling witticisms and singing bawdy songs. They are not an aloof, remote or inscrutable people, the Poles; they might do well, I sometimes feel, in Ireland.

At other moments, though, Warsaw feels a long, long way from Galway; and as the evening draws on, and the progressive playwright closes his typewriter and leaves for a seance with seven eminent philosophers, you may notice a stream of citizens moving intently towards the church which, with its twin angels sustaining the cross on its golden ball, stands in ornate confidence beyond the park. They walk with an air of functional resolution, very different from Ballycommon on Sunday morning, and slip into the church hurriedly, as though they have work to do there, crossing themselves for all the world as a worker clocks himself in at the factory; and if you are patient you will see them emerging again a few moments later, buttoning up their coats, putting on their thick gloves, and hastening away towards the trolley-bus. They look as though they have stopped at a petrol station to get fuel for the evening; and they even remind me – not with irreverence, only sympathy – of addicts on a lost weekend, stocking up at Joe's Bar on Fourth Avenue.

Then the night falls on Warsaw, chill and early, and the dim lights of eastern Europe reluctantly awake. The view from your balcony grows grim and depressing, with the presence of the harsh frozen Vistula always behind your back and only a trickle of prepossessed traffic enlivening the streets. The coffee-shops and restaurants hide their identities behind curtains and closed doors, and few bright lights entice you towards the theatres. The thump of a jazz band may reach you across the snow, but the city feels obscurely muffled and padded, and the gaunt square buildings of the new Warsaw lie there unsmiling in the cold.

Raise your eyes above the rooftops, though, above the angels with their golden ball, and there you will see the big red light on the Palace of Culture and Science, presented to Poland by the Soviet Union, and towering above

124

this grey city like a vast watchman in the dark. And perhaps at the same time if you listen hard enough, closing your ears to the clang of the trams and the rumble of the passing cars, you may hear from some distant student attic the thin thrilling strains of a Chopin polonaise, riding the cold night air like an invocation.

But probably not. I must not romanticize. 'Room service? A cup of coffee, please, two aspirins, and a cable form. That's it, bless you, Room 221.'

The Bristol Hotel is now once again a splendid five-star international hotel. Then it was so immured behind the Iron Curtain that one day during my stay in Room 221 the management asked me if I would write a publicity brochure for it. I did.

The Cold War gave birth to a whole new genre of spy fiction and film, and we newspaper correspondents all saw ourselves somewhere in their pages or sequences. On a journey to Budapest once I was asked by a friend to take a package of books to a diplomat serving in one of the embassies there. I did not ask what the books were, and asked no questions either when it was suggested that I hand them over at a rendezvous in the middle of the Chain Bridge, linking Buda and Pest across the Danube. It was just like a movie. Promptly at the appointed time I set off across the walkway of the bridge, and presently I became aware of a particular figure approaching me from among the pedestrians from the other end. I saw both of us as it were through a long-focus lens, shimmering a little, the distance distorted as we neared each other. We met. We exchanged compliments. We shook hands. I handed over the package, and to dark portentous music – all drums and cellos – I returned to the Buda shore as the credit titles rolled.

The Sixth Fleet

One of the great power factors of the Cold War was the American Sixth Fleet. Its 50 ships, 200 aircraft and 20,000 men constantly roamed the Mediterranean, supplied directly from the United States and constantly shadowed by Soviet ships. For the Guardian *I was flown one day to the brand-new carrier* Saratoga *(65,000 tons), then one of the most powerful warships afloat.*

The captain of the *Saratoga*, a tall, lean man of ecclesiastical bearing, sits in a raised, padded armchair on the port side of his bridge, rather as though he were having his hair cut or being inducted to his see; and thus, by looking through the tilted glass windows to the flight deck beneath, he can survey an historical phenomenon.

The wide air-conditioned bridge is calm and muffled. The Mediterranean is blue and ancient. Away to the west a destroyer steams in placid escort, now and then winking a signal lazily. Behind the carrier a solitary rescue helicopter rides in constant watchful station. But beneath his windows the captain can see the big jet bombers which, at the drop of a hat or a gauntlet, can whisk a hydrogen bomb at 1,000 miles an hour to the soil of Russia itself, and which thus makes the *Saratoga* and her sister ships of the United States Sixth Fleet the most extraordinary instruments of war ever devised.

It is a big, brassy, extravagant, glittering affair, the Sixth Fleet in the Mediterranean. 'This ship,' says the publicity officer of the *Saratoga*, handing you an information folder, an honorary crew membership card, and a flying helmet, 'has enough paint on her to redecorate 30,000 average American homes. If you turned her on end she would reach to the eighteenth floor of the Empire State Building. There are two thousand telephones on board, three escalators, three soda fountains, nine barbers' chairs and 3,676 trouser hangers. We generate enough electricity to service a city the size of Pittsburgh, an industrial city in the state of Ohio. We air-condition enough air to supply twenty theatres the size of Radio City music-hall. Every evening there are eleven film shows on board. Our machines peel a thousand potatoes an hour. You can order a motor-scooter in the ship's store.'

Nevertheless the fleet is in essence an austere conception. It is false to think of the Sixth Fleet, as the world usually does, as a close, grey, earnest phalanx of warships, steaming incessantly towards a false alarm. When the captain looks out from his barber's chair he may see his attendant destroyers, and perhaps the humped, formidable silhouette of the fleet flagship, the cruiser *Des Moines*; but the rest of the ships may be anywhere, off Beirut, in Suva Bay, influencing people in Athens, scrubbing decks in Iskanderun or simply cruising, with the pilots leaping sporadically for their fighters, and the ships' brass bands polishing their trombones.

There is a touch of the theatre to the brilliance and sparkle with which the *Saratoga* is run – a brightness and bustle and enthusiasm to it all that can give you a distinct aesthetic pleasure. Above you the great grey radar installations revolve in silent grandeur, and a thin wisp of vapour emerges from the sunken funnel of the ship. The lean young sailors, in their jeans or overalls, crouch at their stations or lean over the rails with a certain angular elegance, as far removed from the homely postures of the British bluejacket as an avocado pear from a turnip.

On the flight deck the air traffic officers stroll about in yellow sweaters, like impresarios or choreographers, and here and there you come across a couple of waiting pilots, draped in the elaborate trappings of their calling, with yellow life jackets and spherical helmets and close-cropped hair, like benevolent moon-men. Colour is everywhere on this ship, from the fluttering flags to the dazzling images painted on the aircraft. Every now and then, with a whirr of rotors, a shining helicopter drops in and settles itself fussily on the deck, and when it is time for a flight of aircraft to take off, as it very often is, then a new, bitter, theatrical excitement pervades the ship.

A crowd of off-duty onlookers crowd the rail above the flight deck. A preparatory hiss of steam escapes from the catapults. Men in strange helmets or asbestos suiting appear on the deck or crouch in the catwalk. The loud hailers blare. The pilots scramble into their high cockpits. The captain rises from his chair and stands beside his window, and a first violent roar of jet engines reverberates through the carrier, obliterating the faintly perceptible pounding of its own engines far below. ('This ship has seventeen decks,' shouts the publicity officer indefatigably. 'There are more than 7,000 coffee cups on board the giant carrier, which is named from a battleground in the American Revolutionary War.')

Then, with a shattering impact, they are away. Suddenly, as you stand bemused in the breeze, there screams into the corner of your eye a lean silver jet aircraft, violently projected at breakneck speed down the deck and into the blue: and in a moment there seem to be aircraft everywhere, some careering down the angled deck, some straight towards the bows, flashing and roaring and streaming away, as in the great spectacles of Chinese ballet the dancers hurl themselves with violent but impeccable precision across the stage. In a moment or two the whole flight is airborne, and dwindling towards Turkey.

In fact they are going nowhere in particular this morning, these ballistic young men hurtled off deck like cannonballs. Soon they will swing around and plunge back to the ship once more, to hitch themselves with a shudder and a terrifying jolt to the arrester wires stretched across the deck. A few moments more and they will be riding the escalator down to the air-conditioned wardroom, where iced tea and *Time* magazine and solicitous stewards await their arrival. If you stand with the captain on his bridge, though, while the ship steams swiftly on, while the publicity officer tells you about the garbage-grinders and the trash-burners, and a signal lamp flashes from the escort destroyer – as you stand there beside that courteous seaman in the heart of his great ship you may suddenly realize the meaning of that brief dazzling spectacle.

The striking power of the Sixth Fleet is as subtle and sensitive as a panther's, as responsive as radar, as cataclysmic as lightning: a flash, a blast of jets, a dozen young men hurtled brutally past you, and a terrible page of history can almost instantly be written. No wonder the captain of the *Saratoga*, as he returns to the seat of his command, has the air of a thoughtful but authoritative divine.

Helsinki

It was always a pleasure to leave the antipathies of the Cold War for neutral Scandinavia, but in a way it was always an anti-climax too. This essay records the first time I escaped out of Soviet Russia to the Finnish capital so close across the water, but it ends with an ambivalent twist.

Liberal though you may be, and broad-minded, and looking for the best in everybody, nevertheless leaving the grey purlieus of communism constitutes a festivity: an airy, lacy celebration, like having your first swim of the season, or falling in love. They check your baggage very carefully in Leningrad, and thumb laboriously through your manuscripts, and visibly brighten when they come across a chart of the Seven-Year Plan, and send you off to your aircraft feeling obscurely chastened, as though the head-master is not precisely angry with you, only just a little disappointed. But a brief hour in a bumbling Ilyushin, alone with the wistful stewardess (wearing her brown fur-collared coat over her uniform), and at Helsinki you tumble into the other half of the world. The man at the desk merely says 'Passport, please': but bells ring, birds sing, and somewhere a bottle pops.

Here are the things that overjoyed me most, when that kindly man, with a barely perceptible examination of my passport, sent me whistling into Finland, guided by an exquisite airline hostess: Finnish airline hostesses first, for their reviving breath of elegance; clean, glistening architecture second, for its whisper of liberty; nice little houses in a row; Esso and International Harvester, for their welcoming gleam of profit; cars of all nations, driven at a proper pace (in Russia they never seem to exceed thirty, even in the howling spaces); the rosy cheeks of plump burghers, and children playing in their own gardens; shop windows gracefully dressed, well-cut suits, a quayside that anyone can walk along, a jolly polished steam train beside the docks, Simplicity patterns, *My Fair Lady* in Swedish, coffee-pots whose lids, you may be confident, will not fall off with a dismal splash into the coffee-cup.

Even after Leningrad, that loveliest wraith among cities, Helsinki feels marvellously free, easy and undaunted, and down its comfortable streets all the breezes of the West sweep like a cocktail of elixirs. A visit to the city's most famous bookshop, which claims to be the largest in Europe and is bursting with the books of a dozen languages, is like a shot in the arm and a sniff of salts after the drab, dutiful, brownish bookshelves of the Soviet Union. A stroll beside the harbour, where the patient ice-breakers (when they are not on strike) potter stolidly backwards and forwards down the shipping lanes, is wonderfully exhilarating: the wind off a Russian sea feels like a death in the family, but when it blows out of the Gulf of Finland it is only a tingle in the cheek. An hour in a sauna, the Finnish steam bath, where you are slapped periodically with birch and twigs and plunged deliciously from agonizingly hot to shivering cold, is enough to scour the very miasma of Russia from your person and leave you as clean, brisk, and spanking as a magazine advertisement.

After the stocky, buttoned Russians the people of Helsinki seem marvel-lously lithe and light-footed, big but agile, jovial at smorgasbords or loping and sloping across their snow-fields like Tibetan holy men. Their children, slithering about with ice-hockey sticks, give the heartening impression that they came into the world on skis and have not just put them on in the interests of some ideological demonstration. Their wives are as neat as pins, and gossip sharply in expensive coffee-shops. Their hotels are either delectably modern, all pale wood and sliding glass, or fragrantly Edwardian, with murals and cigar-smoked panelling. Their suburbs are posh with provincial snobbery, and they are a people that nobody in the world, not even the heart-throb marching progressive, could possibly feel sorry for. They are as tough as nails, and twice as spiky.

In Helsinki, only an hour from the Winter Palace, you can do exactly what you like. You can take a ride in a sleigh across the frozen harbour, unimpeded by suspicious policemen and pulled by a bleary kind of pony. You can build yourself a little hut on the ice and fish for your dinner through a hole. You can drink mystical liqueurs from the forests, made of berries, pine cones and

Arctic brambles. You can eat, stifling a sentimental tear, smoked reindeer tongue with salad, or guzzle your way through a fish cock – pork stuffed with fresh-water herring, and baked peculiarly into a loaf. You can go to a French film or an American play, and read the English papers with a flourish outside the Presidential Palace (a pleasant minor mansion of the kind described by estate agents as being 'suitable for conversion').

All these many pleasures and stimulants greet you as your taxi skids genially into Helsinki; and all the fun and freedom of the West welcomes you, and all the vitamins and calories are there to bolster your wasted stamina. Most people, when they leave the potato world behind the Curtain, seem to pine for some fresh or virile victual, a lettuce or a pineapple, a cucumber or a pickled egg. My own craving, when I flew into Finland out of eastern Europe, was for raw carrots, and when I arrived in Helsinki I went straight to a grocer, ordered half a pound, washed them in my hotel bathroom, and ate them luxuriously with a glass of schnapps.

But here is an odd and provoking fact: I ate those rich red vegetables with delight, and I wallowed like an emperor in all the milky pleasure of capitalism; but when, later that day, I wanted something to read with my dinner some unexpected instinct guided my choice, a kind of reluctant nostalgia, a niggling trace of respect and affection, and when I sat down to my pig's trotters I found myself dining with Turgenev. (And all that well-dressed little capital, I felt, all that brave and courteous citizenry, could not offer me quite such company.)

Trieste

Another anomaly of the Cold War was the Adriatic seaport of Trieste, disputed by Italy and Yugoslavia after the Second World War, and defined by Churchill as the southern end of the Iron Curtain. By the time I wrote this piece its status had been finally determined, but it remained nevertheless neither quite one thing nor another. It was the first essay I published about a city which was to become part of my personal, my professional and my literary life, and the subject of my final book (not counting this . . .).

'What's become of Waring?' asked Browning's poem about the vanished man-about-town. You may well ask of Trieste (where, in fact, Waring was), for never a city slipped so adroitly out of the world's headlines, or vanished so utterly into the limbo of forgotten crises. Sometimes a traveller returns with a glimpse of the place – a forlorn and demoralized city, he says, without a purpose in life. Sometimes a wandering diplomatist, passing through from Egypt or the East, thinks he recognizes a demarcation line or hears the echo of a Slovene demonstration. For the rest of us, Trieste has simply faded from our acquaintance, and most of us have even forgotten what all the fuss was about.

For fuss there was, for several years after the Second World War, when both Italy and Yugoslavia laid claim to this port, and squabbled so fiercely over it that time and again some sort of half-cock conflict seemed imminent. The dispute fizzled out gradually, inconclusively, point by point, and the *de facto* result is that, while the neighbouring peninsula of Istria has dropped into the maw of Yugoslavia, Trieste is now, in an anonymous and muffled sort of way, part of Italy again. There is still a testy Slovene minority in the city, and there are Slovene schools and cultural centres, but in effect this is an Italian port. Bright little Fiats scurry along the waterfront, smart Italian liners laze beside the quays, and the girls who stroll by arm-in-arm, high-bosomed and languid-eyed, look like so many aspirant Sophia Lorens. The flavour of Trieste today is unmistakably Italianate, and high in the grand old Governor's Palace sits the Commissioner-General, every inch a Roman consul.

There is a slight legal haziness to it all, though, owing to the fact that the United Nations never really made up its mind what to do with the place, and this blurred status perhaps contributes to the torpor of Trieste. It is a dissatisfied, rather petulant city. It is nearly half a century since it lost its old function as the chief outlet of the Austro-Hungarian Empire, but to this day it is always looking over its shoulder to the palmy days of old, the lavish imperial days, when the floodtide of the Empire's prosperity poured into its coffers, and all the urbanity of Vienna spilled over into its salons. Trieste is now the easternmost protrusion of Italy, but it looks central European still, four-square and brooding, and suggests to me one of those impoverished gentlewomen, addicted to piquet and von Hofmannsthal, who are still to be found in stuffy drawing-rooms bewailing the decline of the Habsburgs. 'Of course,' this city seems to say, 'we were used to better things, but there, ha! the world has changed! And how's your poor dear mother?'

For those few years of contention, after the war, Trieste was, if not happy, at least alive and crossly kicking. Its hinterland had been lost, and its position as a great entrepôt centre: but the eyes of the world were upon it, boosting its ego, and the powers argued over its future, gently buttressing its id. Perhaps it was only whistling in the dark, but there was foreign money about in those days, and a well-paid occupying soldiery. They were effervescent, speculative, exciting times, with a riot on Saturday night and a hey-ho for Tito! Today, however, Trieste has subsided into lassitude. By slow stages the Italian government has integrated the port into the affairs of the Republic, and there is nothing special about it any more. It has been domesticated, and lost its fizz. Once it was the seventh port of the world. Now it is only the third port of Italy.

Of course, chance and history have dealt harshly with Trieste. 'Our city is built in a very uncomfortable position,' a Trieste lawyer once remarked to me: and so it undeniably is. Those bleak hills over the ridge are in communist territory. Those waters beyond the headland are the Adriatic, bounded by Marxist shores. Most of the hinterland that should cherish these wharves has been bundled behind the Iron Curtain, and it is many a long uneconomic mile to the factories and markets of Italy. Look at the map of Europe, even so, and you will see why nobody wants to invest capital or enthusiasm in Trieste, poised so precariously between the ideologies.

To be sure, it is still the seaport of Austria – the trains that clank industriously along the promenade have usually come from Graz or Vienna. A reasonable amount of traffic still flows through Trieste. The shipbuilding yards are, when they are not on strike, fairly busy. There are several new local industries. Unemployment is no worse here than it is anywhere else in Italy. The tourists still come in season. People are quite well dressed, and adequately fed. This is still an important insurance centre, and the name of Lloyd Triestino is still familiar on the high seas. Nothing very tragic is happening to Trieste. It is simply pottering. 'Look at Genoa,' say the Triestinos angrily, 'and Bologna, and all the Italian boom-towns! Look at Fiume! Look what the Italians promised us! Look at this bumble-head bureaucracy they've given us! I'll tell you, my friend,' – here a flick of cigarette ash, a drooping of eyelids, an intricate change of inflection – 'there are times, loyal Italian though I am, when I wish our problems had never been solved!'

For it is lack of gusto that mostly strikes you in Trieste today. Neither time nor toil, said Browning's eye-witness, could mar the features of Waring; but Trieste has not been so resilient in its exile from celebrity. Its talented young people are leaving, its old liberal tradition is neglected, its brave commercial instincts are blunted or frustrated. Depressed and half-hearted, it meanders on in disillusionment: not drunk, indeed, or crippled by war, or oppressed, even destitute; just bored, that's all, just bored.

11

South American Frissons

The Guardian *sent me for some months to South America, a sub-continent about which, like most Europeans then, I was appallingly ignorant. The assignment offered me a break from the complexities of the Cold War, and gave me many and varied frissons. I saw a dead body floating disregarded down a river in Colombia, I ate urchins straight from the sea in Chile, I was homesick in Buenos Aires and ravished in Rio. The* Guardian *reprinted my reports in a booklet, and here are three of its city evocations.*

La Paz

Bolivia, as the consequence of a revolution, had recently given social and political equality to every one of its citizens, at least in theory. Nobody knew how long it would last, but for the moment it made La Paz, the political capital of the republic, feel fascinatingly animated.

Southwards from the glistening steel-blue Titicaca runs the highway through the Bolivian Altiplano. To the east stand the splendours of the Andean cordillera, rank upon rank of noble snow-peak, but the road passes through a landscape more lunar than celestial, an arid, drear, friendless kind of country, 14,000 feet above the sea. It is littered with the poor mud huts of the Aymara Indians, and the piles of stones they have scraped and scrabbled from their miserable soil, and sometimes you meet a peasant with his donkeys or his llamas, and sometimes you set the dust flying in an adobe village, and sometimes you see far away across the wilderness some solitary Indian woman, like a huddled witch on a moor, hastening bent-back across the rubble.

For sixty miles the road plods on through this monotony, and then it falls over a precipice. Suddenly it crosses the lip of the high plateau and tumbles helter-skelter, lickety-spit into a chasm: and as you slither down the horse-shoe bends you see in the ravine below you, secreted in a fold of the massif, the city of La Paz. Its red roofs and mud huts pile up against the canyon walls and spill away into the river valley below. All around is the immensity of the Altiplano, and high above it to the south meditates the lovely white mountain called Illimani, where the royal condor of Inca legend folded its great wings in sleep.

La Paz is the highest of the world's big cities, at 12,000 feet. It is a tumultuous, feverish, often maddening, generally harum-scarum kind of place, but nobody with an eye to country or a taste for drama could fail to respond to its excitements, or resist the superb improbability of its situation. After such an approach, in such an environment, you might reasonably expect to find, like the old voyagers, men with three eyes, or heads slung beneath their shoulders. Well, La Paz does her best. Consider a few simple facts about the city:

> The atmosphere of La Paz is so rarefied that virtually the only function of the single municipal fire engine is squirting indelibly coloured water at political demonstrators.

> One of the liveliest institutions of La Paz is a smugglers' trade union, the Syndicate of Frontier Merchants, and by far its best shopping centre is the Mercado Negro, a vast open-air emporium of illegally imported goods in which I recently ran into a Customs official buying himself some illicit gramophone records.

> Half the women of La Paz wear bowler hats, reverently removing them when they enter a church, and among the old-fashioned cottage remedies readily available are foetus of llama, skin of cat and horn of armadillo.

> La Paz has known 179 coups and revolutions in the 135 years of Bolivian independence, and its currency is such that when I emptied my pockets the other day I found myself in possession of 683,700 Bolivianos (I needed a million odd to pay my hotel bill, plus a few thousand, of course, for the bellboy).

There, I am laughing at the place, but only with wry affection, for I have seldom found a city more enthralling. It is anything but comical beneath the veneer. It is pathetic, tragic, stimulating and menacing, and it still retains some of the savage glare and breathless glitter that the

Spaniards brought when they founded it four centuries ago. It is not in itself a beautiful place. Its few old buildings are swamped in half-hearted modernism, and all around it in the bowl of its canyon the Indians have built their terraced streets of mud and corrugated iron. It possesses nevertheless, to an almost eccentric degree, the quality of individualism. There is nowhere else much like La Paz on the face of the earth, but if I had to find an analogy I would suggest some quivering desert city, Damascus, say, or Kairouan, miraculously transplanted to a declivity in the Tibetan plateau.

This is a city of the Andes, and it is the swarming Aymara Indians of the Andes who nowadays set its style. The men are sometimes striking enough, with their ear-flapped woollen hats and Inca faces, but the Andean women are fascinating beyond description. With their rakishly cocked bowler hats, their blinding blouses and skirts, their foaming flounces of petticoats, the babies like tumultuous infant potentates upon their backs and the sandals made of old tyres upon their feet – gorgeously accoutred and endlessly industrious, plumed often with a handsome dignity and assurance, they give to La Paz a flavour part gypsy, part coster and all pungency.

An Indian, highland turbulence keeps this city tense and wary, and makes the midnight curfew more the rule than exception. In the halls of the National Congress, beneath the painted scrutiny of Bolívar, they are mostly Spanish faces, declaiming Latin polemics, but high in the balcony above the debate, peering silently over the railing, are the dark, attentive, enigmatic eyes of the Aymaras. In La Paz you feel everywhere the rising awareness of the Indian people, together with the smouldering of latent violence. It is a city of rumours and echoes. Sometimes the miners of Catavi are about to march upon the capital, dragging their hostages behind them. Sometimes, before daybreak, you may hear the tread of marching feet and the singing of slogans outside your window. Sometimes masked carabinieri, slung about with tommy guns, ransack your car for arms, and sometimes you find a chain slung across the city gate on the hill-top, and a civilian with a rifle vigilantly beside it. Fifteen years ago the mob of La Paz hung the mutilated body of their president from a lamp-post in the Plaza Murillo, and today the old square is stiff with soldiers, in German steel helmets and thick high-collared jackets, self-consciously ceremonious on little platforms outside the Presidency, unobtrusively watchful upon the roof of the cathedral.

All this passion, all this energy, thumps through the city night and day, sharpened into something knifelike and tremulous by the breathless clarity of the altitude. You can feel it on the promenade at weekends, when the wide-eyed girls and men with small moustaches chatter with a kind of gay intensity at the tables of the Copacabana. You can feel it in the conversations of the place, dark with plots but humorous with tall stories, cynical but often secretive. You can sense it in the myriad slogans daubed on almost every wall, with their baffling permutations of political initials and the paint that drips down in frenzied blobs from their exhortations. You can even see it reflected in the smiling, bustling, and wagging of the city's enchanting Carpaccio dogs. The marvellous glacial air of La Paz, which sends the tourists puffing and dizzy to their beds, makes for fizz, bounce and heady enthusiasm, and the isolation of this queer city, mountain metropolis of a land-locked state, gives it a striking sense of introvert obsession.

And most of all you will know the pressure of La Paz if you visit the high Indian quarters after dark. They tumble and straggle dustily upon the hillside, and at night they are tumultuous with activity. It is not a noisy sort of energy – it has a padded, hushed insinuation to it – but it is tremendously purposeful and intent. Crouching along every alley are the indefatigable street-sellers, huddled about some hissing brazier, or sprawling, a confusion of skirts, shawls and babies, behind their stalls of mandarins. Hundreds of candles illuminate the pavement counters; beneath a multitude of canvas awnings, the Indians eat their thick stews or sip their coca tea; outside each dark and balconied courtyard, the caravanserais of La Paz, the lorries are preparing for the dawn journey – down to the steaming Yungas for tropical fruits and jungle vegetables, across the Altiplano for the fabulous rainbow trout of Titicaca.

The scene is shadowy and cluttered, and you cannot always make out the detail as you push through the crowd; but the impression it leaves is one of ceaseless, tireless energy, a blur of strange faces and sinewy limbs, a haze of ill-understood intentions, a laugh from a small Mongol in dungarees, a sudden stink from an open drain, a cavalcade of tilted bowlers in the candlelight – and above it all, so clear, so close that you confuse the galaxies with the street lamps, the wide blue bowl of the Bolivian sky and the brilliant cloudless stars of the south.

But here is an odd thing. When you come to La Paz from the north, over the escarpment, it seems a very prodigy among cities; but if you drive away from it towards Illimani and the south, looking back over your shoulder as you cross the last ridge, why, all the magic has drained from it, all the colour has faded, all that neurosis seems an illusion, and it looks like some drab old mining camp, sluttish among the tailings.

Lima

The capital of Peru evidently gave a disturbing jolt to my conscience, and made me sound (just for once) like a proper Guardian *reporter.*

In Peru you can smell misery, and you need not sniff too hard. Behind Lima, where the arid Andean foothills slouch down towards the sea, there is a hill called San Cristóbal, crowned with a cross of pilgrimage, that commands a famous view of the capital. Splendidly below you lies the City of the Kings, huddled beneath its winter vapours: the gorgeous golden suburbs of San Isidro and Miraflores, the inevitable skyscrapers of the city centre, the towers and plazas and rambling old palaces that made this capital of the Viceroys, for two legendary centuries, the first city of the western hemisphere. Immediately at your feet, however, clustered on the hillside like some nightmare belvedere, there is a quarter very different. Magnificently sited upon that eminence, ironically surveying the grandeur of the prospect, squats a slum so festering, so filthy, so toad-like, so bestially congested, so utterly devoid of water, light, health or comfort, so deep in garbage and excrement, so swarming with scabbed ragged barefoot children, so reeking with squalor that just to wander through its alleys makes you retch into your handkerchief. From these unspeakable stews the stench of degradation rises, veiling the City of the Kings in a kind of haze, and even eddying around the cross on top of the hill.

Lima is ringed by such fearful *barriaras*. Perhaps a quarter of a million people live in them, in a city of 1.2 million, and nowhere in the world have I experienced quite so distressingly the gulf between the immensely rich and the unbelievably poor, with almost nothing homely in the middle – no diligent allotment-gardeners, no chug of second-hand lawnmower, hardly a china seagull winging it across high tea. Peru presents all the stock symptoms of reaction: absentee landlords, enormous semi-feudal estates, widespread illiteracy, political irresponsibility, intricate meshworks of financial interest, snobbery, sophistry, indulgence, ostentation. The symbolism of San Cristóbal is dead accurate. For generations the City of the Kings was as effectively insulated against its bleak hinterland as ever was old St Petersburg: but misery has crept up on it, the penniless Indians and half-castes have swarmed in from the countryside, and today, to the impressionable foreigner if not to the leggy girls on the society pages, it is no longer the grand old churches or the jacaranda gardens that express the meaning of Lima, but the slums at the back of your mind.

The country does not feel on the brink of a convulsion, but it feels as though somewhere far away, in a remote fastness of the Altiplano, perhaps, or in some cell or chamber more distant still, a dampish fuse has begun to smoulder. For this Peru has nobody to blame, as I see it, but her rulers. If ever a revolution does come to Peru, and the proud patricians of Lima are humbled with violence and degradation, they can kick nobody but their own scented selves. Today they are, I am told, reluctantly awakening if not to altruism, at least to self-interest: but by their history, their heedlessness, their vulgar opulence and their exclusivity, they have marvellously qualified themselves for the garrotte.

You will therefore forgive, I hope, a crude and perhaps hasty conclusion from a true-blue British traditionalist. The other day I drove direct from the hideous purlieus of San Cristóbal to have tea at the Country Club in San Isidro. The odour of the slum went with me, clinging to my jacket and the soles of my shoes like some blasphemous travesty of incense, and as I sat there among the little black dresses and the sticky cakes, the greying distinctions and the foppish playboys, the starched nannies and the exquisite children on the lawn, the chic and the cultivation and the chit-chat of urbanity – as I sat there with the squalor still in my hair I could not help remembering, Pharisaical though it seems in retrospect, Dr Johnson's celebrated differentiation: I smell, you stink.

Cuzco

Today everybody knows about Cuzco, in Peru: in 1961 I had never heard of it.

Out of a mountain in Peru fifteen llamas sway down an ancient road, silently pursued by a man in a poncho and knee breeches and a woman wearing a white straw hat, a blazing flurry of petticoats, and a baby-hammock on her back. The man is chewing an opiate wad of the coca leaf, the woman is planning to request the intercession of the Lord of the Earthquakes, whose miraculous figure in the town below is known to sweat in sympathy and weep real tears of compassion.

To the north an elderly American locomotive, with a cow-catcher and an old wail of a whistle, is plunging zig-zag into the valley with a string of cattle-trucks. From the south a clanging of cracked bells rings out of a florid campanile. And as those travellers swing round the last dusty corner, with a soft shuffle of bare feet and padded cameloid hoofs, there below them they see, clear-cut in that Alpine sunshine, the capital of the Land of the Four Quarters.

It could only be Cuzco, a little city of such supreme interest and historical symbolism, of such variety and punch, that in the context of the South American Grand Tour it combines the compulsions of a Stonehenge, a small Barcelona, and a Katmandu. It lies at 11,000 feet in the Peruvian Altiplano, and to reach it from Lima you fly breathtakingly across the Andes in an unpressurized aircraft, nibbling an oxygen tube like a hookah: but its valley is green, the hills around it are as fresh and springy as English downland, and only the testy pumping of your heart at night, and the celestial supervision of the snow peaks, remind you that on the other side of the world the ski-slopes of St Moritz are 5,000 feet lower than your hotel.

Five centuries ago this remote and barricaded place, somewhere between Lake Titicaca and the dreadful Amazon jungle, was the capital of the Incan Empire, the brilliant but baleful organism, part refulgent aristocracy, part deadening discipline, that extended its power over most of the Andean territories, commanding an area as large as France, Switzerland, Italy, Belgium, Holland and Luxembourg all reluctantly put together.

Here the mummified Inca emperors, all entrails sucked out, sat flecked by fly-whisks down the decades in the glittering Temple of the Sun. Here the Chosen Women span their incomparable textiles in imperial virginity, here the ferocious Inca generals marshalled their armies, here the diviners interpreted the intestines of their guinea-pigs, the priests prepared their intoxicated victims for the sacrifice, the marvellous Inca surgeons performed their prodigies of trepanning, amputation and excision.

In the fifteenth century Cuzco was the heart of a civilization so strange, precise and rarefied that nothing remotely like it has even been seen again. The little city was the core of it all – the very name of Cuzco means 'navel' – and everywhere in the town you can still feel the presence of the Incas. Often it is vulgarized in tourism and profit, in Incaland souvenirs, costume jewellery of weird exoticism, schoolgirl vestals with lamps and improbable headdresses at folklore festivals. More essentially, though, it is perpetuated in the massive masonry that still forms, to this very day, the ground layer of

139

Cuzco: vast and impeccably chiselled stonework, like the craft of meticulous giants, with queer unexpected angles and corners of daunting exactitude – the whole looking so new and so contrived that it reminds me of the building material known in England as 'reconstructed stone'.

The basis of the Temple of the Sun remains marvellously rounded beneath a church, and so does the wall of the House of the Chosen Women. There are sacred Inca snakes still above a doorway, and sacred Inca sanctuaries still in a cloister, and brooding above the city stands the enigmatic fortress called Sacsahuamán, incorporating some of the largest chunks of stone ever raised into dubious utility by the ingenuity of man. But all this terrifying structure Pizarro toppled, with no other weapons but bigotry, guts, greed and gunpowder: and on the prostrate capital of the Incas, sans Emperor, sans Chosen Women, sans soothsayers and all, the Spaniards built themselves a second city, dedicated to a very different version of the Sun God.

Gilded, ornate, candle-flickering, snobbish, refulgent with Christian miracles and the titles of grandees, with arches and bell-towers and graceful plazas, with songs from Andalusia and Moorish doors and sizzling coquettes and silver tabernacles – there the Spaniards' Cuzco stands today, triumphant still above the Inca engineers. They called it The Very Noble and Great City of Cuzco, the Most Principal and Head of Kingdoms of Peru, and deep among the canyons of the Peruvian Andes it remains a paradoxical memorial to the virility of Europe.

Returned to its origins it might not be remarkable, but in this utterly alien setting, high on the continental divide, Spanish Cuzco really smacks, as its old divines would wish it, of the miraculous. Fretted, solemn and domineering are the churches that stand around the Plaza de Armas – the dark but glistening cathedral, the arrogant church of the Jesuits, the gloomy shrine of Jesus and Mary beside the Hall of the Inquisition, the aloof Church of the Triumph from which, in 1536, Our Lady emerged with the Christ Child in her arms to disconcert an Indian rebellion. Elaborate and delectable are the mansions of the old magnificos, with their dazzling gardens glimpsed through crooked doorways, their dripping pitchers of flowers, their crested balconies and suggestions of silken solace.

Nearly every corner has its hint of Spanish pride, but the Spaniards do not dominate Cuzco today, for all the flourish of their architecture, and nor do the vanished Incas. Cuzco today is mostly run by mestizos, half-castes of Spanish and Indian cross, but all its living colour and verve is provided by the fuller blooded Quechua Indians of the countryside.

Sometimes they look like gypsies; sometimes, in their trailing skirts, like Navajo Indians from Arizona; sometimes, with their tall white hats and shawls, like ladies out of Borrow's wilder Wales; but to me they usually seem, and sound, and smell, and move like Sherpas out of the Himalayas – less carefree perhaps, less hearty certainly, but still instinct with dung-fires and potatoes, smoky dark interiors, sweat, untanned leather, back-breaking labour, poverty, superstition, resilience, and the viscous alcohol that is brewed in these parts by fermenting maize in women's saliva.

They are all over Cuzco, prostrate before the Lord of the Earthquakes like Tibetans in a tinkling temple, or hastening barefoot through the night, down the shadows of a cobbled alley, bent double with loads of straw. Away in the desolate expanses of the Altiplano the Indians of Peru are usually demoralized, I am assured, often destitute, sometimes actually starving. You would not know it in Cuzco. Their presence is possibly a little wan, but still earthy. Their children are so adorable that I would happily adopt half a dozen myself. Their women, strolling thick-set through the tumbled market in their rakish hats and flounces, spinning their wool as they walk, look to me as though only an ounce of opportunity, only a dram of education, only a year of square meals would release resources of wonderful strength and character. Their menfolk, half-doped as they are by coca, malnutrition, and the degradation of centuries, look as though nothing on earth, from a hostile omen to the most atrocious of hangovers, could deter them from the endless dull drudgery of their lives.

Undoubtedly the Indians win, in this Most Principal and Head of Kingdoms of Peru. Beside them the half-castes look upstart, and the Lima gentry doomed. It will be a long, long time before they come into their own again – if indeed they ever do; but when I run my mind's eye back over the Cuzco scene, away from the snakes above the doorway, away from the smoke-darkened Lord of the Earthquakes, past the campaniles and the fortress on the hill and the puffing wailing train, in the end it rests again on those distant figures on the Inca road, the fifteen lolloping llamas, the man with the plug of coca in his cheek, the barefoot woman in the bright but dusty petticoats, and the infinitesimal baby Quechua on her back, so swaddled in textiles that only one brown pondering eye shows through the muffles, jogging eternally out of the Andes.

12

Oxford 1965

Half-way through the decade I wrote a book about Oxford. I treated the city and its university as though, considered together, they offered a kind of a paradigm of contemporary England as a whole; but it was really the ancient individualism of the university, threatened as it was by changing styles, values and loyalties, that chiefly interested me.

In some ways Oxford University is a gigantic quirk, always out of step with the times. This infuriates those who prize logic above independence, just as the emergence of industry in Oxford offends those who like a city to be all of a piece, all academic or all commercial, all black or lily-white.

The most notorious symbol of Oxford syncopation is All Souls, the all-male graduate college in High Street, which is evil in some people's minds as a seed-bed of Chamberlain's appeasement in the 1930s, and despicable in others as an appalling waste of academic resource. All Souls is theoretically an institute of advanced studies, except that a substantial minority of its sixty or so Fellows need not actually study. They need not do anything at all, indeed, though they are mildly expected to dine in college sometimes and sleep in the bed that awaits them there. Some forty Fellows of All Souls are university academics, some of them professors. Others are young researchers who have won their place in an atrociously difficult examination. Most of the rest, holding different categories of fellowship, only appear at weekends, when they come down from London full of metropolitan gossip and stocked with the expertise of a dozen professions.

No event in Europe can be much sillier, not the most footling country frolic or pointless Anatolian orgy, than the Ceremony of the Mallard at this college – which only takes place every hundred years, to be sure, but is vividly remembered in between. It seems that when they were building All Souls, in the fifteenth century, a mallard duck flapped out of a drain beside its foundations, and this bird has been inexplicably honoured ever since.

Once in every hundred years the Fellows, after a good dinner, seize staves and swords and go looking for its shade, led by a Lord Mallard in a sedan chair, with a dead duck on a pole – up to the roof in the middle of the night, doubtless drunk as so many owls by now, their voices thundering across Radcliffe Square, their torches flickering in the sky, until at last they return to their common room in the small hours, drink a final potation laced with duck's blood, and let the bird lie for another century.

For myself, I would like to see All Souls preserving its fastidious privi-leged character, but packed in every room with eager full-time scholars – the most high-powered, as well as the most sumptuous, of all graduate colleges. The traditional theory is, though, that the give-and-take of thought and controversy, passed week by week across its old oak tables, is itself a sort of English lubricant, fructifying the national life, bridging the gaps between professions, and worth preserving in itself as a late survivor of an old, carefree, valeted England.

Oxford University as a whole, to a less pickled degree, cherishes the same intentions. This is a university still on its own, still half aloof to change. It has tried to adapt an aristocratic tradition to an egalitarian age, and though to the sympathetic observer this generally looks admirable, if a little forlorn, to the critic it is often simply arrogant. Trade unionists, visiting this city for summer conferences, sometimes suggest to outraged college porters that the whole place ought to be blown up, allowing the Ministry of Education to start again from scratch; and the leitmotiv of criticism against Oxford, which never ceases, is the univer-sity's sense of antique superiority – the feeling that, for all its enlightened poses, it only caters for the upper half of the nation, and gives its alumni unfair advantages in life.

Most of it, though, is the wrong end of a stick – a misunderstanding of the gravelly evasiveness of the place, which is only a mask for its tolerance and its fine distrust of sameness (exasperating though it is going to be, for anyone living near Radcliffe Square on the night of All Souls' Day, 2001, when the Fellows clamber up there again behind the Lord Mallard, stamping among the chimney-pots and carrying on about that confounded duck). It is as though a separate little world exists in this city, with its own private time-scale, and in a way this is true: for the Oxford we have been inspecting represents a civilization that is almost gone. Try though you may to see this city as a whole, still the factories and the housing estates feel like intruders upon some ancient preserve. All that is most remarkable about Oxford, setting it apart from other towns, or from other universities, comes from the lost order of the English – essentially a patrician society, stable, tolerant, amateur, confident enough to embrace an infinite variety within a rigid framework. The English gentleman dominates Oxford: not in the flesh, for he has almost vanished from the scene, but in the lingering spirit of the place.

Another England has emerged now, and Oxford is adapting to it, learning to live with the motor plants and the traffic, trying to keep up with the times. There is nothing pathetic to this city, and the new Oxford will doubtless be just as self-satisfied as the old. But as you contemplate its condition now it is as though you are watching the envoi to a majestic play. The great trees planted in the heyday of the English landscape gardeners are now past their prime, and will soon be toppling, and the island character of the English is waning, too, as the wider civilization of the West takes over. Soon it will survive only in the history: but we are not too late, and Oxford stands there still to remind us of its faults and virtues – courageous, arrogant, generous, ornate, pungent, smug and funny.

I am proud to say that when in 2001 All Souls did once again honour the memory of that duck, my description of the ludicrous ceremony was quoted on the cover of the college's commemorative booklet. By then, though, by no means everything in Oxford was as it had been in 1965 . . .

13

Australia

The Guardian *sent me for some months to Australia. I had never been there before. In those days aircraft from Europe generally landed at Darwin to refuel before going on to Sydney or Melbourne; I decided to leave my flight there, and so gave myself a boisterous introduction to Australia.*

Darwin

When you arrive at Darwin, your landfall in Australia, you are given a form to complete for the Customs, and satisfyingly bush-whacking are its demands. Have you any dangerous weapons, like spring-blade knives, daggers, bludgeons, coshes, knuckle-dusters or swordsticks? Are you carrying any saddles, bridles or horse rugs? Are there horns or hoofs in your baggage, dried blood, feathers, germ cultures or microbes? Are you accompanied by insects in any stage of development?

Thus you are pre-conditioned to Darwin, for this is a town that prides itself upon its frontier manners, its horse-rug flavour, its traditions of bludgeon, horn and hoof, the weird animal life that leaps and wallows about it, kangaroo to buffalo, crocodile to dingo. Never did a town greet its visitors more boisterously. Never did the beer flow quite so fast. Nowhere is the traveller treated with such an easy, lolloping, happy-go-lucky, careless and gregarious courtesy. As an introduction to Australia, Darwin is a work of art, for here, carefully fashioned by climate, custom and inclination, is a mosaic of all the reputed Australian virtues, from the instant accessibility of the biggest swell to the determined golden faces of the barmaids. ('But don't judge it all by this place,' its genial citizenry will assure you. 'There's nowhere else in the whole bloody continent like the Top End.')

The Top End: Darwin stands at the very extremity of Australia's Northern Territory, on the shore of the Timor Sea, scarcely a gun-shot from Indonesia and linked with the distant south only by the long lonely road to Alice Springs – 'The Track', as they fondly call it, or 'The Bitumen'. Immediately behind Darwin there begins one of the world's most fearful wildernesses, all desert and dry scrub from here to Adelaide. It is almost exactly a thousand miles to Alice, the next town of any size. Even the railway peters out three hundred miles to the south, and the Darwin telephone district is bounded east west by areas that have, as the directory blandly tells you, no telephones at all. This is an isolated tropical town, twelve degrees south of the equator, blazing and humid in the Australian summer, caressingly warm in July. It is all on its own at the Top End, very fond indeed of its own company, but sometimes uncomfortably aware that several hundred million Asians live in crowded indigence just across the water.

You must not envisage it a Pacific paradise, all palm-fringed and zephyr-blown. Arnhem Land, this bump in the forehead of Australia, is a tough and unlovely place, clad in scrub jungle, with mangrove swamps at the water's edge and a flat monotonous bushland around. Thirty years ago, I am told, this was a whole-hog frontier port, gambling dens, molls, Chinatown and all. Today it is much more respectable. Its principal purpose is government, for it is the administrative centre of the Northern Territory, and some 60 per cent of its people are civil servants. They live in trim uniform government houses, they honour all the hierarchical rules of civil servants everywhere, and they multiply, so the locals say, faster than jack-rabbits. The chief import of Darwin, according to a local proverb, is civil servants: the chief export is empty beer bottles.

But if 60 per cent of the people are conventional enough, the other 40 per cent are marvellously free-and-easy. If Darwin has self-service stores, espresso bars and used-car lots, it also retains some spirited echoes of its roistering days, and many reminders that down the road there still stands an empty continent. The saloon bars are full of handsome sprawling young men in shorts; prickly longshoremen with beer on their breath still lounge around the docks; sometimes a splendid rangy cattleman strides into the Darwin Hotel, with his wide-brimmed hat and his patrician air; and just occasionally one may see in a store one of those tight-lipped taciturn women, in faded floral prints and curlers, who are traditionally the helpmeets of pioneers.

With one eye always cocked towards Asia, Darwin has long since outgrown its racial prejudices. You may observe its tolerant proliferation best on Saturday evening, during the interval at the Smith Street picture house, when the audience pours out to its Cokes and ice-creams in the neighbouring milk bars. This is a people of astonishing variety: black, brown and yellow, Italianate and Chinese, gleaming aborigines, half-castes, women who look like Californians and men who look like gigantic Dutchmen. Up here the notion of White Australia seems ludicrous indeed, and there is nothing strait-laced or loftily Nordic in the air. The illegitimacy rate is extremely high, miscegenation is as old as Arnhem Land, and Smith Street on such an evening fizzes with an almost Brazilian gusto.

Binding all this community together, though, stamping its character, providing the cast for the crucible, is the Australian as we have always thought of him, still recognizably British, and one of the very best and most likeable men on the face of the earth. Here you may see him at his most confident, on the edge of the great Outback. He may be of any age, this 'dinkum Aussie', descended from convicts or new-arrived from Newcastle. He may be a humdrum bank clerk, or a prospector driven wildly in from his shack in the wilderness, to squander his money on drink and loose living – 'riding the vaudeville', as an old fossicker described the process to me. Whoever he is, he is magnificent to meet: as free a spirit as you can find in the world today, shackled by no inhibition of class or disadvantage, with little sense of thrift and still less of decorum, no agonizing reserve, no envy, no contempt, no meanness. He is like some splendid English working man relieved of the burden of the centuries, strengthened and cleansed by the southern sun, and allowed to begin history all over again.

Of course there are blemishes to such a reincarnation. The brewery jokes soon stale, and the beeriness of life itself sometimes borders upon the bestial. For myself I find those steely golden barmaids something less than alluring, and I resent the laboured bandying of my Christian name – 'Nice to know you, Jim' – as though I were participating in a television quiz show. There is a certain air of middlingness to the place, like a boom town without a boom, or perhaps an army without any officers. Darwin does not feel to me a place of spectacular promise, an embryo San Francisco: it is growing all the time, but it remains, after many a long decade of settlement, and many a million gallons of beer down its collective throat, still a small and undistinguished town.

Nevertheless it is a fine introduction to Australia – something fresh, and new, and crackling. It is always alive, always laughing, always full of tall stories and improbable characters, always drinking, always ready to help. The visiting Briton can scarcely help feeling a dude in such a setting, but for myself I respond all too easily to these tolerant and spendthrift philosophies. Perhaps it is some hereditary instinct in the blood, that makes me feel at home and at ease in this wide unfamiliar landscape. Perhaps it is the old yearning of the islander for horizons less cramped, skies less smoky. It may not seem likely, when you hear my effete voice diffidently requesting a second pineapple juice across the bar, but by golly, give me a four-wheel drive and a good bush-woman, and I may well go walk-about myself.

Sydney

I was so ignorant about Sydney that I was never quite sure even how to spell it, and disliked it at first sight. After the publication of this essay it was five full years before the last indignant riposte reached me from down under.

Sydney is a harbour, with a bridge across it that everyone knows by sight, and a city around it that nobody can quite envisage. The origins of Sydney are unsavoury, its history is disagreeable to read, its temper is coarse, its organization seems to be slipshod, its suburbs are hideous and its politics often crooked, its buildings are mostly plain, its voices rasp on the ear, its trumpeted Art Movement is, I suspect, half spurious, its newspapers are either dull or distasteful, and in the end, when you hunger for beauty or consolation in this famous place, you return willy-nilly to the harbour-front, where the ships tread with graceful care towards their moorings, and the great humped bridge stands like an arbiter above the quays.

Harsh words for a stranger to utter, but then there was never a harsher contrast than the disparity between Sydney and its setting. This harbour is not, to my mind, so beautiful as its popularly nominated peers, Rio, Hong Kong and San Francisco, but it is still exceedingly lovely, and to stand upon North Head on a crisp sunshine afternoon, with a swell rolling in from the South Pacific and an idle flurry of yachts beyond Bradley's Head – to stand at the gateway of Sydney on such an afternoon is among the classic experiences of travel: such an ineffable antipodean blue is the sky above you, so unexpected and inviting are the countless coves and fjords of the harbour, so imperturbably do the tankers sweep out to sea, so silent and lordly are the warships in Athol Bay, so grand but monstrous does the crook-back of the bridge protrude above the promontories. It is a San Francisco that such an environment deserves, and sometimes indeed the anxious traveller will find himself reminded of that celestial seaport. He will see affinities in the winter mists, the clap of the water at the end of every vista, the cool green gardens of The Domain above Wooloomooloo, the villas poised so delectably on their cliffsides above the harbour. He will taste, if he meets the right Sydney people, the same careful but seldom humourless diligence, the same meticulous interest in a brief past, comparable cheerful clubs, and, among the cramped espresso bars of King's Cross, similar wayward but resolute Bohemians. Pinchgut Island, with its stone fortress and its dismal recollections, will remind him of Alcatraz, and the bustle of the boats at the Circular Quay, as the Manly Ferry sails away to a tinkle of its resident piano and a quaver of its mendicant violin, may seem a distant homespun echo of Fisherman's Wharf.

This is, though, a San Francisco sadly *manqué*, just as Dorman Long's fine bridge, however sensible and sturdy, is a lumpish substitute for the Golden Gate. Sydney is not one of your absolute cities, and in nothing that I have detected, except perhaps the racing commentaries, is it quite in the first class. It is almost as old as San Francisco, indeed, and bigger than all but a handful of European capitals, but there is something cold and vacuous at its core, something that makes the stranger, however hospitable his acquaintances, feel obscurely lonely in its streets. For most Sydney citizens the purpose of life may perhaps be summarized in the parade of the life-savers on Manly Beach, all bronzed open-air fun on Saturday afternoons, and perhaps it is this paucity of purpose, this lack of lofty memories or intentions, that makes this metropolis feel so pallid or frigid at the soul.

This, and what seems to be a shortage of kindness. The people of Sydney will usually greet you warmly enough, even heartily, but compared with the great immigrant cities of the New World, Montreal, New York or São Paulo, this place feels cruelly aloof. Perhaps it is the origins of Sydney that invoke this sensation – for despite the sophistries of its society ladies, it was founded by the scum of England only six generations ago. Perhaps it is the expressions on the faces of those ladies themselves, so steely, scornful and accusatory, as though they are expecting you (which Heaven forbid) to offer them an improper suggestion. Perhaps it is the intolerance of one citizen to another, sour bus conductor to irritable passenger, cross-patch waitress to graceless customer. Sydney does not feel like a haven. It does not reach out, as New York once did, to receive 'your tired, your poor, your huddled masses yearning to breathe free'. No great ideals of politics or humanity animate its visions, but only starker impulses of self-advancement or survival.

Nor does it even feel content. It seems full of reproach, sneer and grumble. The immigrant from Europe or England all too often feels resented. The dinkum Aussie all too often seems to cherish racial prejudices of the nastiest kind. The sleazy bars of the place, looking like public lavatories and smelling of slopped beer, exude no genial good cheer, but only a mindless and sometimes rather frightening sense of male collusion. A proud new bridge collapsed in Melbourne while I was in Australia, but the Sydney *Daily Telegraph*, in its editorial on the matter, offered not a breath of sympathy, nor even a kindly joke, but only a column of crude and spiteful mockery. The people of Sydney like to think of themselves as a 'weird mob', but they strike me as weird not in any free-and-easy gallivanting way, but only in a sort of twisted uncertainty and isolation. I blush even to consider the numberless exceptions to these hasty generalizations: all the kind and cultivated people who do live in Sydney, all the patient Dutch waiters and merry Italian stevedores, all the charming dons up at the University, all the scholarly attendants at the Public Library, many a jolly taxi-driver and many a thoughtful bookseller, the courteous attendants at the State Parliament, the splendid ferry-captains who stride so grandly, like admirals on a quarter-deck, from one wheelhouse to the other when their boat turns round. The brave new Opera House plan is perhaps a foretaste of more stylish things to come, and each year the influx of Europeans rubs a little elegance into this raw city, and a little gentleness too. Some of the new skyscrapers, though scarcely breathtaking, are handsome enough. Some of the new highways breathe the dash and dazzle one expects of such a young and explosive port.

Even so, Sydney does not yet feel a great city – not a generous, confident, serene city, not a city of any warmth and splendour. Turn your back on the bridge and you will travel through a wilderness of peevish suburbs, a labyrinth of unlovely boulevards, a humdrum desolation, until at last you reach the outskirts of the place, and before you, if you persevere, stretches the emptiness of Australia, which is inescapable, which runs like some chill virus through the bloodstream of this country, and so binds the fragile years together that even now you may sense the presence of the chain-gangs in Sydney, and fancy the punishment cutter striking out to Pinchgut.

It was during my first visit to Sydney, Australia, that I learnt to enjoy food and drink. Until then I had never much cared about either, but an Australian friend gave me a picnic lunch on a lawn overlooking the harbour, and something about the way he ate our simple victuals, slurped our

Australian white wine and broke the crisp loaves between his fingers, suddenly opened my eyes to the delights of gastronomy. When many years later I came to write a little essay about this experience I could remember its sensations exactly – my host's vivid enjoyment of the food, the wide blue sky over our heads, the grand panorama of the harbour below us and above all the white wings of the Opera House spread like a benediction upon the moment. It was only when I had completed the essay that I realized the Opera House hadn't been built then.

Alice Springs

'The Alice' had long been world-famous because of Nevil Shute's 1949 novel A Town Like Alice. *Despite this, even in the 1960s few tourists got there.*

As Florence was to the old Grand Tour, so Alice Springs stands in any Australian itinerary: an apogee, where all that the journey represents is, in theory anyway, consummated at last. The Alice, as they call it in the Outback, must be one of the most famous little towns on earth, and though its origins are strictly functional, conceived as it was as a station on the transcontinental telegraph line, today one treats it as a sort of symbol or slogan, the home of the Flying Doctors, of the aboriginal painters and the Afghan camel-drivers, where the stock-trails converge upon the railhead and the Bitumen strikes out for Darwin and the Timor Sea.

If you have only a day in The Alice you can still extract a proper essence of Australiana, a happy whiff of that dusty, tangy, seat-and-leather flavour that informs the whole Australian myth, and still hangs evocatively around the bush. Contemporary Australia is essentially an urban country, rather flabby in spirit; but up at The Alice, where the wilderness lurches in vast barren formations towards an illimitable horizon – here the legend comes alive again.

You should start very early, when the desert nip is in the air, by walking out to the northern limit of the town, where the sealed road begins. There, if you are lucky, you will see one of the great sights of central Australia, a road train. With a blast of its vast diesel, a rumble of its twenty wheels, a blast of its klaxon and an air of tremendous swank, it will roar past you out of town like a vision of the frontier: fifty yards of cattle-truck, four trailers and a mighty tractor, the biggest thing on any road in the world, and a phenomenon authentically Australian. High in his cab the driver grins at you through the dust swirls, and away he thunders towards the north, headed for the immense stock farms of the interior, where they sometimes number their cattle in hundreds of thousands, and where one property is slightly larger than Belgium.

His is the new Australia, but on the other side of town you may still chance upon the old-school overlanders. Even today the drovers still bring their huge herds week by week across the wasteland to The Alice, and here you can see them at the end of their trail, their fine lean horses tethered beside the track and their breakfasts simmering in the pot. These are Australians as you have always imagined them. I do not believe stronger or more likeable men walk the earth today, so calm and imperturbable are their manners, so infectious their kindly humour, so gauntly handsome their physiques. They are tired and dirty by the time they reach Alice Springs, prickly of stubble and grimy of fingernail, but they rest there like princes among their beasts, people of an enviable fulfilment, Australians to the manner born. But soon you must hurry to the airfield, for there a little aircraft is waiting to fly you to Ayers Rock, like a tourist bus hooting at you impatiently outside the Duomo. In a moment or two you are over the hills, and below you extends the eerie red world of the Australian Centre. It is the most fearful of landscapes, more terrible by far than Sahara or Empty Quarter, painted a queer cruel red and so corrugated by grotesque erosions that it often looks like some ominous belt of fortifications, where no man or animal is permitted to survive.

Strangest of all its strange shapes is the Rock itself, in whose bald shadow you presently alight. It is the biggest of all rocks, the most overbearing of monoliths, standing vast and all alone in a flatland and constantly changing colour with the shifting light – now blue, now pink, now almost crimson in the sunset. Its humped flank is smooth and slippery, and as you scramble up its gullies the wilderness seems to grow around you, ever wider, ever emptier, until at last, when you reach the cairn and the lonely tree upon its summit, with the wind whistling around your ears and the rock pools ruffled at your feet, you feel that you are poised upon an absolute pinnacle of isolation – wreathed in native legend and sorcery, removed from the plane of the ordinary, encamped in some upper attic of the never-never.

For you are in aboriginal territory here. This is one of the reserves of the Northern Territory, and when you have clambered down the Rock again you may visit an encampment of the black people. They are living in tattered jumbled tents, with high-spirited dogs and a couple of camels to keep them company, and they are dressed in raggety European clothes, not unlike gypsies; but they retain, as do these remarkable tribespeople in every stage of their development, an almost creepy sense of detachment, even of mysticism. The headman greets you with a handshake and speaks to you in English, the women, huddled over their untidy fires, smile at you warmly enough; but however hard you try you will feel that your conversation is only sliding off some slithery barrier, deflected like light through a prism, that all around you are wavelengths and cross-currents you do not understand, and that these original Australians, miserably hybrid though their condition seems to be, retain some affinity with their empty landscape that no white man, bound within the confines of logic, will ever be able to achieve.

So you fly back to The Alice feeling a little chilled, as though you have just exchanged glances with a mystery; but a pint of ale at the Stewart Arms will soon restore you to banality, and at the end of your day in Alice Springs you should go back to the beginning, just as the sensible visitor to Florence concludes his visit beside the Arno. A mile or two north of the little town is the site of the original Alice, where the old wooden telegraph station that was its *raison d'être* still meditates in the starlight. Go and end the day there. There will be a rustle of wind in the gum trees, and a croaking of frog armies in the water, and the air is aromatic with dust and foliage, and above you the Southern Cross hangs brilliantly beside the Coal Sack. Down by the water-hole, with a munch and a snort in the half-light, two horses stand sentinel beneath the pepper trees. There is something very sensual about the empty magic of Australia, and such a moment, at the end of The Alice, feels so charged with emotion, echo and pale suggestion that simply experiencing it seems a weak response, and you feel you should really embrace it, ride it, or at least pour it into a tankard and drink it.

14

A New Africa

During the 1960s the European empires continued their retreat from their African footholds, and I reported on independence ceremonies here and there. I remember arriving by air one night at what was evidently a very large metropolis indeed, but whose name I had never even heard of. It took me some baffled moments to realize that Kinshasa had been Leopoldville last time I was there.

Ghana

I had attended the independence festivities of the Gold Coast, later renamed Ghana, in 1957, but went back a few years later to report for the Guardian *on what its now capital Accra was like under the rule of its republican president Kwame Nkhruma.*

Like splendid pickets down the West African coast stand the strongholds of the Portuguese, erected one by one, with guts, bloodshed and slavery, as the caravels of Henry the Navigator probed southwards towards the Cape. They are spacious, flamboyant, arrogant structures, given a sense of dark power by their origins, and a sense of piquancy by the tumble of exotic trees, palm shacks, long-boats and African fizz with which their gorgeous ramparts are now invested: and in their cynical old way they still contribute powerfully to the flavour of those territories, like so many country mansions left high and dry among the housing estates.

I climbed a steep path to the most formidable of these castles, and observed from its walls the distant low confusion of a city. A handsome cheerful cripple, a sort of crystallized crooked smile, led me hobbling up the hill. A man in a blazing blue toga waved at me from a nearby hut. 'Hey, Massa!' shouted the fishermen on the beach below, sinewy black figures among their nets and lean canoes. In the village that spilled down the slope below the castle walls they were celebrating a local holiday: the village chief sat gaudily beneath his ceremonial umbrella, the official linguist brandished his totem of office, the drums thumped away among the mud huts. On the village notice-board it was announced that at the forthcoming obsequies of John Hackman (alias Ankam Tsia), Bishop of the 12th Apostle's Church, the chief mourners would include Prophetess Grase Thannie and Senior Prophet John Elubah Kuwesie. But I strode through them all, undeterred by their distractions, until I reached the uppermost vantage point of the fortress, and could look down the delectable palm-fringed shoreline to that distant metropolis. Only one capital on earth, I thought, could be approached through quite that combination of sensations, that amalgam of history, gusto, colour and immaturity. Only one city possesses quite such a tart hinterland, and they call it Accra: at one time or another a settlement of the Portuguese, the Dutch, the Danes and the British, and now the republican capital of Ghana.

It is not beautiful, but it is inescapably exhilarating, not always for the best reasons: a jazzy, high-spirited, ever bubbly place, whose inhabitants are dressed in dazzling multi-coloured togas and love to dance a slow, blaring shuffle known as High Life. Accra has passed through some queer and cloudy political fluctuations since Ghana attained her liberty, but for all the vagaries of statesmanship it still feels elevated by the very fact of independence, like a young man flourishing his door key still, long after his twenty-first birthday. Many of Accra's gleaming, grinning, vivacious citizens are poor people, very poor, subsisting on dried fish and stringy vegetables, living in squalid tumbledown huts, embroiled in many a medieval tangle of loyalty and superstition: but the city as a whole is well heeled and confident, sustained always by the price of cocoa from the immense plantations of the interior. This is one of those cities that feel inherently lucky, inherently easy-going, where it is all too easy to shrug your shoulders, throw away your statistical pamphlets and go sightseeing.

Or, more pertinently, go gossiping. Accra is not really much to look at, but it never stops talking. Education has bitten deep into its inherited mores, and since it was generally bestowed by Europeans or missionaries, its flavour is sometimes strangely incongruous. The 'youngmen' of Accra (as the Ghanaians like to call those who have ripped themselves away from the old outlooks) cannot often tell you the origins of the Golden Stool of the Ashanti, or the outcome of the battle of Amoafo, but they are often embarrassingly well informed about the House of Tudor or pragmatic sanctions, and are likely to quote Joshua, Shelley or E. M. Forster with disconcerting accuracy. The fine public library of Accra is always busy, and not only with those pallid English housewives, in Horrockses cottons and sandals, to be seen there at tea-time looking for the latest animal best-seller. The press of Accra, reckless, racy, inconsequential, spitting rivalries, ambitions and semi-private jokes, boisterous in misprint, cross-eyed with mixed metaphors, Rabelaisian in abuse and Dickensian in characterization – the indigenous press of Accra is nothing if not vital. The Supreme Court of Accra, during any big hearing, is packed with eager and well-informed enthusiasts, swathed in togas or uncomfortably sealed in reach-me-downs, their big white eyes flickering between the antagonists of a cross-examination like tennis fans at Centre Court. The rich stew of life in Accra is salted always with slander and intrigue, so that any waiter or shop assistant is quite likely to admit you, with a lowering of the voice and a secretive glitter of the pupils, into the latest Cabinet disagreement, and the whole structure of affairs is subject to sudden underhand convulsions, mass arrests or awful denunciations.

Nothing is altogether commonplace in Accra. It is a city of excesses. Public commerce is dominated, physically and figuratively, by the full-blooded, brawny-armed 'mammies' of the market, women of highly tempered economic instincts who play an extraordinarily important part in the progress of Ghana. These *grandes dames* of Accra are flounced in primary colours and half-swamped in dried fish, rolls of dazzling cotton, mounds of murky vegetables, chickens on the claw and cards of elastic, and they are distinguished by a noble Billingsgate spaciousness. Nobody ever hoodwinked an Accra market mammy, except perhaps another one, and no wise politician ignores their interests. It is their money, too, that finances the celebrated 'mammy-wagons' of Accra, perhaps the most memorable of all this city's gay folk spectacles. No form of modern transport is gayer or gaudier than these bright-painted trucks. Their average speed is bone-shakingly high, their cargoes are wonderfully jumbled, and they are emblazoned with curious slogans, some of them pungent ('A Lonely Woman Is a Man's Temptation'), some pious ('Follow the Truth and Obey the Heavens'), some merely enigmatic ('Why?' or 'You Never Can Tell'). You can easily tire of such phenomena, with their brassiness, their clashing colours, their strain of the juvenile: but they do give a kaleidoscopic momentum to the capital, and make you feel as though you are wallowing in a bottle of rather cheap pop.

The Ghanaian House of Assembly is so bursting with African vigour that the very air seems full of sparks, such as fly from silken textiles when the evening is charged with intimacy. Everything is done very fast and very boisterously, rather as the Keystone Kops might think of doing it. The House seems to be in a constant state of motion, honourable members jumping for microphones, ministers leaping to their feet with caustic replies, fans whirling, and outside the open doors and windows kaleido-scopic glimpses of blue-robed women or men in shirt-sleeves. At Question Time this energetic assembly is at its hilarious best. Few inhibitions then govern the give-and-take of parliamentary exchange. Hoots of laughter echo through the galleries. Fists are brandished and quips hurled between the benches. Sometimes there is a sudden moment of uproar, with everyone shouting at once, and sibilant hissings of 'Sit down!' sizzling across the floor, and sometimes you may catch sight of a member pointing with his finger, his shoulders hunched, the whites of his eyes gleaming and his eyebrows raised, as if he is casting some good-natured spell upon the Opposition.

Juvenile? In my reactionary moments, I cannot help thinking so. For all the real pleasures of Accra, all its boisterous kindliness and intelligence, it seems to me the least adult of capital cities. It expresses all that is noisiest and least reassuring about Africa, the melange of primitive or half-understood beliefs, the crossed values, the vacant frivolity. If Moscow is like an old dressing-gown, as Tolstoy thought, then Accra is a fancy-dress pom-pom. This is Africanism almost undiluted, graced by no old Semitic heritage, style of Arab or mystery of Jew, and fast swamping the remnants of imperial order. Historians like to recall that the fascinating Benin bronzes were fashioned only five hundred miles from Accra: but to me, I must confess, this steamy coast of Guinea feels frighteningly devoid of old art, deep wisdom or towering religion, and seems like a nursery shoreline, bickering, giggling and blowing tin trumpets among the gewgaws.

There are still juju murders and Senior Prophets in Accra. There are still magical agencies, seers and wizards. On the lovely bathing beach, among the surfboards and the bathing huts, you may still be shown a palm grove well known to be the domicile of a particularly powerful fetish. In the markets of the city you may still find, brooding among the motor bikes, the snakes' heads, dried rats, chameleons and monkey skulls of the witch-doctors. Now and then a diner of traditional instincts will still excuse himself from the restaurant of the Ambassador Hotel to pour a precau-tionary libation in the garden. The average scholastic standard at the

University of Ghana, I am told, is higher than that of most British universities, but a fearful amount of drivel is uttered by its graduates when they emerge into the fizzle of public life. The slogan 'Freedom and Justice' is written bold across the Triumphal Arch in Accra: but it often rings sour and sorry, when yet another political malcontent is shut away in silence, or yet another travesty of democracy is foisted upon an excited electorate. When three of the most prominent members of the ruling party were suddenly arrested one morning the official newspaper instantly described them as dangerous opportunists, criminal sycophants and diabolical renegades. 'Master-adventurer Adamafio and his tribalist gang, spearheaded by himself, Ako Adjei and Cofie-Crabbe; figured erroneously that they could throw dust into the eyes of the nation. This vile trio today stand condemned as the most inhuman band of lunatic power-seekers and ungrateful tribalist ruffians ever to emerge in the struggle.'

This is vivid and full-blooded stuff, and springs directly out of the Gold Coast's sanguinary past. Accra indeed is full of traditions, from castle walls to chieftaincies, but no certainty of loyalty or purpose underlies them. Adamafio and Cofie-Crabbe figure perennially in the chronicles of these parts, but the old-school abuse of the *Ghanaian Times* reflects something insecure and jejune in the state of Accra. This is partly the fault of the imperial West, with its slave trade, its sometimes misinformed convictions, its thoughtless missionary zeal: but to my mind – *pace* that delightful crippled cicerone, *pace* the friendly fishermen on the beach, *pace* the genial chief beneath his panoply and that splendid view of Accra from the ramparts of the fortress – to my diehard British mind it is mostly only Africa, lovable and terrifying old Africa, which is noble sometimes, and sometimes cruel, but feels so often like a continent playing at history.

Soon afterwards Nkhruma, who had developed dictatorial habits, was deposed by a military coup during his absence in China. He died in 1972.

Nigeria

Nigeria had also recently achieved its independence, and I reported on its celebrations too, but I was more interested in the Islamic city of Kano, in the north, which seemed to have been little affected by the colonial experience anyway.

* * *

As the traveller wanders across the breadth of Africa, through the welter of animisms and tribal faiths, the witch-doctors and sacred stones and fetishes, the gimcrack Christian deviations, the struggling missions and occasional messiahs – as he journeys through this cauldron of devotions he finds himself upon the outer fringes of Islam; and at once the stately order of that marvellous religion brings a fresh dignity to society, and tinges the air with its ornate magic. Such an outpost of the Muslims is Kano, the principal city of northern Nigeria, where the Emir of Kano lives in state in a splendid rambling palace, and the piles of ground-nuts stand like white pyramids outside the walls.

One of the sad results of the Western mission in Africa has been the vulgarization of the continent. Millions of Africans have been weaned from their precarious inherited mores and stuffed with a heady smattering of education and Christianity. It is entertaining, for a week or two, to observe the frothing and the bubbling, the jazzy effervescence that is often the product of this diet: the irreverent gaiety of slogans and posters, the brassy rhythms of High Life jazz in Accra, the unkempt and often scurrilous newspapers, the earnest schoolmasters discussing Sedgemoor or Voltaire, the perky black barristers with their wigs, the fundamentalist preachers playing upon trumpets and foaming at the mouth. There is tremendous vigour to Westernized Africa, especially along the shorelines of Nigeria and Ghana, and a bottomless reservoir of fun.

After a while, though, you begin to feel the pathos of it all, and to realize that these are temporarily rootless peoples, racked by sensations of inadequacy, unfulfilment or frustration, and deprived of the often scratchy cultures that gave them pride of history. It is probably no more than a sorry but inevitable stage in the development of black Africa, and certainly it is balanced by all manner of material blessings, from polio vaccines to pink chiffon: but stroll through the slums of Lagos one day and consider this sad miscegenation of manners, and you may murmur to yourself, as you pass from the dried monkey heads to the blaring radios: 'God help us, what a mess we've got them into!' Stretched between the tribal devils and the deep blue sea of progress, between the old religions and the new, the chieftain's council and Erskine May, many a poor African is a muddle of instincts and aspirations, whistling tunelessly in the dark.

But when you walk through the gates of Kano, with its grassy ramparts running away to the horizon like Mississippi levees, all this vanishes in a trice. Outside the walled city there are communities of Ibos and Yorubas from the south, pagans and Christians of diverse sects, among whom you may often see a young man in a cowboy hat, or hear the thump of ragtime, or even be conducted around a piggery: inside all is Muslim, the throaty quarter-tones of an African muezzin echo from a minaret, and there is a sense of style and latent pageantry. The three provinces of Nigeria have been federated in independence, but Kano feels a different country still, its people have ancient and deeply rooted loyalties of their own, and on ceremonial occasions (or travel posters) the Emir's bodyguard wears ancient chain mail and visors, like the Muslim warriors of antiquity. From the great white mosque near the palace you can catch the pulse of this romantic and remarkable city. A few cheerful convicts, wearing spotless white numbered smocks, lounge in its courtyards vacuously, and on his platform beside the gate the muezzin, black and beturbaned, arranges his robes rather nervously before beginning descent of his ladder. It is not always easy to gain access to the minaret of the mosque, for there has been a small commotion about the numbers of unbelievers who have been climbing its staircase; but after a few moments of breathy negotiation a retainer swathed from head to foot in bright red textiles, like a painted mummy or an indigestible Swiss roll, unlocks the door for you and ushers you upstairs.

The city sprawls below you festooned in heat and dignity. Somewhere across the horizon lies the Sahara, and this is a place like Isfahan or Damascus, subtly impregnated with desert ways, with an echo of cara-vanserai, slave trade and pilgrimage. An enormous higgledy-piggledy market straddles a rivulet in the middle of the city, a wonderful affair, with all the colour of black Africa but little of that fetid smell, compounded of dried fish and obscure medicinals, that brings a touch of the jungle to the great marts of Ibadan and the coast. Across the dusty plains radiate the trade routes that still link this ancient place with the Mediterranean, the Red Sea and Mecca itself. Below you lie the palaces of the great Fulani notables, still the aristocratic rulers of this city. Kano looks exceedingly old from that high eyrie, exceedingly assured, exceedingly grand.

But calm and silent though it may seem, in fact the winds of progress, like the horns of Elfland, are faintly blowing through these walls. The British, in half a century of suzerainty, broadened the basis of princely rule but by no means abolished it. Nor has the Federal Government of independent Nigeria. The Emir and his fellows maintain many of their privileges, but inevitably the people are beginning to look around them. Many of them know the Sudan; thousands have been to Saudi Arabia on pilgrimage; there are old links with North Africa; and there is, as among all

Muslims and speakers of Arabic, a deep interest in the doings of Egypt, at once the patriarch and the showboy of Islam. In the end, I do not doubt, the emergence of Nigeria as a free nation will whittle away the character and the traditional stability of Kano, for this city is not quite as serene as it looks. The distrust of northerner for the southerner is stubborn in Nigeria, and vice versa. The Ibos and Yorubas outside the walls, with their clerkly attainments and school certificates, are anathema to the aloof Hausas and Fulanis of Kano; and in return the outsiders turn up their educated noses at a people so incorrigibly sunk in medieval heritage. No great depth of security supports the grandeurs of the place. Like all such survivals of more spacious times, it lies at the mercy of common sense.

Still, for the moment there is no lack of confidence to Kano's muffled dignitaries, with their amber prayer-beads and their pieties, and no waning assurance to the earnest thumbs-up greeting with which Kano citizens often salute a passing foreigner. It is at the international airport of Kano that many travellers board their aircraft to be swept away to Europe. As they fly northwards to the Mediterranean they will be wise to steal a last valedictory glimpse of this antique city, criss-cross between its grassy walls, like Samarkand beside its Tigris or some lofty market town of Persia. What a farewell to Africa! And what a far-flung triumph, against all the odds of the jazz age and the hucksters, for the old philosophies of Arabia!

The old philosophies of Arabia might have struck me less amiably in the Kano of a few decades later, when more severe and dogmatic forms of Islam were resurgent.

Ethiopia

The greatest anachronism in the changing Africa of the 1960s was the Kingdom of Ethiopia, then still under the rule of the Emperor Haile Selassie. His capital retained some memorials of the brief Italian colonization of the country, thirty years before, but was in most respects decidedly sui generis.

A young lion vetted me in Addis Ababa one morning. He lay at ease in a compound outside the palace of the Emperor of Ethiopia, his paws neatly crossed, his tail straight behind him, and he looked me long, cold, detached and calculating in the eye. I would like to have known his views on the future of Addis, that ebony legend among capitals, but he did not encourage advances. Like the city itself, he looked back at me with an expression not exactly forbidding, and certainly not malevolent, but rather secretive or bemused, as though he had recently swallowed a dormouse, and was determined not to belch.

Addis Ababa, too, is in an indigestive condition, and having some trouble with its juices, but it possesses nevertheless a certain leonine dignity. I cannot call it a handsome city. Its pattern is formless and straggly, its architecture ranges from the mud shack to the pseudo-Corbusier by way of a thousand baroque and Bauhaus aberrations. It is a city without much focus, slums and palaces intermingled – pony-tailed misses streaming out of the lycée, palsied beggars crawling on blistered knees through the market. It offers no shock of vicious contrast, for its separate elements are too intimately fused, but physically it is a faceless kind of place, a little blurred perhaps, a little splodgy.

Among African cities today Addis Ababa is one of the cleanest, one of the least squalid, one of the calmest. This is partly politics, for it is the capital of a patriarchal autocracy not at all encouraging to the effervescence and high jinks; but it is mostly geo-history. Addis compensates for what it is by being where it is, and when. Around it the delightful Shoa highlands lie like a Wiltshire evocation, and groves of junipers, larches, figs and eucalyptus trees sidle into the heart of the city, like the magical forests that invest Kyoto. A glorious half-alpine climate gives a sparkle and a sting to this capital, keeps it free from sludge and stinks, fructifies its shanty slums and humours the wild polychromatic abstracts painted on the walls of its newest apartment blocks. The name Addis Ababa means 'New Flower', because it was founded in the odour of hope towards the end of the nineteenth century; and to this day the city feels young and unexpectedly charming, graced alike by the superb manners and the green fingers of the Ethiopians.

Never was there a more handsome citizenry, since the days of the Assyrian bas-reliefs. I once paused to watch a merchant weighing millet in the marketplace of this city. His wife sat loyally beside him, dressed in a long white gown and a string cap, and three or four labourers in ragged tunics hastened backwards and forwards with their sacks. The merchant sat on a kitchen chair as lordly as any Prester John, bowed gravely over his scales, and when he looked up at me I saw burning black eyes sunk deep between the cheekbones, a nose chiselled like granite, a mouth at once haughty and infinitely delicate, grey hair curling Homerically around the temples, a thin face cold with authority, a look marvellously salted with dry and knowing humour. He smiled when he noticed me, the thin quiver of a smile, and as he did so he slammed the lock of his scales with a gesture terribly final, as though he had ordered the instant expulsion of the Jesuits, or had just beheaded his grandfather.

Addis Ababa is full of faces just as memorable: the resigned, distant, biblical faces of the old men who loiter, leaning lightly on their crooked sticks outside the iron-roofed shacks of the district courts; the intelligent, wary faces of the young bloods home from Europe and America; the aloof, incurious faces of the Muslims washing their feet in the fountains of the mosque; the gentle, empty, haunting faces of the young prostitutes, in virginal white and vicarage embroidery, who wait outside their dim-lit boudoirs (sickly pink, blue, or conventionally red) along the pavements of Churchill Street. This is Africa with Semitic injections. These are not the coarse, laughing faces of Accra. Here there is something extra in the blood, something more restrained and lofty, something that suggests to me the black nobles of legend, or the Magus at the stable door.

For Addis Ababa has nobility; the nobility of a proud but gentle Christian faith, and of an immemorial self-respect. This is a city, like Bangkok, that has scarcely known the long humiliations of colonialism, and has not been obliged to wallow through the sad morass of recrimination, frustration and twisted emotion that belabours the emancipation of subject capitals. Amid all the thump and hubbub of the African renaissance, Addis Ababa stands alone as the capital of an ancient and truly African state. It thus retains a trace of feudal hauteur. There is a Minister of the Pen here, and a functionary called the Mouth of the King. Lions of Judah abound in gilded effigy, and from every hotel office, every restaurant wall, every barber's mantelpiece, there gazes the image of His Imperial Majesty, the Elect of God, Conquering Lion of the Tribe of Judah, splendidly ceremonial in court dress, austerely military in khaki. This is a traditionalism rich and lovable, but flecked with pathos. There are not many kings left on the earth, and it is moving still to encounter one who claims direct descent from Solomon and the Queen of Sheba.

It cannot last, this lion's style. It is fretted, frayed and mocked already. Isolation bred the grandeur of the Ethiopians, but this is a capital no longer remote or mysterious. I can think of half a dozen more difficult to reach, and several more backward and obscure. There is a daily air service nowadays to Europe, and the London Sunday papers get here on Monday. Addis has all the appurtenances of a modern city, from cold-jet dentistry to espresso coffee bars. Americans from Berkeley, Germans from

Frankfurt, sometimes think this an insufferably primitive capital, with its beggars and lepers and bumbling bureaucracy, but to us old hands of Empire and the Third World, us habitual waiters in ante-rooms and addicts of Enterovioform – to wanderers like us Addis Ababa is a haven of convenience.

But the sleazier corrosions of progress are also beginning to show, and a little of the pan-African fizz is bubbling around the inherited certainties. The patriarchal order is doomed, and even the Emperor himself, that grand old warrior-sage, is no longer sacrosanct. Addis Ababa seethes with foreigners, Swedes and Germans and Americans and Englishmen, connecting telephones, teaching woodwork, managing hotels, building roads, squabbling and intriguing and exhorting and complaining and making money and always, night and day, year after year, syllable by syllable, assuring this antique comity that its systems are wrong and its values misguided. Addis is not a passionate city, daubed with slogans and loud with demonstrations; but as this flood of alien energies pours in, as ever more young Ethiopians come home from Harvard, Bonn or Oxford, so we may expect the new hybrid culture of Africa to take root here too, swamp the old gardens of Ethiopia with its jazzy proliferation and reduce this still lofty metropolis to the level of our times.

It has not happened yet. The Emperor still rules in Ethiopia, and this remains a capital of high-flown protocol. There were thirty-five lions in the compound that morning, some young and cuddly, some majestically mature, and as I walked away I fancied the ruminative gaze of each one of them fastened steadily upon my person. They were very silent and absolutely still. It was like that moment of polite but faintly embarrassed hush when the ladies are leaving with a swish for the drawing room, and the men are eyeing the port. Those animals did not really want me there at all, but they were cubs of the Conquering Lion, and they would not dream of showing it.

I saw little of Haile Selassie during this visit to his country. When I went there later his autocracy seemed far more intrusive. When he swept through the streets with his convoy of limousines the citizenry flung themselves face-down on the ground, and I narrowly escaped seeing a public hanging of dissidents. I had set eyes on the Emperor anyway twenty years before, when he had fled from Italian occupation to exile at Bath in England, and I saw him sitting alone, pale, dark-eyed and meditative, in a first-class compartment of a Paddington train.

For all its quandaries and uncertainties, I enjoyed the shifting Africa of the 1960s. In Khartoum, the capital of the Sudanese Republic, I was once given a succinct definition of my proper functions as a reporter. I was interviewing the Minister of National Guidance (later executed for misguiding the nation) and he told me that my duties should be to report 'thrilling, attractive and good news, coinciding where possible with the truth'. I have followed his advice ever since.

15

Manhattan 1969

In the last year of the decade I was commissioned by the Port of New York Authority to go over and write a book for them. I was flattered, and used to display a big aerial photograph I had on the wall at home, prematurely telling myself and everyone else, 'That port's mine!' When my job was done I sailed out by tug to meet the QE2, the last of the classic transatlantic liners, when she entered New York harbour on her maiden voyage. I thought it a properly celebratory conclusion to the writing of my book, The Great Port.

I went on one of the McAllister tugs, sailing from the Battery. The McAllisters are an old New York family of tugboat and harbour men, Irish by origin, ebullient by disposition, and hospitable. Three of their boats sailed that morning in close formation, and they were loaded down with what seemed to me to be several hundred McAllisters – grave elder McAllisters, gay miniskirted McAllisters, gossipy McAllister matrons, virile McAllister bravos. The boats themselves were naturally named for McAllister ladies, and all over their decks, rather loosely kitted out in green kilts and tam-o'-shanters, the pipers of the New York Donegal Pipe Band played in lusty antiphony across the waves. There was a satisfying buffet lunch on board, and plenty to drink, and by the time we had passed beneath the Verrazano Bridge, and saw the elegant and spindly outline of the *QE2* approaching from the open sea, I felt myself an honorary McAllister for the day, and looked out across the water with a Donegal benevolence.

The harbour is the most beautiful of New York's possessions, and nowadays it is one of the last refuges in an unhappy metropolis of that fizz and crackle, that sense of lovers' release, which once used to be synonymous with Manhattan. Here some of the American pageantry survives, and when the *QE2* sailed in that day much of the old American generosity showed too, and the sentimental loyalty. The sea was choppy and the wind rough, but the sun came out just as the ship passed through the

Narrows, and so in a bright flurry of flags and foam our procession passed through the Bay. The liner towered above high, bright and very new, almost fragile. The sky was thick with helicopters and seaplanes, idling happily about there like kites, or paper aeroplanes, and all around us scores of little ships noisily and exuberantly escorted the liner towards her berth.

On the forecastle of the *QE2* the ship's cooks, in their chefs' hats, gazed impassively towards Manhattan, and in an open door in the flank of the liner a solitary white-clad sailor stood silhouetted nonchalant, even bored, against the black inside, as though such spectacles were observable on every voyage. For the rest, everybody seemed to be waving. We waved, all barriers down, at total strangers. We blew kisses all over the place. A girl in a blue dress jumped up and down with excitement on the boat deck, and through the slightly steamy windows of what I took to be some ferociously air-conditioned or centrally heated lounge, I could see pale elderly faces cautiously peering into the open air outside, looking wistfully nostalgic still, I fancied, for mahogany and Palm Court.

What fun it all was! The sirens constantly blew. The flags fluttered from every mast. The Staten Island ferry chugged by with a huge welcome sign hanging from its superstructure. The aircraft buzzed. The Donegal pipers, temporarily abandoning their reels and coming disarmingly apart at the joints of their accoutrements, were to be encountered in odd corners of the tugboat merrily drinking Scotch and swapping badinage. Now and then waves of water sloshed through the scuppers of our boat, washed the legs of the buffet table, and made us all leap on to deck chairs; but nobody much minded, the best came out in all of us, the world was fine, New York was laughing, and as the noble ship paced up the Hudson River and turned into her berth, news came over the tug's radio that Mrs Gerard McAllister, my hostess, had just become a grandmother.

I remembered, as we limped damply but contentedly ashore that afternoon, looking all those months before at my photograph of the Bay, and presumptuously claiming it to be mine. Now, I thought, it really was. No Briton alive, I am sure, had seen more of New York harbour, or knew it better, or felt more at home upon its wide, dirty, magical waters.

It was originally planned that my book would be launched at a party on board the liner in New York harbour, but alas the QE2, *establishing a tradition that she would honour for much of her career, had arrived four months late because of engine trouble.*

The twin towers of the World Trade Center, in lower Manhattan, were commissioned by the Port Authority during my time with it, and the piazza between the two buildings was named after the chairman (and my own patron in the organization), Austin Tobin. This delightful man was nearing retirement, so the office joke was to nickname the immense structures Austin's Last Erection – a joke that went sour when, after his death, the Center was destroyed by terrorists.

The 1970s

For the world the 1970s were years of particularly mixed fortune. In Europe the wretched Cold War still split the nations, but the Treaty of Brussels, signed in 1972, was a majestic step towards the continent's eventual formal unity. In Asia an extension of the great ideological rivalry embroiled the Americans and a few of their allies in the tragic Vietnam War, but in Japan, Korea, Hong Kong and Singapore immense industrial progress was stirring. Africa was in turmoil, periodically plagued by conflict, famine, disease and racial tension, and more or less abandoned by its old colonial overlords. The Middle East was in its usual condition of unease.

For me the decade was a happy one. Professionally I was working on my most ambitious literary project, the Pax Britannica *trilogy about the rise and decline of the Victorian empire: personally I was reaching a solution of my lifelong sexual dilemma. I was still accepting commissions from magazines, but I found my reportage and travel writing metamorphosing more and more into impressionism – perhaps because nothing in world affairs seemed to me so clear-cut as it used to.*

16

Pleasure Places

Around this time, when I was not thinking about Vietnam, the Cold War or the end of the empires, I wrote a succession of articles about particularly enjoyable places – as a sort of relief, I suppose, for I was beginning to think I had observed enough of the world's problem-zones. Here are a couple of these hedonistic essays.

Kashmir

It seems paradoxical that Kashmir, disputed by India and Pakistan and one of Asia's perennial potential flash-points, should also be a paradigm of escape: but so it was then, and I escaped there myself with a dream-like delight.

It was in Kashmir, late in travel and half-way through life, that I first went transcendental. Reality seems distinctly relative in that high and timeless vale, truth bends, distance is imprecise, and even the calendar seems to swing indeterminately by, week blurred into week and Friday arriving unannounced upon the heels of Sunday night.

For my first few days I stuck to the facts, but ever less tenaciously. Nobody else seemed to find it necessary. No decision seemed sacrosanct there, and life was apparently suspended in some limbo between events. I lived myself on a lake of no particular shape or exact location, linked by meandering reedy waterways to a fifteenth-century city down the valley. It took me an hour to get to town, reclining full-length in the cushioned recesses of a boat, while the paddle-man behind me sang high-pitched melodies to himself, took occasional gurgles at a water-pipe, and drank green tea with salt in it. Sometimes I stopped to make an improbable purchase – a jade bangle, a duck for dinner, a chunk of honey off the comb. Sometimes perfect strangers asked me how old my watch was, or told me about their forthcoming examinations in elementary economics. Sometimes, having spent the whole day maundering about the city, I returned to my lake late in the evening with not the slightest recollection of anything specific having happened to me at all.

So in the end I emancipated myself, and soared unimpeded beyond actuality, seldom quite sure where I was, or when, or even sometimes who – answering all questions with abandoned fancy, never seeking a reason or providing a cause. I felt myself disembodied between the green-blue lake and the snow mountains all around, in a gentle Nirvana of my own: nowhere existed, it seemed to me, beyond the celestial vale of Kashmir, and whether the vale existed itself was a matter of individual perception.

I was not the first to enter this airy plane of sensibility. Kashmir has been having such an effect upon its visitors for at least 400 years. The Moghul emperors, who conquered it in the sixteenth century, responded to the vale with a sensual passion, embellishing it with seductive gardens and honouring it with royal dalliances. The British, who became its suzerains in the 1840s, thought it the ultimate retreat from the burdens of empire, and took its magic home with them to the strains of 'Pale Hands I Loved, Beside the Shalimar'. Today's wandering hippies find themselves rootlessly at ease there, and Middle Americans who spend a couple of Kashmir days between Treetops and Hong Kong often feel the interlude to have been an insubstantial dream.

Kashmir has always been more than a mere place. It has the quality of an experience, or a state of mind, or perhaps an ideal. The Muslim sectarians called the Ahmadiya believe that Christ did not die upon the Cross, but was spirited away to Kashmir, the last haven of perfection: and the Moghul emperor Jehangir expressed the wish on his deathbed that Kashmir and Paradise would turn out to be, as he had always thought, one and the same place.

In my more lucid moments, I must here interject, I did not *altogether* agree with the emperor. Looked at hard and realistically, Kashmir falls short of Elysium. Situated as it is high in central Asia, north of Tibet, squeezed between Russia, China and Afghanistan, it can hardly escape the world's contagion. Beside the golf course at Srinagar, Kashmir's capital, one often sees the waiting white cars of the United Nations, chauffeurs patient at the wheel: and there are soldiers about always, and angry politicians, and students with grievances, and un-persuadable men of religion. Kashmir is one of the world's perennial trouble-spots. Though its people are mostly

Muslims, it was ruled until 1947, under the aegis of the British, by a Hindu dynasty of Maharajahs: since then it has been disputed by India and Pakistan. The whole of the vale of Kashmir falls within Indian territory, but sizeable chunks of the outer state are governed by Pakistan, and legal sovereignty of the whole has never been decided. Kashmir is one of those places, deposited here and there in awkward corners of the earth, that never seem quite settled: a bazaar rumour kind of place, a UN resolution place, a place that nags the lesser headlines down the years, like a family argument never finally resolved.

Besides, in my Paradise nobody will be poor: most of the inhabitants of Kashmir are very poor indeed. My Paradise will always be merry: Kashmir is infused with a haunting melancholy. In my Paradise there will be no tourist touts, sharks or hawkers: Kashmir, for more than a century one of the great tourist destinations of the earth, boasts the most charmless touts and indefatigable hagglers in Asia. In my Paradise burgundy will flow like water. In Kashmir all but the most extravagant of Moghuls must make do with Indian Golconda, sixteen rupees a half-bottle from the vineyards of Hyderabad.

Where was I? Drifting, that's right, all but motionless across a Kashmiri lake, preferably in a shikara, a distant relative of the gondola, canopied, low in the water, looking rather stern-heavy and propelled by that boatman with the water-pipe, squatting at the stern. From *outside* a shikara looks like a fairground novelty, brightly coloured and curtained, and generally full of gregarious Indian youths waving and crying 'Hi!', wrongly supposing you to be a research student in comparative ethnology from the University of South Utah. *Inside* the shikara feels a very different vehicle – like a floating capsule or divan, exquisitely cushioned, moving unguently through the water-lilies towards pleasure-gardens and picnics.

Although the vale of Kashmir is 800 miles from the sea, and surrounded on all sides by immense mountains, still its prime and symbolic element is water. The Kashmir thing is essentially a rippling, liquid kind of happening. Geologists say the whole valley was once a lake, and a string of lesser lakes ornaments it still. Srinagar stands in the middle of four, and is crisscrossed too by ancient canals, and intersected by the great river Jhelum. Boats are inescapable in the capital: boats grand or squalid, spanking or derelict; boats thatched, shingled, poled, engined; boats deep with fruit, nuts, timbers, furs, livestock; barges, and punts, and canoes, and skiffs, and elderly motor-boat taxis; above all those floating figures of the Kashmir scene, those vessels of fragrant legend, houseboats.

The Kashmir houseboat has come to be a sort of chalet-boat, or water-villa. It is often gabled, and shingle-roofed. There is a sun-deck on top, with an awning, and the poop is comfortably cushioned, and has steps down to the water. The boat is generally fitted in a Victorian mode: heavy dark furniture, baths with claw feet, antimacassars very likely, hot water bottles for sure. Each houseboat has its own kitchen-boat moored astern, and its attendant shikara alongside, and its staff of resident servants, and its own special smell of cedar-wood, curry, roses and ingrained cigar-smoke: and living upon such a vessel, moored beside the orchard-bank of Nagin Lake, or lying all among the willows of a Srinagar canal, very soon one finds reality fading. The lap of the water takes over, the quacking of the ducks in the dawn, the hazed blue smoke loitering from the cook-boat, the soft water-light, the glitter of the dewdrop in the water-lily leaf, the flick of the little fish in the clear blue water, the dim purplish presence of the mountain beyond the lake, fringed with a line of distant snow.

Time expands in such a setting, and loses its compulsion. The hours dawdle by, as the bearer brings you your coffee on the sun-deck, and the shikara man lies on his own cushions awaiting your instructions, and the peripatetic trading boats sidle into your line of vision – 'You like to see my jewellery, madam? Any chocolates, cigarettes, shampoo? You want a very nice suede coat, sir, half the price of Savile Row? Flowers, memsahib? Haircut? Fur hat? Laundry?' Nothing very particular occurs. A meal comes when you want it. The shikara is always there. The ducks quack. If one considers the matter carefully one finds that the sun rises and sets, and some time between tea and sundowner it does begin to get dark.

Scale, on the other hand, contracts. The focus narrows, within the frame of the Kashmir water-life. The picture gets clearer, more exact, and one finds oneself concentrating upon minutiae, like the number of leaves upon the plucked waterweed, or the twitchy movements of the kingfishers. I took Jane Austen's novels with me to the vale of Kashmir, and perfectly with this delicate awareness of the place did her quill dramas and porcelain comedies correspond.

Sometimes, as I say, I was swishily paddled into town. Then through lily-thick channels we proceeded, willows above us, green fields and apple orchards all around, and as we approached the city the texture of life thickened about us. Barge-loads of cattle glided by to market. Infants sploshed about in half-submerged canoes. Women in trailing kerchiefs, neatly folded about the head, cooked in shanty-boats or washed their clothes at water-steps. Solitary fishermen cast their nets in the shallows: sometimes a man paddled an empty punt along, sitting cross-legged and gnomish in the prow. We passed beneath medieval bridges trembling with traffic, and beside tall houses latticed and mysterious, and past open-fronted waterside stores where merchants sat grandly upon divans, smoking hubble-bubbles and bowing condescendingly in one's direction. We paddled our way, like an admiral's yacht at a review, through flotillas of houseboats, some with tourists jolly on the poop, some all dank and deserted, like funeral boats between rituals.

And presently we would find ourselves upon the muddy water of the Jhelum itself, with its parade of old bridges (Zero Bridge to Eighth Bridge) and the brown jumble of Srinagar all around. Distractedly I disembarked to loiter through the labyrinth of the bazaars, pursued by suggestions proper and profane, and seldom knowing where I was going. Though Srinagar is only seventy minutes from Delhi by daily jet, yet it is a frontier town of central Asia. Here since the start of history the caravans from Sinkiang or Kazakhstan rested on their way to India, and these tangled souks are more like Turkestan than Bengal. Here one feels close to the Uzbeks, the Kurds, the Mongols, the merchants of Tashkent or Bokhara: and often one sees exotic figures from the remotest north swinging through the streets, in goatskin cloaks and fur hats, to remind one of the grand mysteries, Pamir and Hindu Kush, which stand at the head of the valley.

Srinagar has its Westernized quarters, but strewn around and within the bends of the Jhelum, medieval Srinagar magnificently survives. No addict of the mouldering picturesque could complain about these bazaars. They possess all the classic prerequisites of oriental allure – spiced smells, impenetrable alleys, veiled women, goldsmiths, mosques, sages, dwarfs. The air of old Srinagar is heavy with suggestion, and its lanes are so crowded with shrouded and turbaned personages, so opaque with dust and smoke and vegetable particles, that invariably I lost my bearings in them, and wandering fruitlessly among the temples and the cloth merchants, over the Third Bridge and back past the tomb of Zain-el-Abdin, at last I used to clamber into a tonga, and went clip-clop back, to the flick of the whip and the smell of horse-sweat, to my patiently waiting shikara at the Dal Gate. 'Houseboat now?' the shikara man would murmur; and back to the lake I would be unnoticeably propelled, eating walnuts all the way.

Yet it has not been an exhilarating progress. The eye of Kashmir is a brooding, almost a baleful, eye – the eye of the shopkeeper, calculating above his wares, the eye of the military policeman on his traffic-stand, the eye of the floating trader, peering ever and again through the houseboat window in search of victims within.

The Kashmiris are a hospitable people, but not inspiriting. They seem to be considering always the possibilities of misfortune. In the autumn especially, a lovely season in the valley, the fall of the leaf seems a personal affliction to them, and the passing of the year presses them like a fading of their own powers. Then in the chill evenings the women disappear to private quarters behind, and the men light their little baskets of charcoal, tuck them under their fustian cloaks and squat morosely in the twilight, their unshaven faces displaying a faint but telling disquiet. 'Come in, come in,' they murmur, 'come and join us, you are welcome, sit down, sit down!' – but for myself I generally evaded their sad hospitality, preferring Miss Austen's gaiety on the poop.

Yet I was half-ashamed as I did so, for their kindness is very real, and all the truer for its reticence – a flick of the head to disclaim gratitude, a discreetly forgotten bill. There was a touching pathos, I thought, to the Kashmiri style. 'How do you like your life?' I asked one new acquaintance there, when we had progressed into intimacy. 'Excellent,' he replied with a look of inexpressible regret, 'I love every minute of it' – and he withdrew a cold hand from the recesses of his cloak, and waved it listlessly in the air to illustrate his enjoyment.

The vale of Kashmir is like a fourth dimension – outside the ordinary shape of things. About a hundred miles long by twenty miles wide, it is a green scoop in the Himalayan massif, hidden away among the snow-ranges.

For its ultimate aloofness the traveller must climb to the rim of the valley, to the high alpine meadows of Gulmarg or Pahalgam. There the separateness of the place achieves a disembodied quality, and the whole valley seems to be resting in some high cradle among the clouds, supported by the snow-peaks all around. You have to walk to attain this mystic detachment, away from the little chalet-hotels and bazaars of the resorts, up through the silent pine woods, along the banks of slate-grey trout streams, up through the last crude huts of the highland shepherds, beyond the tree line, over the granite scree until you stand among the snows themselves, on the rampart ridge.

Often the vale below is half-veiled by cloud, and one sees only a green patch here and there, or a suggestion of water: but all around the white mountains stand, holding Kashmir on their hips – peak after peak, ridge after ridge, with Nangar Parbat supreme on the northern flank to set the scale of them all. Kashmir is a place like no other: yet even from such a vantage point, high up there in the snow and the sun, its character is curiously negative. It could not possibly be anywhere else, but it might, so it often seemed to me in the hush of those high places, be nowhere at all.

One can judge it only by itself. The fascination of Kashmir is essentially introspective, a mirror-pleasure in which the visitor may see his own self picturesquely reflected, adrift in his shikara among the blossoms and the kingfishers. It is no place for comparisons. Paradise, here as everywhere, is in the mind.

Trouville

I was commissioned to write about Trouville for the international edition of Life *magazine, as one of a series I did for them about historic resorts. I had to look it up on the map, but when I got there I knew it at once – not from any specific book or painting, but from a whole temper or even genre of art.*

There lay the long empty foreshore, with only a few shrimp catchers knee-deep in its sand pools; and there along the boardwalk strolled a group of those women that Boudin loved, blurred and shimmery in flowered cottons; and the beach was lined with a gallimaufry of villas, gabled, pinnacled or preposterously half-timbered; and three fishing boats with riding sails chugged away offshore; and over it all, over the sands and the estuary and the distant promontory of Le Havre, there hung a soft impressionist light, summoned out of moist sunshine, high rolling clouds and the reflection of the sea. I knew the scene at once, from Monet and Bonnard and Proust. The English were the modern inventors of the salt-water resort, and made it fashionable to frequent the beaches; but the French first saw the beauty of the seaside scene, and transmuted into art all its perennial sights – the slant of that white sail, the stoop of that child beside his sandcastle, the preen of the great ladies along the promenade.

This particular aesthetic was born in Trouville. It was among the earliest of the French seaside resorts, for a time it was the grandest, and at the back of our minds it is half familiar to us all.

Not far below the Seine estuary a little river called the Touques arrives unobtrusively at the English Channel. On its right bank, almost at its mouth, there stood at the beginning of the nineteenth century the isolated village of Trouville. The artist Charles Mozin discovered it in the 1820s, and in a long series of affectionate paintings portrayed it in every detail: the horsemen plodding across the river at low tide, the brawny fisherwomen, the bright sails of the boats along the quays, the colonnaded fish market beside the waterfront, and above all the limpid hush that seems to have hovered over the little town. His pictures introduced the world to the charms of a coastline hitherto considered blighted and impossibly primitive, and presently the great caravan of fashion found its way to the Normandy shore, to make the name of Trouville synonymous, for a brief but gorgeous heyday, with the pleasures of the Second Empire. Led by the Empress Eugénie, herself a creature of infinite sensuality, the Empire fell upon Trouville like some overwhelming rich aunt, all scent and furbelows. A boardwalk was laid upon its sands; above it, beneath the bluffs, a parade of hotels and villas arose; and at the point where the river reached the sands, they built a huge casino, a regular monument of a place, with assembly rooms in the latest style, and carriage drives fit for any imperial barouche.

Trouville became a catalyst of the grand and the quaint, and so it was that when I got there I recognized it all: the sea and the sand from the painters, the style from the history books, and the very stance of the hotel manager from the pages of *A la recherche du temps perdu*. Trouville has not much grown since Proust's day, or even since Eugénie's. The countryside behind it remains delectably unspoiled, and the combination of green grass and sand, meeting at the foreshore, still makes the view from the beaches feel like one of those glimpses you get from the deck of a ship, when the passing landscape seems close but altogether unattainable, as though you are seeing it through plate glass.

Trouville was spared by the two world wars, and this impunity means that it has a curiously preserved or pickled air. It is a period piece, more perfect than most. Its balance of commerce and pleasure has been scrupulously maintained, and you can enjoy today almost the same mixture of sensations that the courtiers and the artists enjoyed a century ago. The core of the town remains the Casino. This has aged a little since its ceremonial opening, and has rather gone down in the world. Part of it is a cinema, part of it a salt water spa, part a night club, part a waxwork show, part a fire house, part a shabby kind of tenement. As an architectural whole, nevertheless, it is still imposingly snooty, and looks faintly exotic too – like a Mongol marquee, perhaps, with bobbles and domes and flagstaffs, and its own name in large and ornate letters above the entrance.

On my very first evening in Trouville I made my way to the steps of this old prodigy and leaning against a marble pillar, surveyed the town before me. The square in front of the building, dotted with trees and used as a car park, is asymmetrical, and this splaying of its form makes it look like one of those panoramic postcards popular among our great-grandmothers, in which several negatives were tacked together, and the view came out peculiarly elongated, smaller at the edges than in the middle. From this distorted apex I could see both halves of Trouville. To my left lay the beach and all it represents, the pride, the old grandeur and the space. To my right, the fishing boats were lined up beside the quay, bright awnings ornamented the shop fronts, and all was cluttered intimacy. Both styles were essential, I realized that evening, to the art form that is Trouville; and it is the confrontation of the two, set against the light and scale of the foreshore, that gives the aesthetic of the seaside its especial tangy charm.

I looked to my right first, towards fisherman's Trouville – still as, in the 1820s, any romantic's delight. The tide was high, and the upper works of fishing smacks lined the river boulevard – tangled structures of rope and rigging, hung with flags, buoys, lifebelts, nets and paintpots, and undulating slightly at their moorings. Here and there a crew was unloading its catch in crates upon the quay, while the fish merchant gravely calculated the value, a huddle of housewives knowingly discussed the quality, a few tourists looked on with the glazed fascination that dead fish inspire in almost everyone, and several small boys in their blue school smocks wormed and giggled through the crowd. There were men angling, too, with heavy rods and voluminous canvas satchels. There were porters lounging around the *poissonnerie*, in stained overalls and nautical caps. High-wheeled carts were propped against walls, there was a noise of hammering from a boatyard, and the fish stalls down the street glistened with crabs, lobsters, jumpy things like big water fleas, twitching eels, clams, oysters and mackerel with a cold bluish tinge to their flanks. Fishiness was everywhere – fish smells, fish lore, fish skills, fish in boxes, fish in baskets, and mounds of shellfish upon the pavement tables of the restaurants.

For Trouville is still a working town, and behind the waterfront workaday good sense fills the tight mesh of its streets. There are shops that sell nets and tackle; shops lusciously flowing with the fruits, vegetables and cheeses of Normandy; trim cafés full of mirrors and tobacco smoke; a couple of big chain stores; and up in the grounds of the hospital, overgrown with ivy and embellished with archaic saintly figures, the original church of Trouville, thirteen paces long from door to altar, in whose reverent obscurity the fishing people worshipped for several centuries before the first tourist set eyes upon this place. All the stubborn variety of French provincial life stirs along those streets. Trouville is rich in tough twinkling old ladies, eccentrically dressed and wheeling their groceries on basket trolleys, and in those shabby but courteous old gentlemen of France who might be anything from dukes to retired milkmen, and wear high starched collars in the middle of August. But there are many laughing representatives of the new French generations, too, taller, gayer and more confident than we have ever known French people before, with beautiful children in the back seats of small family cars, and a sense of bright emancipation from a fusty past.

Fisherman's Trouville is never torpid. It admirably illustrates those aspects of the French genius which are unalterably organic – close always to the earth, the sea, the marriage bed and the neighbour's gossip. The Duchesse de Guermantes, the ineffably aristocratic chatelaine of Proust's great novel, loved to tell country anecdotes in a rustic accent: and it is this ancient attachment to earthy things, so vital a part of the French artistic energy, that the right-hand view from the Casino best expresses.

Then I looked to the left, and there lay another France in esplanade. Exuberantly the hotels and villas clustered about the beach – none of them young indeed, but all of them gay, like jolly old gentlefolk, in lace and grey toppers, out to enjoy themselves. It was an elaborate age that made Trouville famous, and the buildings of this resort are flamboyantly individualist. Some are gloriously encrusted with coils, domes and flourishes of classicism. Some are expensively faced in Normandy half-timber, and stand incongruously beside the sands like farmhouses on Fifth Avenue. Others go to wilder excess, and are built like castles, like fairy palaces, even in one case like a Persian caravanserai. The rooftops of this Trouville are punctuated with golden birds, pineapples, crescent moons, spindles, metal flowers and urns, and among the trees the mansions reside in majesty, unabashed by shifts of taste or society, and still looking, behind their ornamental gates and protective shady gardens, almost voluptuously comfortable.

Not much has changed since the great days of the resort. The bright little tents that people put up on the beach are made of nylon nowadays, but with their suggestion of eastern dalliance still recall the enthusiasms of Delacroix or Gautier. The long-celebrated boardwalk, however crowded it becomes in high summer, is still quiet and leisurely. Nobody has erected a skyscraper hotel, or built a bowling alley, and severe instructions affixed to flagstaffs govern the decorum of the sands. The miniature golf course, beside the Casino, is a very model of genteel entertainment, admirably suited to the inhibitions of elastic-sided boots and bustles: with its painted wooden windmill for knocking balls through, its tricky inclines and whimsical hazards, it seems to ring perpetually with the silvery laugh of ladies-in-waiting, and the indulgent banter of colonels.

Having inspected the urban dichotomy I walked behind the great mass of the Casino, and across the narrow river I saw another, larger, more glittering town on the other side. The Duc de Morny, half-brother of the Emperor himself, was paradoxically the originator of Trouville's decline. In the 1860s this enterprising speculator cast *his* eye across the Touques, and saw that the sand on the opposite bank was just as golden, the climate just as sparkling, the sea the same stimulating sea – and the landscape entirely empty. Trouville had reached its peak of fashion; the Parisian elite was beginning to hanker for somewhere more exclusive; in a few years, upon the impetus of the duke, there arose on the left bank of the Touques the excruciatingly posh resort of Deauville. Today it is the smartest watering place in northern France, and it looked to me that evening, from the backside of Trouville's Casino, like a vision of another age. Its clientele nowadays is richer and more cosmopolitan than Trouville's. Its casino has a turnover twice as great. Its street lights come on fifteen minutes earlier. Its race meeting is one of the most important in Europe. No fishermen's cafés soil its elegant promenades, and only yachts and speedboats sail into its basin. It is all resort. Today, if you want to explain where Trouville stands, you can best say that it's over the bridge from Deauville.

So there is a certain pathos to the prospect from the Casino at Trouville – but pathos of a gentle, amused kind. Trouville does not feel humiliated. It is this small town that the artists loved, its image, variously interpreted down the generations, that has entered all our sensibilities – Trouville's sands and sails we all dimly recognize, Trouville's ludicrous mansions that ornament the album pages, Trouville's bright light that gleams so often, with a tang of Channel air, from the walls of so many galleries. In Trouville the sun, the sea, the fishing folk and the high society became an inspiration, and created a tradition of art.

I did not mope that evening, then. I walked back to my hotel, accepted the bows of Proust's pageboys, left a note inviting Whistler and De Musset to join me for a drink at *Les Vapeurs,* and asked the maid to clean my best shoes, in case I bumped into the Empress at the gaming tables after dinner.

I had flown to Trouville with my car on a pioneering air-ferry service from England that then operated from Lympne, in Hampshire. Waiting to board the aircraft on my return journey I fell into conversation with a fellow-motorist also bound for Lympne, but as we chatted he looked up and saw his car at that moment being loaded on to the departing flight for Dublin, which promptly took off. The aircraft was a Bristol Freighter, and a surviving specimen of the marque stands on a plinth at Yellowknife, in Canada, where it is honoured as the first wheeled aircraft ever to land at the North Pole.

17

Ex-Britannica

By the mid-1970s I was deep in the writing of a trilogy about the British Empire called Pax Britannica, *so that many of my travels took me to places where the British had once been rulers, gathering impressions from the present that would illuminate my evocations of the past. I went to most of the countries that had once been dominions of the Crown, in a project that took me, all in all, the whole decade to complete. Many publications financed my journeys, by commissioning articles from around the world.*

Singapore

In some ways the island colony of Singapore – 'the Lion City' – had been the most absolutely imperial possession of them all, because it had been created from scratch by Sir Stamford Raffles in 1819. It had also been one of the most tragic, because when the British surrendered the colony to the Japanese in 1942 it was the most disastrous blow to British arms in the entire history of the empire. By the 1970s Singapore was an independent republic of strikingly un-British temperament.

For the professional traveller there is nothing more agreeable than to reach a place that is altogether on its own, ramparted, defiant and sui generis. Such a place, like it or not, is undeniably the Republic of Singapore, the Lion City. It is like nowhere else. It lives adventurously. It is equally admired and detested. It glitters in the anticipation. It stands on the sea's edge, ostentatiously. It is the last of the city-states – or perhaps, gnomically speaking, the first.

No Florence, though, or Mantua. Flat, steamy, thickly humid, the island lies there in its hot seas, fringed with mangrove swamps, and from the air it looks a slightly desperate place that ought to be uninhabited. It looks an invented place, and so it is, for it was brought to life by the alchemy of empire.

For most Britons of a certain age, I suppose, Singapore remains Raffles's island to this day: but it is poignantly true that although no possession of the old empire was more dashingly acquired, romantically conceived, or successfully developed, still in historical terms Singapore remains a figure of all that was fustiest and snobbish in the colonial empire, all that went with baggy shorts and ridiculous moustaches, with servant problems and Sunday sing-songs at the Seaview, with tennis clubs and beer and meeting for elevenses at Robinson's – with everything that was most bourgeois about the declining empire, and in the end with everything that was most ineffectual. Singapore was the archetype of Somerset Maugham's empire, Noel Coward's empire – an empire that had lost its purpose, its confidence and its will: when it fell to the Japanese in 1942, in effect the empire fell too, and the idea of empire too.

When I landed in Singapore a homing instinct led me direct to the core of this dead colony, the downtown expanse of green called the Padang, and there without surprise I discovered that the imperial ghosts lived on. The last post-prandial members of the Singapore Cricket Club were still sitting with their gin-slings on the veranda, white linen hats over their eyes. There stood the spire of the Anglican cathedral, fretted but still handsome in its close, with small Anglican-looking cars parked outside its offices, and large Anglican-looking ladies coordinating arrangements in its porch. Ineffably conceited barristers, direct from Lincoln's Inn, adjusted their wing-collars or tilted their wigs beneath the colonnade of the Supreme Court: civil servants with briefcases hurried preoccupied into the great offices of government from whose windows, during a century of British rule, expatriate administrators looked out with pride or loathing across the tropic green.

Away to the west, over Anderson Bridge, the lumpish structures of imperial capitalism still breathed the spirit of the thirties, so that I half-expected to see Oxford bags and monocles emerging from revolving doors, or wives in pink cloche hats dropping in on Reggie. Away to the east stood the glorious palms of Raffles Hotel, that grand caravanserai of empire, the Shepheard's of the East, where the Maughams used to drink and the Cowards fizz; where the gin-sling was invented, where there was a Free Dark Room for Amateur Photographers, and Hotel Runners Boarded All Incoming Steamers, where Admiral Skrydloff and the Duke of Newcastle stayed, where generations of Malayan planters intrigued their leaves away, and not a few planters' wives began their tearful journeys home to mother. It is all there still, and the ethos of the dying empire, threadbare, raffish, gone to seed, well-meaning, lingers there forlornly.

It was from the Padang in 1942 that the humiliated colonialists and their wives, mustered by the Japanese, began their cruel march to Changi Prison and often to death: and if I closed my eyes, I thought, I could still hear their voices in the sunshine, courageous or querulous, insisting upon water for the dogs or bursting bravely into 'There'll Always Be An England'. The British Empire went out with a whimper, assiduously though we have disguised the fact even to ourselves, and in Singapore especially it faded away in pathos – or worse still, bathos, for the generals were second-rate, the songs were banal, the policies were ineffectual and even the courage was less than universal.

I find this mixture very moving – the imperial energies debased and enervated, like a very exclusive sport when the masses take it over. The good of empire, like the bad, depended upon force and the will to use it: by 1945 the British had lost that will for ever, and for that matter the force too.

On a masochistic impulse I determined to visit the exact spot where, on 15 February 1942, was sealed the fate of Singapore and thus of the British Empire – which Churchill himself, only a year or two before, had conjectured might last a thousand years. The Japanese had by then captured most of the island, but had only penetrated the outskirts of Singapore City. Short of fuel and ammunition, they were exerting their will upon the hapless British more by bluff than by superior power. They were on a winning streak, the British unmistakably upon a losing one: at seven o'clock that evening General Arthur Percival, wearing his steel helmet and long shorts, walked along the Bukit Timah road to meet General Tomoyuki Yamashita at the Ford Motor Company factory, and surrender Raffles's island to the Great East Asia Co-Prosperity Sphere.

The factory has not much changed since then. The buildings are still modest, low and rather drab, and the man at the gate still raises his barrier with that faintly military manner so characteristic of lesser functionaries under British colonial rule. Inside, the offices have been shifted around somewhat, and separated with glass partitions, and the room in which the surrender was signed has been divided into two. Nevertheless, they said, as they showed me into a fairly gloomy, wood-panelled and teak-furnished executive chamber, this was the very place where the surrender was signed. Even the furniture was the same. There sat Percival and his

three staff officers, hangdog and exhausted, hopelessly, almost obsequiously asking for more time. Here sat the bullish Yamashita in his medal
ribbons and open-necked shirt – 'All I want to know is, do you surrender
unconditionally or not? Yes or no?' The fans whirred heavily above their
heads, and as the sun began to set the dim electric lights came on: in the
long silences Percival stared helpless at his papers, Yamashita's fingers
drummed the table-top. Japanese war correspondents and military
photographers jostled all around the table, Yamashita's commanders sat
impassive beside him. I could see the tired eyes of the British officers,
flinching in the flare of the flashbulbs, as Percival accepted the terms with
a limp 'Yes', and the papers were signed – Yamashita in a bold flourish,
Percival in a cramped schoolboyish hand with what I would surmise to be
a 2s 6d fountain pen.

I felt ashamed to be there, and sorry, and I wished poor General Percival
happier campaigning in his afterlife – 'He looked so pale and thin and ill,'
said General Yamashita later, before they hanged him for his war crimes.
Did many British visitors come to see the room? I asked the Ford people. Not
very many, they said, very few in fact: but seldom a day went by without a
coach-load of Japanese tourists stopping at the factory gate, while their
guide pointed out the historic window, and the cameras clicked.

Hardly anybody in Singapore seems to think about history. The reason
for this is that though the Malays originally owned Singapore, the British
developed it and the Japanese conquered it, it was always the Chinese
who really ran it, providing most of the island's muscles, and much of its
brains. The Chinese are not habitually interested in the past, and the
result is that Singapore essentially lives for the day, and does not much
bother about history. The statues of Raffles and other imperial worthies
survive unmolested, but lacklustrely, as though nobody is quite sure who
they are: and the Singapore Museum, so painstakingly built up by the
imperialists, seems to have fallen into a genteel but unloved decline.

The Chineseness of Singapore is a quality of the overseas Chinese, and
thus stands to the central Chinese tradition, I suppose, rather as
Australianness stands to England. Three-quarters of Singapore citizens are
Chinese, and in effect this is a great Chinese city, one of the greatest.
Everything that is most vigorous about it is Chinese-sponsored, from the
skyscraper to the corner boutique, from the exquisite cuisine of the great
restaurants to the multitudinous eating-stalls which, miraculously as the
sun goes down, spring up in the streets and car parks of the city. It is actually

a fairly ordinary community of the overseas Chinese. It has the organic strength of the commonplace, and it feels absolutely inextinguishable, as though no natural calamity, no historical force, could ever wrest it from the island, or wrench the go-down capitalists from their abaci upon the quays.

It is no surprise that the president of this city-state, the man who has more or less single-handedly re-created it out of the collapse of the imperial idea, is the Chinese politician Lee Kuan Yew. It is not, I think, an attractive republic that he has devised, but it certainly has spirit. It is a tense, tight little state, with the same prickly and defensive excitement as Israel, say, or Iceland – a backs to the wall, let 'em all come, chips down excitement. It is a noisily opinionated little republic, strong on hand-outs, short on tact or sympathy – a harsh and cocky state, setting its own standards, choosing its own styles, and working so hard that its living standards are claimed to be the highest in Asia, excepting only Japan's.

Lee Kuan Yew believes that the whole state must be resolutely directed towards a kind of communal expertise. There is no time for argument. There is no room for dilettantism, nostalgia or party politics. Prosperity is the single aim of the state, and it can be retained only by rigorous discipline and specialization, under the unchallenged authority of an intelligent despotism. Political stability, reasons Lee Kuan Yew, equals foreign confidence, equals investment, equals money for all, which is all the average citizen wants of life and statesmanship.

In some ways this is a Puritan ethic, and both Cromwell and Mao would approve of many of Lee Kuan Yew's policies. Singapore is clean, relatively honest, apparently undecadent. Litter on the streets is savagely punished, drugs are mercilessly kept out, the rock culture is pointedly discouraged. Newspapers must toe the official line or disappear, and dissenting politicians too are apt to find themselves in trouble, or even prison. All this makes, of course, for the usual autocratic drabness. Nothing is more *boring* than a one-party state, and nothing is more dispiriting than to wake up at Raffles Hotel, settling down to papaya, toast and marmalade, and find that there is nothing to read but the *Straits Times*, a newspaper rather less outspoken than *Little Women*.

The great tourist experience of Singapore used to be a visit to Change Alley, the dark covered bazaar, hardly wide enough to stretch one's arms in, through whose gauntlet of Indian shopkeepers and money-changers generations of sailors and globe-trotters picked their bemused and gullible way. I did it once or twice for old times' sakes, stepping into the alley's shadows out of the glare and hustle of the quays, and enduring once more the immemorial banter of the bazaars, that leitmotiv of empire. 'You wanta change money? You want souvenirs? Where you from? You got dollars? You got pounds? Look here, very cheap – come and look, no need to buy, have a cup of coffee with my father!'

Nowadays, though, the excitement of Change Alley comes at the far end of it, where it debouches into Raffles Place. Half-way through I was tempted sometimes to think that nothing changes in the Orient after all, or ever will: but the moment I emerged from that clamorous trap, and saw as in fantasy the new towers of Singapore gleaming in the sunshine, then I knew I was seeing something new in the world: the twentieth-century city-state, within its island ramparts, brazen and self-assured. It was like emerging from a tunnel under the walls, to surface within some extra-territorial civilization where everything was shinier and brassier than life, and new kinds of people were genetically reared.

Let me out! I cried then in my waking dream. Let me out! Where's Reggie?

I wrote this piece for the now defunct London magazine Encounter, *which I later discovered to have been financed by the American CIA as part of a Cold War cultural offensive.*

Ceylon

Presently to be renamed Sri Lanka, Ceylon had played a far less significant role in British imperial history. The colonial style was deeply entrenched there, however, and it was one place in the old empire in which I had some personal stake – my partner in life had been born on the island.

At my window, a shiny-feathered crow; outside, an elderly steam locomotive sporadically snorting; palm trees in the yard, a glimpse of sea, the beginning of a heat haze, four or five distant swathed figures foraging upon the beach. The old electric fan above my head creaked protestingly every third time round. The servant who brought my breakfast shuffled comfortably about in sandals and called me 'Master'. There was a smell of eggs and bacon from below. I was awakening to a morning in Ceylon, from whose medieval name, Serendib, Horace Walpole derived the abstract noun *serendipity* – the faculty, as the *Oxford Dictionary* has it, 'of making happy and unexpected discoveries by accident'.

Not every Ceylonese discovery is happy, for this is an island that has seen better days, and has lately been depressed by addled politics and false finance. Unexpected, though, Ceylon certainly is – a fascinating anomaly of the Indian Ocean, a humped oval island not far north of the equator, with some of the most exquisite scenery in the world and a mountain so holy, to devotees of several religions, that even the agnostic butterflies hazily meander there, when they feel the death-urge coming on. A gently festive air seems to linger over the island, whatever the excesses of its politicians, and leaves in almost every visitor's mind an impression of balanced serenity.

In fact its history has been distinctly rumpled. The Hindu epics peopled Ceylon ferociously with demon-kings and monkey-armies, and in recorded times Indians, Portuguese, Dutchmen and Britons have all invaded the island, with varying degrees of penetration – until the British deposed it by force in 1815 there was still an independent dynasty of kings in the valleys of the interior. Hundreds of thousands of Indian Tamils have crossed the narrow strait to settle in Ceylon, and the island races have been so piquantly compounded that when I looked up the directors of a Ceylonese firm called Tuckers Ltd, I discovered that their names included Kotswala, Aloysius, Fernando and Mrs Mavis Tucker herself. Catholicism has been strong since the first European conquests, Hinduism thrives among the Tamils, and the clash and flare of the devil-dancers still enlivens the street corners of the island, and comforts its timorous villagers.

It is Buddhism, though, that sets the calm tone of Ceylon, and so differentiates it from the frenzied peninsula to the north. The sweet legends of the faith infuse the place and its gentleness still makes the start of a Ceylonese day, whatever the newspaper headlines are screaming, a pleasant prod to one's serendipity. The waiter put down my breakfast that morning, and said he hoped I would have an enjoyable day. I told him I was going to make a pilgrimage to the grave of my father-in-law, a planter who had died in Ceylon during the war.

'By God', he said at once, 'that's good, that's very good – parents is a bigger thing than the Lord Buddha himself,' and picking up my shoes, to clean them for the occasion, he bowed gracefully and withdrew.

The landscapes of Ceylon are overpoweringly varied – landscapes cruel, seductive, grand or intimate in turn, so intricately jammed together that in a morning's journey you can pass from jungle to alp to classic tropical foreshore. Bumpy pot-holed roads link these astonishingly disparate parts with one another. Slow rattly trains labour over impossible gradients. Doomed buses trundle from coast to coast. The package tour has scarcely reached Ceylon yet, the philosophies of tourism are not yet dominant, and the island still feels properly organic. ('Bank Closed' said a chalked blackboard notice when I went to cash a cheque one morning, 'On a/c Full Moon Day'.)

Sometimes the transitions are so abrupt that the colours clash, as though an interior decorator has botched the job, and the emotions of the island, too, are often fierce. The murder rate is among the highest on earth, though crime is nearly always un-premeditated, and is often fired by love or family feud. The clash of dry mountain air and equatorial humidity seems to make for inner resentments. The original Sinhalese resent the immigrant Tamils, the Buddhists resent the Hindus, each wing of every political party conspiratorially resents the other, and there are two Afro-Asian Solidarity Leagues.

The primitive streak is strong: drum beats on the night air, devil worship, queer straggled bands of forest aborigines still eking out, in a few hidden recesses of the island, their last years of the Dark Ages. Ceylon is so dense a country, so dovetailed, so ripe, that it will be generations before the technical civilization of the West finally swamps the place, and I know of nowhere comparably safe or comfortable where you may still feel so close to the gnarled roots of nature. If you have never seen monkeys outside a zoo, their presence along the highways of Ceylon is one of the most delightful experiences of modern travel: so exuberantly, divinely free do they look, as they leap the main road in a couple of bounds, or whisk their babies with merry elegance up a tree-trunk. If an elephant chiefly means to you only a sixpenny ride for the children, or a comic character in an animated cartoon, wait till you see one nobly manipulating logs in a Ceylonese teak forest, or best of all striding in wild grandeur, lordly and untamed, from one forest beat to another.

One can see such animals in greater numbers elsewhere, and in fiercer settings: the glory of Ceylon is that there they exist still in immediate neighbourhood to man himself, in an environment easily accessible and actually rather cramped. The fireflies that waver so haphazard through the shrubbery, as you drink your sundowner, are like friendly envoys from that other world beyond the suburbs, the world of the apes and the elephants: and I once drove five miles through a continuing wavering stream of yellow moths, whose antic progress across Ceylon was a reminder that a right of way is not the exclusive privilege of humans.

And proving this point majestically is the most celebrated of Ceylon's sights and surprises, the great ruined city of Sigiriya, which is frequented now, in its abandonment, by the wild creatures of the bush. In its hushed purlieus, alone and bee-infested in a desolate landscape of the north-east, the drama of Ceylon is enacted most excitingly of all.

Sigiriya, the Lion Rock, is a gaunt and immense column of granite, 400 feet high. It shows from many miles away, theatrically jutting out of a dun countryside, and at first sight seems only to be one of your geological freaks, like Ayers Rock in Australia, or the mushroom buttes of Arizona. But it is a historical freak as well. Fifteen centuries ago the young prince Kasyapa, coveting the throne of Ceylon, buried his father the king alive in a wall: but terrified of the revenge of his brother, who was in India, he set up his own usurping court on the rock at Sigiriya – literally on the rock, for living as he did in perpetual fear of his life, he built a fortress-palace on the very summit, approached by precipitous staircases up the granite, with an audience chamber up there, luxurious apartments, military quarters, water storage tanks and even elephant stables. There the parricide king, his courtiers and his courtesans, lived insulated high above in maniac asylum.

The rock may still be climbed, and in a gallery half-way are the celebrated Sigiriya frescoes, erotic portraits of half-nude women, full-bosomed and heavily jewelled, whom some authorities have assumed to be Buddhist vestals, and others women of royal pleasure. Up you go, clutching the iron railings erected in a less hell-for-leather age, and between the enormous sculpted lion's feet which have given the place its name, up staircase after staircase, through gallery upon gallery, until at last you emerge upon the flat surface of the rock. It is about an acre square, terraced still with the remains of the madman's palace, and at your feet the scrub-land of Ceylon lies empty and unchanged. The hostile world feels impotent indeed, seen from such an eastern Berchtesgaden, and Kasyapa survived up there for eighteen years: but in the end his brother came, and he killed himself while the going was good.

Serendipity! Not always happy, but never failing to surprise. You remember the waiter who brought my breakfast near the beginning of this essay? When he had left the room I hastened to fetch my notebook, to record his observations word for word: but while I was away from the breakfast table, that damned crow flapped in through the window, and stole a slice of toast.

Darjeeling

Darjeeling was a very imperial relic, a hill-resort of the British Raj in India, miraculously preserved. It was proper that I should write this essay for the magazine of the late British Overseas Airways Corporation, BOAC, whose very name now is almost as nostalgic as that of its progenitor Imperial Airways, or for that matter of the Raj itself.

Darjeeling, the most celebrated of the Indian hill stations, is all smallness. It is small physically, of course – hard even to find upon the map of India, so tucked away is it like a trinket on the northern frontiers. But it is still smaller figuratively. It is the most deliberately diminutive town I know, as though it is always trying to make itself less substantial still. One crosses vast scorched plains to reach it from Calcutta, over colossally winding rivers, through a landscape that has no end: but at the foot of the hills Darjeeling sends a toy train to meet you, a gay little blue-painted trundle of a train which takes you indefatigably puffing and chugging up through the forests and the tea-gardens to the town.

Little people greet you at the top. Little ponies canter about little streets. Hundreds and thousands of merry little children tumble all around you. The town is perched upon a narrow ridge, about 7,000 feet up, with deep gorges falling away on either side, and when I arrived there for the first time I found it swirled all around by cloud. It felt curiously private and self-contained – like a childish fancy, I thought, a folly, a town magically reduced in scale and shut off from the world by vapour: but then as to a crash of drums in a *coup de théâtre*, a gap momentarily appeared in the ever-shifting clouds, and there standing tremendously in the background, their snows flushed pink with sunlight, attended by range upon range of foothills and serenely surveying the expanse of the world, stood the divine mass of the Himalayan mountains.

I saw Darjeeling's point, and cut myself down to size.

Some visitors never see the snow-peaks at all, for they are often invisible for days at a time. Anyway there is no need to go on about them. It is enough to say that to see Kanchenjunga and its peers from Darjeeling, in the cool of the morning, is one of the noblest experiences of travel. It is a kind of vision. It has moved generations of pilgrims to mysticism, and even more to over-writing.

Yet it is not the spectacle of the Himalayas that sets the style of Darjeeling. It is simply their presence. The town lives in the knowledge of them, and so acknowledges another scale of things. Its littleness is not inferiority complex, but self-awareness, and it gives the community a particular intensity and vivacity. Darjeeling is built in layers, neatly along its ridge like an exhibition town, from the posh hotels and the villas at the top to the jumbled bazaar quarter at the bottom: and all the way down this dense tiered mass of buildings life incessantly buzzes, hums and fizzes. Darjeeling's energies seem to burn the brighter for their smallness, and not a corner of the town is still, or empty, or dull.

It is a place of astonishing cheerfulness. Everybody seems to be feeling simply splendid. Perhaps they all are, for the air is magnificently brilliant, the heat is seldom too hot and the cold not often icy. The nineteenth-century Welshman who first put Darjeeling on the map saw it from the start as a sanatorium, and the Rajah of Sikkim kindly handed it over to the British Governor-General of India 'for the purpose of enabling the servants of his government suffering from sickness to avail themselves of its advantages'. Today Darjeeling's high spirits never seem to flag. The children never stop playing, the youths never end their horse-play, the tourists never tire of clattering hilariously about the town on hired ponies. The cicadas sing all day long in the gardens, and ever and again from down the hill come the hoots and puffs of the little trains (which prefer to travel gregariously, and come merrily up from Siliguri two or three at a time).

To the stranger it all seems intenser, more concentrated than real life, and especially after dark, when the braziers are aglow in the alleys of the bazaar, and the hotel lights comfortably shine above. Then half Darjeeling turns out for a stroll at Chaurasta, a triangular piazza half-way along the ridge, and on my own first evening in Darjeeling I went and sat on a bench there, and watched the town go by. Beyond the square the ridge fell away abruptly into the night, and there were only the dark foothills out there, and a suggestion of the snowpeaks, and the stars that now and then appeared in unnatural brilliance through the shifting clouds.

To and fro against this celestial backdrop the people of Darjeeling loitered, strolled and gossiped like Spaniards on their evening promenade, or more exotic Venetians at St Mark's. There were tall flashing girls in saris and nose-clips. There were brown gnome-like men in fur caps. There were slant-eyed children of astonishing beauty, and boys with wild eager faces like Genghis Khan. There were monks, and priests, and soldiers, and grand Indian gentlemen in tweeds, and giggly Indian girls in cotton party frocks. There were mountain porters hastening back from work, carrying rucksacks and tent-poles. There were ancient men with plaited pigtails. There were two hippies, and a nun, and four French tourists, and me watching it all, as in hallucination, from a bench beside the bandstand.

It was like a microcosm of the world, assembled up there from the plains and mountains, ushered into that little square, reduced to a neater and more manageable size, and given double shots of adrenalin.

'What is your country?' a man peremptorily demanded, as we met face to face and unavoidably on a narrow hill track, and when I told him Wales, to the west of England, he asked further: 'Is it a high pass to get there?'

Unimaginably high are the passes, indescribably remote the valleys, from which in the century since Captain Lloyd founded Darjeeling the population of the town has found its way to the ridge. This is a frontier settlement. Some of those snow-peaks are in India proper, some in Sikkim and Bhutan, some in the Kingdom of Nepal, some in the People's Republic of Tibet. The town stands on the edge of mysteries, and its people have migrated from many parts of the eastern Himalaya, and from the plains below. The old sanatorium of the memsahibs is far more nowadays: not merely a celebrated resort, but an important bazaar, a centre of local government and a kind of ethnic demonstration.

No little town in the world can show more kinds, and types, and manners of people. The little Lepchas, the original inhabitants of the region, are seldom more than five feet high, but immensely strong and agile. The Sherpas from eastern Nepal, the high-altitude porters of Everest and Kanchenjunga, move with an inexorable striding impetus, as though they can't stop. The Tibetans often look immensely sophisticated, trendy almost, ready for any Chelsea discotheque with their flared pants and impeccable complexions. The Gurkhas look soldiers through and through, always marching, even off parade, with head high and chest out. One sees few sleepy or dullard faces among these Mongoloid peoples of the north: all seem eminently capable – straight square-set people, who look as though, deposited in a Brooklyn back-alley or one of the remoter villages of the southern Urals, they would instantly find their feet.

But they are only one element in the Darjeeling melange. There are many other kinds of Nepalese, for instance – Gurungs, Magars, Tamangs, Newars. There are refugees from Tibet proper, and Indian Army soldiers from the Punjab and Rajasthan. Here comes a slim dark girl in blue pyjamas, who might be Annamese, or perhaps Malay. Here are four Rajput officers of the garrison, with their thin black Sandhurst moustaches and their suede boots. The Hindu holy man beside the lane is smeared mysteriously with yellow ochre. The Bengali family being hoisted on to its ponies is all guileless anticipation, proud young father holding the baby (who wears a pink peaked cap with yellow velvet ribbons), mother in gold and red sari assiduously combing the already immaculate hair of a small boy apparently dressed for an exceptionally extravagant wedding. The eyes that peer at you between bushy beard and bundled turban are, of course, the eyes of a Sikh: the shy porcelain smile from the lady at the next table is a smile from the palm trees and sands of Madras.

In the autumn they have races at Darjeeling, and then one may see this demographic jumble at its most cheerful. The racecourse is endearingly claimed to be the smallest in the world: at the end of a race the competitors run breakneck off the course into the approach road, an unnerving experience for newcomers. The meetings are not very formal. Young men play football in the middle of the track. Between races the horses graze casually on grassy spaces round about. A dribble of racegoers stumbles down the mountain track from the town above, carrying umbrellas and race cards, and a stream of jeeps and rattly taxis blasts its way along the motor-road.

Still, the traditional procedures are honoured. The races are run by the Gymkhana Club of Darjeeling, and in the official stand the stewards and judges, mostly army officers, sit in well-cut elegance with immensely superior ladies. Sometimes the senior steward takes a stroll about the enclosure, moving with the lordly benevolence common to racing bigwigs from Longchamps to Kentucky Downs. The race card is printed with every refinement of the racegoer's jargon and the rules are, of course, severe ('Trainers and Jockeys are hereby notified that Riotous Behaviour, Intemperance, or other Improper Conduct, although not occurring on the Race Course, will be taken cognizance of by the Stewards'). It would take an iconoclast indeed to defy the decrees of the Darjeeling Gymkhana Club.

The bell rings; the flag drops; hurtling around the track in billows of dust come three or four little Tibetan ponies, ridden at desperate speed and with savage concentration by fierce little high-cheeked jockeys – brilliantly liveried in scarlets and yellows, visors low over their eyes – rocketing around that little track, as the crowd rises tip-toe with excitement, until they shoot out of sight, with cheers, laughter and catcalls, behind the grandstand and off the course. It is as though the scouts of Attila have passed through. The stranger may feel a certain sense of shock, but the stewards do not seem disconcerted. 'Jolly good show,' they say to each other. 'Hell of a good race, what?'

For the most dogmatic progressive will not deny to little Darjeeling a tug of nostalgia. It is harmless. It is only a fragrance of earlier times, a Victorian bouquet still lingering up here along the ridge. Darjeeling is largely built in that gabled semi-chalet style so dear to Victorian pleasure-seekers, and imposed upon its gallimaufry of peoples is a decorous, poke-bonnet, tea-and-biscuits style. Nobody in their senses would wish it otherwise. It is an essential part of Darjeeling's minuscule mystique, and used to suggest to me a musical-box town, where pretty little melodies would tinkle in the sunshine, while clockwork figures in top hats and bustles jerkily proceeded along the Mall. The very names of the place carry this old evocation – the Esplanade, a Happy Valley, Step Aside – and the main road to the plains is still known in Darjeeling as the Cart Road.

Some of the hotels are deliciously Victorian. The porridge at the Windamere [sic] Hotel is, I am told by unimpeachable authorities, unsurpassed in Scotland, while the tea at the Mount Everest is tea, my dear, just like we used to have it. Shopping in Darjeeling, too, is agreeably old-school. Patiently attentive are the assistants, instantly to hand is the chair for memsahib, and one almost expects to find, winging it across the Kashmiri shawls and the Tibetan prayer-wheels, one of those wire-pulley change receptacles one used to see in provincial English drapers' long ago.

Most of Darjeeling's pleasures (I except the illicit joys of the bazaar quarter) would perfectly satisfy our grandparents. There is the classic pleasure, for instance, which I abstemiously denied myself, of getting up at three in the morning to see the sunrise and the top of Everest from Tiger Hill. There are the pleasures of Excursions to Places of Interest, like Ghoom Rock or Kaventer's Dairy Farm. There are the pleasures of identifying wild flowers and trees, or sketching, or looking at animals in the outdoor zoo (where the Llama and the Siberian Tiger, returning one's inspection morosely from their enclosures, look as though they wish the Victorian era had never dawned). There are pony-rides, of course, and there is miniature golf, and when I was there *Ruddigore* was being performed by the pupils of St Paul's School.

Above all there is the pleasure of walking. In most of Darjeeling no cars are allowed, and this is one of the walkingest towns on earth. One may walk decorously around the town itself, or through the Botanical Gardens. One may walk into the foothills for a picnic. Or one may, stacking up with tinned pineapple and sleeping bags, engage a team of Sherpas and stride off into the distant mountains. Every year more and more people go trekking from Darjeeling, and a very healthy pastime it must be. 'No place like Darjeeling,' one stalwart matron reproachfully observed as, staggering beneath the weight of her accoutrements, she passed me doing nothing in particular over a glass of lemonade – 'nowhere like Darjeeling for blowing the cobwebs away!'

As I say, our grandparents would have loved it: and sometimes Darjeeling's scrapbook essence can be, to the sentimental visitor, distinctly moving. On Jalapahar Hill, at the eastern end of the ridge, there is a small military cantonment, complete with parade ground, garrison church and shops for the soldiery. I was once walking through this camp, enjoying its display of the military aesthetic – polished brass, regimental signs in whitewashed pebbles, the clump of ammunition boots and the bristle of sergeantly moustaches – when an unexpected sound reached me from the parade ground behind. With a slow and melancholy introductory wail, the Gurkha pipe band broke into the sad, sad music of a Highland lament. I stopped dead in my dusty tracks, and the tears came to my eyes: for what generations of my own people, I thought, had stirred to that music in their exiles long ago, and how strange and sweet and lonely it sounded in these hills of the Indian frontier!

'Can I help you?' inquired a passer-by, seeing me standing there. 'You are not ill?' Not ill, I assured him as I moved on up the hill. Only susceptible!

Every morning before breakfast I used to walk up Observatory Hill. This wooded hump, rising directly above the Chaurasta, is holy to the Buddhists, who have a shrine upon its summit. All along the steep and winding path to the top mendicants invite the contributions of the pious – grave holy men who bow like archbishops, jolly old crones, coveys of chirpy inquisitive children. Two grinning stone lions guard the entrance to the holy compound, the trees are hung all over with white prayer flags, and mysteriously from the recesses of the shrine one may hear the incessant murmur of prayers and tinkling of bells. There are always people up there.

Some are praying, some meditating, some reading sacred scripts, and one I met each day used to stand all alone among the bushes looking towards Tibet and writing in a large black notebook.

If the weather is clear there is a glorious view of Kanchenjunga and its peers, and while they were cooking my eggs in the hotel down below I used to sit on the grass alone and marvel at the immunity of Darjeeling. It has, it seemed to me, *escaped*. It knows its own dimension, and is satisfied. Though its name is famous everywhere, still it remains a small town of the Himalayan foothills, very close to the soil and the temple. There is material squalor enough, but seldom I think despair, still less degradation. The loads may be crippling, but still the porters find the energy to smile. The children and the chickens may be in and out of the kitchen, but the mothers never seem to get cross. The girls laugh as they laboriously chop firewood in the thickets, and the bundles of hay piled upon the backs of the labourers are speckled all over with flowers of pink and blue.

It is as though by an unconscious exertion of values Darjeeling has selected what it wants from the world below, and rejected all the rest. One feels better and kinder for a visit to Darjeeling. Those stupendous mountains in the clouds have set the scale right, and adjusted the balance. It's no good fussing, they seem to say. It can't last. And this sententious thought, which occurred to me every morning after ten minutes or so upon the hill, used to remind me that my eggs were waiting for me down the lane – and down I would hurry, past that merry line of beggars, tagged by swarms of children and encouraged by avuncular sages, to where the waiter in his red turban and his polished brass badge, looking anxiously from the dining-room door, was waiting to whisk the cover off my porridge.

During my stay in Darjeeling I often saw a young American dressed in the habit of a Buddhist monk. He was studying at a nearby seminary, I was told, and wore the brown cloak, the sandals and the hair-bun as to the manner born. Nobody appeared the least surprised by this anomalous figure, and even his father, who was paying him a visit from the States, seemed entirely at home with the phenomenon. 'I'm going to drink, Jimmy,' I heard him saying to his son one day, puffing at his cigar and raising his glass, 'I'm going to drink to all these wonderful, wonderful people of Dar-jeeling!' (And 'Say,' he tactfully added as he put his glass down, rather hastily I thought, 'is this Indian wine? Delicious!')

Many years later I was back at the Windamere in Darjeeling making a television film, with my son Twm and a cosmopolitan Welsh, English and Polish crew. When we left I wrote a grateful poem in the hotel's visitors' book, and I am honoured to learn that it is now framed upon a wall.

Delhi

The greatest of all the post-imperial destinations was Delhi, the mighty seat of British dominion in India, which had been the headquarters of countless dynasties before, and was now the capital of the largest demo-cratic republic on earth. I wrote this essay for the New York magazine Rolling Stone.

'You see,' said the government spokesman, 'you may liken Delhi to the River Ganges, it twists and turns, many other streams join it, it divides into many parts, and it flows into the sea in so many channels that nobody may know which is the true river. You follow my train of thought? It is a meta-physical matter, perhaps. You will do best to burrow under the surface of things and discover what is not revealed to us ordinary mortals! In the meantime, you will take a cup of tea, I hope?'

I took a cup of tea, milkless, very sweet, brought by a shuffling messen-ger in a high-buttoned jacket with a scarf around his neck, and between pleasantries I pondered the spokesman's advice. Indians, of course, love to reduce the prosaic to the mystic. It is part of their Timeless Wisdom. For several centuries the tendency has variously baffled, infuriated, amused and entranced travellers from the West, and India is full of pilgrims come from afar to worship at the shrines of insight. But *Delhi*? Delhi is not just a national capital, it is one of the political ultimates, one of the prime movers. It was born to power, war and glory. It rose to greatness not because holy men saw visions there but because it commanded strategic routes from the north-west, where the conquerors came from, into the rich flatlands of the Ganges delta. Delhi is a soldiers' town, a politicians' town, a journalists', diplomats' town. It is Asia's Washington, though not so pic-turesque, and lives by ambition, rivalry and opportunism.

'Ah yes,' he said, 'what you are thinking is quite true, but that is the *surface* of Delhi. You are an artist, I know, you should look *beyond*! And if there is anything we can do to help your inquiries,' he added, with an engaging waggle of his head, 'you have only to let us know. You may telephone us at any time and we will ring you back with requisite information in a moment or two. We are here to help! That is why we are here! No, no, that is our duty!'

Certainly Delhi is unimaginably antique, and age is a metaphysic, I suppose. Illustrations of mortality are inescapable there, and do give the place a sort of nagging symbolism. Tombs of emperors stand beside traffic junctions, forgotten fortresses command suburbs, the titles of lost dynasties are woven into the vernacular, if only as street names.

Delhi is scarcely an innocent city, for on every layer it is riddled with graft and intrigue, but it is distinctly organic, to an atavistic degree. An apposite introduction to the city, I think, is provided by Map Eight of the *Delhi City Atlas*, which marks a substantial slab of the municipal area as being Dense Jungle: though this is now a city of a million inhabitants, it feels near the bush still. From many parts of it the open plain is in sight, and the country trees of India, the feathery tamarisks and ubiquitous acacias, invade every part of it – the animals too, for squirrels are everywhere and monkeys, buffaloes, cows, goats and a million pi-dogs roam the city streets peremptorily.

There is simplicity everywhere, too, for rural people from all India flock into Delhi for jobs, for help, to see the sights. There are Sikhs and sleek Bengalis, Rajputs ablaze with jewellery, smart Gujaratis from the western coast, beautiful Tamils from the south, cloaked Tibetans smelling of untanned leather, clerks from Bombay smelling of aftershave, students, wandering sages, clumping soldiers in ammunition boots, black-veiled Muslim women, peasants in for the day from the scorched and desiccated Punjab plains. Endearingly they trail through their national monuments, awe-struck, and the attendants intone their monologues hoping for tips, and the tourist buses line up outside the Presidential Palace, and the magicians prepare their levitations and inexplicable disappearances in the dusty ditch below the ramparts of the Red Fort.

Delhi is a city of basic, spontaneous emotions: greed, hate, revenge, love, pity, kindness, the murderous shot, the touch of the hand. Its very subtleties are crude: even its poverty is black and white. On the one side are the organized beggar children who, taught to murmur a few evocative words of despair like 'hungry', 'baby' or 'mummy', succeed all too often in snaring the susceptible stranger. On the other are the courtly thousands of the jagghis, the shanty towns of matting, tentage and old packing cases which cling like black growths to the presence of Delhi.

The voice of the people, Gandhi used to say, is the voice of God. I doubt it, but I do recognize a divine element to the Indian poverty, ennobled as it is by age and sacrifice. Indians rationalize it by the concept of reincarnation, and I see it too as a half-way condition, a station of the cross. 'In the next world,' I suggested to my driver after a long and exhausting journey into the country, 'I'll be driving and you'll be lying on the back seat,' but he answered me with a more elemental philosophy. 'In the next world,' he replied, 'we'll *both* be lying on the back seat!' For even the inegality of Delhi, even the pathos, often has something robust to it, a patient fatalism that infuriates many modernists but is a solace to people like me. It is disguised often in Eastern mumbo- jumbo, preached about in ashrams to gullible Californians and exploited by swamis from the divine to the absurd: but it is really no more than a kindly acceptance of things as they are, supported by the sensible thesis that things are not always what they appear to be.

But pathos, yes. Delhi is the capital of the losing streak. It is the metropolis of the crossed wire, the missed appointment, the puncture, the wrong number. Every day's paper in Delhi brings news of some new failure, in diplomacy, in economics, in sport. While I was there I developed an unsightly boil in my nose, and the side of my face swelled up like a huge bunion. In this condition, self-consciously, I continued my investigations, and at first I was touched by the tact with which Indians in the streets pretended not to notice. After a day or two, though, I realized that the truth was more affecting still. They *really* did not notice. They thought my face quite normal. For what is a passing grotesquerie, in a land of deformities?

'Certainly,' said the government spokesman, perusing my list of questions, 'by all means, these are all very simple matters. We can attend to them for you at once. As I told you, it is our duty! It is what we are paid for! I myself have to attend an important meeting this afternoon – you will excuse me, I hope? – but I will leave all these little matters with our good Mrs Gupta and all will be taken care of. I will telephone with the answers myself without fail – or if not I myself, then Mrs Gupta will be sure to telephone you either today or tomorrow morning. Did you sign our register? A duplicate signature here if you would not mind, and the lady at the door will issue you with the requisite application form for a pass – it will make everything easier for you, you see. Have no fear, Mrs Gupta will take care of everything. But mark my words, you will find the spiritual aspects of our city the most rewarding. Remember the River Ganges! As a student of history, you will find that I am right! Ha ha! Another cup of tea? You have time?'

Even he would agree, though, that the spiritual aspect is hardly predominant in New Delhi, the headquarters of the Indian government and seat of Indian sovereignty – the newest and largest of Delhi's successive capitals. This was built *by* the British, and despite one or two sententious symbolisms and nauseating texts – *Liberty will Not Descend to a People, A People Must Raise Themselves* to *Liberty* – it is a frank and indeed noble memorial to their own imperial Raj. It is not anomalous even now. For one thing it was built in a hybrid style of East and West to take care of all historical contingencies, and for another, Britishness is far from dead in Delhi. Delhi gentlemen, especially of the sporting classes, are stupendously British still. Delhi social events can be infinitely more English than Ascot or Lord's.

Seen early on a misty morning from far down the ceremonial mall, Rajpath, New Delhi is undeniably majestic – neither Roman, its architects said, nor British, nor Indian, but *imperial*. Then its self-consciousness (for its mixture of styles is very contrived) is blurred by haze and distance and by the stir of awakening Delhi – the civil servants with their bulging briefcases, the multitudinous peons, the pompous early-morning policemen, the women sweepers elegant in primary colours, the minister perhaps (if it is not *too* early) in his chauffeur-driven, Indian-built limousine, the stocky Gurkha sentries at the palace gates, the first eager tourists from the Oberoi Intercontinental, the entertainer with his dancing monkeys, the snake charmer with his acolyte children, the public barber on the pavement outside Parliament, the women preparing their washing beside the ornamental pools, the man in khaki who, approaching you fiercely across the formal gardens, asks if you would care for a cold drink.

Then the power of India, looming above these dusty complexities, is unmistakable: not only created but instinctive, sensed by its foreign rulers as by its indigenous, and aloof to history's permutations. Of all the world's countries, India is the most truly prodigious, and this quality of astonishment displays itself afresh every day as the sun comes up in Delhi. Five hundred and eighty million people, 300 languages, provinces from the Himalayan to the equatorial, cities as vast as Bombay and Calcutta, villages so lost in time that no map marks them, nuclear scientists and aboriginal hillmen, industrialists of incalculable wealth and dying beggars sprawled on railway platforms, three or four great cultures, myriad religions, pilgrims from across the world, politicians sunk in graft, the Grand Trunk Road marching to Peshawar, the temples of Madras gleaming in the sun, an inexhaustible history, an incomprehensible social system, an unfathomable repository of human resource, misery, ambiguity, vitality and confusion – all this, the colossal corpus of India invests, sprawls around, infuses, elevates, inspires and very nearly overwhelms New Delhi.

Nehru said that modern Western civilization was ersatz, living by ersatz values, eating ersatz food: but the ruling classes of Delhi, the politicians, the businessmen, the military, have mostly adopted those values without shame. Gandhi said that his India would have 'the smallest possible army', but Delhi is one of the most military of all capitals: when I looked up some friends in the Delhi telephone book, I found that under the name Khanna there were four generals, an air commodore, twelve colonels, a group captain, twelve majors, three wing commanders, four captains, one commander, three lieutenant commanders and a lieutenant.

As it happens, I am rather an addict of power. I do not much enjoy submitting to it or even exerting it, but I do like observing it. I like the aesthetics of it, coloured as they so often are by pageantry and history. I am everybody's patriot, and love to see the flags flying over palace or parliament, Westminster or Quai d'Orsay. Somehow, though, I do not respond to the old magic in India. The British, rationalizing their own love of imperial pomp, used to claim that it was necessary to retain the respect of Asiatics. It availed them nothing, though, against the 'half-naked fakir', as Churchill called Gandhi, and now too the magnificence of Delhi seems paradoxically *detached* from India. How remote the great ensigns which, enormously billowing above their embassies in the diplomatic enclave, testify to the presence of the plenipotentiaries! How irrelevant the posturings of the grandees, hosts and guests alike, the Polish Defence Minister greeted by epauletted generals, the Prince of Wales inevitably winning his polo match, the resident Congress Party spokesman puffed at one press conference, the visiting Minister of National Reorientation condescending at the next.

And most detached of all seems the unimaginable bureaucracy of Delhi, battening upon the capital – a power sucker, feeding upon its own conse-quence or sustained intravenously by interdepartmental memoranda, triplicate applications, copies and comments and addenda and references to precedent – a monstrous behemoth of authority, slumped immovable among its files and tea-trays. Much of it is not concerned with practical reality at all but with hypotheses or dogma. Forty government editors are engaged in producing the collected works of Gandhi, down to the last *pensée* – they have got to volume 54. Hundreds more are concerned with plans, for there was never a capital like Delhi for planners. Big Brother is everywhere, with a slide rule, a clipboard and warning in small print. 'This map,' says one Delhi tourist publication severely, 'is published for tourists as a master guide and *not as legal tender*' – and there, in its mixture of the interfering, the pedantic, the unnecessary and the absurd, speaks the true voice of Indian officialdom.

There is a species of telephone operators' English, often heard in Delhi, which is not exactly an articulated language at all, but a sort of elongated blur. Indian English proper, of course, is one of India's cruellest handicaps, for it is so often imperfect of nuance and makes for an unreal relationship between host and visitor, besides often making highly intelligent people look foolish ('Chinese Generals Fly Back to Front', said a celebrated Indian headline long ago). But the elliptical, slithery kind is something else again, and has another effect on its hearers. It makes one feel oddly opaque or amorphous oneself, and seems to clothe the day's arrangements in a veil of uncertainty.

This is proper. One should not go fighting into Delhi, chin up and clear eyed. Here hopes are meant to wither and conceptions adjust. A single brush with a noseless beggar is enough to change your social values. Just one application for an import licence will alter your standards of efficiency. After a while graver mutations may occur, and you will find yourself questioning the Meaning of It All, the Reality of Time and other old Indian specialties. 'You will see, you will see!' Most disconcerting of all, you may well come to feel that the pomp and circumstance of Delhi, which struck you at first as illusory display, is in fact the only reality of the place. All the rest is mirage! Everything else in the Indian presence, north, east, south, west, across the Rajasthani deserts, down to the Coromandel beaches, far away to the frontiers of Tibet, everything else is suggestion, never to be substance.

Preoccupied with its own diurnal round of consequence and command, Delhi is paradoxically protected against the dust storm of controversy, threat and misfortune that hangs always, dark and ill-defined, over the Indian horizons. That blur or slither of Delhi, which begins as a mystery and develops into an irritation, becomes in the end a kind of reassurance. After trying three times, you give up gratefully. After expostulating once or twice, it is a pleasure to accede. You think you can change the system? Try it, try it, and when the elaborations of Delhi have caught up with you, when you realize the tortuous significances of the old method, when it has been explained to you that only Mrs Gupta is qualified to take the money, that Mr Mukerjee is prevented by custom from working beside Mr Mukhtar Singh and that Mr Mohammed will not of course be at work on Fridays, when it dawns upon you gradually that it has been done more or less this way, come conqueror, come liberation, since the early Middle Ages, with a relieved and affectionate smile you will probably agree that perhaps it had better be left as it is.

As it is! India is always as it is! I never despair in Delhi, for I feel always all around me the fortification of a profound apathy. The capital is essentially apathetic to the nation: the nation is aloof to the capital. By the end of the century there will be, at the present rate of increase, nearly 1,000 million people in India, and I think it very likely that there will have been a revolution of one complexion or another. But the traveller who returns to Delhi then will find the city much the same, I swear, will respond to much the same emotions, indulge in just the same conjectures, bog down in just the same philosophical quagmires, and reach, if he is anything like me, about the same affectionate and inconclusive conclusions.

'You see? You see? Did I not say so? You are thinking metaphysically, as I foretold!' Well, perhaps. But the government spokesman proved his point better himself, for neither he nor Mrs Gupta ever did ring.

18

Casablanca: A Change of Sex

In 1974 I published a book, Conundrum, *about my lifelong conviction that I had been born into the wrong sex, and about my eventual change of sexual role. This had been gradually happening for some ten years, under the influence of hormone treatment, and it had culminated in 1972 with surgery in a clinic run by a Dr B. at Casablanca, Morocco. The book was intensely personal, of course, but did perhaps have some wider significance as a symptom of the more liberated sexual ethics emerging in what was later to be called, generally disparagingly, the Permissive Age. I did not know Dr B.'s address, but when I arrived in Casablanca I looked him up in the telephone book, and was told to come round to his clinic next afternoon. So I had time to wander about the town.*

As a city Casablanca is something less than romantic, being mostly modern, noisy and ugly in a pompous French colonial way. The experience I was to have there, though, struck me then as it strikes me now as romantic to a degree. It really was like a visit to a wizard. I saw myself, as I walked that evening through those garish streets, as a figure of fairy tale, about to be transformed. Duck into swan? Scullion into bride? More magical than any such transformation, I answered myself: man into woman. This was the last city I would ever see as a male. The office blocks might not look much like castle walls, nor the taxis like camels or carriages, but still I sometimes heard the limpid Arab music, and smelt the pungent Arab smells, that had for so long pervaded my life, and I could suppose it to be some city of fable, of phoenix and fantasy, in which transubstantiations were regularly effected, when the omens were right and the moon in its proper phase.

I called upon the British Consul in the morning. It occurred to me that I might die in the course of changing my sex, and I wanted him to let people know. He did not seem surprised. Always best, he said, to be on the safe side.

* * *

The clinic was not as I imagined it. I had rather hoped for something smoky in the bazaar, but it turned out to be in one of the grander modern parts of the city, one entrance on a wide boulevard, the other on a quiet residential back street. Its more ordinary business was gynaecology of one sort and another, and as I waited in the ante-room, reading *Elle* and *Paris Match* with a less than absolute attention, I heard many natal sounds, from the muffled appeals of all-too-expectant mothers to the anxious pacings of paternity. Sometimes the place was plunged in utter silence, as Dr B. weighed somebody's destiny in his room next door: sometimes it broke into a clamour of women's Arabic, screechy and distraught somewhere down the corridor. At last the receptionist called for me, and I was shown into the dark and book-lined presence of the maestro.

He was exceedingly handsome. He was small, dark, intense of feature, and was dressed as if for some kind of beach activity. He wore a dark blue open-necked shirt, sports trousers and games shoes, and he was very bronzed. He welcomed me with a bemused smile, as though his mind were in St Tropez. He asked what he could do for me. I told him I thought he probably knew very well. 'Ah, I think that's so. You wish the operation. Very well, let us see you.' He examined my organs. He plumped my breasts – '*Très, très bons.*' He asked if I was an athlete. 'Very well,' he said, 'come in this evening, and we shall see what we can do. You know my fee? Ah well, perhaps you will discuss it with my receptionist – *bien, au revoir*, until this evening!'

I paid the money, all in advance, and I signed the usual form absolving Dr B. from any responsibility if he happened to make a mess of it, and clutching my suitcase and a copy of that morning's *Times*, for I was not beaten yet, an hour later I was led along corridors and up staircases into inner premises of the clinic. The atmosphere thickened as we proceeded. The rooms became more heavily curtained, more velvety, more voluptuous. Portrait busts appeared, I think, and there was a hint of heavy perfume. Presently I saw, advancing upon me through the dim alcoves of this retreat, which distinctly suggested to me the allure of a harem, a figure no less recognizably odalisque. It was Madame B. She was dressed in a long white robe, tasselled I think around the waist, which subtly managed to combine the luxuriance of a caftan with the hygiene of a nurse's uniform, and she was blonde herself, and carefully mysterious. She talked in a dreamy way, and was anxious to confirm that I had signed the travellers' cheques. It was a lot of money, I ventured to murmur. 'A lot of money! What would you have? He is a great surgeon, one of the great surgeons! What could you do,' she theatrically demanded, throwing out her white arms like a celebrant, 'if this great surgeon could not operate on you?' Go home to England, I said, and get it done there – 'But let us not talk about the money,' she interrupted hastily, and sweeping me into her ambience she opened a small door set in a corner of what appeared to be her salon, and led the way down a spiral staircase. Instantly the atmosphere changed again. In the private quarters all had been shimmer and Chanel: down here, as we emerged into the corridor beneath, it was all clinical austerity. It was like going from the seraglio to the eunuch's quarters, not a bad simile I thought at the time.

It is true that the room numbers were painted on flowered enamel, the colour scheme was pinkish, and in the corridor there stood a baby's crib, ribboned and cushioned. But an air of stern purpose informed the place, for these were the operating quarters. There was the operating theatre itself, said Madame, gesturing towards a mercifully closed door, 'And even now,' she thrillingly added, 'at this moment an American is under surgery. My husband works always.' She opened the door of No. 5, the end room in the corridor, and bidding me a soft but frosty good night, for she was offended I think about the money, left me to my fate.

It was dark by now, and the room was uninviting. Its lighting was dim, its floor was less than scrupulously clean, and its basin, I soon discovered, never had hot water. Outside the window I could hear a faint rumble of traffic, and more precise street noises from the alley below. Inside the clinic seemed to be plunged into a permanent silence, as though I was shut away and insulated from all other life – not far from the truth, either, for the bell did not work, and there was no other patient on the floor. Nobody came. I sat on the bed in the silence and did the *Times* crossword puzzle: for if these circumstances sound depressing to you, alarming even, I felt in my mind no flicker of disconsolance, no tremor of fear, no regret and no irresolution. Powers beyond my control had brought me to Room 5 at the clinic in Casablanca, and I could not have run away then even if I had wished to.

Late at night two nurses arrived, one French, one Arab. I was to be operated on later, they said. They had come to give me a preliminary injection, and in the meantime I must shave my private parts. 'You have a razor? Undress, please, and shave yourself. We will wait.' They sat on the table, swinging their legs, the one holding the hypodermic syringe, the other a sterilizing bowl. I undressed and took my razor, and miserably in that bare light, with the cold water from the tap and a cake of Moroccan soap, I shaved the hair from my pubic region, while the girls watched sardonically, sporadically chatting to each other. I can see them now, swinging their legs there, while I struggled uncomfortably on, a lonely naked figure in the middle of the room, where the light was brightest.

At last it was done, and they injected me upon the bed. 'Go to sleep now,' they said, 'the operation will be later.' But when they had gone I got out of bed rather shakily, for the drug was beginning to work, and went to say goodbye to myself in the mirror. We would never meet again, and I wanted to give that other self a long last look in the eye, and a wink for luck. As I did so a street vendor outside played a delicate arpeggio upon his flute, a very gentle merry sound which he repeated, over and over again, in sweet diminuendo down the street. Flights of angels, I said to myself, and so staggered back to my bed, and oblivion.

When I awoke it was pitch dark, and there was no sound, inside or out. I was instantly alert, but when gingerly I tried to explore the condition of my body, I found I could not move a muscle. I was pinioned in some way to the bed. My arms, stretched away from my body, seemed to be strapped to the bed itself, and I no longer appeared to have any legs. I could lift my head a little, but it did no good, for the blackness was impenetrable. I might just as well be in the grave. There was absolutely no sign of life in the clinic. If I had screamed my head off nobody would have heard. I wondered mildly if something had gone terribly wrong, and I was in fact dead: but no, I seemed to be breathing all right, my mind worked, and sure enough a cautious clenching of the abdominal muscles seemed to tell me that I was heavily bandaged, perhaps tubed, down below. It seemed to me that on the whole I was alive, well and sex-changed in Casablanca.

I have always thought of my conundrum as a matter of the spirit, and others have declared it to be all in the mind: but some thirty years later Dutch scientists, after examining the autopsied brains of six transsexual men, discovered that in every case a particular region of the hypothalamus, at the floor of the brain, was abnormally small for a male, and in fact smaller than most females'. This seemed to show that there was some physical, as against psychological reason for the phenomenon, but I still prefer the mystic explanation though.

19

London 1975

The character of London, England's ancient capital, has always eluded me, and seemed to me particularly evasive in the transitory atmosphere of the 1970s. This essay, written for Rolling Stone, *is only one of many attempts I have made to grasp it.*

One of the flight-paths to London Airport, Heathrow, goes straight over the middle of the capital, east to west. The city does not look much at first: just a drab sprawling mass of housing estates, terraces and industrial plants, nibbled at its edges by a fairly grubby green – just mile after mile of the ordinary, splodged here and there with the sordid.

Presently, though, the route picks up the River Thames, sinuously sliding between the eastern suburbs, and one by one landmarks appear that are part of the whole world's consciousness, images familiar to every one of us, reflecting the experience of half mankind. The Tower of London squats brownish at the water's edge. Buckingham Palace reclines in its great green garden. The Houses of Parliament, of all famous buildings the most toylike and intricate, stand like an instructional model beside Westminster Bridge. There are the swathes of London parks, too, and the huge Victorian roofs of the railway terminals, the cluttered hub of Piccadilly, the big new block of Scotland Yard, and always the river itself, twisting and turning through it all, out of the city centre into the western purlieus, until the first of the country green appears again on the other side, with gravel pits and motorways. Windsor Castle appears tremendous on its hillock, and the aircraft, slightly changing its tone of voice, tilts a wing over Slough and begins the last descent to the airport.

It is the city of cities that we have flown over. Like it or loathe it, it is the daddy of them all. If New York is ethnically more interesting, Moscow or Peking ideologically more compelling, Paris or Rome more obviously beautiful, still as a historical phenomenon London beats them all. It has been itself, for better or for worse, for a thousand years, unconquered by a foreign army since William the Norman was crowned King of England in Westminster Abbey in 1066. It has spawned and abandoned the greatest empire known to history. It was the first great industrial capital, the first parliamentary capital, the arena of social and political experiments beyond number. It is a city of terrific murders and innumerable spies, of novelists, auctioneers, surgeons and rock stars. It is the city of Shakespeare, Sherlock Holmes, Dr Johnson, Churchill, Dick Whittington, Henry VIII, Florence Nightingale, the Duke of Wellington, Queen Victoria, Gladstone and the two Olivers, Cromwell and Twist. Mozart wrote his first symphony in London, and Karl Marx began *Das Kapital*. London has five great symphony orchestras, eleven daily newspapers, three cathedrals, the biggest subway on earth and the most celebrated broadcasting system. It is the original world capital of soccer, cricket, rugby, lawn tennis and squash. It is where Jack the Ripper worked. It is the home of the last great monarchy of all, the House of Windsor, likely to be outlived only, in the expert judgement of the late King Farouk of Egypt, by the Houses of Hearts, Diamonds, Clubs and Spades. London is nearly everything. If you are tired of London, Dr Johnson once remarked, you are tired of life.

It is a gift of London, or rather a technique, that through the dingy and the disagreeable, the fantastic habitually looms. Illusion breaks in! Its principal agency is that monarchy, whose heraldic lions, unicorns, crowns, roses, thistles and Norman mottos are as inescapable in this city as Leninist quotations in Moscow.

Monarchy in London is part religion, part diplomacy, part make-believe; if the gleaming standards above the royal residences are like prayer flags or talismans, the ramrod soldiers stamping and strutting between their sentry boxes are pure Sigmund Romberg. The mystique of London's royal presence, the fetish feel, the mumbo jumbo, colours the sensations of this peculiar city, and often makes it feel like a place of pilgrimage, a Lourdes or a Jerusalem, or more exactly, perhaps, like one of those shrines where a familiar miracle is regularly re-attested, the saintly blood is annually decongealed or the hawthorn blossoms each Christmas morning. The world flocks in to witness the mystery of London, enacted several times a year in the ceremonial thoroughfare called the Mall. The pavements then are thick with foreigners, and far away up Constitution Hill the tourist buses, emblazoned with the emblems and registration plates of all Europe, stand nose to nose in their shiny hundreds. The guardsmen lining the Mall are like acolytes at the shrine; the patrolling policemen, sacristans.

The beat of a drum is the start of the ritual, somewhere up there in the blur of gold, grey and green that is Buckingham Palace. The beat of a drum, the blare of a band, and presently a procession approaches slowly between the plane trees. A drum major leads, in a peaked jockey cap and gilded tunic, as impassive on his tall white horse as a time drummer on a slave galley. Then the jangling, clopping, creaking, panting cavalry, black horses, brass helmets, plumes, anxious young faces beneath their heavy helmet straps, the skid and spark of hoofs now and then, the shine of massive breastplates, sour smells of horse and leather. Three strange old gentlemen follow, weighed down beneath fat bearskin hats, with huge swords bouncing at their sides; they ride their chargers rheumatically stooped, as though they have been bent in the saddle like old leather.

Another plumed squadron . . . a pause . . . a hush over the crowd . . . and then, bobbing high above the people, almost on a level with the flags, the familiar strained and earnest face of the mystery itself, pale beneath its heavy makeup. It is like the Face on the Shroud, an image-face. Everybody in the world knows it. It is a lined and diligent face, not at all antique or aristocratic, but it possesses its own arcanum. The crowd hardly stirs as it passes, and the murmur that runs down the pavement is a tremor less of astonishment or admiration than of compassion. It is as though a martyr is passing by. She rides, she bleeds, for us!

There is something fatalistic about the spectacle. The ritual is so old, so very old, so frozen in so many conventions and shibboleths. The Queen bobs away with her guards, her captains and her bands towards whatever elaborate and meaningless ceremonial her major-domos have prepared for her beyond the trees, but she leaves behind something stale. Her martyrdom is the suffering of a tired tradition, and if the royal flummery is the saving fantasy of London, it is the city's penance too. London seems often to be labouring beneath the weight of its own heritage – year after year, century upon century, the same beat of the drum-major's drum, the same jangle of the harnesses, the same bent old courtiers on their chargers lurching generation after generation down the Mall.

Like many another celebration of faith, it is an act, and this perpetual posturing around the royal palaces, like the swishing to and fro of surpliced priests around a reliquary, pervades the rest of the capital too.

More than any other city in Europe, London is a show, living by bluff and display. People have always remarked upon its theatrical nature. In Victorian times it was Grand Guignol, and the smoky blackness of the city streets, the rat-infested reaches of the river, coupled with the lively squalor of the poor, that powerfully impressed susceptible visitors. In the blitz of the 1940s it was pure patriotic pageantry: the flames of war licking ineffectively around the mass of St Paul's, Churchill in his boiler-suit giving the V-sign from the steps of 10 Downing Street, Noël Coward singing 'London pride has been handed down to us' or 'A Nightingale Sang in Berkeley Square . . .'

Today we are between the great civic performances that have punctuated London's history, but the greasepaint is always on, and the sensation of theatre is still endemic to the place. It is a city of actors always, as it has been since the days of Will Shakespeare and his troupers down at the Globe. You can hardly spend a day in London without seeing a face you recognize, and in this city, famous actors are not mere celebrities or glorified pop stars, but great men. They are figures of authority, honoured or ennobled. Laurence Olivier sits as a baron in the House of Lords. Sir Ralph Richardson lives like a grandee in his Regency house by the park. Sir Alec Guinness, Sir Michael Redgrave, Sir John Gielgud – these are the truest nobility of this capital: people who, like the admirals of an earlier English age, frequently sail abroad to do their country honour, fighting the Queen's battles in Rome or Hollywood, but who return always, full of glory, to this their natural estate.

The histrionic art is the London art *par excellence* – the ability to dazzle, mimic, deceive or stir. Look now, as you step from the restaurant after dinner, across the blackness of St James's toward Westminster. There is the floodlit Abbey, that recondite temple of Englishness; and there is the cluster of the Whitehall pinnacles; and there, the flash of the neons pinpoints Piccadilly and intermittently illuminates Nelson on his pillar in Trafalgar Square; and riding above it all, high over the clockface of Big Ben in the Palace of Westminster, high in the night sky, a still small light, all alone, burns steadily above the city. It is the light that announces the House of Commons, the mother of all parliaments, to be in session below. There's theatre for you! There's showmanship!

Or pay a visit to the High Court in the morning, and see the performers of London law present their daily matinee. No professional actors ever played such unfathomable, judicial judges as the justices of Her Majesty's Bench, wrinkled like turtles beneath the layered carapaces of their wigs, scratching away at their notes on their high seats, or intervening sometimes with polysyllabical quips. No prime-time mimic could outdo the sharpest of the London barristers, who play their briefs like instruments, hold themselves whenever possible in profile and wrap their robes around them in the ecstasy of their accomplishment, like so many Brutuses assembling for the kill. Laughter in a London court is frequent and often heartless; there is a regular audience of hags and layabouts, and so infectious is the atmosphere of theatre that often the poor accused, momentarily hoisted into stardom, wanly smiles in appreciation.

With luck one may still see Cockneys in performance. The Cockney culture survives only precariously in the city of its origins, as the taxi-drivers, marketmen and newspaper vendors move out to the suburbs, are rehoused in high-rise apartments, or find their accents, their loyalties and their humour swamped in the sameness of the age. It is many years since officialdom cleared the flower sellers from Piccadilly Circus, and even the buskers of the London tradition, the escape artists who used to entertain the theatre queues, the pavement artists outside the National Gallery, are slowly being chivvied on to oblivion. But the culture *does* survive, and remains among the most truly exhibitionist of all traditions.

Sometimes at fêtes and functions, even today, you may see the pearly kings and queens, the hereditary folk monarchs of the Cockney vegetable-barrow trade, dressed in the curious livery, decked all over in thousands of mother-of-pearl buttons, which is their traditional prerogative. Better still, any Sunday morning, in the vast outdoor market of Petticoat Lane, among the shabby mesh of streets that lies to the north of the Tower, you may watch the Cockney salesmen exuberantly in action. Theirs is an art form straight from the music hall, or vice versa, perhaps; in their timing, in their sly wit, in their instinctive rebound from a failed joke, in their exhilarating air of grasping insouciance, the Cockney hustlers stand directly in the line of the gaslight comedians.

London is a stage! The big red buses of this city, moving with such ponderous geniality through the traffic, are like well-loved character actors. The beefeaters outside the Tower, holding halberds and dressed up like playing cards, are surely extras hired for the day. And most theatrical of all are those London functions which are not merely quaint, or orna-mental, but really integral to the status of this capital, close to the political power of it.

I went one day to the installation of a new member in the House of Lords, the upper chamber of the British Parliament. He was a prominent politician ennobled for his party services, and I was taken to the ceremony by another peer, of more literary distinction. We were late and hurried through the vast, florid halls of the Palace of Westminster, past multitudi-nous busts and forbidding portraits ('my great-great-great-grand-father', panted Lord J. as we passed William III, 'illegitimately, of course',) down interminable carpeted corridors, through chambers enigmatically labelled, between gigantic murals of swains, maidens, liege lords and war horses, until up a winding stone staircase, through a creaking oak door, he shoved me precipitately into the visitors' gallery.

Inside a dream was in progress. The rest of the peers and peeresses indeed looked mundane enough on their benches below: thick-set party reliables, jowly former ministers, a handful of flinty and talkative women, a bishop with heavy-rimmed spectacles and a resolutely ecumenical expression. But slumped eerily with his back to me, the Lord Chancellor of England sat like a dummy on his woolsack, the big woollen bag which has for 600 years and more sustained the Chancellorian rump. Dark robes blurred the shape of him, a black tricorn hat was perched on top of his judicial wig, and he suggested to me the presiding judge of some sinister hearing, with a hint of that magisterial caterpillar with his hookah, on top of the mushroom in *Alice*.

Just as I entered, the new peer, appearing silently out of nowhere, approached this daunting figure. He was dressed in red and ermine, escorted by two colleagues and preceded by a functionary in black knee breeches holding a silver wand. Spooky things ensued in the silence. The three peers sat down, but almost at once they rose again, in dead silence, and in unison bowed toward the woolsack, simultaneously removing their hats. The Lord High Chancellor removed his in return, adjusting his posture on his sack and bowing slightly, almost frigidly, in their direction. Twice more, without a sound, the ritual was repeated – down, up, hats off, bow, hats on, down – while we in the galleries, perhaps even the other peers and peeresses in their benches below, watched almost aghast, so arcane was the spectacle.

This was not a charade. This was a contemporary political occasion, London style. As soon as it ended I hastened out of the gallery and down the steps in time to bump into Lord J. emerging from the chamber below. 'Good gracious me,' I could not help saying, 'however long have they been doing that?' 'I believe it began,' he replied quite seriously, 'with the Druids.'

Whether London is a success just at the moment or a failure, a rich city or a poor one, nobody quite knows. It is, surprisingly, a very volatile capital: the US ambassador recently diagnosed it as manic-depressive, on top of the world one day, all despondency the next. Sometimes the kingdom, of which it is not just the heart, but the mind, lung and belly too, is represented to us as almost bankrupt. At other times it stands on the brink of incalculable wealth, revivified by the promise of oil from the North Sea. One month its accounts are disastrously in debit, the next month it has an enormous surplus. The vaults of London burst with money, the gold reserves in the Bank of England are higher than ever, but much of it is foreign wealth, deposited there for security and quick returns, and easily withdrawable.

All this is nothing new. Despite its reputation for stability, calm and balance, London has always lived precariously. Dickens's Mr Micawber, always confident that something would turn up, was a true son of this city. It is essentially a market for invisible commodities, services performed, expertise. Insuring, banking, auctioneering, valuing, analysing – these are the archetypal functions of the place. They are fluid functions, hard to assess, and they are fragile too, since they depend upon the state of the world; so the prosperity of London is never certain, even in euphoric periods, but seems to fluctuate, apparently dependent upon the weather, the news or the mood of Europe that day.

It is a neo-socialist city, its economy a mixture of state and free enterprise, and the one constant in its progress since the war has been the decline of the bourgeoisie, which in previous generations was its bulwark. This process is apparent always. Walk into a Whitehall pub, say, any sunny lunchtime, and you may observe it for yourself. Outside the door, the tide of the city flows busily by – the rumbling buses, the shirt-sleeved tourists reading to each other from guidebooks – but inside the early drinkers are slumped heavily over their beers. They are businessmen and bureaucrats, senior enough to be able to slip out around twelve, sufficiently successful to have a club round the corner in Pall Mall. They are all men, all middle-aged, and would be instantly recognizable as English wherever they went in the world.

An aggrieved or embattled air attends them in the shadowy recesses of the front bar, as though they have retreated into this dim enclave off the streets to be among their own kind, to lick their wounds, perhaps. They do not talk much, but when they do it is generally to complain: about the state of the country, the beer, the young, the weather. Up the road their wives, in a break from shopping, are having their cups of coffee (or more exactly, the price of coffee being what it is, their cups of chicory extract). History has hit them harder still. Time was when a trip into town for a morning shopping was a treat; they wore their best hats and coats and took a friend along. Now, all too often, they sit alone, and their clothes have lost their colour. Their faces, though kind, look strained. They wear head scarves and solid shoes, and each year they seem to lose a little of their class identity, and it becomes harder to tell whether the lady opposite you is married to a factory hand or a schoolmaster.

Yet in those streets outside, there are signs of opulence wherever you look. Rolls-Royces are two a penny. Your cab-driver tells you about the holiday he is planning in Tunisia, the record shops are jammed with the free-spending young, up-and-coming executives in BMWs invariably beat you to the parking space. In the upper-crust restaurants the comfortable conventions of old London are sustained by the magic of the expense account, and businessmen who scarcely know a tithe from a ptarmigan are treated with all the homely respect once reserved for the landed gentry. 'Certainly, my lady' is a stagey phrase that still drops easily from the lips of London lackeys, and if the English rich have been driven from their traditional haunts in Mayfair and Knightsbridge, they are still as snug as ever, with their nannies, their Filipino cooks and their Swedish *au pair* girls, in the villas of St John's Wood or Little Venice.

All these contrasts and anomalies help to give London its febrile air. Between performances! Stripped of its enormous empire, neither quite part of Europe nor altogether insular, socialist but capitalist too, hankering for its glory days, clinging to its ritual loyalties, London feels unsettled, unfulfilled, as though unsure which role to accept next. Is the old trouper 'resting', reading scripts, past it or about to launch another smash hit? Nobody is sure. Radical decisions are always in the air but never quite happen. There is always an election pending, a strike threatened, a settlement in sight, a ring road about to be built, a demolition started.

Some of it is certainly loss of confidence. The thirty years since the Second World War have been rotten years for London. Rich or poor, this city is no longer the greatest capital of the world, as it could still claim to be before the war, just as the pound sterling is no longer the world's criterion of security. The consequence and authority of London, which are expressed in so many memorials and institutions, so many horseback statues, is a dream now. Even the Scots and the Welsh challenge the primacy of this capital today, and a city that once decreed the destinies of a quarter of the earth is reduced to the somewhat testy direction of 50 million souls. The political style is accordingly rather wilted. Nowadays when prime ministers emerge from their celebrated threshold, 10 Downing Street, with attendant policemen like caryatids beside the door, they do so almost

217

apologetically, or scuttle away into their waiting limousines as though they have just discovered their flies undone.

After dinner with friends one night, we wandered round the market area of Covent Garden, now in the first pangs of rebirth, the vegetable stalls and fruit wagons having migrated south of the river. In London the removal of an old and beloved landmark is an especially traumatic experience, and the gap left by that most celebrated of markets, where opera rubbed shoulders so romantically with cabbages, and Eliza Doolittle was originally picked up by Professor Higgins, is now being tentatively filled in – to me a disturbing phenomenon, like a numbed corner of the brain. We found a whimsical pottery shop, a very smart books store and the Rock Garden Café, through whose seventeenth-century arcade eponymous music thumped loudly through the night, suggesting to me less a corner of old London than a bit of some resuscitated ghost town living only by the summer trade.

The Opera House was being cleaned, and shone phosphorescent through its scaffolding, and to complete my sensation of dislocation, alienation perhaps, a solitary laser beam hung flickerless over London like a single wire of an imprisoning mesh. Didn't they feel it too? I asked my friends. Didn't they sense, in the condition of their city that night, symptoms of disintegration? It was like someone who had suffered a breakdown, I said, whose personality is split, splintered or possibly in abeyance.

'It's that damned laser beam,' my host replied. 'It's enough to give any-one the creeps.'

Once the robustly English capital of the English kingdom, among the most homogeneous of the great cities of the earth, London is now one of the most international of capitals. It is not international in a generous way, opening its arms to the hungry yearning to breathe free, but only under protest. Evelyn Waugh anathematized modern London as a 'vulgar cos-mopolitan city'; the alienation of London is not just an after-dinner fancy, but a sociological fact.

In the winter it may not particularly strike you. The West Indian and Pakistani bus conductors, the black inspectors on the Underground, have become so thoroughly Londonized by now that they seem an organic part of the scene, as indigenous as the buses themselves. It is no longer a surprise to be greeted with a cheery Cockney 'hullo, ducks' by a jet-black functionary from Barbados, and London Airport would not be its familiar self without the melancholy commiserations of the Indian ladies sweeping up the sandwich crumbs, or sometimes the sandwiches, from the coffee-bar floors.

But in the summer things feel very different. Then Londoners write letters to the editor of *The Times*, wryly complaining that they can't find another Englishman to talk to. Then, even to the most liberal mind, the foreigners seem to infest London like so many insects, and Waugh's definition becomes uncomfortably true. Across the ancient face of the city the strangers are inescapable, wherever a deal is to be struck, an old church inspected, a work permit obtained, a ceremony to be observed, a property acquired or (as Londoners would murmur) a queue to be jumped. On every double yellow line, it seems, a diplomatic car is imperviously parked. In every Marks and Spencer store, relays of Frenchwomen hold sweaters against each other's busts for size. Round the edges of Petticoat Lane aged oriental ladies sit in the backs of big black cars, watching the passing crowds as through *mashrabiya* windows, while their servants foray among the stalls for bargains.

All around Eros in Piccadilly Circus, the scruffy young of a dozen nationalities squat upon the statue's pedestal – its fountain spilling incontinently about their feet – or lie flat on the ground sustained by rucksacks, while a few yards away the visiting bourgeoisie wait in interminable lines for the open-topped tourist buses. Then the beefeaters stand like island bastions against the polyglot sea of sightseers, and the foreign bankers return purposefully to their offices from the steakhouses, carrying black fibre briefcases with combination locks and talking to each other in unknown tongues.

This is not just the usual internationalism, common to all great capitals and essential, of course, to immigrant cities like New York. This is something more. This has to it a strong feeling of takeover or possession, which is why, for the first time in many years, the average Londoner is showing symptoms of xenophobia. London used to be the most self-sufficient, the most proudly separate of all capital cities: as the celebrated London *Times* headline is supposed to have said, VIOLENT STORM IN THE ENGLISH CHANNEL; CONTINENT ISOLATED. Now the alien worms have turned, and at this particular juncture in its history. London depends upon foreigners more than ever to keep it solvent. It depends upon the pundits of the International Monetary Fund, upon the bankers of the European central banks, upon the tourist trade, and not least upon the

Arabs, yesterday's wogs or Ayrabs, who now provide incalculable funds for the London money market and have actually bought large slabs of the capital itself. London is momentarily in fee to the Arabs, and there are parts of the city that the Arabs actually seem to have colonized, thus turning the wheel of empire full cycle. In particular, Knightsbridge, that plush network of streets that lies between Kensington Gardens and Hyde Park Corner, has become a little Arabia. From Knightsbridge, the tracks of the London Beduin criss-cross the capital, linking the merchant banks of the City, the Oxford Street stores, the shoemakers of St James's, the shirt-makers of Jermyn Street and the antique dealers of Bond Street, with their lairs, pads and harems around Harrods department store.

Sardonic Londoners claim it is easy to differentiate them. The Jordanians and the Palestinians, they say, are the charmers. Only the Saudis maintain the authentic plutocratic sneer in all circumstances. To most citizens, though, they seem a kind of dour unity, as Europeans once appeared to them, from the black-veiled ladies silent in the dentist's waiting room to the plump small boys in expensive grey flannel ogling the shop-girls at Selfridges, or for that matter, the princelings, perfectly at ease in their beautiful tweeds, who offer, from time to time, slinky half-smiles in hotel lobbies.

By the standards of contemporary London many of these foreigners are unimaginably rich, and many indeed seem to have no sense of money at all. They spend without thinking, without trying. And if this tide of alien opulence rankles Londoners, it also corrupts them. It breeds envy and resentment and brings out the lickspittles. The sycophancy directed by Londoners to English lords and knighted actors is now extended to Japanese industrialists and illiterate sheiks. Fawning and visibly fattened are the chauffeurs, sons of the stalwart Cockneys, seen handing white-gowned tribesmen from their Mercedes; bland are the faces of the bell-boys as they accept from yet another impassive client a gratuity beyond the remotest bounds of equity.

London is in flux more than usual just now, and out of the uncertainty ugly things are sprouting. The slums have almost vanished, but they have been replaced by ill-constructed tower blocks, where the lifts are all too often out of order, the walls are habitually covered with obscene graffiti, and every apartment seems fortified against the rest. This is a state of affairs common in other cities, but new to London: and in these dislocated communities, where nobody need be destitute but nobody seems content, violence and prejudice fester. For the first time in London's history there are sizeable segments of the city where foreign-born citizens are in a majority – and not just foreign-born, but actually black or brown, a different category of alien to the intensely race-conscious English. Racial bigotry thrives and indeed seems to fulfil some sort of psychological need; it is different in kind, I think, from the American variety and often seems not exactly a social attitude, even less a political conviction, but rather a category of sport.

I was walking with a friend one Saturday down Lewisham Way, a blighted thoroughfare south of the river, when we felt in the air some hint or tremor of trouble. The street indeed seemed built for trouble. As far as we could see it was lined with nothing in particular: apparently makeshift blocks of shops and offices, car parks that were mere extensions of ancient bomb sites, isolated terraces of Victorian houses left high and dry by social history, and occupied now by multitudinous tenants. Sure enough, that afternoon trouble approached. Far in the distance we descried a Union Jack, held high, crooked and bobbing, and we faintly heard above the Saturday traffic strains of that grand patriotic anthem, 'Rule Britannia'.

'You'd better watch it, mate,' said a shopkeeper, standing in the door of a store that appeared to specialize in second-hand saucepans. 'That's the National Front, that is. They're not funny, you know. They don't mind who they bash.' But we walked gingerly on, and presently the flag disengaged itself from its dingy background, and the sensation of impending evil was embodied in a clutch of short-cropped youths in jeans, high boots and spangled leather jackets, holding the flag between two poles above their heads and striding northward towards the river with a certain jauntiness, like apprentice boys in Northern Ireland. Over and over again, as they drew nearer, they sang the same couplet of the song, as though they knew no more: Rule Britannia, Britannia rules the waves, Britons never never never shall be slaves . . . 'What's happening?' we asked as they passed, and they stopped at once, without resentment, and clustered around us as though they had discovered some street curiosity, and were about to learn something themselves. They spoke a particular kind of debased Cockney and tended all to talk at once.

'Big rally dahn the High Street, innit? Us against the Socialist Revolutionaries, know what I mean? Coupla football games in tahn, too.'

'What's it all about, then?'

'Well it's a bit of a punch-up, innit? Look, the coons and the reds give us a bit of aggro, know what I mean? The Paks and them, the nig-nogs and the football mobs, then we're in there, aren't we? Bit of violence, know what I mean? That's what it's all abaht, innit? Nig-nogs Saturday night!'

They laughed, but not maliciously – rather engagingly, as a matter of fact – and they clustered around us eagerly, as though we were visiting parents at a school match. There was a sort of chill innocence to their frankness. They were like moon children. 'Wanna come and watch?' they kindly suggested. 'You won't get no aggro. Just stand back, know what I mean?'

They laughed again, the laughter degenerating at the fringe of the posse into uncontrollable giggles, and for a moment we just stood and stared at them, and they at us. From the ear of one boy, I noticed, hung a small golden cross, and it swung rhythmically while its owner tunelessly whistled, occasionally nudged a neighbour in the ribs when something comical occurred to him or tapped a booted foot upon the pavement. I smiled at him wanly, and he responded with an inept wink, as though he had not quite mastered the knack; and then abruptly, with the Queen's flag borne skew-whiff above their heads, off they swung again, raggle-taggle down the street.

They were pure riot fodder, a demagogue's dream, thick as potatoes, gullible as infants, aching for a fight, not without courage, not without gaiety either. They were too slow to understand that the affray to which they were so boisterously heading – a clash between Right and Left, between the neo-fascists of the National Front and the frank communists of the Socialist Revolutionary Party – was more than just a Saturday afternoon bust-up, but an ideological confrontation which might one day ravage the capital. Know what I mean?

The riot, deliberately planned, turned out to be the worst in London for many years. I watched it on television that evening. By the standards of Paris, Berlin, Calcutta or Detroit, it was a modest disturbance. Nobody was killed. Only a few cars were set on fire. But in London, the city of so many ordered centuries, it came as a nasty shock: the muddle of billboards and banners in the shabby streets; the knots of youths, black and white, lashing out at each other like tomcats; the occasional scream, the sudden blood-stained figures; the thick, blue lines of helmeted policemen, sheltered behind their transparent shields from the showers of stones and bottles; the mass chanting; the smoke of burning cars. And the horsemen – especially the horsemen, who, suddenly appearing upon our screens and advancing at a deliberate trot upon that terrified and infuriated crowd, were horribly evocative of more terrible events elsewhere in history.

It was as though that certain indefinable malaise of London, that laser beam across the evening sky, was erupting just for an hour or two into fulfilment, and in the middle of it all I noticed something odd. Three hatless policemen, ties askew, helmets half off, were struggling with a youth, whose ferocious writhings, kickings and mouthings made him look the very embodiment of a snarl. They dragged him off my screen in the end, but just before he disappeared, I saw, under the heavy arm of one constable, over the sweating forehead of another, a small gold cross in a horny ear, vigorously joggling.

A city between performances. Not The City – for that title, for so long the prerogative of Constantinople, must now go to New York, a world epitome – but still, to my mind, the most enthralling of them all. I have described the neuroses I sometimes feel in London now, and the air of resignation which, to my mind, attends the pageantry of crown and state these days. But I know in fact that these are only on the surface, and do not reflect the real meaning of this city. Behind its shifts of fortune and history, London is impelled by a sharp expediency very different from the accepted images of the place. V. S. Pritchett, a Londoner himself, once wrote that the chief characteristic of London was *experience*. I am from Wales, a place of sea and mountains, and to me the unchanging essential of the capital is an eye for the main chance. London is hard as nails, and it is opportunism that has carried this city of moneymakers so brilliantly through revolution and holocaust, blitz and slump, in and out of empire and through countless such periods of uncertainty as seem to blunt its assurance now.

It is a calculating city behind it all, a city of intelligence agents, a matchless centre of political and military information. Its knowledge of the world is as exact and deliberate as ever it was in the days of empire. I was lunching one day with a chap from the foreign office, at Beoty's, the Greek place in St Martin's Lane, when he happened to mention, as foreign office chaps do, a hotel in Canton called the Ding Sang – formerly, as I might perhaps remember, the Yang Cheng, Goat City, a name he person-ally preferred. What did the new name mean? I wondered – 'Ding Sang? Oh, it means "The East Is Red". It's actually the theme phrase, so to speak, of one of the best-loved Maoist patriotic songs, dear to every Chinese heart.

'At least,' he then added thoughtfully, laying down his knife and fork, 'at least I *think* it's the main theme,' – and here a change came over his face, and for a moment he began to look oddly oriental himself. His eyes were screwed up at the corners, and his cheekbones seemed curiously to rise. Faintly over the buzz of the restaurant I heard him, in a high, cracked

223

tenor, softly singing to himself an eastern tune, quavery and half toned. As he sang he mouthed the words. 'Yes,' he said presently, in a satisfied voice, returning to the squids, 'I felt sure it was. It provides the principal refrain of the song.'

This is the London expertise, to adapt deftly, if necessarily surreptitiously, to the changing times. Tradition in front, utter pragmatism behind. In the past ten years or so some of this inner steeliness has, so to speak, been revealed by the dispersion of London's smoke. Ever since the Industrial Revolution the nature of London has been masked by fog and murk. It has been a city of black suggestiveness, choked often in impenetrable mists off the river, against which the splendours of the kingdom were paraded in pungent contrast. The very name London used to sound echoing and foggy, and every Hollywood film about the place had it thick with murderous fog.

Now the smoke has gone, and with it some of the romantic mystery, the camouflage. The city has been steam-cleaned all over. The river has been so brilliantly cleared of pollution that in 1977 the first salmon ran upstream through London from the sea. There is a new glint to London now, and its clarity tells a truer story than the swirls and opacities of old. The best place to look at London is not in the Mall after all, where the Queen rides by, and certainly not in Knightsbridge or Lewisham Way, but half-way across London Bridge – *new* London Bridge. The previous one now resides in Arizona, the one before that – the one with the shops, houses and turrets on it, and the malefactors' heads dripping blood at its gates – having been pulled down in 1832.

It is in fact the fourth London Bridge we are going to, completed only a few years ago, but still spanning the Thames in exactly the same spot as the ford by which, two thousand years ago, the Romans crossed to found their Londinium on the north bank. It is always, of course, an intensely busy place. The road is busy above, the river below. Distorted loud-speaker voices echo from beneath the bridge as the tourist launches chug their way to Greenwich or the Tower. Dirty squat tugs with lines of barges labour against the tide toward the Isle of Dogs. Downstream lies the superannuated cruiser *Belfast*, speckled with the unseamanlike pinks and yellows of tourists, while upstream indistinct flotillas of small craft seem to be milling purposelessly about in the distant haze of Westminster. But when we reach the middle of the bridge, and discover the north bank spread there before us, the Thames seems hardly more than a country stream, a pleasure pond, beside the gleaming vulgarity, the harshness, the concentration of the new City of London, the square mile that is the financial heart of the capital and its true core of constancy.

It is new, because most of it has been rebuilt since the Second World War; only now are the last bomb sites being filled in, to complete its sense of packed intensity. It is a cramped, ugly, jostling, bitter, clever square mile, jammed there on the waterfront. Its buildings look as though they have been forcibly hammered into the landscape in successive stages, century by century, forcing less virile structures back from the river or into the ground. It is a terrific spectacle, to my mind the most startling urban view in Europe, and it is given touches of nobility by its hoary landmarks: the majestic dome of St Paul's, the austere fortress turrets of the Tower, the fairy-tale silhouette of Tower Bridge, the spires of all the City churches squeezed in there among the concrete.

But it is not a nice scene, not a nice scene at all. There is something vicious to it. Every street you see down there is full to its attics with money-men, bankers, stockbrokers, agents, accountants, exchange specialists, economists, financial journalists and entrepreneurs. History does not much faze these adept Englishmen, and they are inhibited by no ideological qualms. Once the very champions of laissez faire, they have adapted with consummate flexibility to the advance of socialism, and would soon adjust again, I do not doubt, if communism ever took over this state. The City of London is the most subtle and perhaps the most vehement of all the world's financial bazaars, even now, and it emanates a sense not of power, or responsibility, but of unremitting self-interest. It is chock-a-block full, one feels, of gentlemanly cunning.

The poet Wordsworth, surveying London in an earlier century from another of its river bridges, was moved to ecstasy by the sight. Earth, he exclaimed, had nothing to show more fair! One could not say the same, looking out from London Bridge in 1978, but I'll tell you this, for sure: earth has nowhere more capable of looking after itself, than this aged and incorrigible deceiver!

By now this essay is decidedly a period piece. Since its time London seems to have deliberately abandoned its old character, whittling away at its traditional institutions, smoothing away its quirks and anomalies, half-forgetting its past and becoming an overwhelmingly multi-cultural capital. The House of Lords is not very lordly now and racism has acquired a new dimension since that day my friend and I encountered it on the Lewisham Road.

As for the monarchy, it was soon to lose much of its arcane magic – and its remoteness. Years later I was a guest at a Buckingham Palace reception for publishers and writers, and at the end of the evening, wishing to leave, looked around for somebody to thank. Queen, princes, dukes and all seemed to have gone elsewhere, so I left anyway, and at the palace gates I found a policeman. 'I was brought up,' I told him,' to say thank you for having me when I'd been to a party, so as I can't find the Queen or anybody to say it to, I'll say it to you instead. Thank you for having me.'

He replied stylishly, I thought, but in the new palace mode. 'Not at all, madam. Come again.'

Post-Glory: The USA

During the 1970s I wrote about several American cities for Rolling Stone, *and found the USA a very different place from the gloriously confident and benevolent republic I had first encountered in the 1950s. The founder and owner of the magazine, though, the brilliant Jann Wenner, still displayed the old American panache. When, at lunch one day in San Francisco, I expressed my admiration for the restaurant's wicker chairs, he instantly summoned a waiter and asked for a pair of them to be sent to me in Wales.*

Los Angeles

I had been to Los Angeles in 1954. I had introductions then to some of the Hollywood film community, had enjoyed its social whirl, but had gone away thinking of it as rather a silly and superficial sort of place. My responses twenty years later were very different.

Los Angeles is the city of Know-How. Remember 'know-how'? It was one of the vogue words of the forties and fifties, now rather out of fashion. It reflected a whole climate and tone of American thought in the years of supreme American optimism. It stood for skill and experience indeed, but it also expressed the certainty that America's particular genius, the genius for applied logic, for systems, for devices, was inexorably the herald of progress. As the English thought in the 1840s, so the Americans thought a century later. They held the future in their hands and this time it *would* work. Their methods and inventions would usher not only America herself but all mankind into another golden age. Know-how would be America's great gift to history: know-how to rescue the poor from the poverty, to snatch the coloured peoples from their ignominy, to convince the nations that the American way of free enterprise was the best happiest way of all. Nothing was beyond know-how. Know-how was, if not actually the substance of God, at least a direct derivative.

One city in America, above all others, came to represent this enviable conviction. There has never been another town, and now there never will be, quite like El Pueblo de Nuestra Señora la Reina de Los Angeles de Porciuncula, Southern California, where the lost American faith in machines and materialism built its own astonishing monument.

Los Angeles, in the generic sense, was a long time coming. It is not a young city. Spaniards were here before the United States was founded, and I never get the feeling, as I wander around LA's vast, amorphous mass, that it lies thinly on the ground. It is not like Johannesburg, for instance, where almost within living memory there was nothing whatsoever. Nor does it feel transient or flimsy, like some of those towns of the Middle West, which seem to have no foundations at all, but await the next tornado to sweep them away in a tumble of matchwood. In Los Angeles there are reminders of a long tradition. There is the very name of the city, and of its euphonious streets and suburbs – Alvarado, El Segundo, Pasadena, Cahuenga Boulevard. There is the pattern of its real estate, still recognizably descended from the Spanish and Mexican ranches of long ago. There is its exotic taste in architecture, its patios and its deep eaves, its arcades, its courtyards. There are even a few actual buildings, heavily reconstructed but still authentic, which survive from the first Spanish pueblo – swarmed over by tourists now, but frequented too, I like to think, by the swaggering ghosts of their original caballeros.

A sense of age informs the very setting of LA. From the air the city looks like some enormously exaggerated pueblo itself: flat, sprawling, rectilinearly intersected, dun-coloured, built of mud brick by some inconceivable race of primitives, and behind it the tawny mountains run away in a particularly primeval way, a lizardy, spiny way, their dry expanses relieved only by the flicker of white on a snow peak here and there, or the distant glimmer of a lake. In a huge amphitheatre the city lies, accessible only by passes through the surrounding ridges, rather like a gigantic mining camp: and through the veil of its own artificial mist, suggestively whirled about and blended with the California sunshine, it looks across its golden beaches toward that most enigmatic of oceans, the Pacific (never called the sea in Los Angeles, always 'the ocean').

There is nothing Johnny-come-quick to this scene. Los Angeles is a complex merger of separate settlements, containing within its scrambled presence eighty different municipalities, and sprawling district by district, decade by decade, over its central plain and into its foothills. Though I would guess that nine-tenths of its buildings were erected in the twentieth century, still Los Angeles is, like some incurable disease, a balefully organic phenomenon. Its streets are forever nibbling and probing further into its perimeter hills, twisting like rising water ever higher, ever deeper into their canyons, and sometimes bursting through to the deserts beyond. If the city could be prised out of its setting, one feels, it would be like a dried mat of some bacterial mould, every bump, every corner exactly shaped to its landscape.

This is partly because the landscape itself is so individual, so that unlike Chicago, say, or Paris, Los Angeles is inconceivable anywhere else. But it is also, I think, because this city genuinely springs out of its own soil, possesses a true genius loci and forms a kind of irreplaceable flashpoint: the point on the map where the intellectual, the physical and the historical forces of American history met to produce – well, combustion, what else? Whatever happens to LA, it will always be the city of the automobile and the radio, showbiz and the Brown Derby restaurant, the city where the American ideal of happiness by technique found its folk art in the ebullience of Hollywood. It is essentially of the forties and the fifties, and especially perhaps of the Second World War years, when the American conviction acquired the force of a crusade, and sent its jeeps, its technicians and its Betty Grables almost as sacred pledges across the world. Los Angeles then was everyone's vision of the New World: and so it must always remain, however it develops, a memorial to those particular times, as Florence means for everyone the spirit of Renaissance.

Across the car park from the remains of the original Spanish pueblo, where the Mexican souvenir shops now huddle profitably along Olvera Street, there stands Union Station. This was the last great railway depot to be built in the United States, completed in 1939, and one of the most handsome. Cool, tall, elegant, and nowadays restfully unfrequented by trains, it has patios green with flowers and trees, shaded colonial-style arcades, and is rather the sort of railway station a multi-billionaire might devise, if he wanted one at the bottom of the garden. In this it is very proper, for while paying graceful respect to LA's origins and pretensions, it honours too the first and fundamental quality of this city: organized, stylized movement.

It was not liberty that Los Angeles cherished in its prime, or at least not absolute liberty. A spiritual culture can be anarchical, a material culture must be disciplined. Implicit to the promise of technological fulfilment was the necessity of *system*, and LA soon became a firmly ordered place. The original Los Angeles public transport system, the electric trains and streetcars of the early twentieth century, drew together the scattered settlements of the time, bringing them all into cityness.

When the car arrived the mesh was tightened, and LA built its incomparable freeways. These remain the city's grandest and most exciting artefacts. Snaky, sinuous, undulating, high on stilts or sunk in cuttings, they are like so many concrete tentacles, winding themselves around each block, each district, burrowing, evading, clambering, clasping every corner of the metropolis as if they are squeezing it all together to make the parts stick. They are inescapable, not just visually, but emotionally. They are always there, generally a few blocks away; they enter everyone's lives, and seem to dominate all arrangements.

To most strangers they suggest chaos, or at least purgatory. There comes a moment, though, when something clicks in one's own mechanism, and suddenly one grasps the rhythm of the freeway system, masters its tribal or ritual forms, and discovers it to be not a disruptive element at all, but a kind of computer key to the use of Los Angeles. One is processed by the freeways. Elevated as they generally are above the flat and centreless expanse of the city, they provide a navigational aid, into which one locks oneself for guidance. Everything is clearer then. There are the mountains, to the north and east. There is the glimmering ocean. The civic landmarks of LA, such as they are, display themselves conveniently for you, the pattern of the place unfolds until, properly briefed by the experience, the time comes for you to unlock from the system and take the right-hand lane into the everyday life below.

The moment this first happened to me, Los Angeles happened too, and I glimpsed the real meaning of the city, and realized how firmly it had been disciplined by the rules of its own conviction.

Confusing, nevertheless, the Santa Ana with the San Diego Freeway, missing the exit at Bristol, mistaking Newport Avenue for Newport Boulevard, getting in the wrong lane at Victoria, miscounting the traffic lights on 22nd Street, an hour late exactly I arrived for lunch with the world's greatest authority on European naval history in the early twentieth century.

Through apparent chaos to unmistakable authority. This was a not uncharacteristic Los Angeles experience. Expertise is the stock in trade of this metropolis, and behind the flash and the braggadocio, solid skills and scholarship prosper. There are craftsmen everywhere in LA, craftsmen in electronics, in film-making, in literature, in social science, in advertising, in fashion. Here Lockheed makes its aircraft. Here NASA makes its space shuttle orbiter. Here is UCLA, one of the most fertile universities in the Western world. Here the McCulloch Corporation has patented a device to pop the golf ball *out* of the hole, to save its owner stooping. This is no place for dilettantes. Even sport is assiduously, sometimes grimly, pursued: the tennis players of Beverly Hills joylessly strain towards perfection, the Malibu surfers seldom lark about, but take their pleasures with a showy dedication.

I went one morning to Burbank Studios to see them filming Neil Simon's macabre comedy, *Murder by Death*. This is one of those movies in which everyone is a star, and the set was cluttered with familiar figures. There was Truman Capote, described in the studio publicity as 'acclaimed author and international celebrity', huddled with a young friend in a corner and wearing a wide-brimmed hat. There was Peter Falk, charmingly chatting with Elsa Lanchester. Alec Guinness looked truly gentlemanly, David Niven looked almost too elegant. Ray Stark the producer looked preternaturally successful, Robert Moore the director looked alarmingly gifted.

I am antipathetic to the famous, though, and I found that my eyes kept straying from these luminaries to the two sound technicians who, just off the set, sat nonchalantly over their equipment wearing headsets and reading the trade papers. One was called Jerry Jost, the other Bill Manooth, and they had both been in the business twenty years and more. How calm they looked, I thought, how sure of themselves, how easily aware of the fact that nobody in the whole world could do their job better than they could! They had seen the stars come and go, they had helped to make flops and winners, they had suffered every temperament, they had seen the film industry itself in boom and decline. Sometimes they looked up to exchange a pleasantry with a passer-by, sometimes they turned a page of the *Hollywood Reporter*: but they were always alert when the moment came, always watching their quivering instruments, always ready to mouth the magic word 'Speed!' – which, with its assurance that they had got things right, gave the signal to that whole assembly, director, cameraman, actors, Capote and all, to proceed with their flamboyances.

For somewhere near the heart of the LA ethos there lies, unexpectedly, a layer of solid, old-fashioned, plain hard work. This is a city of hard workers. Out on the hills at Santa Monica, overlooking the Pacific Ocean, the writer

231

Christopher Isherwood and the painter Don Bachardy share a house, sunlit and easy-going, with a view over the rooftops and shrubberies of the canyon. In such a place, with such occupants, in such warm and soothing sun, with the beach down the road and Hollywood up the freeway, it might seem a house for cultivated indolence, interminable wit around a swimming pool, long cool drinks with worldly neighbours before lunch. Not at all. 'We are *working* people,' Isherwood says, and so they literally are: each at his own end of the house, each with his art, the one surrounded by his books, the other by his brushes and pictures, carefully and skilfully they work through the day, friends and fellow labourers.

I very much like all this. It suggests to me, unexpectedly, the guild spirit of some medieval town, where the workers in iron or lace, the clockmakers and the armourers, competed to give their city the glory of their trades. All the mechanisms of Los Angeles are like apprentices to these matters: the robot lights and the TV cameras, the scudding helicopters, the labouring oil pumps bowed like slaves across the city, or the great telescopes of Mount Wilson, brooding among their conifers high above the city, which in the years before the Second World War more than doubled man's total knowledge of the physical universe.

It is true that this expertise is sometimes rather dated, but then LA is essentially a survivor of earlier times, and one is constantly plucked back to that simpler world of the forties, when values were surer than they are now, and the attainment of wealth or fame seemed a true gauge of contentment.

Nostalgia blurs the realities of Hollywood, the Versailles of Los Angeles, and peoples it for ever with the royalty of another era, the Astaires, the Tracys, the Garbos, and nobles of even earlier vintage. Now as always the tourist buses circumnavigate the Homes of the Stars, and the touts peddle their street plans on Sunset Strip. Now as always Hollywood feeds upon narcissism, cosseted in sycophancy and sustained by snobbery. Scattered over the Hollywood Hills, and over the Santa Monica Mountains into the San Fernando Valley, the houses of the movie people stand sealed and suspicious in the morning, the only sounds the swishing of their sprinklers, the snarling of their guard dogs, or perhaps the laboured breathing of their gardeners: and in their garages the cars are profligately stacked, Jag beside Merc, Rolls upstaging BMW. Hollywood prefers its own world to ours, loving and living, generation after generation, its own fairly tawdry legend.

I stayed in the middle of it all, and soon came to feel how period a piece it was. My hotel was the Chateau Marmont, a monument in itself, built in the French manner half a century ago, and directly overlooking Sunset Boulevard. Everyone in Hollywood knows the place. That's where Bogart proposed to Bacall, they say, that's where Garbo used to stay, Howard Hughes had a suite there, Boris Karloff loved it, Valentino preferred the penthouse. It is impregnated with showbiz, from the gigantic antiques in the downstairs lounge to the strains of the electronic organ from the pop group practising in the garden bungalow: but what seems to the aficionado amusingly evocative seemed to me only a little threadbare, and I often found myself pining for an honest downtown motel, where never a Gable raised his eyebrow or a Garland threw a tantrum.

Every morning, too, I walked across the boulevard to have my breakfast at Schwab's, 'The World's Most Famous Drugstore'. Everyone knows Schwab's, too. Schwab's is where Lana Turner was discovered, sitting on a barstool. Hardly a Hollywood memoir is complete without a reference to Schwab's, and it is heavy with the old mystique. Elderly widows of émigré directors reminisce about Prague over their cornflakes. Young men in jerkins and expensive shoes ostentatiously read *Variety*, or greet each other with stagey endearments and expletives. Ever and again one hears across the hubbub, in the whining intonations peculiar to not very successful actors offstage, an exchange of critiques – 'I love her, she's a fine, fine actress, but it just wasn't *her*' – 'Well, but what can you expect with Philip directing, she needs *definite* direction' – 'True, but shit, it just made me *puke*, the way she did that last scene . . .' I used to drink my coffee at the counter, until I found its instinct for intimacy too cloying for comfort, and took to sitting at a table with the divorced wife of a Mexican set designer who shared my enthusiasm for Abyssinian cats.

If fetish and nostalgia often make for vulgarity in LA, they often make also for homeliness, in the English sense of the word – a community feeling, a domesticity. Even Hollywood is far less repulsive in its private aspects than in its public goings-on. This is largely because Los Angeles is a haven, to whose doors people have come from all over the world. It is a fraternity of refugees. Isherwood, showing me the view from his window one day, remembered the days when Stravinsky, Schoenberg, Brecht and Aldous Huxley had all lived in the city out there. Hardly a day goes by without the death of some celebrated European resident, driven here long ago by war, ambition or persecution, and the British consul-general told me that within his area there live more than 50,000 British subjects, some of whom fly Union Jacks from their roofs. San Francisco, up the coast, has an intimacy of a totally different kind, a hereditary or environmental

233

closeness, bound up with the beauty of the place and the allure of its traditions. There is no such grace to the brotherhood of LA. This is a charmless city really, humourless, often reactionary, a city without a gentry. Its comradeship lies only in a common sense of release or opportunity, tinged with a spice of holiday.

I used to buy my bread at Farmer's Market, a rambling enclave of stalls and tables off Wilshire Boulevard, and sitting over an orange juice afterwards, nibbling bits off the end of my loaf, loved to watch the Angelenos go by. Often, of course, they were not Angelenos at all, but Japanese business-men being shown around by bored local agents, or package tourists in wild sunglasses and kerchiefs, or bookish Europeans from UCLA deep in *Sociological Ratios in Southern California*. But there were always plenty of indigenes too, and they were instantly recognizable, not so much by their looks as by their posture, for they displayed all the somewhat impatient complacency of people who have discovered a Promised Land, and don't want to miss a minute of it. Though there are obviously lots of unhappy people in LA, lots of dispossessed blacks, unemployed layabouts, junkies and nuts and winos, still by and large this strikes me as a happy population – determinedly happy, perhaps. Nobody I met wanted to go back to New York or Detroit. With its Middle West squareness, its Manhattan bitterness, its imported touch of the European and its glorious Pacific sun, LA seems to please most people in the end – or for the moment.

In particular it provides a cheerful refuge for the jollier kind of American widow or divorcee, and many of these belatedly liberated souls frequent Farmer's Market. I often talked to them. There was a certain sameness to their appearance: in their bright blouses, leather jerkins, rather too tight slacks and rather too rakish sailor caps, bowed often by arthritis but reso-lutely vigorous of step, most of them looked more or less like Mr Capote except, of course, for the layered make-up ineffectually disguising their cod-skin complexions. To their attitudes though there was a sprightly element of freedom. Briskly, gaily, talkatively they walked around the stalls, a pumpernickel loaf here, a bag of cashews there, and often they exchanged rather throaty comments with acquaintances about last night's movie or tomorrow's meeting of the Democratic Party.

For such citizens LA offers an unexpected security, for its hard efficiency provides a bedrock, so to speak, upon which they can safely reconstruct their lives. It is nourished by the certainties they were weaned upon, like the pre-eminence of gadgetry or the goodness of capitalism. For all its cosmopolitan excitement, to a far greater degree than Chicago or San

Francisco, let alone New York, it is still a provincial American town. 'Did you know,' one Farmer's Market lady asked me, supposing me, I imagine, to be a bit lost for social satisfactions, 'did you know that the telephone company offers a free tour every day? My, that's a rewarding way of spending an afternoon.'

I went one night to one of those Hollywood parades one used to see on newsreels long ago. Nothing much had changed. The long motorcade crawled down Hollywood Boulevard in a welter of self-esteem, with drum majorettes and elephants and Scottish pipers and US Marines and belly dancers and coveys of movie personalities in antique cars who stopped now and then to be interviewed by TV men – 'Hey, Bob, great to see you! How's everything? Isn't this a great parade?' 'Sure is, Jim, fantastic, just great, and I wantya to meet my family, Jim, my wife Margie, this is my son Jason, my daughter Laureen!' 'Great, fantastic, great to meet all you folks, nice talking with you, Bill.' 'Sure thing, Jim, sure is a great parade, fantastic . . .' The echoes of the bands trumpeted across town, the belly dancers spangled their way past Grauman's Chinese Theater, and overhead the helicopters clanked and circled, playing their search-lights upon the junketings below.

I was touched by the crowd that watched this display, for I felt in it a truly innocent wonder. Its people came from everywhere. There were a few of my Market friends ('I forgot to mention this morning, dear, that the Municipal Cleansing Department offers a very interesting lecture tour Tuesday mornings'); but there were Mexicans, too, in bright ponchos with babies on their backs, and lots of Italians, and Hindus talking impeccable English, and Greeks talking Greek, and there was a Scotsman in a kilt looking maudlin when the pipers went by, and a man who looked like a Zulu chief, and a voluble family who seemed to be talking Finnish, or perhaps Basque, and there were thousands of that particular neo-American blend, of no particular colour, no specific race, no exact dialect, the *Homo californii*; and though the cops strode up and down fiercely slapping their nightsticks against their thighs, still everybody seemed genuinely, guilelessly delighted to be participants in such an unmistakably Angeleno spectacle.

I stayed till the very end, and the last I saw of the parade were the winking red lights of the police cars which brought up the rear, blinking away slowly down the boulevard as the crowds flooded off the sidewalks to follow them.

* * *

Hollywood itself, its fact and its reputation, its studios and its publicity machine, is a family of sorts, not always very loving indeed, and frequently incestuous, but still bound by a common loyalty to its own legend. Its members often speak of it with true affection, especially if they are old. As the glamour of success fades, as the meaning of money blurs, so Hollywood memories acquire a mellower force, and elderly directors, dowager stars, speak of old Hollywood as others might remember happy school days, or Edwardian society. Age is paradoxically venerated in Hollywood, and one is told without pejoration that so-and-so is living in a home for aged actors, or assured with respect that Miss Estelle Winwood really *is* in her 93rd year. The new breed of entertainer often seems awkwardly anomalous, almost alienated, in this hierarchical community: which is why the Hyatt hotel on Sunset Boulevard, where the rock bravos tend to congregate, was long ago nicknamed the Continental Riot House.

And unexpectedly, when I examine my feelings about this tremendous and always astonishing city, I find them inextricably shot through with regret. LA is full of vitality still, full of fun and wealth. The refugees are still flocking to this haven beyond the deserts, the men of brilliance are still at work in labs and laboratories and studios from Malibu to Irvine. Almost every development of Western thought, from space research to comparative linguistics to Transcendental Lung Control, finds its niche, its expression and its encouragement somewhere in this metropolis. Surveyed in the morning from one of its mountain belvederes, Los Angeles really does look one of the classic cities, one of the archetypes. Its streets and houses and bridges and buildings seem to lie there *differently* – massed differently, differently integrated, sprouting here and there peculiarly with the clumps of their urban centres, and hung over already, as the sun rises over the deserts, with the particular chemical haze whose very name, smog, was a Los Angeles invention. Then it looks unmistakably a world city: and it will represent for ever, I think, the apogee of urban, mechanical, scientific man, rational man perhaps, before the gods returned.

For it is past its prime already. It has lost the exuberant certainty that made it seem, even when I first knew it, unarguably the City of the Future, the City That Knew How. None of us Know now, the machine has lost its promise of emancipation, and if LA then seemed a talisman of fulfilment, now it is tinged with disillusion. Those terrific roads, those thousands of cars, the sheen of the jets screaming out of the airport, the magnificent efficiency of it all, the image building, the self-projection, the glamour, the fame – they were all false promises after all, and few of us see them now as the symptoms of redemption.

There is one monument in LA which hauntingly commemorates this failing faith. It is the queer cluster of pinnacles called the Watts Towers, and it stands in one of the shabbier parts of town, way out on 107th Street, beside the railway tracks. Simon Rodia, an Italian immigrant, built these arcane artefacts single-handedly, taking more than thirty years to do it. He made them of cement, stuck all over with bits of glass and pottery, strengthened by frames of scrap metal and wound about with curious studded spirals, rather like precipitous roller coasters. When he had built them he surrounded them with an irregular cement wall, like a row of tombstones, so that the whole ensemble has the air of a temple or shrine, rather oriental in nature.

It is very dusty there, and all around are the unpretentious homes of black people, so that you might easily suppose yourself to be in some African railway town, in the Egyptian delta perhaps. Few cars go by. You can hear children playing, and dogs barking, and neighbours chatting across the way. It is like a simple country place, before technology arrived, and the Watts Towers, years before their time, were a symbolic *cri du coeur* against the computer tyrannies to come. Mr Rodia was a prophet: and when he had built his towers he slipped away from Los Angeles once and for all, and went to live somewhere quite different.

Manhattan

What I had thought about Manhattan in the 1950s, I thought still in the 1970s. Whatever the condition of America, however I felt about its policies or its values, this was one American city that never let me down.

Sometimes, from the high windows of the *Rolling Stone* offices in Manhattan, you can make out a faint white blob in the green of Central Park far below. It is like the unresolved blur of a nebula in the night sky: and just as through a telescope the fuzz in Andromeda resolves itself into M31, so that whitish object in the park, defined through binoculars, becomes a phenomenon hardly less spectacular. It is the polar bear in the Central Park Zoo, and even as you focus your lenses, bringing his indistinct physique into clarity, with a shaggy shake of his head he swings his great form vigorously from one extremity of his cage to the other.

The bear lives alone in his compound down there, and I am told that he is a character of weird and forceful originality – sadly neurotic, some informants suggested, genuinely imaginative, others thought. He is a bear like no other, and it is not the fact of his captivity that makes him so, I am sure, but its remarkable location. Destiny has deposited that animal plumb in the middle of Manhattan: you might say he is the central New Yorker. He affects me profoundly whenever I see him, and when I put my binoculars down, and only the suggestion of him remains, apparently inanimate among the trees, all around him in my mind's eye the marvellous and terrible island of Manhattan concentrically extends, ring after ring of cage, ditch or rampart, precinct limit and electoral boundary, Hudson, East River and Atlantic itself – the greatest of all the zoos, whose inhabitants prowl up and down, like victims of some terrific spell, for ever and ever within it.

For Manhattan really is an island, even now, separated from the mainland still by a channel just wide enough for the Circle Line boats to continue their pleasure circuits, and it is this condition of enclave that gives the place its sting. Like the bear, its citizens are heightened, one way or another, by their confinement. If they are unhappier than most populaces, they are merrier too. If they are trapped in some ways, they are brilliantly liberated in others. Sometimes their endless pacing to and fro is sad to see, but when the weather is right and the sap is rising, then it assumes an exhilarating rhythm, and the people of Manhattan seem to dance along their avenues, round and round the city squares, in and out the sepulchral subway.

Images of confinement certainly haunt me in Manhattan but the first thing that always strikes me, when I land once more on the island, is its fearful and mysterious beauty. Other cities have built higher now, or sprawl more boisterously over their landscapes, but there is still nothing like the looming thicket of the Manhattan skyscrapers, jumbled and overbearing. Le Corbusier hated this ill-disciplined spectacle, and conceived his own Radiant City, an antiseptic hybrid of art and ideology, in direct antithesis to it. His ideas, though, mostly bounced off this vast mass of vanity. Tempered though it has been from time to time by zoning law and social trend, Manhattan remains a mammoth mess, a stupendous clashing of light and dark and illusory perspective, splotched here and there by wastelands of slum or demolition, wanly patterned by the grid of its street system, but essentially, whatever the improvers do to it, whatever economy decrees or architectural fashion advises, the supreme monument to that elemental human instinct, Free-For-All.

But the glowering ecstasy of it! No other city, not even Venice, projects for me a more orgiastic kind of allure. I do not mean the popular phallic symbolism of the place, its charged erections thrusting always into the sky. I am thinking of more veiled seductions, the shadows in its deep streets, the watchfulness, the ever-present hint of concealment or allusion. The clarity of Manhattan is what the picture postcards emphasize, but I prefer Manhattan hazed, Manhattan reticent and heavy-eyed.

I like it, for instance, on a very, very hot day, a day when emerging into the streets from the air conditioning is like changing continents. Then a film of chemical vapour seems to drift around the city, fudging every edge, and gauzing every vista. Exhausted, half-deserted, the island seems to stand stupefied in the haze: but sometimes flashes of sunlight, piercing the humidity, are reflected momentarily off windows or metal roofs, and then I am reminded of those uncertain but resplendent cities, vaporous and diamond-twinkling, which stand in the backgrounds of all the best fairy tales.

Conversely on a grey lowering day it is like some darkling forest. The tops of the buildings are lost in fog, and only their massive bases, like the trunks of so many gigantic oaks, are to be seen beneath the cloud base. I feel a mushroom feeling in Manhattan then, and the huddled scurry of the people on the sidewalks, the shifting patterns of their umbrellas, the swish of cars through pothole puddles, the blinking of the traffic lights one after another through the slanting rain, the plumes of steam which, like geysers from the subterranean, spout into the streets – all this speaks fancifully to me, here in *urbanissimus*, of clearing, glade and woodland market.

But best of all, for this reluctant and secretive beauty of the island, I like to walk very early in the morning down to Battery Park, the southernmost tip of it, its gazebo on the world, looking out across the great bay towards the Narrows and the open sea. This is a melancholy pleasure, for the shipping which used to make this the busiest basin on earth has mostly been dispersed now. Most of the Atlantic liners sail no more, the freighters mostly berth elsewhere around the bay, and of the myriad public ferries which used to bustle like so many water insects to and from Manhattan, only the old faithful to Staten Island survives.

So early in the morning, the scene down at the Battery is not likely to be bustling. If it is misty, it is likely to be a little spooky, in fact. The mist lies heavy over the greyish water, muffled sirens sound, somewhere a sound-buoy intermittently hoots. Perhaps a solitary tanker treads cautiously toward Brooklyn, or a pilot boat, its crew collars-up against the dank, chugs out toward the Narrows. Early commuters emerge blearily from

239

the ferry station; two or three layabouts are stretched on park benches, covered in rags and newspaper; a police car sometimes wanders by, its policemen slumped in their seats dispassionately.

It seems eerily isolated and exposed, and you feel as though the few of you are all alone, there at the water's edge. But as the morning draws on and the mist clears, something wonderful happens. It is like the printing of a Polaroid picture. The wide sweep of the bay gradually reveals its outlines, the Statue of Liberty appears unforeseen upon her plinth, lesser islands show themselves, and as you turn your back upon the water, glistening now in the freshening breeze, it turns out that the tremendous presence of Manhattan itself, its serried buildings rank on rank, has been looking over your shoulder all the time.

I was walking one day down Sixth Avenue (as New Yorkers still sensibly prefer to call the Avenue of the Americas) when I saw a lady taking a bath, fully clothed, in the pool outside the Time-Life Building. This struck me as a good idea, for it was a hot and sticky day, and I approached her to express my admiration for her initiative. I did not get far. When she saw me step her way she sat bolt upright in the pool, water streaming off her lank hair and down the clinging blue fabric of her dress, and screamed obscenities at me. It was unnerving. Shrill, wild and dreadfully penetrating, her voice pursued me like an eldritch curse, and everyone looked accusingly at me, as though I had insulted the poor soul, and deserved all the imprecations she could command (and her repertoire, I must say, was impressive).

Nobody, I noticed, looked accusingly at *her*. She was evidently mad, and so unaccusable. Confined like that bear on their own rock, the people of Manhattan are the most neurotic community on earth. The twitch, the mutter, the meaningless shriek, the foul-mouthed mumble, the disjointed shuffle – these are native gestures of the island. Pale and ghostly, violently made up or sunk in despair are thousands of its faces – clowns' faces, chalk white and crimson, or haunted faces that have survived concentration camps, or faces alive with a crazy innocence, like those of murderous infants.

Every great city has its bewildered minority – the confused are always with us. Manhattan, though, is the only one I know that sometimes seems on the brink of general nervous breakdown. Intensely clever, cynical, introspective, feverishly tireless, it has all the febrile brightness, alternating with despondency, that sometimes attends insomnia, together with the utter self-absorption of the schizophrenic. Few residents of Manhattan really much care what happens anywhere else. Backs to the sea and the waterways east and west, theirs is a crosstown outlook, focusing ever closer, ever more preoccupied, upon the vortex of the place – which is to say, themselves. 'Does dyslexia', I heard an interviewer say in all serious-ness on television one day, 'crop up in other parts of the country, or is it pertinent only to Manhattan?'

Lord Melbourne, when he was Queen Victoria's Prime Minister, was once asked by an anxious acquaintance for his advice on how best to cope with the problems of life. 'Be easy,' was all the statesman said. 'I like an easy man.' He would have to look hard for one in Manhattan, where the old gamblers' precept 'Let it ride' has long been rejected. Analysis, I some-times think, is the principal occupation of Manhattan – analysis of trends, analysis of options, analysis of style, analysis of statistics, analysis above all of self. Freud has much to answer for, in this island of tangled dreams, and the women's movement has evidently liberated all too many women only into agonized doubt and self-questioning.

But actually, like most people, New Yorkers like to be thought a bit crazy. When they had a poll in New York and Los Angeles, each city complacently claimed its own population to be madder than the other. I know a business corporation in Manhattan – I dare not mention its name – which seems to me to be run entirely, top to bottom, by people off their balance. The minute I enter its offices, an uneasy suggestion of collective therapy assails me. Concealed and unapproachable behind his monumental mahogany doors sits the president of this corporation of nuts, mad as a hatter himself, and in hierarchy of psychosis his subordinates hiss and fiddle their days away below. Sometimes a whole department is fired: sometimes a surprised and hitherto unnoticed employee is plucked from obscurity and made the head of a division for a month or two; sometimes the company, which deals (let us say) in commodity shares, suddenly invests a few million dollars in a Chattanooga umbrella factory, or a grocery chain in Nicaragua.

They have all been driven off their heads, I suppose, by the needling and hallucinatory pressures of Manhattan, the prick of ambition, the fear of failure: and in their eyes I see, as they contemplate the future of their lunatic careers, just the same fierce but loveless passion that one sees in the eyes of brainwashed cultists – a blend of alarm and mindless dedica-tion, dimly tinged with tranquillizers.

I say hallucinatory pressures, because to the outsider there is much to Manhattan that seems surreal. This is not a place of natural fantasy, like Los Angeles – its spirit is fundamentally logical and rationalist, as befits a city of merchants, bankers and stockbrokers. But its daily life is spattered with aspects and episodes of an unhinged sensibility, of which I record here, from a recent two-weeks' stay on the island, a few by no means extraordinary examples:

Item: An eminent, kind and cultivated actress, beautifully dressed, taking a cab to an address on Second Avenue. Cabdriver: 'Whereabouts is that on Second Avenue, lady?' Actress, without a flicker in her equanimity: 'Don't ask me, bud, you're the fucking cab-driver.'

Item: At the headquarters of the New York police, which is at police Plaza, and is approached along the Avenue of the Finest, there is a functionary called the Chief of Organized Crime. I heard an administrator say to a colleague on the telephone there: *You're going sick today? Administrative sick or regular sick?*

Item: A young man talks about his experiences in a levitation group: *Nobody's hovering yet but we're lifting up and down again. We're hopping. I've seen a guy hop fifteen feet from the lotus position, and no one could do that on the level of trying.*

Item: Coming down in the hotel elevator at the New York Hilton is a delegate to the American Urological Association convention. He is on his way to a presentation on Pre-Lymphadenectomy Staging of Testicular Tumors, and his name, I see from his lapel card, is Dr Portnoy.

Item: An aged court-appointed lawyer, down at the state courts, histrionically convinces the judge, with a florid wealth of legal jargon and gesture, that an adjournment is necessary, but spotting a row of hostile witnesses as he passes through the courtroom on his way out, loudly offers them a comment: *Too bad, assholes.*

Item: Graffito in Washington Square. YIPPIES, JESUS FREAKS AND MOONIES ARE GOVERNMENT OPERATED.

Item: Four angry ladies are trying to enter St Patrick's Cathedral by the wrong entrance for the celebration of the cathedral's centenary, to be attended by three cardinals and eight archbishops. Their way is barred, but as the chanting of the mass sounds through the half-closed door, I hear them responding with a genuine *cri du coeur*: *We must get in! We must! We're tourists from Israel!*

Item: The terrifyingly ambitious, inexhaustible girl supervisor at one of the downtown McDonald's. Over the serving counter one may see the glazed and vacant faces of the cooks, a black man and a couple of Puerto Ricans, who appear to speak no English: in front that small tyrant strides peremptorily up and down, yelling orders, angrily correcting errors, and constantly falling back upon an exhortatory slogan of her own: *C'mon, guys, today guys, today . . .!* The cooks look back in pained incomprehension.

Item: I feel a sort of furry clutch at my right leg, and peering down, find that it is being bitten by a chow. *Oh Goochy you naughty thing*, says its owner, who is following behind with a brush and shovel for clearing up its excrement, *you don't know that person.*

Item: At nine in the morning, on a smart street in the East Seventies, a highly respectable middle-aged lady leans against the hood of a black Mercedes, meditatively scratching her crotch.

Item: It is night, and drizzling. I am crossing Park Avenue on my way home, and looking to my left to the mass of the Grand Central Terminal, see a sort of vision: piled on top of the New York General Building, and silhouetted floodlit against the monstrous Pan Am tower behind, the pinnacled cupola of the structure looks, just for a moment, like a shrine – a stupa, perhaps. I pause in astonishment, half expecting to hear mystical prayer bells sounding, until a passing cab, hooting its horn and showering me with mud from an adjacent gutter, scuttles me back to realism.

How small it is! Thirteen miles long from tip to tip, two and a half miles across at its widest point – at 86th Street, I believe. It would be hard to be anonymous for long in Manhattan, if anyone well known ever wanted to be. When I was here last I went to see Mr Woody Allen's masterpiece *Manhattan*, the truest contemporary work of art I know about the island: after the show I went next door for a cup of tea at the Russian Tea Room, and there, large as life, toying with what I assume to have been a blini, was Mr Allen himself.

Sometimes it is hard to remember that this is one of the earth's most powerful cities, for in some ways it is oddly parochial. The *New York Times* is half a newspaper of international record, and half a parish magazine, with full obituaries of respected local insurance managers, and blow-by-blow accounts of the engagement of Miss Henrietta Zlyman to Edward Twistletoe III. Like all great metropolises, Manhattan is divided into lesser enclaves, each with its own personality and purpose, but the skinny shape of the island, the rigidity of its grid and the flatness of it all, make it impossible for any district to feel remote from any other. You can easily walk from Central Park to Battery Park in a gentle morning stroll; I boarded a bus recently with an acquaintance in the very heart of Harlem, all dingy tenements and apparently abandoned stores, and before he had finished telling me his war experiences we had arrived outside the Plaza Hotel. Besides, the great landmarks of the place, the Empire State Building, the twin towers of the World Trade Center, are so enormous that they are visible almost everywhere, and give the island a foreshortened sort of intimacy.

All crammed in like this, it is no wonder that the inhabitants of Manhattan sway to and fro, as though with minds linked, to the shifting tunes of fashion. No city in the world, I think, is so subject to the diktats of critics, snobs and arbiters of taste. Manhattan feeds upon itself – intravenously, perhaps. A very public elite dominates its gossip columns and decors, the same faces over and over, seen at the same currently fashionable clubs and restaurants, Stork Club in one generation, Studio 54 another, drinking the statutory drinks, *kir* yesterday, Perrier today, using the same ephemeral 'in' words – when I was here last, for example: 'schlep', 'supportive', 'copacetic', 'significant others'.

I was taken one evening, at my own request, to the saloon currently the trendiest in town, Elaine's on Second Avenue. Everyone knows Elaine's. Secretaries hang about its bar, in the hope of being adopted by wild celebrities, young executives talk about it the morning after, and even the most intelligent of public people, it seems, literate directors and scholarly critics, unaccountably think it worth while to be seen there. No such phenomenon exists in Europe, for Elaine's is neither very expensive nor exactly exclusive – anyone can go and prop up the bar. I detested it, though: the noise, the jam-packed tables, the showing-off, the gush, the unwritten protocol which gives the best-known faces the most prominent tables, and banishes unknowns to the room next door. The beautiful people looked less than beautiful shouting their heads off in the din. The waiter resisted my attempts to have scampi without garlic (not liking garlic is infra dig in Manhattan).

I felt fascinated and appalled, both at the same time: but more surprising, I felt a bit patronizing – for all of a sudden, as I observed those bobbing faces there, wreathed in display or goggled in sycophancy, fresh as I was from my little village on the north-west coast of Wales, I felt myself to be among provincials.

Not a sensation I often get in New York. More often, when I am at large in this incomparable city, I feel myself to be among ultimates. *How're they gonna get me back on the farm?* This is, after all, The City of our times, as Rome was in classical days, as Constantinople was through centuries of Mediterranean history. This is everyone's metropolis, for there is no nation that has not contributed something to Manhattan, if only a turn of phrase or a category of bun. I went one day to the street festival which is held each May on Ninth Avenue, one of the most vividly cosmopolitan thoroughfares on the island, and realized almost too piquantly what it means to be a city of all peoples: smell clashing with smell, from a mile of sidewalk food stalls, sesame oil at odds with curry powder, Arabic drifting into Ukrainian among the almost impenetrable crowds, Yiddish colliding with Portuguese, and all the way down the avenue the discordant blending of folk-music, be it from Polish flageolet, Mexican harmonica or balalaika from Sofia.

Nothing provincial there! And if over the past 300 years the clambering upon this huge raft of refugees, adventurers, idealists and crooks from every land has given Manhattan always a quality of paradigm or fulcrum, so when it comes to the end of the world, I think, most people can most easily imagine the cataclysm in the context of this island. The great towers crumpling and sagging into themselves, the fires raging up the ravaged boulevards, the panicked rush of the people, like rats or lemmings, desperately into the boiling water – these are twentieth-century man's standard images of Doomsday: and in my own view, if God is truly going to sit one day in judgement upon the doings of mankind, he is likely to set up court on the corner of Broadway and 42nd Street, where he can deal first (and leniently I am sure) with the purveyors of Sextacular Acts Live on Stage.

We live in baleful times, and it is a pity that Manhattan, that temple of human hope and ingenuity, should be obliged to fill this particular role of parable. There is no denying, though, that there often passes across the face of this city, like a shudder, a sense of ominous portent. I read one morning in the *Times* that a woman, walking the previous day down a street near City Hall, had been attacked by a pack of rats 'as big as rabbits'. I leapt into a cab at once, but Manhattan had beaten me to it: already a small crowd was peering with evident satisfaction into the festering abandoned lot from which the rodents had sprung. Already one of your archetypal New Yorkers had appointed himself resident expert, and was pointing out to enthralled office workers one of your actual rats, *almost* as big as a rabbit, which was sitting morosely in a wire trap among the piled rubbish. What became of the original victim? I asked. 'I guess she was some kind of screwball. She just drove off screaming . . .'

I would have driven off screaming too, if those rabbit-rats had attached themselves to me, but around the corner, almost within excretion distance of the rat pit, business was brisk as ever at the neighbourhood takeout food store. New Yorkers are hardened to horror, I suppose, and perhaps it is this acclimatization that gives their island its sense of fated obliteration. It might be designed for nemesis, and suggests to me sometimes an amphitheatre of pagan times, in which ladies and rats, like gladiators and wild beasts, are pitted against each other for the rude entertainment of the gods.

Everything comes on to the island: nothing much goes off, even by evaporation. Once it was a gateway to a New World, now it is a portal chiefly to itself. Manhattan long ago abandoned its melting-pot function. Nobody even tries to Americanize the Lebanese or the Lithuanians now, and indeed the ethnic enclaves of the island seem to me to become more potently ethnic each time I visit the place. Nothing could be much more Italian than the Festival of St Anthony of Padua down on Mulberry Street, when the families of Little Italy stroll here and there through their estate, pausing often to greet volatile contemporaries and sometimes munching the soft-shelled crabs which, spread-eagled on slices of bread like zoological specimens, are offered loudly for sale by street vendors. Harlem has become almost a private city in itself, no longer to be slummed through by whities after dinner, while Manhattan's Chinatown is as good a place as anywhere in the world to test your skill at that universal challenge, trying to make a Chinese waiter smile.

So the lights blaze down fiercely upon a tumultuous arena: but its millions of gladiators (and wild beasts) are not in the least disconcerted by the glare of it, or daunted by the symbolic battles in which they are engaged, but are concerned chiefly to have swords of the fashionable length, and to be seen to advantage from the more expensive seats.

Back to the park. At the centre of the world's present preoccupation with Manhattan, for one reason and another, stands Central Park. 'Don't go walking in that Park,' they will warn you from China to Peru, or 'Tell me frankly,' they ask, 'is it true what they say about Central Park?'

The Park is the centre of the island too, no man's land amid the surrounding conflict of masonry – on the postal map it forms a big oblong blank, the only portion of Manhattan without a zip code. To the north is Harlem, to the south is Rockefeller Center, on one flank is the opulence of the Upper East Side, to the west are the newly burgeoning streets that sprout, teeming with artists, agents, Polish grocers and music students, right and left off Columbus Avenue. It is like a big rectangular scoop in the city, shovelled out and stacked with green. It covers eighty-four acres, and it is almost everything, to my mind, that a park should not be.

This is a heretical view. Central Park is enormously admired by specialists in planning and urban design. The architectural critic of the *New York Times* calls it the city's greatest single work of architecture. It was laid out in 1856 by Frederick Law Olmsted and Calvert Vaux, and ever since everybody has been saying how marvellous it is. 'One of the most beautiful parks in the world,' thought Baedeker, 1904. 'This great work of art,' says the *AIA Guide to New York City, 1978*.

Not me. With its gloomy hillocks obstructing the view, with its threadbare and desolate prairies, with its consciously contrived variety of landscapes, with its baleful lake and brownish foliage, with the sickly carillon which, hourly from the gates of its appalling zoo, reminds me horribly of the memorial chimes at Hiroshima, Central Park seems to me the very antithesis of the fresh and natural open space, the slice of countryside, that a *city* park should ideally be.

Nevertheless the world is right when, invited to think of Manhattan, it is likely to think first these days of Central Park. If I deny its ethereal beauty, I do not for a moment dispute its interest. It is one of the most interesting places on earth. 'It is inadvisable,' warns the Michelin guide, 1968, 'to wander alone through the more deserted parts of the park': but wandering alone nevertheless through this extraordinary retreat, dominated on all sides by the towering cliffs of Manhattan, is to enjoy one of the greatest of all human shows, in perpetual performance from dawn through midnight.

You want tradition? There go the lumbering barouches, their horse smells hanging pungent in the air long after they have left their stands outside the Plaza, their Dutch trade delegates, their Urological Association conventioneers, or even their honeymooners from Iowa, somewhat self-consciously sunk in their cushions, and their coachmen leaning back, as they have leant for a century or more, whip in hand to ask their customers where they're from.

You want irony? Consider the layabouts encouched apparently permanently on their bundles along the East Side, beyond the open-air bookstalls, prickly and raggedy, bony and malodorous, camped there almost in the shadow of the sumptuous Fifth Avenue apartment houses, and more tellingly still perhaps, actually within earshot of the feebly growling lions, the cackling birds and funereal carillon of the zoo.

You want vaudeville? Try the joggers on their daily exercise. Dogged they lope in their hundreds around the ring road, generally cleared of traffic on their behalf, like migrating animals homed in upon some inexplicable instinct, or numbed survivors from some catastrophe out of sight. Some are worn lean as rakes by their addiction, some drop the sweat of repentant obesity. Some flap with huge ungainly breasts. Some tread with a predatory menace, wolflike in the half-hour before they must present that memo about ongoing supportive expenditures to Mr Cawkwell at the office. Sometimes you may hear snatches of very Manhattan conversations, as the enthusiasts labour by – *So you're saying* (gasp) *that since* 1951 (pant) *there's been no meaningful change whatever* (puff) *in our society?* Sometimes you may observe a jogger who has taken his dog with him on a leash, and who, obliged to pause while the animal defecates behind a bush, compromises by maintaining a standing run, on the spot, looking consequently for all the world as though he is dying for a pee himself.

But no, it is the sinister you want, isn't it? *'It is inadvisable to wander alone, despite the frequent police patrols on horseback or by car . . .'* That is what Central Park is most famous for these days, and it is not hard to find. I have never been mugged in Central Park, never seen anyone else harmed either, but I have had my chill moments all the same. More than once, even as the joggers pad around their circuit, I have noticed perched distantly on the rocky outcrops which protrude among the dusty trees, groups of three or four youths, silently and thoughtfully watching. They wear dark glasses, as likely as not, and big floppy hats, and they recline upon their rock in attitudes of mocking but stealthy grace, motionless, as though they are fingering their flick-knives. I waved to one such group of watchers once, as I walked nervously by: but they responded only by looking at each other in a bewildered way, and shifting their long legs a trifle uneasily upon the stone.

All around the city roars. Well, no, not roars – buzzes, perhaps. The energy of Manhattan is less leonine than waspish, and its concerns are, for so tremendous a metropolis, wonderfully individual and idiosyncratic. Despite appearances, Manhattan is an especially human city, where personal aspirations, for better or for worse, unexpectedly take priority. Perhaps this is because, unlike either of the other global cities (for in my view there are only two, Paris and London) – unlike its peers, New York is not a capital. True, the headquarters of the United Nations is down by the East River, but architecturally it is the perfect reflection of its lacklustre political self, and one hardly notices it. True too that the municipal affairs of this city, being on so momentous a scale, are equivalent I suppose to the entire political goings-on of many lesser republics. But it is not really a political city. Affairs of state and patriotism rarely intrude. Even the state capital is far away in Albany, and Manhattan conversations do not often turn to infighting within the Democratic Party, or the prospects of Salt III.

There is not much industry on the island, either, in any sociological or aesthetic sense: few blue-collared workers making for home with their lunch boxes, few manufacturing plants to belch their smoke into the Manhattan sky. This is a city of more intricate concerns, a city of speculators and advisers, agents and middlemen and sorters-out and go-betweens. Many of the world's most potent corporations have their headquarters here, but their labour forces are mostly conveniently far away. Fortunes are made here, and reputations, not steel ingots or automobiles.

The pace of New York is legendary, but nowadays in my opinion illusory. Businessmen work no harder, no faster, than in most other great cities. But New Yorkers spend so much time contemplating their personal affairs, analysing themselves, examining their own reactions, that the time left for business is necessarily rushed. Do not suppose, when the Vice-President of Automated Commercial leaves his office in such a hurry, that he is meeting the Overseas Sales Director of Toyuki Industries: good gracious no, he is leaving early because he simply must have it out face to face with Brian about his disgraceful behaviour with that Edgar person in the disco last night.

More than any other place I know, to do business in New York you must understand your colleagues' circumstances. They often need worrying out. There are some tell-tale signs indeed, like tribal tattoos – short hair for Brian and Edgar, for example, droopy moustaches and canvas shoes for aspirant literary men, rasping voices and nasal intonations for girls who hope to get into television, hands in trouser pockets for Ivy League executives. But you should take no chances. The tangles of Manhattan marital and emotional life, which provide inexhaustible hours of instruction to the social observer, set the tone of this place far more than torts, share prices or bills of lading.

There is hardly a citizen of Manhattan, of any race, creed or social class, who does not have some fascinating emotional imbroglio to relate – and hardly a citizen, either, who fails to relate it. Nitter-natter, chit-chat, *you would hardly believe it, so I said never, so she said absolutely* – sibilantly across this city of gossip, from Wall Street clubs to bars of Harlem, one seems to hear the tide of confession and confidence, unremitting as the flood of the traffic, rattly as the clang of the subway trains which now and then emerges from grilles beneath one's feet.

Is this inbreeding? Certainly there is something perceptibly incestuous about Manhattan, now that the diversifying flow of immigration has abated. This is no longer the lusty stud of the world. Ellis Island, through whose lugubrious halls so many millions of newcomers passed into the land of fertility, is only a museum now, and ethnically Manhattan has lost its virile momentum. You feel the migratory thrust far more vividly in Toronto, and most of New York's contemporary immigrants are hardly immigrants at all, in the old risk-all kind, but are Puerto Ricans joining their relatives, or Colombians co-operatively financed by the drug-rings of Jackson Heights.

They are seldom inspired, as their predecessors were, by any flaming spirit of release or dedication, and they very soon fall into the Manhattan mode. 'Well it's like I say, see, I got this lady I used to know back in Bogotá. She says to me, "Leon," she says, "I wantya to know, I'm fond of you, truly I am, but there's this problem of Juan's baby, see?" "To hell with Juan's baby," I says, "what's Juan's baby to me?" And she says, "Leon honey," she says, "listen to me . . . "'

'Give me your tired, your poor, your huddled masses yearning to breathe free . . .' An occasional Russian dissident appears in New York these days, to endure his statutory press conference before being whisked away to CIA debriefing or associate professorship somewhere. But the loss of the grand old purpose, so stoutly declaimed by the Lady of Liberty out there in the bay, means that Manhattan is recognizably past its prime. Every city has its heyday, the moment when its purpose is fulfilled and its spirit bursts into full flower, and Manhattan's occurred I think in the years between the Great Depression, when the indigents squatted in Central Park, and the end of the Second World War, when the GIs returned in splendour as the saviours of liberty. In those magnificent years this small island, no more than a fantastic dream to most of the peoples of the world, stood every-where for the fresh start and the soaring conception. Manhattan was Fred

Astaire and the sun-topped Chrysler Building! Manhattan was the Jeep and Robert Benchley! Manhattan was rags-to-riches, free speech, Mayor La Guardia and the Rockettes!

No wonder nostalgia booms on Broadway. Those were the days of the American innocence, before responsibility set in, and every dry and racy old song of the period, every new Art Deco furniture boutique, is an expression of regret. European Powers pine for their lost glories with bearskin parades or jangling cavalry: New York looks back with *Ain't Misbehavin'*, or the refurbishing, just as it was, of that prodigy of Manhattan gusto, Radio City Music Hall (whose designer reportedly had ozone driven through its ventilator shafts, to keep its audiences festive, and toyed with the idea of laughing gas too . . .). Fortunately the old days come quickly in a city that is not yet 300 years old, and the authentic bitter-sweetness is relatively easy to achieve. I was touched myself by the furnishing of a restaurant equipped entirely with the fittings of one of the old Atlantic liners, those dowagers of the Manhattan piers, until I discovered that the ship concerned was the *Caronia*, whose launching I remember as clear as yesterday.

The memories of that time are legendary already, and moving fast into myth. Nothing in travel stirs me more than the dream of that old Manhattan, the Titan City of my childhood, when the flamboyant skyscrapers soared one after the other into empyrean, when John D. Rockefeller, Jr, pored over the plans for his Center like a modern Midas, when the great liners stalked through the bay with their complements of celebrities and shipboard reporters, and the irrepressible immigrants toiled and clawed their way up the line of Manhattan, from Ellis Island to the Lower East Side to the Midtown affluence of their aspirations. Its monuments are mostly there to see still, newly fashionable as the buildings of the day before yesterday are apt to become, and sometimes even now you may stumble across one of its success stories: the waiter proudly boasting that, since arriving penniless and friendless from Poland, he has never been out of work for a day – the famous publisher, in the penthouse suite of his own skyscraper, whose mother landed in Manhattan with a placard around her neck, announcing her name, trade and language.

Rockefeller Center is the theatre of this mood. Raymond Hood, the creator of its central structure, the RCA Building, was reminded one day that he had come to Manhattan in the first place with the declared intention of becoming the greatest architect in New York. 'So I did,' he responded, looking out of the window at that stupendous thing, jagged and commanding high above, 'and by God, so I am!' The magnificent brag, the revelatory vision, the ruthless opportunism, the limitless resource – these were the attributes of Rockefeller Center, as of Manhattan, in the heady years of its construction: and when at winter time they turn the sunken café into an ice rink, then in the easy delight of the skaters under the floodlights, some so hilariously inept, some so showily skilful, with the indulgent crowd leaning over the railings to watch, and the waltz music only half drowned by the city's rumble – then I sometimes seem to be, even now, back in those boundless years of certainty.

If the conviction is lost, the abilities remain. This is the most gifted of all the human settlements of the earth, and there are moments in Manhattan when the sheer talent of the place much moves me. I happened to be in the Pan Am Building recently when an orchestra of young people was giving a lunch-time concert in the central concourse. This is a common enough event in Manhattan, a place of inescapable music, but somehow it seized my imagination and twisted my emotions. No other city, I swear, could provide an interlude so consoling. The brilliant young players were so full of exuberance. The audience listened to their Brahms and Vivaldi with such sweet attention. The music sounded wonderfully tender in the heart of all that stone and steel, and seemed to float like a tempering agent down the escalators, through the bland air-conditioned offices, of that great tower of materialism. ('How beautifully they play,' I remarked in my delight to a man listening beside me, but in the Manhattan manner he brought me harshly down to earth. 'They gotta play beautifully,' he replied. 'Think of the competition.')

The cities of Europe have mostly lost their artists' quarters, swallowed up now in housing estates or ripped apart by ring roads. In Manhattan, Bohemia flourishes still, in many an eager alcove. This is a city of the streets and cafés, where human contact, carnal or platonic, is still easy to arrange, where no young artist need feel alone or benighted for long, and where no ambition is too extravagant. Manhattan probably has more than its fair share of artistic phonies, and SoHo, currently the most popular painters' quarter, certainly exhibits an adequate proportion of junkyard collages or knobs of inadequately sandpapered walnut labelled 'Significant Others 3'. But tucked away in the attics, cheap hotels, apartment blocks and converted brownstones of this island myriad genuine artists and craftsmen are at work, impervious to trend and disdainful of sham.

I like to spend Sunday mornings watching the alfresco circus down at Washington Square, the gateway to Greenwich Village, where wandering musicians and amateur jugglers compete for the attention of the sightseers with virtuoso Frisbee throwers, classical in their skills and gestures, impromptu demagogues, chess players, itinerant idiots and Rastafari bravos. Often and again then, when I am sitting on my park bench watching this colourful world go by, I spot a fellow practitioner of my craft, alone on *his* bench with *his* notebook, and as our eyes meet I wonder if I ought to feel compassion for him, as the struggling artist from his austere garret somewhere, or envy, as the author of tomorrow's runaway best-seller.

Contrary to the world's conceptions, New York is rich in people of integrity. In a city of such attainments it has to be so. This is a city of dedicated poets, earnest actors and endlessly rehearsing musicians. Draft after draft its writers are rejecting, and there are more good pianists playing in New York every evening than in the whole of Europe – smouldering jazz pianists in the downtown clubs, crazy punk pianists on Bleecker Street, stuffed-shirt romantic pianists in the Midtown tourist spots ('Would you mind lowering your voice to a whisper, please, during Mr Maloney's renditioning?'), smashing student pianists practising for next year's Tchaikovsky competition, jolly young pianists accompanying off-Broadway musicals, drop-out pianists, drunk ruined pianists, mendicant pianists with instruments on trolley wheels, Steinway pianists flown by Concorde that afternoon for their concerti at Lincoln Center.

So I am never really deluded by the charlatan inanities of New York. I disregard the fatuous interviewers and repellent respondents of what we are gruesomely encouraged to think of as NBC's Today Family. I sneer not at the sellers of Instant Ginseng. I am not deceived by the coarse-grained editors, hag-ridden by their own accountants, or the ghastly company of celebrities. 'Creativity' is so degraded a word in Manhattan that I hesitate to use it, loathing its translation into salesmen's acuity or publicity gimmick. But creative this place truly is: not in the old audacious style perhaps, but in the quieter, introspective, muddled but honest way that is more the Manhattan manner now.

It would seem inconceivable to Hood or John D., Jr, let alone Commodore Vanderbilt or Pierpont Morgan, but actually in 1979 Manhattan feels a little old-fashioned. The Titan City has come to terms, and recognizes that everything is *not* possible after all. They build more thrilling buildings in Chicago now. They do more astonishing things in

Houston. There are more aggressive entrepreneurs in Tokyo or Frankfurt. It is no good coming to Manhattan for the shape of things to come: Singapore or São Paulo might be more reliable guides. In the days of the Great Vision the New Yorkers built an airship mast on the top of the Empire State Building almost as a matter of course, sure that the latest and greatest dirigibles would head straight for Manhattan: it was years, though, before New York was reluctantly persuaded, in our own time, to allow supersonic aircraft to land at JFK.

Manhattan is no longer the fastest, the most daring or even I dare say the richest. For a symbol of its civic energies now, I recommend an inspection of the abandoned West Side Highway, the victim of seven years' municipal indecision, which staggers crumbling on its struts above a wilderness of empty lots, truck parks and shattered warehouses, the only signs of enterprise being the cyclists who cheerfully trundle along the top of it, and the railway coaches of the Ringling Bros, Barnum and Bailey Circus which park themselves habitually underneath.

The falter came, I believe, in the fifties and sixties, when Manhattan began to see laissez faire, perhaps, as a less than absolute ideology. Doubts crept in. The pace slowed a bit. The sense of movement lagged. All the great ships no longer came in their grandeur to the Manhattan piers; the New York airports were far from the island; today even the helicopters, which were for a couple of decades the lively familiars of Manhattan, are banned from their wayward and fanciful antics around the skyscrapers. Bauhaus frowned down upon Radio City Music Hall, in those after-the-glory years, and most of Manhattan's mid-century architecture was, by Hood's standards, timid and banal. The truly original buildings were few, and worse still for my taste, the swagger-buildings were not built at all.

The fashionable philosophy of smallness has strongly appealed to New Yorkers, in their new mood of restraint, and nowadays when citizens want to show you some innovation they are proud of, they generally take you to a dainty little kerbside park with waterfalls, or Roosevelt Island, an itsy-bitsy enclave of sociological good taste. Suavity, discretion and even modesty are the architectural qualities admired in Manhattan now, and the colossal is no longer welcomed.

And believe it or not, *quaintness* approaches. Mr Philip Johnson's latest building is to be crowned with a decorative device like the back of a Chesterfield sofa: so does old age creep up, all but unsuspected, upon even the most dynamic organisms – Time's A-Train, hurrying near! Manhattan is no longer critical in the atomic sense: 'No Nukes' is a proper slogan for this gently decelerating powerhouse.

It is not a sad spectacle. I find it endearing. If New York has lost the power to amaze, it is gaining the power to charm. It happened that when I was in Manhattan, Bonwit Teller, for generations one of the smartest stores on Fifth Avenue, closed its doors to make way for a building development. I went along there on the last day, and what a sentimental journey that was! Tears came to saleswomen's eyes, as they pottered for the last time among the atrocious hats, unsellable ceramics, belts and bent coat hangers which were all that remained of their once-delectable stock: and an elderly customer I was buttonholed by in the elevators seemed almost distraught – something beautiful was going out of her life, she said, 'a bit of New York, a little bit of me'.

Bonwits was quick to remind us, in the next day's *New York Times*, that they have plenty of stores elsewhere, but still the event really did touch some heart-cords in New York. Sentimentality, eccentricity, Earl Grey tea – all these are signs of a society growing old, but doing it, on the whole, gracefully. There is much that is jaded or curdled, of course, to the culture of Little Old New York. Violence really is a curse of the place, circumscribing the lives of hundreds of thousands of people, and blighting whole districts of the city – when the donor of the East River Fountain was asked why it had not been spouting recently, he said he assumed it was clogged with corpses. More people in Manhattan, as it happens, suffer from human bites than from rat bites – 764 recorded in 1978, as against 201 from the rats.

Yet I am of the opinion all the same that Manhattan, whose very name is a byword for the mugging, the fast practice, the impossible pressure and the unacceptable vice, has become in its maturity the most truly civilized of the earth's cities. It is where mankind has, for good or for bad, advanced furthest on its erratic course through history, and in unexpected places, in unforeseen situations, its mellowness shows.

They used to say of it that it would be a fine place when it was finished. I think in essentials they have completed it now. They are no longer tearing down its buildings, and throwing up new ones, with the fury of their youth. Whole districts are no longer changing character year by year under the impact of the immigrants. Manhattan has jelled, I think. A feeling not of complacency but perhaps of wry experience pervades Little Old New York now.

Let me end with one more visit to the Park, that zipless blank at the heart of Manhattan, for a lyrical *envoi* to this piece. I chanced one day, off the joggers' circuit, to come across a young black man fast asleep upon a bench below the lake. His overcoat was thrown over him, his boots were placed neatly side by side upon the ground. His head upon his clasped hands, as in kindergarten plays, he was breathing regularly and gently, as though bewitched.

Even as I watched, a grey squirrel, skipping across the green, leapt across his legs to the back of the bench, where it sat tremulously chewing, as squirrels do: and suddenly, almost at the same time, there arose one of those brisk gusts of wind, tangy with salt, which now and then blow a breath of the ocean invigoratingly through New York. A scatter of leaves and fallen blossoms came with it, flicked and eddied around the bench. The squirrel paused, twitched again and vanished. The black man opened his eyes, as the breeze dusted his face, and seeing me standing there bemused, smiled me a slow sleepy smile. 'Be not afeared,' I said ridiculously, on the spur of the moment, 'the isle is full of noises.'

'Yeah,' the man replied, stretching and scratching mightily in the morning. 'Bugs, too.'

The essays I wrote during the 1970s for Rolling Stone *were later published as a book,* Destinations, *jointly by the magazine itself and by Oxford University Press. Its unusually matched patrons threw a joint party to launch it, at the* Rolling Stone *offices overlooking Central Park, at which half the hosts were bedecked in beads, talismans and all the paraphernalia of what was then known as the New Age, and the others wore collars, ties and pin-striped suits. In my memory the pin-striped gentlemen were all from* Rolling Stone. *The Oxonians wore the beads.*

21

South African Black and White

All Africa was in a mess in the 1970s, as its many young states struggled through a morass of poverty, corruption and historical confusion to find modern identities. In the Republic of South Africa, which I had first visited twenty years before, one could see working itself out that seminal human conflict, the antipathy of colour. There the supremacy of the white minority was being sustained, to the disapproval of the whole world, by the pseudo-ideology of apartheid *– literally 'separateness' – which made the Afrikaner whites politically supreme, the British-descended whites ever more uncertain of themselves, and the black and coloured citizens utterly impotent.* Rolling Stone *commissioned me to see for myself.*

High above Pretoria, the administrative capital of the Republic of South Africa, there stands a squat bulbous monument on a hill, commanding the wide windswept highlands of the Transvaal – 5,000 feet up on the high veld, 400 miles from the sea, in one of the most splendidly African parts of the African continent. This is the supreme shrine of the White Man in South Africa. Built into its massive stonework, as coins and newspapers are buried beneath the foundations of bridges, is the deepest rationale of apartheid, the intricate political device – part mysticism, part economics, part confidence trick, by which the white race maintains its supremacy over the blacks in the southernmost part of the continent. Everywhere else the white race, once master of half the earth, has withdrawn from its conquered territories, but in southern Africa it stands intransigent upon its privileges against the terrible and majestic swell of black unrest. The Voortrekker Monument explains and expresses that intransigence: for it stands there so uncompromisingly on its *kopje*, seems to be socketed so deeply into the soil, is so buttressed with vaults, arches and ceremonial steps that it looks as though nothing short of cataclysm could ever destroy it.

On the face of it the monument commemorates the Great Trek, the legendary *hegira* of the Afrikaner people away from the coast into these remote and tremendous uplands, where in the early nineteenth century they established their own independent republics and rooted their culture in the soil. But its meaning is deeper. In withdrawing so far into Africa the Afrikaner were deliberately disavowing the values of the world outside, declaring their resolve to live in their own way in their own inviolate homeland: and in particular they were rejecting once and for all the thesis, pressed upon them by the pragmatic British on the coast, that all human beings were equal before God. It was basic to Afrikaner reasoning that all men were *not* equal, and in particular that the black indigenes of the country were divinely ordained to be inferiors, hewers of wood and drawers of water. The Great Trek of the Afrikaner zealots, lurching in their ox wagons ever further into the harsh hinterland, was a journey that led them and their little nation directly, against all hazards, with much splendour of spirit, toward the squalid racial impasse, whites balefully confronting blacks, which now engulfs their country.

The monument is an arcane edifice, like a place of pledge or sacrifice. The Afrikaner Volk, it proclaims, have overcome the forces of Evil to achieve this hefty consummation on the veld, and they alone have carried the torch of true civilization into these savage territories There is an eternal flame burning in the crypt to prove it, and once a year, at midday on 16 December, a shaft of sunlight penetrates the high roof of the building and falls upon a great stone cenotaph which, like Napoleon's tomb at Les Invalides, stands sombre in its subterranean chamber, mystically to illuminate the oath inscribed enormously upon its granite: ONS VIR JOU, SUID-AFRIKA – 'We for Thee, South Africa'.

December 16th: the day when, in 1838, an Afrikaner force of fewer than 500 men utterly defeated an army of 20,000 black Zulus at the Battle of Blood River in Natal. They had made a covenant with Providence, and 16 December is celebrated as a day not just of military victory, but of spiritual commitment – statistical procedures, we are assured by the Monument Handbook, show that there was only a 1 per cent chance of Afrikaner success at Blood River, 'supporting the belief that this Victory was an Act of God'. Over the years the historic meaning of Afrikanerdom itself came to be embodied in this divinely sponsored triumph over the Powers of Darkness, visibly and symbolically expressed in the black skins of the defeated adversaries, and the Voortrekker Monument was erected to perpetuate the message for posterity. The divine privilege of being white is demonstrated in a slaughter of blacks, achieved against all statistical odds by the direct intervention of God.

258

Standing inside this portentous structure, with the Lamp of Civilization burning steadily in its glass reliquary, the images of battle and dedication all around, the wind of the high veld moaning through the casements and the sun shaft imperceptibly moving through its high orifice, minute by minute toward the next anniversary, one begins to understand the almost occult reluctance of the Afrikaner government of South Africa to admit its black subjects to equality. The Voortrekker Monument is no place for conciliations or second thoughts. It is more like a setting for *Götterdämmerung*, and all around it there stands a barricade of sculpted ox wagons, encircling the shrine in perpetual watchful laager, as if to imply that the Battle of Blood River is not over yet.

Today the white man is absolutely supreme. Not a single black or coloured man has a vote for the National Parliament in Cape Town, no non-European can rise high in business or in government, there are racial restrictions and discriminations so elaborate and so all-pervasive that they affect every facet of life, dividing the races absolutely and making it almost impossible for an ordinary black family to be friendly with an ordinary white. It is not a colonial arrangement, an elite of expatriates exploiting the natives. *All* these peoples are natives, and the racial order is something far more organic, deeply entrenched in history and religion, and supported paradoxically by the very riches of the country itself – riches which give the white man his power and make him so unwilling to change his style of life.

It is the most tantalizing of countries – a country permanently denied serenity, it seems, by the fact of race. Even now, when its antagonisms seem to be sliding toward catastrophe, there are parts of it where one may experience a melancholy sense of might-have-been – especially in Cape Province where, not so long ago, blacks, browns and coloureds seemed to have established a congenial equilibrium. Cape Town still feels like a civilized city in a civilized country – a touch of San Francisco, a slight tang of Sydney. People of all races walk its streets, and there are flower stalls about, and bookshops, and a symphony orchestra, and four daily papers of varying views. Above the city Table Mountain gloriously crouches, often swirled in cloud, frequented by nature ramblers and lugubrious baboons. Offshore the supertankers of the world steam by, never pausing on their long pilgrimage to the oil countries, but supplied with mails and medicines, like passing sadhus accepting offerings, by helicopters from this munificent shore.

259

And better still, you may glimpse the elusive idyll of South Africa in the delectable winelands to the northeast of Cape Town, where the Cape plain rises gently toward the summits of the Du Toit's Kloof. Here is the enchanting university town of Stellenbosch, the oldest seat of the Afrikaner culture, all Dutch gables, oaks, stinkwood furniture and musty, vinous smells. Here the fields of Riesling, Steen or Pinotage stretch away, meticulously tended, to plain white farmhouses at the mountain edge, and the very names on the map have an Arcadian ring – Bonfoi, Sir Lowery's Pass, the Jonkershook River or the Botterlary Hills.

Even here, though, up the winding dirt lanes, come rumours of riot, blood-shed and repression, for the inescapable reality of South Africa today, the truth around which all else revolves, is the suppression of the huge black majority by the whites, and the inescapable slow movement of the blacks toward revolution. The racial conflict dominates every conversation, as it dictates every political act and every economic decision. Every day its shadow grows more ominous, and every day its symptoms break into the newspapers – more deaths in the Cape Town black townships – another student riot – a militant black paper is launched – a policeman is killed by a grenade – another batch of black protestors is charged under the Terrorism Act, or the Suppression of Communism Act, or the Internal Security Act, or they are detained incommunicado without charge, or placed under house arrest, or banned from public life indefinitely. The segregated black townships, on the edge of the white cities, are littered now with the wreckage of arson and communal violence, and the country is tense with apprehension, as though an enormous thunderstorm is brooding over it, sometimes spilling heavy raindrops on the sidewalk.

The blacks are angry, and this is something new to South Africa. After generations of slights and injuries, voteless, propertyless, under-paid, overworked, confined to vast monotonous ghettos with rotten houses and second-rate schools – after generations of all this the black masses of South Africa have remained, until now, astonishingly good-natured. It is only within the past year, as news of the black risorgimento has filtered down from Angola and Mozambique, as Black Consciousness has at last fired the imagination of the African young, that the blacks have burst into open militancy and turned to violence. It is as though a monumental public patience has cracked at last, never to be soothed again.

The Grand Plan of Afrikanerdom does not allow for anger, for apartheid is essentially an intellectual conception, theologically tinged. It postulates that if the coloured peoples of the country are allowed to integrate with the whites, they will presently take over the state and fundamentally alter its character. The alternative it proposes is the division of South Africa into separate, autonomous entities, one white and eight black, to be economically united but politically, socially and culturally distinct. This is a vision different in kind from the old American idea of segregation, and when it was first defined by the academics of Stellenbosch there seemed a certain nobility to it.

But if the scholars devised it idealistically, the politicians interpreted it in expedience. For them it was a device of white supremacy. The delineated black 'homelands' were small and poor, and anyway more black people lived in the huge rich areas reserved for the whites, where their labour was indispensable: these people were to be deprived of all citizenship rights for ever, remaining there as convenient helots. The Grand Plan was to be upheld too, when the politicians put it into practice, by a vast and preposterous edifice of racial discrimination, legalizing the basest instincts of the bigots, and ensuring that in death as in life, in urinating as in buying a postage stamp, in boarding a bus, in making love, in writing a sonnet on a bench, black and white were to be irrevocably kept apart. As the years passed the whole project became more obviously delusory. By 1970, the year of the last census, well under half the black people lived in their own allotted territories, and today even some of the Stellenbosch theorists admit that the whole idea was an enormous miscalculation, almost a historical hoax.

Yet it is still being laboriously implemented, as though nobody knows how to stop it, while the resentment of the blacks surges toward explosion, and the South African government, in shiny brochure and policy broadcast, insistently declare it the True Way of racial progress.

Far away beyond the Drakensberg mountains, beyond the wide pastoral uplands of the Orange Free State, so heartless in winter, so delicately flowered in spring, there stands a very different creation of apartheid: Soweto, Southwest Townships, the vast black ghetto, several segregated cities splotched into one, which supplies the labour force for Johannesburg and the gold mines of the Rand.

There is nowhere else in the world like Soweto. It is something like a disused exhibition, something like an open prison, something like a gypsy encampment, something like a construction camp and something like a slum. With a population of more than a million – twice the size of

Johannesburg itself – Soweto is one of the great cities of Africa, but it does not feel like a city at all, for it has no centre. Mile after mile, in interminable geometrical lines, curves and circles, the shabby little brick houses of the blacks extend across the treeless veld, linked by rutted mud roads, unkempt, unpainted, each section indistinguishable from the next, the whole seeming to possess no recognizable shape or limit. There is no focus to Soweto, no complex of stores and offices, no cathedral tower or television mast: it is like a haggard dream, in which one is always on the edge of somewhere, but never ever gets there. In Soweto, in the summer of 1976, began the series of township riots which have already changed everything in South Africa, giving notice, so to speak, that the great black reactor was going critical. Here the whole structure of apartheid is seen as no more than a tyrannical device, and Matanzima and his kind are branded not merely as Uncle Toms, but as traitors. The black dynamic burns furiously in Soweto now. White people may enter the township only with special permits, prominently stamped AT OWN RISK, and the security forces watch the place almost as they might watch an enemy salient on a battlefront. Deep in that shabby maze the unknown revolutionaries are at work, and the place seethes with plots and rivalries and vendettas, and crawls with police informers.

A few years ago the Soweto blacks seemed like shadow people. They seemed to have no fervours of their own, except when they indulged in tribal dances, football matches or violent crime. In the daytime one saw them expressionless at their menial tasks in Johannesburg, at night-time they vanished altogether. Now they seem very different. They crowd uninhibitedly through the shops of Jo'burg. They say very nearly seditious things at public meetings. They riot. They visibly grope out of their poverty toward a contemporary elegance, and have already achieved, in their command of the gaudy and the surprising, an excitement of bearing beyond the range of the whites. They are beginning to seem the salt of the place, the fizz of it, providing just those elements of brilliance, fun and response that white South Africans, on the whole the least vivacious people I know, so dispiritingly lack.

The young people of the townships are the first blacks of South Africa to achieve a revolutionary cohesion. 'We don't need any communists to teach us,' as one burning young activist told me in Soweto. 'We know what we want, and we know what to do about it.' They are as much like Puritans as they are like Maoists – contemptuous of their elders' servility, austere and earnest in their lifestyles. They have furiously attacked the township speakeasies, the 'shebeens', which have been for generations the emblems of black degradation, and they have imposed upon the townships a macabre regime of mourning for the victims of the riots. Thousands of them have boycotted school, in protest against the educational system, thousands more have escaped from the country altogether, over the borders into the independent states of Lesotho, Botswana or Swaziland. They have been imprisoned by the hundreds, beaten up, reviled, herded about like animals, tear-gassed and snatched from their homes by security police: yet in all the years of apartheid theirs has been the first group of citizens to risk all in opposing the system, and to resist institutional violence by violence in the streets.

It is not all sublime idealism. It has often been vicious. Innocent blacks have been bullied and intimidated. Children have been frightened out of school. Above all, black racialism, which for so long seemed almost a contradiction in terms, has been given an ominous new impetus.

There was a moment in the 1930s when observers of the Indian scene realized that, though the British Empire still held all the guns, in a deeper sense the Indians had already won their struggle for independence. I think this is true in South Africa now. Though their oppressors are far more ruthless than the British ever were, already the black Africans feel like winners. They see Black Power supreme throughout most of Africa; they observe the world unanimous in their support; they realize at last that though the white South African looks powerful and important when he towers across the charge desk, bullies you from the prosecutor's stand or floods your school with poison gas, he is not important really, nor anything like omnipotent. The White Man's Magic has evaporated in this last segment of his empire.

There is no missing this new black assurance. It is everywhere, in the swagger of young men in the street, in the startling outspokenness of black leaders, in the progressive collapse, absurdity by insult, of petty apartheid. 'We will take no more nonsense,' one young black swore to me, assuring me that he no longer even bothered to carry his pass book, once the sine qua non of black existence in South Africa, 'no more nonsense at all.' Even the housemaid at my hotel in Johannesburg, when I asked her how she felt about her situation in life, answered me in one conclusive word: 'Angry.'

The tables are turning. To the black militants the concessions already won are contemptible, and the slow relaxing of petty apartheid means nothing – it is not separate lavatories or demarcated bathing beaches that matter, but the realities of power. The blacks no longer wish merely to enter the white man's world, but actually to take it over. The papers are full of terrorist training camps, of schoolboys spirited away for Marxist indoctrination, of border infiltrations and secret armoires. Sometimes casualty lists appear from the running conflict, misted in secrecy, being waged by the South African security forces on their northern borders, or heroes of the battle are honoured with bands, medals and patriotic addresses. Gatsha Buthelezi, leader of the 4 million Zulus, openly and with impunity calls for mass civil disobedience, and says of himself, as a man speaking not out of weakness but of strength: 'I am the hand that my people offer in friendship, but I am also the hand they will withdraw in their anger.' Sometimes the rioters of the townships will let a white man pass if he gives the Black Power salute; and this seems proper enough, for the most profound recognition in South Africa today is the dawning realization, among blacks and whites alike, that *force majeure* works both ways.

There are still moderate, liberal blacks about, pro-white blacks even, but they begin to seem indecisive, dated people. The conviction of compromise lacks bite, and no fiery black evangelist has yet made the middle way, the conciliatory way, seem virile and exciting. A Christ might achieve it, but not even a Gandhi, I fear, could convince the blacks of South Africa that moderation is the best policy. The very suggestion of cooperation with whites, even the most enlightened whites, is enough to blight a reputation among the fiercest of the young black patriots.

It is not one of your planned revolutions, organized from some central cell. It is happening organically, almost seismically, as though Nature herself is restoring a balance. In twenty years, by current trends, there will be 37 million black people in South Africa, outnumbering the whites seven to one. 'What will happen to us then?' replied a government official when I asked him the eternal South African question. 'We'll be bred into the sea, that's what!'

Still, it is upon the Afrikaners, they of the Sacred Flame, that the whole future of South Africa depends: they hold the power still, they have the jets and the machine guns, and they alone can dictate, by opting for conciliation with the blacks or persevering with oppression, what becomes of this marvellous and miserable country. The issue is gigantic – who is going to be boss, the black man or the white? – and the Afrikaner understands it instinctively, as part of his heritage.

Among all the tribes of Africa, the most formidable is this white tribe of the Afrikaners, who have a right to be called Africans since they have been indigenous to this soil almost as long as there have been white men living in North America. They are truly tribal people. They have their own atavistic version of the Christian god, their own distinctive mores, their own colourful language – not a very old one, it is true, having started life in the eighteenth century as a kind of kitchen Dutch, but still recognizably a tongue of its own, with a lively, growing literature and a fine lexicon of phrases like *Foeitog* ('What a pity!') or *Reddingsbaadjie Onder U Sitplek* ('Life Vest under Your Seat'). They are bound by a rigid sense of kin and origin, and the concept of the Volk, which enters so many of their usages, is more than just 'the people' in the American constitutional sense, but is something nearer to cult or fraternity – the innermost society of Afrikanerdom is actually called the Broederbond.

There are only 2.5 million Afrikaners. They form a very introspective community, and the development of their culture, the fostering of their history, the formation of their national purpose, have all been highly self-conscious processes. Little in Afrikaner history is haphazard. It is a history of extremes and abruptness, a constant instinct toward separateness – no blurs, no blends, no overlaps. Until now the Volk have prospered by these uncompromising techniques, and have turned all their disadvantages into success. Having been defeated by the British in war, they used the subsequent peace to turn the tables. Being vastly outnumbered by the blacks, they subdued them by sheer arrogance. Every attempt to dominate or alter their society they have fought off or sidestepped – by trekking ever deeper into the African hinterland, by starting their own business enterprises, by the calculated instrument of apartheid. They have fought their battles all alone, and so far they have won through.

All is now at risk, because of the one great error in the Afrikaner creed. Those forces of darkness, so graphically conjured in the mysteries of the Voortrekker Monument, are *not* the black men after all. God did not mean it that way. The revelation is mistaken, and the conviction that Afrikaner society can survive only by the perpetual subjection of the black African is the one fatal flaw in the courageous outlook of the Volk. It has brought out the worst in them, the narrowness, the intolerance, the bigotry that goes with their patriotism and their religion. It has muddled their thinking and coarsened their merits. And though it has served them well enough during the first 300 years of their history, it is almost inconceivable that it can succeed much longer. They are in their last laager, symbolically represented in that circle of ox wagons around the monument. They have nowhere else to retreat, and they cannot fight on for ever.

Time passes, the whole towering edifice of white supremacy sways, and apartheid proves itself to have been one of the most terrible of all historical miscalculations. Its system is cracking anyway, by the momentum of history, and the blacks are forcing their way into the white man's world by plain force of circumstance. 'Change', which Afrikaner last-ditchers call a communist word, is nevertheless on every politician's lips, for it is evident that the apparatus of racialism is doomed. Three decades of apartheid have been a tragic waste of time and life and passion. It has not worked. It is a fateful moment, a breathless moment, for nobody knows whether the Afrikaners will submit to history or defy it. Perhaps they are going to hang on after all, whatever happens elsewhere. They are unlikely to be toppled by internal revolution, however inflamed the blacks, and they may well be right when they claim that the capitalist West will save them from invasion. Besides, the spirit of laager still excites the Afrikaners, the urge to ultimate defiance, even to national self-immolation perhaps, holding the Eternal Flame while savagery, atheism, communism and barbarism burn the wagons and storm the shrine.

But they will be defeated in the end anyway, if not by force then by the misery of it all, by the relentless threat of catastrophe which debilitates the life of the country, by the demoralizing boycott of the world, by the slow decay of their own certainties and the awful realization of error. Why, I asked an old black man once, did not Mr Vorster, the Prime Minister of South Africa, frankly admit the misjudgement of apartheid and make a fresh start while there was still time? His answer I suspect, came somewhere near the truth. 'Because,' he said, 'it would make him look a fool.'

It would make him look silly: more pertinently still, it would reveal the whole Afrikaner mystique, so full of pride and achievement, so inspired and so genuinely inspiring, to be fallible after all – as though that mystic sunshaft, one fine December noonday, were to miss the hole in the roof altogether, owing to an inaccuracy in the mathematics.

Three decades later the blacks control South Africa. It happened without violence after all, but we have yet to see if the races will ever be truly reconciled.

During one of my visits to the country I drove in a rented convertible to Stellenbosch University, the intellectual cradle of apartheid, where I had arranged to meet a group of intensely segregationist intellectuals. The weather was lovely, the sunshine benign, and I found those stern theorists awaiting me on the steps of their department as I drove showily into the campus with the roof down. They looked disapproving already, perhaps because my radio was blaring a hit song of the day, Cole Porter's 'Love Forever True'.

The 1980s

In the 1980s the Cold War came to an end with the symbolical opening of the Berlin Wall, but it was not altogether an easy decade. There were troubles in the Middle East, as usual, there was a small war in the Falkland Islands – the last British imperial war. And there were the first portents of a hazy world-wide movement towards terrorism as an instrument of politics – assassinations and assassination attempts, the taking of innocent hostages and the hijacking of aircraft. I felt myself to be well out of it all, and the books I wrote took me, by and large, into more peaceable parts of the world – or in some cases, into dream-places.

22

On Wistful Whims: Virtual Places

Feeling myself rather bewildered by the state of everything, and suspecting that I had never scratched below the surface of places I had written about, in the 1980s I sometimes turned to virtual places, so to speak – places that did not seem quite real in the context of the time. For example I went searching, on a wistful whim, for Anthony Trollope's fictional cathedral city of Barchester, which I seemed to find half-reincarnated in Somerset.

Wells

I craved the Trollopian scene not for itself exactly, but for its myth of a Golden Age. Of course I wanted the incidentals too, the bells across the close, the fine old ladies taking tea beneath college rowing groups featuring, at stroke, their uncle the late Precentor. I wanted the mingled smell of dry rot and market cabbage. I hoped to catch a glimpse of the Organist and Choirmaster, pulling his gown over his shoulders as he hurried across to evensong. But like many other romantics, all over the Western world, I hungered really for the hierarchal certainty of the old England, that amalgam of faith, diligence, loyalty, independence and authority which Trollope mischievously enshrined in the legends of his little city.

At least Wells looks impeccably the part. As one descends from the spooky heights of Mendip, haunted by speleologists and Roman snails, it lies there in the lee of the hills infinitely snug and wholesome. No motorway thunders anywhere near. It is fourteen miles to the nearest railway station. Though Wells has been a city since the tenth century, it is still hardly more than an ample village, dutifully assembled around the towers of the cathedral: and although beyond it one may see the arcane bumps and declivities of the Glastonbury plain, there is nothing very mystical to one's first impression of the place. Its accent is homely Somerset, and its aspect rubicund.

In no time at all I had found myself a room, low-beamed and flower-patterned, in the Crown Hotel overlooking the Market Square, where a rivulet swims limpidly down the gutter past the old town conduit: and hardly less promptly, as it happened, I found myself fined £2 for parking too long outside Penniless Porch, through whose squinted archway the great grey mass of the cathedral itself looked benignly down upon traffic-warden and miscreant alike.

Almost at once, too, I met the Dean, actually in the shadow of the Porch. Eton, Oxford and the Welsh Guards, he was not hard to identify. In the cathedral, I later discovered, they call him 'Father Mitchell', a disconcerting usage to one of my purposes, but I certainly could not complain about his authenticity *qua* Dean. With a splendid concern his voice rang out, as we sat there on the beggars' bench watching the citizenry pass by. 'Good morning, good morning! Lovely day! What a success yesterday – what *would* we have done without you? Morning, Simon! Morning, Bert! Morning, John! (*John Harvey, you know, our greatest authority on medieval church architecture . . .*)'

The Dean of Wells is a very busy man indeed. He showed me his diary, and it was chock-a-block – even Thursday, resolutely marked as his day off, was nibbled into by a meeting of the Judge's Lodgings Committee. It seemed more the life of an impresario than a cleric, and this is because a cathedral nowadays is far more than just a shrine, but is partly a social centre, partly a concert hall, partly a tourist attraction, and in the case of Wells, very largely a National Concern. A few years ago it was realized that the west front of Wells Cathedral, incorporating an unrivalled gallery of not very exciting but undeniably medieval statuary, was crumbling away: the consequent appeal, launched by an urbane firm of professional appealers, suddenly made Wells, like Venice, better-known for its decay than for its survival, and added a new dimension to the life of the Very Reverend the Dean.

It crossed my mind, indeed, so ubiquitous were the symptoms of restoration, that the cathedral's chief function had become its own repair. The building itself, clouded with scaffolding, tap-taps with the hammers of the masons. One frequently sees the Dean, cassocked and umbrella'd, gazing with solicitous eyes at a leprous evangelist or precarious cornice. Outside the west doors there stands a superannuated Victorian pillar box, painted bright blue, for the acceptance of contributions, and hardly a week seems to pass without some fund-raising function beneath the bold inverted arches of the nave (themselves a restorative device, for they were hastily erected when, in 1338, the central tower lurched twelve feet out of true).

But no, the Dean reassured me over lunch, the true focus of cathedral life remained the daily services which, however infinitesimal the congregations, are held now as always in the panelled seclusion of the choir. Behind the scenes the immemorial functions of the cathedral continue, each with its titular chief: the Baron of the Exchequer, the Chancellor, the Master of the Fabric, the Communar, the Chief Steward. The Dean still presides over the Quinque Personae of his Chapter. The Priest-Vicars, the Lay-Vicars, the Canons Residentiary, the vergers, the twenty-one choristers, all are there to offer their gifts and energies to the daily affirmation of the faith.

I took him at his word, and went that afternoon to evensong: or rather, like nearly everybody else in sight, I loitered about the interior of the cathedral while evensong proceeded beyond the narrow entrance of the choir, allowing me, from the dimmer recesses of the nave, suggestive glimpses of surplices, shaded lamps, anthem sheets and musical motions within. It was magical. The rest of the great building lay in hush, haunted only by self-consciously shuffling groups of sightseers, and encapsulated there in their bright-lit chamber, as though in heavenly orbit, the Dean, his canons, the musicians and a handful of devoted worshippers performed their evening ritual.

The anthem was S. S. Wesley's 'Thou Wilt Keep Him', among the most lyrical in the repertoire, and it was touching to see how many of the tourists leant in silence against pillars, or paused thoughtfully in their decipherment of epitaphs, as the sweet melody sounded through the half-light.

'Can I go and meet Daddy now?' I heard a voice say from the cathedral shop, near the west door. 'He's bound to be down from the loft by now.' He was, the last note of the voluntary having faded away into the Lady Chapel, and presently the Organist and Choirmaster, his wife, his two daughters and I were comfortably before a fire in Vicars' Close, the exquisite double row of fourteenth-century houses which runs away to the north of the Chapter House (and which is the only part of the Wells cathedral precinct properly called the Close). Here was Barchester all right! An Oxford print hung above the fireplace; a cat luxuriated on the hearth; books, musical instruments, edibles and Cinzano were all equally at hand. 'Aren't we lucky?' said the children. 'Don't we live in a lovely place? Isn't this a lovely house? We tidied it all up specially for you!'

It was by no means the only musical house in the neighbourhood, for the cathedral precinct of Wells, if it sometimes suggests showbusiness, and often package tours, sometimes feels like one gigantic conservatoire. Muffled from within the cathedral walls, any hour of the day, one may hear the organ rumbling. Celestial through the open doors come snatches of 'Thou Wilt Keep Him'. From old grey houses around the green sound snatches of string quartet, trombonic arpeggios or tinkles of Czerny. Hardly has the Organist and Choirmaster finished one performance than he is up there again with his choristers, high in their medieval practice room behind Penniless Porch, rehearsing Wood in C Minor for the following day.

If faith is the reason for Wells, music is its most obvious diligence. Wells Cathedral School is one of the three schools in England offering specialist education for musically gifted children, tracing its origins to a Song School of the thirteenth century, while the music of the cathedral itself is intensely professional. I much enjoyed this feeling of disinterested technique, so remote from commercial competition or union claim. I saw something truly noble to the spectacle of that daily choral celebration, performed to the last degree of excellence, attended by almost nobody but the celebrants themselves: a practice more generous, more frank, more *English* (I ventured to suppose) than monasticism or meditation – and more acceptable actually, one might think, to the sort of gods I myself cherish, the gods of the stones and the lavender, than to the Christian divinity to whom it has, for a thousand years, uninterruptedly been offered.

Before I left Vicars' Close, the children invited me to write something in their autograph books. Visitors always did, they said. I looked with interest at the previous entries, expecting to find there, as one would in a Barchester book, the names of visiting politicians, magnates or men of law: but no, they were musicians almost to a scrawl – the composers, the instrumentalists, the teachers who pass in a constant stream these days through the busy precincts of Wells. (When I saw what witty things they had written there, I could think of nothing comparably pithy to say myself, so I drew a couple of pictures of the cathedral instead. 'Thought you said you couldn't draw,' the children kindly said. 'We think you're *jolly good*.')

The loyalty essential to the myth of Englishness is of course embodied in Wells in the fabric of the cathedral itself, and the enclosure of grass, garden and old stone that surrounds it. For a millennium there have been people in Wells who have devoted themselves to this structure, and it seemed to me that this corporate possession of the little town, like some grand totem or fetish, must powerfully augment the citizenry's sense of community or comradeship.

How easy it would be, I thought, to fall in love with such a building, and to spend one's life getting to know it, or more usefully perhaps, keeping it there! In the shadow of such permanence, surely life's transient miseries would pass one by? The Master-Mason of the cathedral smiled enigmatically, when I expressed this thought. He is a very practical man. He first fell victim himself to the enthralment of the cathedral when as a small boy he wriggled through a prohibited aperture somewhere in the masonry, and so discovered for himself the infinite complexity of the place. Now he knows it all, its unsuspected corridors and hidden galleries, its vaults and its cloisters, and through his yards and offices pass all the architects, the restorers, the masons, the accountants, the surveyors and the builders' merchants perpetually engaged, as they have been for so many centuries, in maintaining the holy structure. He was like the Master-at-Arms on a warship, I thought, beneath whose experienced eye the workaday life of the vessel goes on, leaving the men on the bridge above, like those priests and choristers at evensong, free to attend to the navigation.

Then there is the Horologist. The most beloved single artefact in Wells Cathedral, I would say, is the medieval Great Clock in the north transept. It is claimed to possess the oldest working clock in Europe: whenever it strikes the hour four little horsemen, whirring round and round, knock each other off their wooden horses with lances, while a dead-pan character called Jack Blandiver, sitting stiffly on his seat high on a wall near by, nods his head, hits one bell with a hammer, and kicks two more with his heels.

Every morning at half past eight or so, if you hang around High Street, you may see the Horologist on his way to wind this endearing timepiece. His father did it before him, his son will doubtless follow, and never was a labour more cherished. 'There's old Jack,' he says affectionately as he unlocks the door to the clock gantry, and looks up at the quaint old figure on the wall: and when you have climbed the narrow winding steps, looking through the inverted arches to the empty nave beyond, then he opens the big glass doors of the mechanism as one might open a cabinet of treasures. The works are Victorian, the originals being in the Science Museum at South Kensington, and the Horologist admires them enormously. What workmanship! What precision! Look at those cogs! Feel how easily the handle turns! I caught his mood at once. Everything felt wonderfully *hand-made* up there, so rich in old wood and dressed stone, with that elaborate gleaming mechanism slowly ticking, and the beautiful cool space of the cathedral beneath one's feet.

'Wouldn't it be good,' I said, 'if *everything* in life felt like this?' 'Ah wouldn't it,' said he, resuming his coat after the exertion of the clock-winding. 'But you have to work for it, you see. It doesn't look after itself! Come here now, look down here,' – and he showed me down a little shaft to the circular platform on which the four knights of the Great Clock, relieved from their eternal joust until the next quarter-hour, were resting woodenly on their arms. 'Now those fellows down there take a lot of looking after. They break so easily, you see. Well they would, wouldn't they, hitting each other with their lances every quarter of an hour? You can't expect them to last for ever, knocking each other about like that!'

In a curious way, I felt, the cathedral was more the property of the Town than of the Close. Bishops, Deans and Canons come and go, but the shopkeepers and the businessmen, the farmers, even the traders who bring their vans and stalls to Wells Market every week – these people live all their lives in the presence of the great building, and must feel it to be part of their very selves. Wells has its own magnificent parish church of St Cuthbert, often mistaken by the tourists for the cathedral itself. It has a substantial landed interest and some thriving small industries. But still every street seems to look, every alley seems to lead, almost every conversation seems somehow to turn, to that ancient presence beyond Penniless Porch.

To discover how jealously Wellensians, as citizens of Wells complicatedly call themselves, regard the affairs of the Close, I went to see the newspaper editor. Like nearly everything in Wells, his office is only a step or two from the cathedral, almost opposite the Star (and just up the road from the King's Head which has been unnervingly metamorphosed into a Chinese restaurant). The paper is shortly to move to more modern premises, but for the moment its funny old gimcrack buildings are in High Street, all ramshackle and disjointed, like the kitchen quarters of some dilapidated mansion. How knowingly, I thought, those Linotypes chattered! What intrigues, vendettas and innuendos had found their way through those presses, during the 128 years in which the *Wells Journal* has kept its eye impartially on precinct and marketplace!

Ah yes, said the editor wryly. There was never a shortage of gossip in Wells, or controversy either. They were an independent sort, the Wellensians. Why, I should have heard the fuss when the Bishop took to culling the wild duck in his moat by shooting them out of his window! Or when they built those dreadful new canons' houses, all trendy streaked concrete, behind the Old Deanery! Oh, yes, Wellensians often resented the airs of the clergymen Up There: though it was not strictly true that the precinct was walled in defence against the assaults of the townspeople, often enough it felt like it.

The Alderman vehemently agreed – the controversial Alderman, everyone called him, who turned out to be a fiery Welshman, bred by the Parachute Regiment out of the Swansea valleys, whose passionately conservationist views during his period as Mayor had led him into bitter conflict with the cathedral. Vividly he recalled those old affrays for me. Had he not threatened to take the Dean to court when he chopped down the Mulberry Tree? Was it not he who instructed his Council, when the Bishop was late for a civic function, to take their seats without his Lordship? The Alderman clearly loves a fight, and I rather wished he was engaged in one just then, so that I could see the sparks fly for myself. But no, though he spoke to me movingly of an erroneous new sewage scheme, all was quiet in Wells just then. He sounded rather disappointed, and so was I; for Barchester is not Barchester, after all, without a battle on its hands.

Or, for that matter, without a Mrs Proudie. It was when I reached the Bishopric at last that I felt my pilgrimage had failed. Faith I had certainly found in Wells, diligence, loyalty, pride: but the sense of authority, of an established order unbreakable and supreme, which is essential to the Romantic view of England, is lost with the winds of social change and historical necessity. In Trollope's allegories that old discipline was represented if not by the person, at least by the office of the Bishop, splendidly identified by his accoutrements, his circumstances and his privileges; but the Anglican Bishop of tradition, gloriously fortified by material well-being and spiritual complacency – that grand figure of fancy has long gone the way of the Empire-builder and the top-hatted Station Master.

As it happens the Bishop's Palace at Wells is perhaps the most splendid Bishop's Palace of all. Surrounded by its own moat, its own castellated walls, its own parkland beyond, it stands on the edge of Wells, in the flank of the cathedral, looking across green fields into the depths of Somerset. It is like a fortress, and though the enormous banqueting hall is now only a picturesque ruin, still the palace is a terrific spectacle. Duck of many varieties paddle its moat, and swans deftly ring the gatehouse bell for their victuals. The palace itself stands grandly around its yard, with a huge pillared refectory, and a fine library, and a private chapel in which, within living memory, daily choral services were held for the Bishop, his family and his servants.

But no majestically awful Mrs Proudie greeted me at the palace door. Nobody greeted me at the main door at all, for the Bishop of Bath and Wells now lives only in the north wing of the structure, the rest being devoted to conferences and other useful activities. Gone are the days when the Bishop and his family ate all alone in splendour in the centre of the vast undercroft, surveyed by a gigantic gilded mitre above the fireplace. Gone are those daily services in the private chapel – nowadays the Bishop prays there alone. Gone is the daunting approach to the episcopal presence, never to be forgotten by curates of long ago, when after treading the long stately corridors of the palace, through the dark gallery lined with portraits of earlier prelates, they timidly opened the door of the great study to discover his Lordship, against a serried background of theological treatises, tremendously at his labours.

The Bishop himself recalled that vanished consequence for me. Now he and his distinctly un-Proudean wife live more modestly, more sensibly no doubt, more Christianly I suppose, but undeniably less impressively in their nicely done-up wing. His new study, furnished in pale woodwork by the Church Commissioners, is unexpectedly emblazoned, around the tops of its bookcases, with a text not from Leviticus or the Sermon on the Mount, but from King Alfred. His visitors' book, when I signed it, contained on the previous page the signature of the actor Peter O'Toole. His car is a Rover – 'such a blessing when you're overtaking on our narrow Somerset roads'. This is a very modern, very functional bishopric.

Here at the core the times have overtaken Barchester. The majesty has left the palace. Crowds of people throng to those conference rooms, taking their cafeteria luncheons on canteen tables in the undercroft (where the gilded mitre looms large as ever, but anomalous). Often the gardens are open to the public, and at any time of day sightseers are to be observed hanging over the gate which, inside the great gatehouse above the moat, inadequately (to my mind) asserts the privacy of the bishopric.

Nobody could represent these changes more persuasively than the present Bishop and his wife, who sit in their modest private corner of the gardens as a Bishop and his lady should, relishing the green and the grey of it all, the long mellow line of their ancient wall, the sweep of the trees and the droop of the trumpet vine, the Turneresque pile of the ruined banqueting hall, the silent towers of the cathedral beyond. But it is not the same. Atavist that I am, yearning sometimes from the austerity of Wales for some of the gorgeous and heedless assurance that used to characterize our magnificent neighbour – nostalgic in this way for the England I am just old enough to remember, I missed the purple swagger and the swank.

For it was partly the conceit of it, Trollope's hubris of the cloth, that captured our imaginations once – now gone it seems, for better or for worse, as utterly from Barchester as from Simla or Singapore.

San Francisco

My second virtual place was San Francisco, which for many years I had seen as a kind of ideal city. I spent some time there in the 1980s as a guest of the San Francisco Examiner, *which had started a programme of Writers-in-Residence, rather like a university. My only duty was to write a weekly essay for the paper about the city – or as San Franciscans like to say, the City – but I had to admit that this dream was half empty . . .*

And coming down from Sonoma in the evening light, as in a resplendent dream I see the City.

At such revelatory moments, warranting the opening not just of a sentence, but of an entire essay with a conjunction – at such moments the city of San Francisco deserves the capital letter its citizens, I notice, like to give it. I have been experiencing that mystic initiation intermittently for thirty years, and it never fails to exalt me – so full of hope does the City look, so incomparably felicitous on its hills above the sea, like the city of all desires in the closing pages of an allegory.

All the more puzzling, then, that when I actually enter the streets of San Francisco, this time as always I find my responses peculiarly ambivalent. The vision lets me down. There is nothing illusory to the loveliness of the place, but at closer quarters the allegory fades, and something soft, something pallid seems to muffle the excitement. Whenever I come here – more so every time – San Francisco strikes me as being at once the most heart-wrenchingly beautiful and the most tantalizing of all the great cities of the world.

Ah, but *is* it a great city? Certainly the streets look properly metropolitan – boulevards lined with banks, posh stores and hotels where Sinatras stay, neighbourhoods authentically equipped with ethnic eateries and adult bookstores, back alleys urbanely nooky, flowered and burglar-alarmed. But the buildings themselves, however imposing, strike me as oddly tentative or temporary of feel, buildings without foundations, buildings not made to last. In some obscure and perhaps seismically related way, San Francisco feels too flimsy to be a metropolis.

Besides, where have all the people gone? Half the city seems uninhabited, as though some impending new catastrophe has emptied it of its residents, leaving only disposable strangers to be swallowed up or incinerated. Even in Union Square on a Saturday evening, about the loudest noise is the clanking of the cable-car cables in their grooves. Even the financial quarter at high noon seems eminently chattable, strollable and ready for lunch. Like city people everywhere, San Franciscans love to boast of their traffic problems and crime rates, but to a visitor the pressures of this city seem, if not actually small-town, at least decidedly provincial.

The colours of San Francisco are gentle pastel colours, not the golds and crimsons of capital consequence. The light is a washed sea light, filtered always, one feels, through early morning mists. Even the local ocean never seems to me a proper whole-hog, titanic ocean, but is more like a vaster Great Lake, so that surveying its surf-fringed rocks from the heights above, I often catch myself wondering if it really is salt water down there.

They call all this laid-back, and so it is. For my tastes, though, it is a kind aesthetic betrayal. The City of my dreams, that half-imaginary shining city of the Sonoma road, is anything but laid-back, but blazes always with fires of aspiration. Think of Rio, or Sydney, or Hong Kong, or Manhattan – all cities of glorious visual impact too, but cities as thrilling at intermission as they are when the curtain goes up. Of all the supremely handsome cities I know, only San Francisco greets you, after the dazzle of its first impression, not with urge, but with relaxation . . .

San Francisco has its thrills, too, and once it was among the most vital and thrusting of all cities. But not even its fondest citizens could call it that now, and when I ventured to suggest to one of them that his beloved town might benefit from having a couple of thousand more people in it, he answered with a fine San Franciscan retort. 'Might it not possibly be,' he almost solicitously answered, 'that you are by temperament an LA person?'

But so lovely, so essentially decent, so exquisitely mannered! Even as I write these incivilities I bite my tongue, for the values that are traditional to San Francisco are the very values that I most admire: tolerance, individuality, courage, a graceful sense of fun. And yet, and yet . . .

I went one day to an anniversary party for the venerable survivors of the 1906 earthquake, on a sunny morning in Union Square. Nothing could have been jollier. Jazz bands played, free champagne was distributed by white-gloved waiters to one and all, a Clark Gable look-alike entertained the somewhat baffled veterans from the stage. ('Isn't he just great?' cried the compère. 'Yeah,' dazedly murmured the survivors in response.)

Around the flanks of this celebration two senior citizens of independent instincts separately cavorted to the music – one a lithe but cadaverous old gent in a baseball cap, the other a plump matron wearing pink slacks and sneakers. He was energetically hamming it up for the audience, waving a flag, stepping high; she was dancing all for herself, privately, singing under her breath; and so the pair of them, oblivious to each other, shimmied and trucked in the sunshine while the band played on.

At first I thought, how charming! How San Francisco! But the longer I watched those aged jitterbugs, the more they began to seem to me like death's heads grinning there, grotesquely prancing parodies of youth, in a *danse macabre* of Union Square. Once again the City had disenchanted me, and what had seemed to be eternal joy turned out to be mere senility.

But then San Francisco often trivializes what it touches. There was a time, twenty years ago, when this city seemed to be leading us all into a new age of idealism – remember the Age of Aquarius? To watchers far away it seemed that in San Francisco a truly historical moment of liberation and enlightenment was occurring, but for most of its activists, it now appears, it was only a game after all, just a frolic with history, fuelled by drugs and rock and roll, superseded as the years passed by careers in computers or associate professorships.

There is no dismissing San Francisco's regard for human variety in all its manifestations. This really is the city of few rebuffs! Where else do elderly ladies bear themselves with such sprightly confidence, sure of their place in society? (At the theatre the other night the usher was so elderly that she had to use a magnifying glass to check my seat number.) Where else would a young woman walk into a bookshop and ask with such blithe and loud aplomb, as I recently heard one ask, 'D'ya have any books like *How to Enjoy Sex Successfully?*' Compassion really does seem to be a San Francisco characteristic, and nothing in the contemporary scene is nobler than the loving care with which, as I understand it, this city's gay community cares for its Aids victims.

Yet even among the fringe people, the people I generally like the best, I am nagged by San Francisco's fatal element of sham. Your true eccentric is totally unaware of any oddity in himself, but here eccentricity is all too often debased into exhibitionism – the strutting of show-off dandies, the posturing of self-conscious weirdos. Worse still, I am disturbed by San Francisco's undeserved propensity for tragedy. It will end in tears, as all our mothers used to say. Today it is Aids, and from the once festive coffee shops of Castro Street one sees only pale and anxious faces looking out. Yesterday it was drugs, and when, sitting on a San Francisco bench, I see another ruined and ravaged victim of the '60s shambling by, I think: O City, City, I can sometimes hear, your siren song of Haight and Ashbury!

Then the sunshine comes, that particular pure sea-sun through my curtains! It holds me here, as it holds everyone else, and just a glimpse of it in the morning, just the idea of San Francisco awaiting me out there, is enough to make me cancel my flight and keep the room another day. It is not, of course, Malibu or Waikiki sun. Like the city itself, it is much more subtle and evasive than that. The palm trees in Union Square are fraudulent – this is anything but a tropic city. I think of it indeed as the southernmost city of the North – the westernmost eastern city, too, and the most Atlantic of the cities of the Pacific.

Is this, it now occurs to me, the source of that enigma? Does San Francisco know precisely *what* it is? Tourism has created a San Francisco, of course, of very pronounced identity – tourism, which turns even tourists themselves into pretend people, and drives whole cities, whole countries into pastiche. But behind the familiar images, Coit and cable car, Fisherman's Wharf and Alcatraz, lies – what? Is this it, I often find myself asking in San Francisco. Is this all there is?

Perhaps I am demanding too much, and should be content with the charm and kindness of this most charming and kindly of cities, the happy disorientation of its hills and waters, the ever-surprising vistas at the ends of its streets, the bleached cleanness of everything, the fine old ladies, the celestial setting, the innocent pretence of it all, its sense of easygoing detachment from a harsh and greedy world.

Perhaps. Looking out my window the other morning over the cluttered tourism of the Wharf, it seemed to me that everything I saw was some kind of sham. A superannuated sailing ship lay at a pier no longer working. The flag of a defunct republic flew. A couple of sightseeing boats sailed out towards a disused prison, and the cable cars that passed were not really cable cars at all, but buses in disguise. Synthetic grass surrounded the swimming pool below me. From restaurants around I could smell, if only in fancy, the odours of de-frozen swordfish and plastic-packaged clams. Is *nothing* real, I rudely wondered, in silly San Francisco?

But at that very moment there entered my field of view a submarine: a very black, very sinister, all too real and active submarine, on its way no doubt through the Golden Gate to missile patrol in the Pacific. Instantly my perceptions changed. All of a sudden the frivolous scene below my window acquired a new and grander meaning. A shame-faced sense of ingratitude overcame me, and watching that mean black warship sliding by, 'Well,' said I reproachfully to myself, 'there goes reality, if that's what you'd prefer . . .'

Rio de Janeiro

My third virtual city was, I suppose, real enough. Not everything about Rio de Janeiro is idyllic, but as I had written thirty years before, on my first acquaintance with the city, 'Great God! I will swap you a dozen prim and thrifty boroughs for one such lovely greatheart!' I went back to see how the seduction had lasted.

On the steps of the Teatro Municipal in Rio de Janeiro, a Dutch combo plays Dixieland jazz. It is an extremely white, blonde and stalwart combo, and on its flank four Dutch airline hostesses (for it is in the nature of an advertising session) oscillate to the music with a well-built air of carnival. I sit beside them on the steps, and between the lot of us, so blatantly northern European, so patently un-Dixie, we present a comically incongruous spectacle, in the heart of the great Brazilian city, at the height of the noonday rush.

But it does not matter in the least. The city effortlessly absorbs us anyway. Some thirty or forty people of all ages, all colours, are stomping, clapping and laughing with us at the foot of the steps, and very soon the occasion is more or less taken over by an elderly, half-crazed man who prances with rhythmic grace up the steps, singing the while and grinning inanely to universal applause.

The legendary fizz of Rio is not merely infectious, but actually possessive. It seizes one, sets one wriggling and jerking to the beat of things and often leaves one laughing when one should really be crying. When that band went off, still trumpeting, to its next stand, pursued by its own poor Fool, I stood up myself and found the back of my shirt splodged with some chocolaty sticky substance. The crowd examined it with interested concern. Whether it had been sprayed on me by a disgruntled street hawker, or dropped upon me by some arcane Brazilian bird, they were unable to decide, but they took me off to a small ornamental pond where I might wash it off.

I dipped my handkerchief into the scummy water and found it to be alive with tadpoles: a thousand incipient Brazilian frogs there beside the Avenida Rio Branco, squirming indefatigably as I washed the stuff off my shirt, and the music of the Dutch sounded fainter and fainter across the effervescent city.

Wiping off the last of that muck, and a few tenacious tadpoles with it, I walked around the corner into the nineteenth century. Rio is not all travel-brochure glitz. It is an old merchant city, a seaport, and its downtown is venerable with offices, banks, warehouses, bars where the businessmen go for lunch, city alleys and squares with statues in them. In old photographs this busy commercial area *is* Rio de Janeiro, and a solid, sensible, business-like place it looks.

A surviving glory of that era is the Colombo on Rua Gonçalves Dias, one of the best cafés in the world. Clad as grandiloquently in mirrors as Versailles itself, it is a very palace of refreshment. Its ceiling is of stained glass, its floors are tiled and it gleams with glass cabinets full of bottles, cakes, cookies and neatly stacked table linen. Clusters of old-fashioned lamps illuminate it, and fans laboriously keep it cool.

The multitudinous bow-tied waiters of the Colombo look as though they have spent their whole lives in its service, and at lunchtime they are all old-school professionalism, scurrying and skirting through the tables that jam the huge floor space, bowing here, waving a response there, pushing in and out of the kitchen doors or dimly to be glimpsed attending to the customers who sit, precariously it seems, at gilded tables on the high, narrow balcony above.

The noise is terrific, and the clientele ranges from the stately to the alternative, by way of many eccentric and atavistically made-up dowagers. Things have hardly changed here, I suspect, since the place opened in 1894. Rio, however, is Rio, and the atmosphere is peculiarly relaxed. When I finished my meal, I walked out past the cake cabinets, and there, leaning against a counter, brushing crumbs from his black jacket, was the waiter who had just served me, taking time off to eat a cake himself. I wished him *bon appétit*, but he could only smile and bow slightly in response, for he had his mouth full.

Youth, of course, is the thing in Rio. It is an old-young city – he was an old-young waiter – and on the beach at Copacabana, any weekend morning, the human ageing process seems mysteriously disrupted. Here I stroll along the famous beach, eating a banana, and all around me the laws of nature are defied.

It is clearly impossible, physically impossible, for that grand motherly lady to touch her toes so easily. It is positively unnatural for that group of aged gents to throw themselves about with such agility in their game of ball: their faces are wizened, their hair is white, but some weird Brazilian alchemy has kept their muscles iron-taut and their movements uncannily springy. Then what about these geriatric couples striding along the promenade? By what dispensation do they wear shoes, hats and swimsuits a couple of generations too young for them, yet get away with it so stylishly? There is an old dear on the beach who would surely be, in another society, confined if not to the back kitchen at least to the church flowers committee; here at Copacabana she is oiling herself sinuously on her sunbed, wearing a wide yellow hat and rhinestoned sunglasses, and now and then drinking from a can she has embedded in the sand like a bottle of champagne in an ice bucket.

The young, too, seem younger still upon this magic shore. They plunge more frantically into the surf. They scamper more merrily around the sunshades. They build big platforms of sand on which they sit cross-legged like gurus, playing cards or squabbling. They play ever more demanding games: for example, a ferocious kind of volleyball in which the ball may be touched by any part of the body except the head, requiring such excruciating leaps and contortions that it makes me breathless just to watch them.

Out at sea a haze of spray hangs over the breakers and half obscures the islands beyond. Through it a squadron of white-sailed yachts scuds and tacks, and presently a grey warship appears around the point and disappears into the Atlantic. It looks a wild southern sea out there. The sun goes slowly, very slowly down. The madcap rejuvenations of Copacabana continue apace. Crossing the street to one of the cafés behind, I order a

Brazilian drink of great potency that instantly restores me to youth myself.

There Fagin's boys are hanging around, looking for likely victims, nice American tourists with watches to be snatched or handbags to leave lying around on the beach. They are all too obvious little rascals – like stage villains, making over-acted gestures to each other, whistling conspiratorially across street corners and posing only in the most perfunctory way as bootblacks or sellers of trinkets.

Alas, they are not in the least lovable. There is not an Oliver among them. They look perfectly horrid, and swarming around them I fancy always the flies and fleas of the slums they come from – whose greyish shambled precincts one can see from this very beach, like spills of garbage tumbling down the hillsides. Christ himself stands high above, arms outstretched on the summit of Corcovado, but the shanty-towns below, like those small thieves on the beach, look utterly beyond his benediction.

A streak of loveless abandonment runs through the life of Rio, and not least through its exhilaration – through the panache of the street crowds, through the disturbing hyperactivity of the beach, through all the luxuries of the Rio rich. The city is scrawled over with unsightly graffiti. Some proclaim political slogans, but most are senseless squiggles and scrawls, reaching to the second floors of houses sometimes, when daring nihilists have climbed up trellises or hung upside-down from balconies. This mindless mess suggests to me a message from the void, telling us always of the helplessness, amounting to a kind of communal exhaustion, that lies beneath the glitter of Rio de Janeiro.

I sit now in a motionless bus near the foot of the Sugar Loaf, at a place where a small park runs down to the sea. There are military offices near by, and in constant twos and threes colonels and captains walk by carrying briefcases. A few children are there with their mothers, too, and tourists come and go from the funicular station, but my eye is captured by a solitary middle-aged man hanging about at the edge of the park. He bears himself elegantly, slim and erect in a well-cut grey suit, but there is something wrong with him.

It seems to be partly physical, partly mental, and partly, perhaps, too much coffee. He can never get comfortable. If he sits on a bench, after a moment he gets up again. If he takes a turn around the grass, he abruptly stops. Sometimes he looks up at the hill above, but it seems only to disappoint him, as if he cannot see what he is looking for up there. He inspects the passing officers keenly (was he once a colonel or captain himself?) but he recognizes none. He gazes longingly out to sea, but the sun gets in his eyes. When my bus starts, and we move away from the park, I wave at him through my window, and he waves abstractedly back – but not at me, I think, not at me.

23

Sydney 1983

I went back to Australia in the 1980s, to write a book about Sydney, and while I was there wrote this essay for Rolling Stone. *Many people I met remembered the last piece I had written about the city, a quarter of a century before.*

'Kev. *Kev!* Time you got going.'

'Jeez, Sandra, it's raining out there.'

'TV says it's fining up. You're not crook are you, Kev? It's all that booze you know, Kev, you know what the doctor said, cut down on the booze, he said, no wonder you're crook in the mornings, the human body can take only so much . . .'

But Kev has slipped out by now, and with his office gear slung in his backpack is away, and up the steps, and half-way along the approach to the great bridge.

If he was crook, he is crook no more, for the TV was right, the rain clears as if by magic, and all the glory of the winter morning unfolds over the water as he breaks into his jog along the sidewalk. He is joining the stream of life itself! To his right the suburban trains clatter, the commuter cars lurch in fits and starts towards the city. To his left ferries bustle across the harbour, the first hydrofoil is streaking in a foamy curve towards the sea, the very first yacht is slipping from its moorings, and a tug is on its way, riding lights still burning, to meet the towering freighter just appearing around the headland.

On the harbour bridge there are already plenty of people about. He overtakes briskly walking businessmen with briefcases and identical moustaches. He is overtaken by huge athletes in sweatbands and sloganed shirts. Archetypal schoolboys loiter their way, satchels dangling, reluctantly towards their education. An elderly lady in a mackintosh cries 'Grand to see the sun again!' in an exaggeratedly Irish brogue. Another pack of giants comes panting and sweating past. Another covey of schoolboys kicks a pebble here and there. Ahead of him, between the massive pylons of the bridge, the city towers are beginning to gleam in the sun, and there is a flashing of upper windows, and a fluttering of flags in and out of shadow, and a golden shine from the observation deck of the tallest tower of all.

It is as though the innocence of the morning has infected the whole scene, and made everything young. A pristine vigour is on the air, very fresh and good for you, like orange juice. By the time Kev reaches his office on the seventeenth floor, he feels he's never drunk a tinny of Foster's in his life: and looking back upon the scurrying ferries of the Circular Quay, the flying white roofs of the Opera House, the traffic still streaming across the bridge, the rising sun and the water and the green park-lands all around, silently he congratulates himself once more, as he does every morning as a matter of principle, upon his great good fortune in being born an Australian.

The city he surveys is a very concentrate of that condition. The whole matter of Australia, history, character, reputation, attitude, finds its best epitome in this particular corner of the great land mass, where Sydney stands beside its fjord-like harbour. When the world thinks of Australia, it thinks of that bridge, that Opera House, that wake-frothed and yacht-flecked harbour. When the world thinks of an Australian, it thinks, more or less, of Kev.

Australian society is overwhelmingly urban, and Sydney is Australia *urbanissima*. Canberra is the capital, Adelaide is a delight, Perth holds the America's Cup, Melbourne people believe their city to be at least as mature, civilized and unutterably lovely, but only Sydney has the true metropolitan presence. An enormous spread of suburbia around an intensely packed downtown, it stands upon its marvellous haven in the stance of proper consequence. A glittering business quarter makes one feel it is keyed in to the Wall Street–London–Zurich–Hong Kong circuit of profit. The inescapable presence of virtually the whole Australian Navy, moored beside its dockyards or glamorously returning from sea with ensigns flying and radars twirling, gives it a front-line air. It is equipped with all the statutory metropolitan tokens – city marathon, revolving restaurant, supine veiled figure by Henry Moore, breakfast TV and Bahai temple.

Its stature really resides, though, not in its universality, not in its membership in the league of big cities, but for better or worse, like it or not, in its unchallengeable Australian-ness. It is a metropolis sui generis. Take its looks for a start. Architecturally Sydney is no great shakes. Its suburbs are at best pleasantly ordinary, enlivened only, here and there, by wrought iron and engaging terracing. Its downtown is handsome but unexceptional, the usual cubes, cylinders, plazas and mirror-walls of contemporary urbanism surrounding the usual clumps of nineteenth-century florid. It has no elegant set pieces of civic planning, and has crudely degraded its waterfront on Sydney Cove, the site of its beginnings and still the focus of its life, by building an expressway slap across it.

Yet it is one of the most beautiful cities in the world, specifically because it is Australian. That winding, nooky, islanded, bosky harbour thrillingly reminds one always that Sydney stands on the shore of an island totally unlike anywhere else on earth. The pale pure light of the Sydney winter seems to come straight from the bergs and ice mountains of Antarctica. The foliage of Sydney's parks and gardens is queerly drooped and tangled, apparently antediluvian fig trees overshadow suburban streets, and the perpetual passing of the ships through the very heart of the city gives everything a tingling sense of remoteness. The water goes down the plug-hole the other way in Australia, and it really is possible to imagine, if you are a fancifully minded visitor from the other hemisphere, that this metropolis is clinging upside-down to the bottom of the earth, so subtly antipodean, or perhaps marsupial, is the nature of the scene.

The supreme Sydney experience, for such a traveller, is a walk on a brisk sunny morning around the headland called Mrs Macquarie's Chair, through a complex of park and garden beside the harbour. Except only for Stanley Park in Vancouver, this seems to me the loveliest of all city park-lands, but its loveliness is of a sly, deceptive kind. It is like a park in the mind. The grass is almost too vividly green, the trees look curiously artificial, parakeets squawk viciously at each other in the shrubbery. The shifting scene around you, as you walk the park's perimeter, seems more ideal than actual – water everywhere, and those grey warships at their quays, and glimpses of Riviera-like settlements all around, and a sham castle in a garden, and the inescapable passing of the ferries.

And slyest of all is the prospect as you round the point itself, where the families are spreading their picnics on the grass, and a solitary ibis is burrowing for edibles in a rubbish can; for there suddenly like an aerie fantasy the Sydney Opera House, most peculiar of architectural masterpieces, spreads its white wings in the sunshine, light as some unsuspected water-bird, with the massive old harbour bridge, a beast to its insubstantial beauty, all brutal heft above.

* * *

Those two unforgettable structures, the one rooted so powerfully in the bedrock, the other aspiring to the state of levitation, represent the nature of this city more than aesthetically. Upon Sydney's foundation of absolute British Australian-ness has been superimposed a prismatically ethnic super-structure, making this city, formerly one of the most homogeneous and stodgy in the world, a fascinating mix of the complacent and the tentative, the almost immovable and the practically irresistible. Once it used to suggest nowhere else. Now it is full of alien allusion. It reminds me often of Stockholm. As Sydney is to the South, Stockholm is to the North, and Sydney's Australia is Stockholm's Scandinavia – I am not surprised that the Danish architect of the Opera House clearly had in his memory, as he planned his prodigy, Stockholm's Town Hall upon an inlet of another sea. The light of this southern fjord is not unlike the light of the Baltic; a pallid freshness is common to both cities; sitting snugly out of the sunlight in Sydney's Strand Arcade, all fancy balustrades and tessellated paving, sometimes I almost expect to see the shoppers shaking the snow from their galoshes, breathing in their hands to restore the circulation, and ordering themselves a schnapps.

At other moments Sydney reminds me of somewhere in central Europe; any Saturday morning in the plush waterside suburb called Double Bay, for example, when the rich immigrants assemble in the street café of the Cosmopolitan, talking loudly in Ruritanian, or deep in the financial pages of the *Sydney Morning Herald*. Like the bourgeoisie of old Prague or Budapest they while the hours away in chat and exhibitionism – here four men with coats slung over their shoulders, smoking small cigars and passionately arguing about President Beneö –here a couple of leathery ladies, furred and proudly diamonded, sitting in lofty silence over aperitifs – a young poseur in a deer-stalker hat, smoking a cigarette in a long jade holder, a gaggle of Double Bay socialites in the swathed ragbag fashion, faintly Martial Arts in suggestion, rampant in Sydney at the moment.

Lebanese proliferate in Sydney, and Greeks, and Filipinos, and Indonesians. The Vietnamese, they tell me, are shifting out of the western suburbs towards East Sydney. Maori gays, gossip picturesquely maintains, are taking over Bondi. The Spanish Club advertises itself with a picture of Don Quixote and Sancho riding out of a golden Outback. Sydney's Chinatown booms with investment from Hong Kong, and the Chinese taste for unexpectedly mixed foods seems to have infected the entire municipal cuisine, so that perfectly true-blue Aussie restaurants are likely to offer you hot buttered pumpkin and orange soup with peppercorns floating in it, or quail in a sauce made of red wine and bacon. The Sydney Municipal Board sometimes likes to announce itself in all the languages of its tax-paying citizenry, and these arcane proclamations, attached to some lumpish municipal pile of mid-Victorian imperialism, pungently illustrate the state of things.

Still dominant nevertheless, as the bridge looms high over the Opera House, stand the likes of Kev. The flow of immigration has softened, eased and illuminated Sydney, but it came too late ever to displace the original bloodstream of this city. Half a century ago 98 per cent of Sydney people were of British descent, and it is they, the Old Australians, who still set the anthropological tone. Sit long enough among the Ruritanians at the Cosmopolitan, and some beefy young Ocker will arrive to steal the scene and drink his beer out of the bottle. Go to *La Traviata* at the Opera House, and my, what an unexpectedly hearty and robust chorus of ladies and gentlemen will be attendant upon Violetta in the opening act, their crinolines and Parisian whiskers delightfully failing to disguise physiques born out of Australian surf and sunshine, and names like Higginson and O'Rourke – while even La Traviata herself, as she subsides to the last curtain, may seem to you the victim of some specifically Australian variety of tuberculosis, since she looks as though immediately after the curtain-call she will be off for a vigorous set of tennis with the conductor, or at least a grilled lobster with orange sauce and caramel.

Such is the strength of Kev's sub-species, into which the children of all those immigrants, too, are inexorably mutated. Years ago, waiting for the Manly ferry, I caught the eye of a young Italian working at a coffee-stall, and I remember distinctly the wiry black Latinate quality of his person. I went down there again the other day to see if he was still about, and I found him not just aged and plumped, but altogether altered by the Kev Effect – his face pulled into a different shape, his sparkle replaced by something more wary or blunted, or perhaps dreamier. And when he spoke, the last traces of Neapolitanism were all but hidden beneath the virile twisted vowels of Australian English.

Language they say is the badge of nationality, and above all else it is the language of Sydney that binds this fissile society into a recondite unity. It is many years since the writer Monica Dickens, at a Sydney signing session, famously inscribed a volume to Emma Chissett, misunderstanding a lady who wanted to know the price of the book, but fundamentally the vernacular has not changed: 'Emma Chissett?' I make a point of asking now, when I want to buy something, and the shop assistants never give me a second glance, taking my dinkum Aussiness for granted, and frequently confiding in me their grievances about the train service from Parramatta.

Or from Woop Woop perhaps, an imaginary township which has become a Sydney generic for the back of beyond. Sydney English is full of such fantasies and in-jokes, and consciously perpetuates itself in self-amusement, hardly a year passing without another new dictionary of the argot. Usages change constantly – out goes *she'll be apples* ('it'll be OK'), in comes *throwing a mental* (losing one's temper) – and there is almost nobody in Sydney, schoolboy to sage, who is not eager to discuss the present state of the vernacular. Why do Sydney women end all their sentences, even the most definite, with a rising interrogative inflection? Because they're so put down they daren't say anything for sure. What's the true definition of an Ocker? 'A man who watches the footy on TV with a terry-towel hat on his head and a tinny of Foster's balanced on his belly.'

The language makes the man, and makes the city too. Without his language your Sydney citizen (he no longer calls himself a Sydneysider) might be taken for a Scandinavian, a Californian or even sometimes an Englishman: with it even a second-generation immigrant can be mistaken for nobody else, and the fizz and the fun of the tongue reflects Sydney's particular strain of constancy. The pubs of this city are loud with jazz and rock music, deafening the packed saloons within, blaring over the sidewalks. Often the thump of it drives the customers into a frenzy, and the bars are full of strapping young Ockers throwing their hands above heir heads, whoopeeing and beating their enormous feet. They are not at all like roisterers of Europe or America, partly because they all seem to be, like that opera chorus, in a condition of exuberant physical well-being, partly because the tang of their language pervades everything they do, and for a time I thought their burly disco to be something altogether new out of Sydney, an Australization specifically of the 1980s.

But emerging half-shattered one day from the Observer Inn, having weaved a perilous way among those flailing limbs and stomping size 14s, I chanced to see, in a shop down the road, a print of early Sydney settlers living it up 150 years ago. They wore floppy slouch hats and check shirts, were heavily bearded, and were probably celebrating their recent release from hard labour in the prisons: but they were kicking their legs about in that self-same Sydney fandango, in just the same heavyweight high jinks, and were yelling their songs and cheerful obscenities, I am sure, in similarly rank and entertaining distortions.

* * *

For even Sydney has a past. It began in the 1780s with the arrival of the first British convicts, put ashore here in their chains to serve as the reluctant and incongruous Founding Fathers of Australia. It ended in the 1950s with the mass landings of the European immigrants, disembarking after their government-subsidized passages to transform Australia from semi-emancipated colonialism into Pacific cosmopolitanism. By then the penal colony had developed into a city of great but somewhat unlovely character, chauvinist to an almost comical degree, with an elite of often snobby and vulgar monarchists, and a labour force so powerful that unionists everywhere called this the Worker's Paradise. In those days any Sydney matron worth her social salt boasted of her distant connection with the Earl of Mudcastle, while the Sydney proletariat was as rough, as ready, as truculent, as contemptuous of earls and as militantly Irish as a self-respecting proletariat ought to be.

Today that society has mostly gone underground. If you want a symbolic demonstration of it, try going to the subterranean railway station beside the Town Hall: for there behind the trendily creeper-covered walls of the sunken plaza, all waterfalls and canopies, the station itself survives as a very museum of the Old Australia – brass knobs, Bakelite switches, Instructions to Employees in copper-plate script behind brass-framed glass, bare electric bulbs lighting up to announce the next train to Pymble or Hornby. The Sydney railways are very Old Australia. So are the ferries, and the less liberated pubs, and the memorials to kings and queens and Robbie Burns. The granddaughters of those well-connected matrons still curtsey with a preposterous zeal when Prince Charles drops by. Go-slows on the Woop Woop line, heavy-jowled men with placards demanding a Fair-Go For Aussie Ships, recall the heyday of the Worker's Paradise. The old beery machismo has not been entirely subsumed in white wine and unisex hairdressing.

More importantly, out of the Old Australia comes Sydney's sense of order and fair play, which underpins the shifting vigour of this city. *Kindness and Courtesy* is still the motto of Double Bay School, and to a remarkable degree the old values obtain. You might expect this haven on a creek at the bottom of the world to be a seamy, wild and reckless place, and of course Australians, like city people everywhere on earth, talk with dismay of rising crime rates and drunken driving. By most standards, though, Sydney is good as gold. The streets are much safer than most, the traffic is generally demure enough, even jay-walkers look guilty, and the city comports itself, at least to visitors, with unfailing politesse.

These are legacies based, *au fond*, upon parliamentary democracy and the Common Law, and their survival is a tribute to their strength: for what has happened all around them, in the last three decades, is nothing less than a social revolution. Sydney has become a different city, different in style, in aspiration, in loyalty, in taste. A generation ago, it seemed to me, the very core of the Sydney ethos was the memory of the sacrifices its men had made in the two world wars, fighting in a cause almost quixotically remote to them, yet made poignantly real by their devotion to Crown, Flag and Empire. The heroic ordeals of Gallipoli and Alamein stood somewhere near the root of the civic pride, and the Returned Servicemen's League was sacrosanct and inescapable.

But on a recent winter Sunday I revisited the great war memorial in Hyde Park which was the shrine of those epic memories, and found its tragic magnetism dispersed. It stood there still of course, grey, powerful and sombre among the trees; the sad sculpted soldiers still looked down, sitting like thoughtful gods around the parapet; but the people in the park somehow seemed to shy away from its presence, as though it had been put out of their minds by some process of re-education, or sealed up, with all its toxic energies, like an expended reactor.

It seems only proper that the motto of another Sydney school, *I Hear, I See, I Learn*, should translate into Latin as *Audio, Video, Disco*, for the young have boisterously discarded the old image of Sydney, and have remoulded it again in their own. Today this city is one of the world's great promises, a pledge of better things, living in a state of ill-defined but perpetual expectancy. It is a very young city: not just young in manners and accomplishment, but exceedingly young in person. Sometimes indeed it seems to be inhabited chiefly by schoolchildren, children kicking pebbles across bridges, children racing fig leaves down the channels of ornamental fountains, children clambering like invading armies all over the Opera House, or mustered in their thousands in the New South Wales Art Gallery. They seem to me a stalwart crew. 'Now this is a Picasso,' I heard a teacher say in the gallery one day, 'I'm sure you all know who Picasso was.' 'I don't,' piped up a solitary small Australian at the back, and I bowed to him as the only absolutely honest soul in sight.

It is a city attuned to young ideas – 'Barefoot shoppers,' sensibly decrees one of the grandest department stores, 'must not use the escalators' – and its youthfulness is so pervasive as to be almost hallucinatory. The magistrate in the petty sessions court looks like a second-year law student, the prosecuting attorney might just have invested in his first motor bike, and surely the accused, who is charged with public indecency, has not yet reached the age of puberty? As for the Stock Exchange, it appears to be run by several hundred athletes, helped by a few go-go girls in miniskirts, and the old men in the public gallery upstairs, ostensibly examining the shares board through their binoculars to see how Consolidated Metals are doing, look to me less like speculators than plain voyeurs.

The youthfulness of Sydney, like all youthfulness, is a little schizo, being half brash, but half timid. In a posh Sydney hotel, for instance, or an upstage Sydney restaurant, customers tend to behave with a detectable sense of reverence, talking in undertones to each other and gratefully accepting the wine-waiter's recommendation – it would be a maître d's delight, were it not for the fact that in Sydney even that insufferable guild behaves with a becoming inhibition. Australians always used to be accused of inferiority complex, and though their image in the world is very different now, still Sydney has not reached the free fine assurance of absolute civic maturity – 'When I go to California,' a very attractive and intelligent Sydney girl said to me, 'I feel like a mouse.' And the mouse instinct erupts some-times, of course, as it always does, into absurd expressions of self-assertion. Sydney people are far less vulnerable to criticism than they used to be, but they are hardly less sensitive to the patronizing or the aloof. In Europe, one Sydney intellectual told me severely, ignorance about Australian affairs was abysmal, *abysmal* – why in London, he had been assured, reputable art critics had never even heard of Brett Whiteley!

'Brett Who?' I could not resist inquiring (remembering the boy in the art gallery) for this aspect of the Sydney style can be a bit relentless. One is told a little too often of the Whiteley genius, one tires of the gossip about the Sidney Whites and the Patrick Nolans; yes, one did realize that the author of *Schindler's List* was a local man; for myself I feel lucky to have missed the recent Sydney fashion show, about which I heard so much, which featured a ballet performance to aboriginal music, songs with flute accompani-ment against a background of wrecked cars, and some extreme examples of the Bundled Jap look.

But then youth, hope and silliness go together, in cities as in people, and it is the hope that counts. The hope is what Kev unconsciously feels, as he jogs over the bridge in the morning, and what nearly every stranger feels too, on a first foray into the streets of Sydney. How young and strong the city! How magnificent the promise! One forgets sometimes that even in the Land of Oz, youth is not eternal . . .

* * *

The Reeperbahn or 42nd Street of Sydney is King's Cross, a mile or two south-east of Sydney Cove. This used to be an entertaining Bohemian quarter, but has degenerated lately into a nasty combination of squalor and pathos. Among the usual Reeperbahn company of pimps, pornographers, strippers, tattooists and transvestites, bathed in the conventionally sinful half-light, gaped at by the inevitable visitors from Woop Woop, through King's Cross after midnight there now move some more heart-rending figures: child-prostitutes, hardly in their teens, desperately made up and not very expertly soliciting the passing drunks and lechers.

John Gunther, the great reporter, used to ask, wherever he went in the world, 'Who runs this place?' It is my practice to ask who (or in print, perhaps, *whom*) I ought to be sorry for. In some cities – think of Calcutta, think of Johannesburg! – the question is superfluous. In many another the tender heart is wrung by terrible poverty, or political oppression, or general gloom of environment. In Sydney there is hardly any abject poverty. Politically the people of this city are free as air, socially they are as emancipated as anyone on earth. Their town is clean and mostly safe, their climate is a dream, and though they grumble a good deal about the effects of recession, and frequently go on strike, by the standards of the world at large they live magnificently.

So who should I be sorry for? Sydney people are puzzled by the question, and sometimes can't think of anyone at all. Sometimes they reply with jokes about unsuccessful football players or politicians in eclipse. 'Me,' says Kev, but he does not mean it. A few propose those poor children of King's Cross, there are vague references sometimes to derelicts ('derros') or exploited immigrants. And in the end it occurs to most people that I should give a thought to the abos, the aborigines, whose names are all around one in Sydney, in Woolloomooloo, in Parramatta or in Woop Woop, but whose physical presence is but a wisp or a shadow in the thriving city.

Most of the aborigines of these parts were exterminated, by imported disease or by brute force, within a few decades of the first white settlement. Yet two centuries later a few hundred cling to their roots in Sydney, at the very site of the European coming. They are called 'coories' here, and like the water of the harbour, like the exotic foliage of the parks and headlands, they are a reminder of stranger, older things than Kev and his kind can conceive. To some Australians the aborigines are a blot on the conscience, to others just a pain in the neck: still, in the end most people thought the coories were worth feeling sorry for, and feel sorry for them I did.

297

Though their community has produced some celebrities in its time, notably boxers, they live mostly in more luckless quarters of the town, and do not show much as a rule. As it chanced, however, while I was in Sydney this time they celebrated Aboriginal Day. The aboriginal flag of gold, black and yellow flew, to the consternation of Old Australians, side by side with the national flag on Sydney Town Hall, and a march through town was announced, to be followed by a rally at Alexandria Park. Alas, all this went sadly awry. Nobody seemed to know where the march was to begin, or when, somebody pulled the flag down from the Town Hall, not everyone seemed to have mastered the rally chant – *What do we want? Land rights! What have we got? Bugger all* – and the arrangements ran so late that when the time came for speeches everyone had gone home. 'They are a *random* people,' was the convincing explanation I was given, when I asked if this was true to coorie form.

By the time I reached Alexandria Park Aboriginal Day seemed to have fizzled out altogether, and all I found was a small huddle of dark-skinned people around an open bonfire, surrounded by litter on the edge of the green. They greeted me with a wan concern, offering me beer out of an ice-bucket, sidling around me rather, and occasionally winking. A small thin boy with cotton wool stuffed in one ear wandered here and there leading a black puppy on a string. Others kicked a football about in the gathering dusk, and around the fire a handful of older men and women looked sadly into the flames. A strong smell of alcohol hung over us, and the man with the bucket urged me quietly, again and again, to have one for the road, dear. Had the rally been a success? I asked. 'Yeah,' they said, and looked into the fire.

I *did* feel sorry for them. They were like last wasted survivors from some primeval holocaust, whose memories of their own civilization were aeons ago expunged. Did they have a Sydney all their own, I wondered, long ago near the beginnings of time? Did their flag fly braver then? When I said goodbye and drove away ('Go on, dear, just one') the lights of the down-town tower blocks were shining in the distance: but in the shadows at the edge of the park the bonfire flames were dancing still, and the frail figures of the indigenes moved unsteadily in the flicker.

One morning I went to Iceland, the skating rink, to watch the Sydney people skating. They did it, as they do most things, very well. Their tall strong frames looked well on the ice. Once more I was struck by the Scandinavian analogy, so Nordic does an Australian look when you put

298

him in cold circumstances, but eventually my attention was gripped by a figure who, it seemed to me, could be nothing else but Aussie.

He was about five years old, blond, lively, tough and unsmiling. He could not, it seemed, actually skate, but he was adept at running about the rink on his blades, and his one purpose of the morning was to gather up the slush that fell off other people's boots, and throw it at passing skaters. This task he pursued with skilful and unflagging zeal. Hop, hop, he would abruptly appear upon the rink, and picking a lively target, staggering his way across the ice, inexorably he would hunt that victim down until *slosh!* the missile was dispatched – and hobble hobble, quick as a flash he was out of the rink again, gathering more material.

I admired him immensely. He hardly ever fell over, he seldom missed, and he did everything with a dexterous assiduity. When I asked him his name he spelt out GORGE with his finger on the rail of the rink; when I asked him if he was enjoying himself he just nodded grimly; and in my mind's eye I saw him thirty years from now, exploding into a company meeting perhaps, with an irresistible take-over, or relentlessly engineering the resignation of a rival under-secretary. I kept my eye firmly on him as I walked out of Iceland, for instinct told me he was assembling slush for me.

Australia was not built by kindness, nor even by idealism. Convicts, not pilgrims, were its Fathers, and Sydney remains rather steelier than it looks. It is not a very sentimental city, and not much given I fear to unrequitable kindness. There is a certain kind of Sydney face, especially among women, which at first sight looks altogether straight, square and reliable, but which examined more carefully (surreptitiously if possible, over the edge of a newspaper from the next table) reveals a latent meanness or foxiness inherited surely, I tell myself in my romantic way, from the thuggery of the penal colonies.

Behind the pleasant façade of this city, harsher things are always happening. Inexplicable political scandals excite the newspapers. Numberless Royal Commissions investigate improprieties. Through this apparently egalitarian society stalks a handful of gigantic capitalists, with tentacles that seem to extend into every cranny of city life, and make you feel that whatever you are doing, whether you are buying an ice-cream or booking an airline ticket, you are making the same rich Australians richer yet. Immigrants say that your older Ocker is a terrible bigot still, and even now they tell me a foreign accent often gets snubs and indignities – and not only a European accent, for the favourite Sydney witticism of the day is the New Zealand Joke ('How d'you set up a New Zealander in a small business?' 'Give him a big one, and wait').

Sydney people strike me as essentially cautious or suspicious in their social attitudes. They lack the gift of spontaneous welcome or generosity. They are too easily embarrassed. Invariably smiling and helpful though this citizenry seems, and quite exceptionally polite, I sometimes think that if I were in real trouble, friendless, destitute and passport-less in the streets, I might feel less abandoned in Manhattan. I considered making the experiment as a matter of fact, and presenting myself on the Circular Quay to beg passers-by for my ferry fare: but I remembered that look in the eye of the ladies at the next table, and lost my nerve.

Even now, two centuries after the event, a streak of bad origins is still apparent in Sydney. Truth will out! It has been smudged in the historical memory – if you can believe the Australians, none of the transported convicts ever did anything worse than poach a squire's salmon, or tumble his daughter in the hay. It has been romanticized, too – in the figure of the larrikin for instance, the Sydney street urchin of ballad and anecdote who used to strut picturesquely about these streets in bell-bottom trousers and pointed shoes, fighting merry gang wars and picking pockets. Today it has been varnished over with layer upon layer of gentility and sophistication, but it is there all the same, and if you want to see it plain, try going to the park on a Sunday afternoon, when the Sydney soap-box orators give vent to their philosophies, and the hecklers to their interruptions. In most countries I love these arenas of free expression – they are rich in picaresque episode and eccentricity, and sometimes even in wisdom. I left Sydney's Speakers' Corner, though, with a shudder. The free speech was too grossly free, too crudely spiteful, sexist and foul-mouthed. The arguments were bludgeonly, the humour was coarse, and all around the soap-boxes there strode a horribly purposeful figure, wearing a beret tipped over his eyes, and holding a sheaf of newspaper, whose only purpose was to shout down every speaker in turn, whatever the subject or opinion, with a devastating loutishness of retort – never silent, never still, hurling offensive gibes at speaker and audience alike with a flaming offensive energy.

Now where, said I to myself, have I seen that fellow before? And with a pang I remembered: GORGE the indefatigable ice-slosher, up at the ice-rink.

Away to the west of Sydney, over a long innocuous hinterland of suburbs, neither ugly nor beautiful, neither poor nor rich, with Lebanese laundries, and pubs with names like the Gladstone Arms or the Lord Nelson, and ladies in flowered housecoats exercising their dogs at lunch-time, and pizza houses with blown-up pictures of Vesuvius behind their counters, and streets called Myrtle Street and Merryland Road – out there beyond the western suburbs you can see the outline of the Blue Mountains. Snow falls up there sometimes, and log fires burn in resort hotels: and beyond them again, beyond Orange and Dubbo, there begins the almost unimaginable emptiness of Australia, extending mile after mile after mile of scrub, waste and desert into the infinite never-never of the aborigines. Nearly all Australia is empty. Emptiness is part of the Australian state of things, and it reaches out of that wilderness deep into the heart of Sydney itself, giving a hauntingly absent sense to the city, and restraining the responses of advertising executives in elevators.

The scrub is always near. The splodges of green everywhere make this metropolis feel, even now, like an interloper in the wasteland, and people commute daily into Sydney from country that is almost virgin bush. Only just outside the metropolitan limits, up on the Hawkesbury River, are communities that still cannot be reached by road, to which the mail goes out each day on a chugging river-boat, nosing its way among the creeks and channels, between woodlands where wallabies leap and koalas ruminate, to be unloaded on rickety wharfs at hamlets of shacks and bungalows, and hobbled away with by aged oystermen – the air-conditioned towers of Sydney itself barely out of sight, beyond the gum trees!

The sea everywhere, insidiously entering the city in a myriad inlets, seems a vacuous kind of ocean, which seldom brings the tang of a salt breeze into the downtown streets, and often looks to me indeed like fresh water all the time. The history of Sydney, like the history of Australia, is essentially blank, very little of interest ever having happened here, and there is a sort of bloodlessness even to the very success of the place, and a pallor to its style, and a curious suggestion of muffle even at rush-hour, which reminds one repeatedly of that immense desolation beyond the hills.

This sensation preoccupies many Australian artists, and affects me very strangely. Sometimes in Sydney I feel I am not looking directly at the city at all, but seeing it through glass, or perhaps reflected in a mirror. Its edges seem oddly ill-defined when I am in such a mood, its pellucid light is lacking in refraction, without the opacity of dust, breath, history and regret that hangs on the air of most great cities. The wind seems to have been filtered through some pale mesh of the south. Even the seafood, however imaginatively garnished with strawberries or avocado, seems to lack the tang of the deep sea and the tides. Even the Australian language sometimes sounds to me echo-like, as though it is reaching me from far, far away, or out of another time.

Sydney can be exhilarating, but it is a *moderate* exhilaration. It can stir the heart, but not quite to the point of ecstasy. You do not dance along these streets, or thrill to the beat of the place. Its faces, in repose, are neither kind nor cruel, but just expressionless. People seldom seem surprised in Sydney, and for that matter they are seldom very surprising themselves: though it is astonishing that so grand a place should exist down here at all, so handsome, so complete a metropolis on the edge of nowhere, still it never gives the impression, as other young civic prodigies do, that it has burst irresistibly out of the sub-soil into life.

Here are two old Hungarians walking on a Sydney beach. They wear hats, camel coats and signet rings. They came here half a lifetime ago out of the shambles of Europe, and they have lived happily ever after. They escaped the murder of war and the miseries of communism to prosper in this peaceful haven of the Antipodes. Their wives are taking coffee at the Cosmopolitan – remember the two in furs, silent over their Camparis? Their sons, daughters and grandchildren are probably out in their boats. They are very lucky, and know it. 'We are very lucky,' they say. 'Sydney is a beautiful city. Australia is the Best Country in the World.' They do not say it *con amore*, though, or even *cantabile*. They seem unlikely to kiss the soil they walk on, or raise their hands in gratitude to the Australian dream. 'Let us hope the world stays in peace,' they simply conclude, as if to say, let's hope our luck lasts out – just give us ten more years, O God of the Southern Sun!

Most people like Australia, but in this city of the numbed reflex, the blank eye, few will open their hearts about the place.

Far up the coasts of Sydney, north and south of the Sydney Heads that form the spectacular portal of Australia, comfortable villas of the well-to-do lie encouched in fig trees, gums and lawns of buffalo grass. They are seldom ostentatious houses. They are not like the garden palaces of Cap d'Antibes, or the monastically enclosed pads of Hollywood. Though it is true that the Sydney *jeunesse dorée* is given to things like flying by sea-plane to take lunch in suburban restaurants, or giving birthday parties for favourite Ferraris, still history, temperament and politics have combined to ensure that this is not a city of conspicuous consumption. Its extremely rich are seldom visible, if only because they are in Europe or California; and its glossiest mansions cannot be seen either, because they are country houses set in 25,000 acres of sheep country somewhere over the hills. All this gives the city an air of calm stability: the very idea of economic collapse, still less revolution, seems preposterous, as I look out of my hotel window now to see the white yachts at play in the harbour, yet another laughing horde of schoolchildren storming the terraces of the Opera House, and Kev at his window in his shirt-sleeves, preparing himself psychologically for the long jog home.

Short of another world catastrophe, I think, this place has reached its fulfilment. This is it. It will probably get richer, it will certainly get more Asian, but aesthetically, metaphysically, my bones tell me I am already seeing the definitive Sydney, the more or less absolute Australia. A few more tower blocks here, an extra suburb there, a louder Chinatown, more futuristic ferry-boats perhaps – otherwise, this is how Sydney is always going to be. That bland pallor of personality will survive, that seen-through-a-glass quality, and visitors from the north will always be able to fancy, as they look out at the harbour's odd foliage and wide skies, that they have been deposited upside-down on the obverse of the world. The strain of shyness, the old streak of the brutal, will be held in balance still: another zealot will always be collecting slush at the ice-rink, another generation of satisfied entrepreneurs will ask destiny for just another decade of happiness, just long enough to live out their lives in the Best Country in the World.

I have been at pains to draw the warts of Sydney in, but on the whole, I have to say, few cities on earth have arrived at so agreeable a fulfilment. Those old Hungarians are right – they are very lucky people, whose fates have washed them up upon this brave and generally decent shore. But just as no man is a hero to his valet, so no city is a paragon to its inhabitants, especially at the end of a hard day in the office, and by 5.30 Kev's morning euphoria has long worn off. The ferries down there are jammed to the gunwales with commuters. The bridge looks solid with traffic. It is drizzling again. Bugger it, Kev remembers, tonight's the night for Andrew and Marge – avocados again, you can bet your life, and they'll probably bring that snotty brat Dominic to crawl around the table. 'Night, Mr Evans.' Night, Avril, silly cow. 'Night, Kev.' Night, Jim, you pot-bellied Ocker. 'Just before you go, Kev, heard this one? There's this New Zealander . . .'

Jeez this rain is miserable. Get out of the road, you silly sod. Christ, who dreamed up that Opera House? (We all know who paid for it, don't we?)

Avocado and prawns, you can bet your life. What was that woman on about in the elevator? Warm Salad! Shit! Look at that traffic! Look at that madman in the Fairmont! Who'd live in a town like this, I ask you. Warm Salad! We must all be bloody loonies . . .

'Kev! Kev, is that you? Marge and Andrew are here, dear, and they've brought little Dominic with them.'

I thought this essay fairly friendly on the whole, but far, far fewer Australians wrote to me about it than had written about my first and much less admiring Sydney essay, all those years before . . .

24

O Canada!

I escaped some of the unsettling realities of the Old World in Canada. I spent much of the 1980s there, writing a series of articles for the Toronto magazine Saturday Night. *Canadians liked to say the twentieth century was Canada's century. When I had visited their country in the past I had generally thought it dispiritingly provincial, but after this more protracted exposure I reached the conclusion that while Canada might not be the most thrilling of countries it did have a genuine claim to be considered the best. Certainly the four Canadian essays that follow are (for what it's worth) among my own favourite things in this book.*

Ottawa

At first, with its spiked and stippled towers above the ice-cold river, Ottawa reminded me of Stockholm. Then on a windy Sunday afternoon I caught the savour of frying potatoes from a chip wagon in Confederation Square, and was transported for a moment to Aberdeen. And finally I found myself thinking ever and again of Cetinje.

Cetinje? Cetinje was an obscure mountain village of Montenegro until, in the nineteenth century, the princes of that country made it their capital, supplied it with palace and opera house, stately mall and proud memorial, and summoned to it the emissaries of the Powers. In no time at all it had legations on every other corner, while its rulers married so successfully into better-known monarchies of Europe, and implanted their personalities so ornately upon the little city, that in the end Cetinje found itself immortalized in *The Prisoner of Zenda* as the capital of that indestructible kingdom, Ruritania.

I am not suggesting, dear me no, that there is any element of comic opera to Ottawa. No capital is more innocent of foolish pomp and feathered canopy. But often enough the city does seem to me, in its own self-deprecatory way, almost as exotic as Cetinje – almost as deeply in the middle of nowhere, almost as fiction-like in its nuances, just as well equipped with the metropolitan trappings, as well supplied with home-grown heroes, and embellished at least as adequately with halls of government and diplomacy.

Consider, before we go any further, a few improbable facts. In Ottawa mankind ate its first electrically cooked meal. In Ottawa one of the world's first bi-directional elevators takes visitors slightly askew up the parliamentary tower. In Ottawa I was offered one day, without a smile, pears poached in Earl Gray tea. Ottawa mints the coins of Papua New Guinea. Ottawa is inscribed all over with logos, acronyms and cabalistic initials, and is dotted with buildings named for dead knights – the Sir Richard Scott Building, the Sir Guy Carleton Building, the Sir John Carling Building . . . An eminent prime minister of this capital maintained spiritualist contact with his departed terrier, Pat. The head of state to which Ottawa now owes allegiance lives several thousand miles away across an ocean, but its first presiding authority was the Great Hare of the Ottawa Indians, lop-eared creator of all things.

Isn't it a bit like Ruritania? I felt repeatedly in Ottawa that fantasy, or at least originality, was trying to break through, kept in check always by the Canadian genius for the prosaic; and I was gratified to discover not only that the distinguished Ottawa law firm of Honeywell and Wotherspoon actually lists a partner named E. Montenegro, but that the Anglican cathedral in Sparks Street, believe it or not, was designed by King Arnoldi. Could anything be more Cetinje than that?

Certainly, for a start, no half-mythical Balkan metropolis was ever more baffling in its arrangements than Ottawa, capital of the most famously logical and sensible of modern states. If you stand exactly in the middle of the Alexandra bridge, spanning the Ottawa River in the middle of this conurbation, you may experience a decidedly disorienting sensation – may well wonder indeed where in the world you are. Have a care, before you move an inch. Your left foot is certainly subject to the common law familiar to all English-speaking travellers, but in some respects your right foot is subject to strictures of the Napoleonic Code. If a policeman approaches you from the west, to charge you with improper loitering in a public place, he will probably charge you in French; if from the east, to make sure you are not planning acts of sabotage, probably in English.

Several separate legislatures are responsible for your right side, several others care for your left. Three different flags at least are flying all around you, and you stand simultaneously within the mandate, so far as I can

make out, of the Canadian federal government, the provincial govern-
ments of Ontario and Quebec, the National Capital Commission, the
regional municipalities of Ottawa-Carleton and Outaouais, the city
administrations of Hull and Ottawa, and for all I know half-a-dozen other
boards and commissions that I have never heard of.

Outside Canada I doubt if one educated person in ten thousand could
place Ottawa with the remotest degree of accuracy upon a blank map.
Most foreigners might just as well do what Queen Victoria is supposed to
have done when she chose this singular spot for Canada's capital, namely
shut her eyes and stabbed the atlas with a hatpin. Even here on the bridge,
if you are anything like me, you may feel hardly the wiser. You seem to
be in a kind of extraterritorial limbo, swirled all about by overlapping
administrations, rival bureaucracies, ambivalences of geography, politics,
the obscurer reaches of history. Only the reassuring buildings of the
Canadian confederacy, whose shape everybody knows from childhood
stamp collections, make one moderately certain what city this is.

But ever-palpable is the immensity of the landscape all around – one of
the most monotonous landscapes on earth, but one of the most challenging
too. Bears sometimes turn up in Ottawa suburbs, beavers impertinently
demolish National Capital Commission trees, the air is pellucid. Best of all,
here and there around the capital you may see, as a white fuzz in a distant
prospect, the fierce white waters of Canada – those thrilling hazards which
have haunted the national imagination always, which have meant so
much in the history of this wanderers' country, and which remind the
stranger still, even when tamed with sightseeing bridges, picnic sites or
explanatory plaques, that this is the capital of the Great Lone Land.

In some ways nothing is more dullening for Ottawa than being a capital. It
has to reflect the mores, the aspirations, the styles of the country as a
whole, and if there is one thing that is debilitating about Canada, it is the
feeling that through no fault of its own this nation is neither one thing nor
the other.

The British affiliations of Ottawa are fast fading, its citizens keep
assuring me, naïvely supposing that I care twopence one way or the other.
You would not know it in the church of St Bartholomew in New Edinburgh,
a small and pretty Anglican church which has traditionally been the place
of worship of Ottawa's governors general. This seems to me almost as
much a shrine of monarchy as a house of God. The Governor-General has
a crested pew, there are flags and escutcheons everywhere, generals and

noblemen are pictured all along the cloister, and there are signed portraits of royal persons, more normally to be found on the lids of grand pianos in ambassadorial residences, at the very portal of the sanctuary itself – as if to demonstrate once more that royalness really is next to godliness.

Still, despite those knighted office blocks there is a strongly republican feeling to this capital: even the royal crests on official buildings do not dismay me, for they seem to be merely expressions of constitutional convenience. If the old spell from the east is waning, the magnetism of the south is inescapable. Directly opposite the front gates of Parliament, like an ever-watchful command post, stands the United States embassy, flag on the roof, iron posts in the sidewalk to discourage suicide drivers who might otherwise be tempted to come careering down the path from the Peace Tower to explode themselves at the front door. The symbolism of the site is brutal, but not unjust, for there is scarcely a facet of this city, scarcely an attitude, an opinion, a restaurant menu, that is not recognizably affected by the presence of that vast neighbour to the south.

Ottawa first became nationally important as an *un*-American place. The Rideau Canal, around which the town coalesced, was built to give Canada a strategic route beyond the reach of predatory Americans. Today the US seems just down the road – if that. Nowhere in the world, of course, is now insulated against American culture. In Ottawa, though, there is no escaping the fact that the United States is physically close at hand too, almost in sight, like a huge *deus ex machina* just over the horizon. Working men in Ottawa have holiday homes in Florida – they call it simply 'down south' – and half the people I meet in this city seem to have just come from, or be at that moment about to leave for, Washington, DC. They suggest to me pilgrims, coming and going always from a shrine, and some of them indeed speak of the experience with a solemnity almost reverential.

Not that Ottawans are at all American. They seem to me by and large quite particularly Canadian – in bearing, in manner, in response.

I went one evening to a public citizenship court, at which newcomers to the city, having completed the necessary preliminaries, were sworn in as Canadian citizens. The ceremony took place in a cavernous echoing hall, like the most gigantic of all parish assembly rooms, beneath the stadium of the Civic Centre. Was there ever an odder affirmation? At one end the great room was laid out with café tables, and among them Turkish children romped, Croatian musicians rehearsed national melodies, a Tibetan bistro offered brick tea with meat dumplings, and ladies in peasant aprons stood about munching hereditary sandwiches. At the other end, upon a stage, a solitary Mountie in full *Rose Marie* gear provided a lonely and slightly self-conscious element of pageantry, while an almost excessively benign lady dignitary, in gown and white tabs, welcomed the new Canadians to their fulfilment.

One by one those fortunates stepped to the rostrum, to swear allegiance to the monarch-over-the-ocean. The Croatians swung into another verse at the far end of the hall, and the Mountie shifted his weight, poor fellow, surreptitiously from one foot to the other. There were immigrants from fifteen countries, Poland to Hong Kong. To me it seemed, like all processes of naturalization, somehow a little degrading, but to those actually undergoing the experience it was evidently an occasion of pure delight. There were smiles in every row, and enthusiastic applause came from mathematicians and housewives alike. Eager children examined the documents their parents brought back from the rostrum, which looked to me suspiciously like income tax forms, and when everything was done, and all were, as the lady said, 'fully fledged members of our Canadian family', and the Mountie had stood at the salute without a tremor throughout the national anthem – when all the formalities were over, the new citizens settled down with happy anticipation for the ultimate test of Canadian aptitude, a multi-ethnic folklore performance.

I laugh at it – I have an ironist's licence, not being Canadian myself – but I was touched really, and slipping hastily off before the first clash of Lebanese cymbals, from my heart wished all those hopeful people well. One of the true pleasures of Ottawa, actually, is its gentle cosmopolitanism. This really is a bi-cultural capital now, and when I went to the closing night of the Ottawa Book Festival in the National Library, to my delight it turned out to be a bi-literary occasion. Two literatures were being honoured side by side. True-blue Anglo matrons launched into painstaking French before my eyes, gaunt and furious Quebecois relapsed without complaint into English. The winner of the non-fiction prize was one of God's own French Canadians, a handsome, merry, and amiable man who told me he had spent much of his life either in jails or escaping from them, but who did not even bother to inquire if I spoke French – such a relief, I always think, when conversing with francophone bank robbers of literary accomplishment.

Shortly before that event I developed a snivelling cold, and finding myself short of handkerchiefs I took along to the National Library a face flannel from my hotel instead. What fun it was to observe the good Canadians when, feeling the need to blow my nose, I produced this huge yellow square of absorbent fabric! One or two of them paused for a moment, but only a moment, in their conversation; some could not resist nudging a neighbour; most of them resolutely looked in the opposite direction, willing themselves not to notice. Blowing one's nose with a yellow face flannel is not, it seems, altogether the done thing in Ottawa.

Quite right too – it is not a pretty habit. Still, the reactions of those party-goers did entertainingly illustrate Ottawa's public personality. After a century of capital status, this is still on the face of things a decorous, tentative, discreet, conventional, sensitive and charming city. It is by no means lacking in fun, but is rather short of panache. Its humour is leisurely. It is very kind. It is incorrigibly modest, and it bears itself with such careful dignity that even its flags seem to fly undemonstratively. Inevitably security is tighter than it used to be, but even now it is mounted in a familial, almost apologetic way. A woman in yellow taking pictures at a political demonstration readily identified herself to me as a member of the police, collecting identity photographs for the files, and her male colleagues from the plain-clothes division, with their gunslinger stances and high CIA-type collars, might just as well have come wearing policemen's helmets. ('You guys are hiding everywhere today,' I overheard a uniformed officer tactfully remark to these less than indistinguishable operatives.)

The demonstration, as it happened, turned out to be a very Ottawan spectacle – there is a demonstration every ten minutes on Parliament Hill. This one was protesting against American policies, but it was not terribly savage, and was easily confined by the police to the opposite side of the street from the United States embassy. When four or five protesters peeled off from the others and tried a flank approach, I heard the following exchange.

Police Inspector: Are you a part of this demonstration, which is forbidden as you know to go any closer to the American embassy?
Protester: No sir, we are just Canadian citizens exercising our right of free movement.
Inspector: Why are you carrying that placard, then?
Protester: Oh, that's simply an expression of my own personal views, as a Canadian citizen.
Inspector: I see. All right, go ahead then.
Protester: Thank you, sir.
Inspector: You're welcome.

* * *

So it goes in Ottawa – demonstrators given harmless leeway, police polite, confrontation avoided and free opinion maintained. The protesters went and chanted a few mantras outside the embassy door – *Reagan Reagan is no good, send him back to Hollywood* – and, having made their point, rather effectively I thought, peaceably dispersed.

Can it be all, this common sense, this universal amiability? Surely not. One must remember that this is the capital of compromise – or of equivocation if you prefer. Canada is permanent compromise, it seems to me. Province must be balanced against province, languages kept in kilter, immigrants smilingly welcomed, protesters warily tolerated. After a few days in Ottawa I began to think that perhaps some recondite accommodation kept this city itself in balance – that some unwritten compact between the prosaic and the fantastic sustained its bland composure.

I suppose it could be said, actually, that the most interesting thing about Canada is its alliance, whether fortuitous or contrived, between the fearfully dull and the colossally romantic. I dropped in one morning upon the Supreme Court. The cases it was discussing were not very interesting, its judges (two men and a woman) said nothing pithy, the few spectators seemed torpid, the press seats were empty, the room was imposing without being exalting, and I was just about to leave when something astonishing happened. Suddenly the bench was bathed in an ethereal light, and simultaneously there appeared on TV screens ranged down the courtroom an attorney in Winnipeg, Manitoba, assuring Their Lordships, Her Ladyship, too, that his client was without a doubt, under sub-section 22 of the relevant act, entitled to an appeal.

I was witnessing Lex Canadiana – electronic justice, projecting the images of guilt and innocence, truth and falsehood across sixty degrees of longitude to this grey building on the Ottawa bluffs. It was a process, I thought, of truly imperial splendour, and it turned the judges up there, who had until then struck me as a fairly parochial kind of magistracy, into an almost celestial tribunal.

So I swung here and there, between poles of ennui and surprise, throughout my stay in Ottawa. It was like being torn (in a considerate way, of course) between moods, and it may surprise the more abjectly diffident of Ottawans to hear that my visit ended most distinctly *con brio*. This is how it happened:

I am by vocation a wandering swank – I love to walk about the places I am describing as though I own them – and it cannot be said that Ottawa is a town for swanking. Its Ruritanian aspects never get out of

311

hand, its peculiarities do not generally show, and altogether it is too well-mannered a city for showing off, even to oneself. Besides, when I was there the weather was unusually balmy, making it feel rather less than its most dramatic self, and so even less conducive to delusions of superbia.

But on my very last day in Ottawa the *Citizen* warned us to expect the chilliest day ever experienced for that time of year, in all the recorded annals of the capital's climate. Instantly I sprang out of bed, put on three or four sweaters, and hastened down to the river past the canal locks. Wow, it was cold! I walked briskly along the water's edge, climbed the steps near Queen Victoria's statue, and found myself standing before the central door of Parliament itself, surveying the awakening city before me.

The sun shone. The flag flew with an altogether unaccustomed flourish. The cold stung my cheeks and sharpened my spirits. And in the glory of the morning, there at the very apex of Canada, a mighty sense of swagger seized me. Down the wide steps I went in shameless pride, and the great building rose behind me, and the eternal flame awaited me beside the gates, and all along Wellington Street the towers and turrets saluted as I passed. Nothing seemed ordinary now! As I paraded that bright icy morning through the streets of Ottawa, whistling all the way and blatantly wiping the drips off my nose with my yellow face flannel, it dawned upon me that if this went on too long, and if I were not extremely careful, I might start getting sentimental about the place.

But fortunately I had to catch a midday flight, so it never came to that.

Toronto

In the 1980s Toronto was the most popular immigrant destination in the entire world, and had already developed the techniques of multi-culturalism by which other countries later coped with the ever-increasing movement of peoples around the globe. I wrote this essay to commemorate Toronto's sesquicentennial, a category of anniversary I had never heard of before.

As I waited for my bags at the airport carousel, I considered the faces of my fellow-arrivals. They mostly looked very, very Canadian. Calm, dispassionate, patiently they waited there, responding with only the faintest raising of eyebrows or clenching of gloved fingers to the loudspeaker's apology for the late delivery of baggage owing to a technical fault, edging gently, almost apologetically inwards when they spotted their possessions emerging from the chute. They looked in complete command of their emotions. They looked well fed, well balanced, well behaved, well intentioned, well organized, and well preserved. Sometimes they spoke to each other in polite monosyllables. Mostly they just waited.

But like a wayward comet through these distinctly fixed stars there staggered ever and again a very different creature: a middle-aged woman in a fur hat and a long coat of faded blue, held together by a leather belt evidently inherited from some earlier ensemble. She was burdened with many packages elaborately stringed, wired, and brown-papered, she had a sheaf of travel documents generally in her hands, sometimes between her teeth, and she never stopped moving, talking, and gesticulating. If she was not hurling questions at those expressionless bystanders in theatrically broken English, she was muttering to herself in unknown tongues, or breaking into sarcastic laughter. Often she dropped things; she got into a terrible mess trying to get a baggage cart out of its stack ('You – must – put – money – in – the – slot'. 'What is slot? How is carriage coming? Slot? What is slot?'); and when at last she perceived her travelling accoutrements – awful mounds of canvas and split leather – erupting on to the conveyor, like a tank she forced a passage through the immobile Canadians, toppling them left and right or barging them one into another with virtuoso elbow-work.

No, I have not invented her – touched her up a little, perhaps, as I have heightened the characteristics of the others, in the interests not so much of art as of allegory. I don't know where she came from, whether she was in Canada to stay or merely to visit her favourite married nephew from the old country, but she represented for me the archetypal immigrant: and she was arriving at the emblematic immigrant destination of the late twentieth century, Toronto, whose citizens are certainly not all quite so self-restrained as those passengers at the airport, but which is nevertheless one of the most highly disciplined and tightly organized cities of the Western world.

I watched that first confrontation with sympathy for both sides: and though I lost sight of the lady as we passed through Customs (I suspect she was involved in some fracas there, or could not undo the knots on her baggage), I often thought of her as we both of us entered Toronto the Good in its sesque– sesqua– sesqui– well, you know, its 150th year of official existence.

* * *

There are moments when Toronto offers, at least in the fancy, the black and terrible excitements of immigration in the heyday of the New World. I woke up the very next morning to such a transient revelation. A lowering mist lay over the downtown city, masking the tops of the great buildings, chopping off the CN Tower like a monstrous tree-trunk; and under the cloud the place seemed to be all a-steam with white vapours, spouting, streaming with the wind, or eddying upwards to join the darkness above. Lights shone or flickered through the haze, the ground everywhere was white with snow, and the spectacle suggested to me some vast, marvellous, and fearful cauldron, where anything might happen, where villains and geniuses must walk, where immediate fortunes were surely to be made, where horribly exploited Serbian seamstresses probably lived in unspeakable slums, and towering manufacturers swaggered in huge fur coats out of gold-plated private railway cars.

The mist cleared, the cloud lifted, even the steam subsided as the first spring weather came, and it was not like that at all. Toronto has come late in life to cosmopolitanism – even when I was first here, in 1954, it seemed to me not much less homogeneous than Edinburgh, say – and as a haven of opportunity it is unassertive. No glorious dowager raises her torch over Lake Ontario, summoning those masses yearning to breathe free, and conversely there are no teeming slums or sweatshop ghettos, still less any passionate convictions about new earths and heavens. I heard no trumpet blast, no angel choirs perform, as I took the streetcar downtown.

The promise of Toronto, I presently realized, was promise of a more diffuse, tentative, not to say bewildering kind. On a modest building near the harbour front I happened to notice the names of those entitled to parking space outside: D. Iannuzzi, P. Iannuzzi, H. McDonald, R. Metcalfe and F. Muhammad. 'What is this place?' I inquired of people passing by. 'Multicultural TV,' they said, backing away nervously. '*Multi-what* TV?' I said, but they had escaped by then – I had yet to learn that nothing ends a Toronto conversation more quickly than a supplementary question.

Multi-culturalism! I had never heard the word before, but I was certainly to hear it again, for it turned out to be the key word, so to speak, to contemporary Toronto. As *ooh-la-la* is to Paris, and *ciao* to Rome, and *nyet* to Moscow, and hey you're looking *great* to Manhattan, so multi-culturalism is to Toronto. Far more than any other of the great migratory cities, Toronto is all things to all ethnicities. The melting-pot conception never was popular here, and sometimes I came to feel that Canadian nationality

314

itself was no more than a minor social perquisite, like a driving licence or a spare pair of glasses. Repeatedly I was invited to try the Malaysian vermicelli at Rasa Sayang, the seafood pierogi at the Ukrainian Caravan, or something Vietnamese in Yorkville, but when I ventured to suggest one day that we might eat Canadian, a kindly anxiety crossed my host's brow. 'That might be more difficult,' he said.

A whole new civic ambience, it seems, has evolved to give some kind of unity to this determined centrifugalism – I never knew what a heritage language was either, until I came to Toronto – but I soon got used to it all. I hardly noticed the street names in Greek, or the crocodiles of school children made up half and half, it seemed, of East and West Indians. I was as shocked as the next Torontonian, three days into the city, to hear a judge tell a disgraced lawyer that he had betrayed not only the standards of his profession but also the trust of the Estonian community. I was not in the least surprised to see a picture of the Azores as a permanent backdrop for a Canadian TV newscast, or to find the ladies and gentlemen of the German club swaying across my screen in full authenticity of comic hats and *Gemütlichkeit*. 'My son-in-law is Lithuanian,' a very WASPish materfamilias remarked to me, but I did not bat an eyelid. 'Only on his father's side, I suppose?' 'Right, his mother's from Inverness.'

But multi-culturalism, I discovered, did not mean that Toronto was all brotherly love and folklore. On the contrary, wherever I went I heard talk of internecine rivalries, cross-ethnical vendettas, angry scenes at the Metro Guyanese political rally, competing varieties of pierogi, differing opinions about the Katyn massacre, heated debates over Estonian legitimacy, the Coptic succession, or the fate of the Armenians. There turned out to be a darkly conspiratorial side to multi-culturalism. I have never been able to discover any of those writers' hangouts one is told of across the world, where the poets assemble over their beers; but in Toronto I felt one could easily stumble into cafés in which plotters organized distant coups, or swapped heavy anarchist reminiscences.

But this is not the sort of fulfilment I myself wanted of Toronto. I am not very multi-cultural, and what I chiefly yearned for in this metropolis was the old grandeur of the North, its size and scale and power, its sense of wasteland majesty. Fortunately now and then I found it, in between the Afro-Indian takeaway, the Portuguese cultural centre and the memorial to the eminent Ukrainian poet in High Park. Here are a few of the signs and symbols which, at intermittent moments, made me feel I was in the capital of the Ice Kingdom:

Names such as Etobicoke, Neepawa Avenue, Air Atonabee, or the terrifically evocative Department of Northern Affairs.

Weekend breaks to go fishing in the frozen lake at Jackson's Point ('All Huts Stove-Heated').

The sculpted reliefs on the walls of the Bay Street postal office, thrillingly depicting the state of the postal system from smoke-signals and an Indian-chased stagecoach to an Imperial Airways flying-boat and Locomotive 6400.

High-boned faces in the street, speaking to me of Cree or Ojibwa. 'Raw and Dressed Skins' in a furrier's window, taking me to forests of fox and beaver.

The great gaunt shapes of the lake freighters at their quays, with huge trucks crawling here and there, and a tug crunching through the melting ice.

The fierce and stylish skating of young bloods on the Nathan Phillips rink, bolder, burlier, faster, and more arrogant than any other skaters anywhere.

And best of all, early one morning I went down to Union Station to watch the transcontinental train come in out of the darkness from Vancouver. Ah, Canada! I knew exactly what to expect of this experience, but still it stirred me: the hiss and rumble of it, the travel-grimed gleam of the sleeper cars, the grey faces peering out of sleeper windows, the proud exhaustion of it all, and the thick tumble of the disembarking passengers, a blur of boots and lumberjackets and hoods and bundled children, clattering down the steps to breakfast, grandma, and Toronto, out of the limitless and magnificent hinterland.

These varied stimuli left me puzzled. What were the intentions of this city? On a wall of the stock exchange, downtown, there is a mural sculpture entitled *Workforce*, by Roben Longo: and since it expresses nothing if not resolute purpose, I spent some time contemplating its significance.

Its eight figures, ranging from a stockbroker to what seems to be a female miner, do not look at all happy – the pursuit of happiness, after all, is not written into the Canadian constitution. Nor do they look exactly inspired by some visionary cause: it is true that the armed forces lady in the middle is disturbingly like a Soviet Intourist guide, but no particular ideology seems to be implied. They are marching determinedly, but joylessly, arm-in-arm, upon an undefined objective. Wealth? Fame? Security? The afterlife? I could not decide. Just as, so Toronto itself has taught us, the medium can be the message, so it seemed that for the stock exchange workforce the movement was the destination.

Well, do cities have to have destinations? Perhaps not, but most of them do, if it is only a destination in the past, or in the ideal. Toronto seems to me, in time as in emotion, a limbo-city. It is not, like London, England, obsessed with its own history. It is not an act of faith, like Moscow or Manhattan. It has none of Rio's exuberant sense of young identity. It is neither brassily capitalist nor rigidly public sector. It looks forward to no millennium, back to no golden age. It is what it is, and the people in its streets, walking with the steady, tireless, infantry-like pace that is particular to this city, seem on the whole resigned, without either bitterness or exhilaration, to being just what they are.

Among the principal cities of the lost British Empire, Toronto has been one of the most casual (rather than the most ruthless) in discarding the physical remnants of its colonial past. On the other hand there is no mistaking this for a city of the United States, either. If that lady at the airport thought she was entering, if only by the back door, the land of the free and the home of the brave, she would be taken aback by the temper of Toronto. Not only do Torontonians constantly snipe at all things American, but this is by no means a place of the clean slate, the fresh start. It is riddled with class and family origin. Humble parentage, wealthy backgrounds, lower-class homes and upper-class values are staples of Toronto dialogue, and the nature of society is meticulously appraised and classified.

For it is not a free-and-easy, damn-Yankee sort of city – anything but. Even its accents, when they have been flattened out from the Scots, the Finnish, or the Estonian, are oddly muted, made for undertones and sur- mises rather than certainties and swank. There is no raucous equivalent of Brooklynese, no local Cockney wryness: nor will any loud-mouthed Torontonian Ocker come sprawling into the café, beer can in hand, to put his feet up on the vacant chair and bemuse you with this year's slang – Sydney has invented a living language all its own, but so far as I know nobody has written a dictionary of Torontese.

It is as though some unseen instrument of restraint were keeping all things, even the vernacular, within limits. One could hardly call authority in Toronto Orwellian – it seems without malevolence; but at the same time nobody can possibly ignore it, for it seems to have a finger, or at least an announcement, almost everywhere. If it is not admonishing you to save energy it is riding about on motor-bike sidecars looking for layabouts; if it is not hoisting one flag outside city hall it is hoisting another outside the Ontario Parliament; in the middle of shopping streets you find its incongruous offices, and no one but it will sell you a bottle of Scotch. I have heard it address criminals as 'sir' ('I'm going to send you to prison, sir, for three months, in the hope that it will teach you a lesson') and say 'pardon' to traffic offenders (Offender: 'Well, hell, how'm I supposed to get the bloody thing unloaded?' Policeman: 'Pardon?'). Yet it is treated by most Torontonians with such respect that if the Bomb itself were to be fizzing at the fuse on King Street, I suspect, they would wait for the lights to change before running for the subway.

Toronto is Toronto and perhaps that is enough. I look out of my window now, on a bright spring afternoon, and what do I see? No Satanic mills, but a city clean, neat, and ordered, built still to a human scale, unhurried and polite. It has all the prerequisites of your modern major city – your revolving restaurants, your Henry Moore statue, your trees with electric lights in them, your gay bars, your outdoor elevators, your atriums, your Sotheby Parke Bernet, your restaurants offering (Glossops on Prince Arthur Avenue) 'deep-fried pears stuffed with ripe camembert on a bed of nutmeg-scented spinach'. Yet by and large it has escaped the plastic blight of contemporary urbanism, and the squalid dangers too.

Only in Toronto, I think, will a streetcar stop to allow you over a pedestrian crossing – surely one of the most esoteric experiences of travel in the 1980s. Only in Toronto are the subways quite so wholesome, the parks so mugger-less, the children so well behaved (even at the Science Centre, where the temptation to fuse circuits or permanently disorient laser beams must be almost irresistible). Only the greatest of the world's cities can outclass Toronto's theatres, cinemas, art galleries and newspapers, the variety of its restaurants, the number of its TV channels, the calibre of its visiting performers. Poets and artists are innumerable, I am assured, and are to be found in those cafés where writers and painters hang out, while over on the Toronto Islands, though permanently threatened by official improvements, a truly Bohemian colony still honourably survives, in a late fragrance of the flower people, tight-knit, higgledy-piggledy, and attended by many cats in its shacks and snug bungalows.

I spent a morning out there, watching the pintail ducks bobbing about the ice and the great grey geese pecking for worms in the grass; and seen from that Indianified sort of foreshore the achievement of Toronto, towering in gold and steel across the water, seemed to me rather marvellous: there on the edge of the wilderness, beside that cold, empty lake, to have raised itself in 150 years from colonial township to metropolis, to have absorbed settlers from half the world, yet to have kept its original mores so recognizable still! For it is in many ways a conservative, indeed a conservationist achievement. What has *not* happened to Toronto is as remarkable as what *has* happened. It ought by all the odds to be a brilliant, brutal city, but it isn't. Its downtown ought to be vulgar and spectacular, but is actually dignified, well proportioned, and indeed noble. Its sex-and-sin quarters, where the young prostitutes loiter and the rock shops scream, are hardly another Reeperbahn, and the punks to be seen parading Yonge Street on a Saturday night are downright touching in their bravado, so scrupulously are they ignored.

The real achievement of Toronto is to have remained itself. It says something for the character of this city that even now, 150 years old, with 300,000 Italian residents, and 50,000 Greeks, and heaven knows how many Portuguese, Hungarians, Poles, Latvians, Chileans, Maltese, Chinese, Finns, with skyscrapers dominating it, and American TV beamed into every home – with condominiums rising everywhere, and a gigantic hotel dominating the waterfront, and those cheese-stuffed pears at Glossops – it says something for Toronto that it can still be defined, by an elderly citizen over a glass of sherry, with a Manx cat purring at her feet and a portrait of her late husband on the side-table, as 'not such a bad old place'.

So this is the New World! Not such a bad old place! Again, for myself it is not what I would want of a Promised Land, were I in need of one, and when I thought of that woman at the airport, and tried to put myself in her shoes, wherever she was across the sprawling city, I felt that if fate really were to make me an immigrant here I might be profoundly unhappy.

Not because Toronto would be unkind to me. It would not leave me to starve in the street, or bankrupt me with medical bills, or refuse me admittance to discos because I was black. No, it would be a subtler oppression than that – the oppression of reticence. Toronto is the most undemonstrative city I know, and the least inquisitive. The Walkman might be made for it. It swarms with clubs, cliques and cultural societies, but seems armour-plated against the individual. There are few cities in the

319

world where one can feel, as one walks the streets or rides the subways, for better or for worse, so all alone.

All around me then I see those same faces from the airport carousel, so unflustered, so reserved. I caught the eye once of a subway driver, as he rested at his controls for a few moments in the bright lights of the station, waiting for the guard's signal, and never did I see an eye so fathomlessly subdued – not a flicker could I raise in it, not a glint of interest or irritation, before the whistle blew and he disappeared once more into the dark. It takes time, more time than a subway driver has, for the Toronto face, having passed through several stages of suspicion, nervous apprehension, and anxiety to please, to light up in a simple smile. Compulsory lessons in small talk, I sometimes think, might well be added to those school classes in Heritage Languages, and there might usefully be courses too in How to Respond to Casual Remarks in Elevators.

Sometimes I think it is the flatness of the landscape that causes this flattening of the spirit – those interminable suburbs stretching away, that huge plane of the lake, those long grid roads which deprive the place of surprise or intricacy. Sometimes I think it must be the climate, numbing the nerve ends, or even the sheer empty vastness of the Toronto sky, settled so conclusively upon the horizon, wherever you look, unimpeded by hills. Could it be the history of the place, and the deference to authority that restrains the jaywalkers still? Could it be underpopulation; ought there to be a couple of million more people in the city, to give it punch or jostle? Could it be the permanent compromise of Toronto, neither quite this nor altogether that, capitalist but compassionate, American but royalist, multi-cultural but traditionalist?

Or could it be, I occasionally ask myself, me? This is a city conducive to self-doubt and introspection. It is hard to feel that Torontonians by and large, for all the civic propaganda and guidebook hype, share in any grand satisfaction of the spirit, hard to imagine anyone waking up on a spring morning to cry, 'Here I am, here in T.O., thank God for my good fortune!' I asked immigrants of many nationalities if they liked Toronto, and though at first, out of diplomacy or good manners, they nearly all said yes, a few minutes of probing generally found them less than enthusiastic. Why? 'Because the people is cold here.' 'Because these people just mind their own business and make the dollars.' 'Because the neighbours don't smile and say hullo, how's things.' 'Because nobody talks, know what I mean?'

Never I note because the citizenry has been unkind, or because the city is unpleasant: only because, in the course of its 150 years of careful progress, so calculated, so civilized, somewhere along the way Toronto lost, or failed to find, the gift of contact or of merriment. I know of nowhere much less merry than the Liquor Control Board retail stores, clinical and disapproving as Wedding Palaces in Leningrad. And even the most naturally merry of the immigrants, the dancing Greeks, the witty Poles, the lyrical Hungarians, somehow seem to have forfeited their *joie de vivre* when they embraced the liberties of this town.

Among the innumerable conveniences of Toronto, which is an extremely convenient city, one of the most attractive is the system of tunnels which lies beneath the downtown streets, and which, with its wonderful bright-lit sequences of stores, cafés, malls, and intersections, is almost a second city in itself. I loved to think of all the warmth and life down there, the passing crowds, the coffee smells, the Muzak, and the clink of cups, when the streets above were half-empty in the rain, or scoured by cold winds; and one of my great pleasures was to wander aimless through those comfortable labyrinths, lulled from one Golden Oldie to the next, surfacing now and then to find myself on an unknown street corner, or all unexpectedly in the lobby of some tremendous bank.

But after a time I came to think of them as escape tunnels. It was not just that they were warm and dry; they had an intimacy to them, a brush of human empathy, a feeling absent from the greater city above our heads. Might it be, I wondered, that down there a new kind of Torontonian was evolving after all, brought to life by the glare of the lights, stripped of inhibition by the press of the crowds, and even perhaps induced to burst into song, or dance a few steps down the escalator, by the beat of the canned music?

'What d'you think?' I asked a friend. 'Are they changing the character of Toronto?'

'You must be joking,' he replied. 'You couldn't do that in a sesquicentury.'

He's probably right. Toronto is Toronto, below or above the ground. And you, madam, into whatever obscurely ethnic enclave you vanished when we parted at the airport that day, have they changed *you* yet? Have they subdued your peculiar accent? Have they taught you not to push, or talk to yourself, or hurl abuse at officialdom? Are you still refusing to pay that customs charge, or have they persuaded you to fill in the form and be sure to ask for a receipt for tax purposes? Are you happy? Are you homesick? Are you still yourself?

Whatever has happened to you, destiny has not dealt you such a bad hand in bringing you to this city by the lake. You are as free as we mortals can reasonably expect. Street cars will stop for you, there are dumplings on your dinner plate and a TV in your living room, if not classic fluted columns in a sunken conservatory. Your heart may not be singing, as you contemplate the presence around you of Toronto the Good, but it should not be sinking either. Cheer up! You have drawn a second prize, I would say, in the Lottario of Life.

Vancouver

The Canadian piece of mine that has been most often quoted back at me appeared in an essay about Vancouver, but really had a more general application.

All Canada, of course, is reserved, undemonstrative, unassuming. I put it down variously to the size of the country, the generally daunting climate, the lingering influence of the British and their debilitating traditions, and the presence of the marvellous, mighty, and terrible neighbour to the south. In Vancouver, however, decorum assumes a new dimension, and gives the whole city (to a stranger's sensibility, anyway) a peculiarly tentative air.

Consider the Smile Test. This is the system I employ to gauge the responsiveness of cities everywhere, and it entails smiling relentlessly at everyone I meet walking along the street – an unnerving experience, I realize, for victims of the experiment, but an invaluable tool of investigative travel journalism. Vancouver rates very low in the Smile Test: not, heaven knows, because it is an unfriendly or disagreeable city but because it seems profoundly inhibited by shyness or self-doubt.

Pay attention now, as we put the system into action along Robson Street, the jauntiest and raciest of Vancouver's downtown boulevards. Many of our subjects disqualify themselves from the start, so obdurately do they decline eye contact. Others are so shaken that they have no time to register a response before we have passed by. A majority look back with only a blank but generally *amenable* expression, as though they would readily return a smile if they could be sure it was required of them, and were quite certain that the smile was for them and not somebody else. A few can just summon up the nerve to offer a timid upturn at the corners of the mouth, but if anybody smiles back instantly, instinctively, joyously, you can assume it's a visiting American, an Albertan, or an immigrant not yet indoctrinated.

Whenever I have been back to Vancouver people have asked me how they're doing nowadays in the Smile Test. I respond with a nervous smile myself.

St John's

St John's, Newfoundland, was the place I liked best in Canada – one of the places I like best in the whole world, and for my tastes perhaps the most entertaining town in North America.

Thwack! Despite it all the personality of St John's hits you like a smack in the face with a dried cod, enthusiastically administered by its citizenry.

The moment you arrive they take you up Signal Hill, high above the harbour, where winds howl, superannuated artillery lies morose in its emplacements, and far below the ships come and go through the rock gap of the Narrows. Within an hour or two they are feeding you seal-flipper pie, roast caribou, partridge-berries or salt cod lubricated with pork fat. They show you the grave of the last Beothuk Indian and the carcass of the final Newfoundland wolf. They remind you that they, alone in continental North America, live three and a half hours behind Greenwich Mean Time.

They chill you with tales of the corpses lying in Deadman's Pond. They warm you up with Cabot Tower rum. They take you to the site of the city's first (hand-operated) traffic signal. They show you the house into which the Prime Minister of Newfoundland escaped from a lynch mob in 1932, and the field from which the aviators Harry G. Hawker and Kenneth Mackenzie-Grieve failed to cross the Atlantic in 1919. They guide you down higgledy-piggledy streets of grey, green, yellow and purple clapboard. They explain to you in detail the inequities of the 1948 Confederation referendums. They tell you repeatedly about their relatives in Boston, and involve you in spontaneous and often incomprehensible conversations on street corners.

Such is the nature of this city; windy, fishy, anecdotal, proud, weather-beaten, quirky, obliging, ornery and fun.

I start with 'despite it all' because St John's is undeniably a knocked-about sort of town. Economic slumps and political hammerings, tragedies at sea, sectarian bigotries, riots, fires, poverty and unemployment have taken their toll, and make the little city feel a trifle punch-drunk. The very look of it is bruised. The outskirts of St John's are much like the purlieus of many another North American city – malls, car dealers, airport, duplexes, a big modern university – but its downtown is bumpily unique. Set around the dramatically fjord-like harbour, overlooked by oil tanks and fort-crowned heights but dominated by the twin towers of the Catholic basilica, its chunky wooden streets clamber up and down the civic hills with a kind of throwaway picturesqueness, suggesting to me sometimes a primitive San Francisco, sometimes Bergen in Norway, occasionally China and often an Ireland of long ago.

'Either it's the Fountain of Youth,' said a dockyard worker when I asked him about a peculiarly bubbling sort of whirlpool in the harbour, 'or it's the sewage outlet.' St John's is nothing if not down-to-earth, and the best efforts of the conservationists have not deprived the town of its innate fishermen's fustian. The first dread fancy lamp-posts and orna-mental bollards, the first whiff of novelty-shop sachets, the arrival on the waterfront of that most ludicrously incongruous architectural cliché, mirror-glass – even the presence of Peek-a-Boutique in the premises of the former Murray fishery depot – have so far failed to make St John's feel in the least chichi. It remains that rarity of the Age of Collectibles, an ancient seaport that seems more or less real.

I hear some expostulations. 'Fishermen's fustian,' indeed! For all their hospitality, I get the sensation that the inhabitants of St John's may prove prickly people to write about, and there is a prejudice I am told among some of the grander St John's persons against the city's association with the fish trade. Yet even the loftiest burghers' wives could hardly claim that this is a very sophisticated place. It is like a family city, meshed with internecine plot, but still somewhat reluctantly united by blood, history, and common experience. It is the poorest of the Canadian capitals; it has little industry and few great monuments; its responses are those of a permanently beleaguered seaport on a North Atlantic island – which is to say, responses altogether its own.

Actually within the city limits of St John's there are pockets of the Arcadianism that Newfoundland picture postcards so love to show. Small wooden houses speckle seabluffs, dogs lie insensate in the middle of steep lanes, and here and there one may still see the fish stretched out to dry, as they have been stretched for 400 years, on the wooden flakes of tradition. Almost within sight of Peek-a-Boutique I met a hunter going off to the hills in search of partridge, buckling his cartridge belt around him, hoisting his gun on his shoulder, just like a pioneer in an old print. And immediately outside the windows of one of the city's fancier restaurants ('Step Back in Tyme to Dine') one may contemplate over one's cods' tongues the whole rickety, stilted, bobbing, seabooted, genial muddle that is the classic image of maritime Newfoundland.

It is a community of cousins. It happened that while I was in town St John's was celebrating its centenary as a municipality with what it called a Soiree. The festivities closed with a public party at the St John's Memorial Stadium that powerfully reinforced the familial sensation, and suggested to me indeed an enormous country wedding – everyone someone else's in-law, everyone ready to talk, with no pretence and no pretension either. Jigs and folk songs sounded from the stage, miscellaneous bigwigs sat stared-at in the middle like rich out-of-town relatives, and when people seemed slow to dance the jolly Mayor of St John's took the floor alone, offering free booze coupons to any who would join him – 'You have to get them half-tight,' he remarked to me as he handed out these inducements, jigging the while himself.

I puzzled, as every stranger must, about the mingled origins of this pungent civic character, and the first strain I identified was undoubtedly the Irish. The simplicity of St John's is streaked, I came to sense, with a particularly Irish reproach, wit, and irony – sometimes I felt that Ireland itself was only just out of sight through that harbour entrance. The prickly pensioners and layabouts who hang around on Water Street, 'The Oldest Continuously Occupied Street in North America', look pure Cork or Wexford. The instant response that one gets from nearly everyone is Ireland all over. And the complex of buildings that surrounds the Basilica of St John the Baptist, episcopal, conventual, didactic, societal buildings, is a reminder that here Irish values and memories, however dominant the British colonial establishment of the place, proved always inextinguishable.

But that establishment too still flies its flags – literally, for at city hall they flaunt not only the ensigns of the city, the province, and the Confederation but actually the Union Jack too, for reasons defined for me as 'purely sentimental'. As a sign reminds us on the waterfront, The British Empire Began Here – when Sir Humphrey Gilbert established the first permanent settlement of New Founde Land in 1583 – and the city is appropriately rich in heroic memorials, commemorative plaques, royally planted trees or dukely laid foundation stones. Newfoundland was a self-governing British possession within my own lifetime (no school stamp collection of my childhood was complete without the 1¢ Caribou of our oldest colony), and within the city centre it is still easy enough to descry the old power structure of the Pax Britannica. The governor's mansion is recognizably the social fulcrum that it was in every British possession. The garrison church is spick-and-span. The Anglican cathedral is authentically unfinished, like all the best Anglican cathedrals of the Empire. The old colonial legislature is properly pillared and stately.

The general view seems to be, all the same, that the British Empire never did much for its oldest colony. Most people I asked said that emotionally at least they would prefer to enjoy the island independence signed away to Canada in 1949, but a good many told me that if they had the choice they would opt for union with the US. This did not surprise me. In some ways St John's is very American. It does not feel to me in the least like Canada, being altogether too uninhibited, but I can conceive of it as a half-Irish, half-Empire Loyalist backwater of New England.

A century ago the Newfoundlanders were all for free trade with the Americans, at least, and would have got it if the British government had not intervened. Today half the people I met seemed to have American connections of some kind or another, mostly in Boston. When I suggested to one elderly lady that closer links with the United States might in the end mean more corruption, exploitation, and general degradation, she seemed quite affronted. 'That's only the fringe of things down there,' she said. But I looked her in the face as she said this, and I rather think I detected in it, through the patina of the years, the bright eager features of a GI groupie of long ago. 'I can assure you that at heart the Americans are very good people,' my informant firmly added, and as we parted I swear I heard, as in historic echo, a giggle in the shadows of McMurdo's Lane, and a distant beat of 'In The Mood'.

These varied inheritances and associations save St John's from any suggestion of provincialism. History does it, one might say. The fateful gap of the Narrows is like a door upon a world far wider than Canada itself, while the city's particular kinds of expertise, to do with ships, and fish, and ice, and seals, and perilous navigations, make it a place beyond condescension. Memorial University of Newfoundland has a formid-able reputation, the Marine Institute is world famous, and ships of many nations and many kinds, perpetually coming and going through the harbour, give the town a cosmopolitan strength – rust-streaked fishing vessels from the deep Atlantic grounds, hulking coastguard ships, coastal freighters, ocean research vessels, container ships and warships and ships bringing salt for the winter roads – ships in such ceaseless progress that each morning of my stay, when I walked down to the waterfront before breakfast, I found that some new craft had come out of the night like a messenger while I slept.

The historical continuity of St John's, too, allows it a status beyond its size. The world has been passing through St John's certainly for a longer time, and perhaps with a greater intensity, than through any other Canadian city – from the Basques, Dutch, French, and English of the early years to the GIs of the Second World War and the Russian and Japanese seamen who are familiars of the place today. All their influences have been absorbed, in one degree or another, into the city's persona. No wonder St John's, though long reduced to the condition of a provincial capital, remains so defiantly itself. There is no false modesty here. 'You're right, but it isn't true of St John's,' a man told me when I remarked that the citizens of most Canadian cities wanted to talk about nothing but themselves – and he went on to rehearse in loving and elaborate detail all other superiorities of the civic character.

In fact the people of St John's are irresistible talkers about themselves, and their peculiar accent, which strikes me as a cross between Irish, Devonian and Atlantic Seal, makes the flow of their infatuation all the more unguent. Since everyone seems to know nearly everyone else, throughout my stay I felt myself encompassed within a web of overlapping reminiscence, amusement, and complaint. Gossip flows lively in St John's; images of scandal, joke, and mischief passed before me like figures on a wide and gaudy screen. The moneyed dynasties of the town were dissected for me in richest idiom whether living or extinct; politicians suffered the sharp sting of Newfoundland iconoclasm; as I was guided around the streets one by one the pedigrees and peccadillos of their structures stood revealed. Here was the store which was all that was left of the Xs' fortunes, here the mansion where the wildly successful Ys resided. One of the less estimable of the lieutenant governors lived in this house, a whiz-kid entrepreneur had lately installed eight bathrooms in that.

All this makes life in the city feel remarkably *immediate*. There is no lag, it seems, between introduction and confidence. By my second day in town I was being given under-the-counter comments on the local judiciary by a well-known politician. By my third day I was being treated to the lowdown about some spectacular financial goings-on. Hardly had I been introduced to a member of one of St John's oldest families, who has one house in town and another on its outskirts, in a kind of Newfoundland version of the transhumance system – hardly had I met this distinguished citizen and his wife before they were explaining why their cat is named after – well, I had better not say who it's named after, let alone why.

1 *Extend Arm* (says a notice at a pedestrian crossing outside City Hall)
2 *Place Foot on Street*
3 *Wait Until Cars Stop*
4 *Thank Driver*

This strikes me as a quintessentially St John's announcement, with its blend of the amiable, the unexpected and the tongue-in-cheek. If reading this essay makes you too feel rather as though you are being slapped in the face with a dried codfish, that is because I was beguiled by almost everything about the city and its inhabitants.

I was conscious always all the same, as I wandered so enjoyably through the city, that life and history have never been easy here. Beneath the charm there lies a bitterness. St John's is full of disappointment, and is an exposed and isolated place in more senses than one. One afternoon, by driving the few miles out to Cape Spear, I made myself for a moment the easternmost person in North America, and was chilled to think, as I stood there in the wind, that while at my back there was nothing but the ocean, before me there extended, almost as far as the imagination could conceive, the awful immensity of Canadian rock, forest, prairie, and mountain. St John's is the edge of everywhere, the end and start of everything. The sign for Mile 'o' of the Trans-Canada Highway stands immediately outside city hall.

And to this day, though much of the activity of St John's has moved inland, everything in this city looks down, if only metaphorically, to the Narrows. Even the stolid Confederation Building, erected with a becoming diffidence well back from the bloody-minded seaport, peers cautiously from its distance towards that dramatic fissure. I found myself bewitched by it, repeatedly driving up to its headlands, or around the southern shore to the lighthouse at the end, or waving goodbye to the ships as they trod carefully between the buoys towards the open sea – a distant slow wave of an arm, from wheelhouse or forecastle, returning my farewell as seamen must have responded down all the centuries of Atlantic navigation.

Once I was contemplating that hypnotic view from the bar of the Hotel Newfoundland, which looks immediately out to the Narrows and the Atlantic beyond. It was evening, and the prospect was confused by the reflection, in the plate-glass windows, of the people, plants and ever-shifting patterns of hotel life behind me. Beyond this insubstantial scene, though, I could see the stern outline of the cliffs, the floodlit Cabot Tower on Signal Hill, the white tossing of the ocean breakers, and the slowly moving masthead light of a ship sliding out to sea.

The hotel pianist was playing Chopin – and as he played, with the recondite inflections of Newfoundland conversation rising and falling around me, mingled with laughter and the clink of glasses, somehow the riding light of that ship, moving planet-like through the mirror images, brought home to me with a frisson the grand poignancy that lies beneath the vivacity of St John's. I thought it sad but exciting, there in the air-conditioned bar.

I first went to St John's in the 1960s. In the Newfoundland of those days, still a British colony, it was necessary to find a local guarantor before one could cash foreign money orders. Knowing nobody in town, and discovering that the public library possessed a book of mine about Venice, I introduced myself to the librarian and asked if she would endorse a traveller's cheque. How could she confirm, she sensibly said, that I was who I said I was? By a simple literary test, said I: surely nobody else on earth could recite by heart the last line of my Venice book, which she had upon her own shelves. Solemnly she reached for the volume. Nervously I stood at her desk while she turned to the final page and ran her eye down the paragraphs to the end of it. Well, she said? I cleared my throat. The concluding words of my book were not very stately. 'No wonder,' I mumbled then, feeling distinctly disadvantaged, 'no wonder George Eliot's husband fell into the Grand Canal.' Without a flicker that librarian of old St John's closed the book, returned it to the shelf and authorized my money.

In London my book about Canada was called O Canada!, *but hardly anyone bought it amyway – 'Canada! What on earth could you find interesting to write about in Canada?' In Toronto its publishers honoured the national reputation by calling it* City to City . . .

25

There Stood China

*I had been repeatedly rebuffed in my attempts to get to China, and when I
did manage it in 1983, for* Rolling Stone *magazine, the country was still getting over the nightmare of the Cultural Revolution, and reeling rather after
the death of Mao Zedong and the start of the allegedly liberalizing policy
called the Open Door. I sailed there on a coastal steamer from Hong Kong.*

And in the distance, through the porthole, there stood China.

Of course wherever you are in the world, China stands *figuratively* there,
a dim tremendous presence somewhere across the horizon, sending out
its coded messages, exerting its ancient magnetism over the continents. I
had been prowling and loitering around it for years, often touched on the
shoulder by its long, long reach – watching the Chinese-Americans
shadow-box in San Francisco, say, or being dragged screaming and kicking
to the Chinese opera somewhere, or interviewing renegade patriots in
Taiwan, or debating whether to go to the fish-and-chip shop or the
Cantonese take-away in Dublin. It had seemed to me always the land of
the grand simplicities, pursuing its own mighty way through history,
impassive, impervious, where everything was more absolute than it was
elsewhere, and the human condition majestically overrode all obstacles
and reversions. I had wondered and marvelled at it for half a lifetime: and
here I was at last on my way to meet it face to face, on a less than spanking
Chinese steamship, rust-streaked, off-white, red flag at the stern, steaming
steadily northward through the blue-green China Sea.

My fellow-passengers assiduously prepared me for the encounter. They
showed me how best to suck the goodness out of the smoked black carp at
dinner. They taught me to count up to ten in Mandarin. They drew my
attention to an article in *China Pictorial* about the propagation of stink-bugs
in Gandong Province. Mrs Wang, returning from a visit to her sister in
Taiwan, vividly evoked for me her hysterectomy by acupuncture ('when
they slit me open, oh, it hurt very bad, but after it was very *strange* feeling,

very *strange* . . . '). The Bureaucrat, returning from an official mission to Hong Kong, thoroughly explained to me the Four Principles of Chinese Government Policy.

Around us the sea was like a Chinese geography lesson, too. It was never empty. Sometimes apparently abandoned sampans wallowed in the swell, sometimes flotillas of trawlers threshed about the place. Red-flagged buoys mysteriously bobbed, miles from anywhere, grey tankers loomed by high in the water. Islands appeared, islands like pimples in the sea, like long knobbly snakes, islands with lighthouses on them, or radio masts, or white villas. And always to the west stood the hills of China, rolling sometimes, sheer sometimes, and once or twice moulded into the conical dome-shapes that I had hitherto supposed to be the invention of Chinese calligraphers. Ah, but I must go far inland, the Bureaucrat told me on our third day at sea, I must go to Guangxi in the south, to see such mountains properly – mountains like no others, said he, the Peak of Solitary Beauty, the Hill of the Scholar's Servant – 'But look' (he interrupted himself) – 'you notice? The water is turning yellow. We are approaching the mouth of the Yangtze!'

So we were. In the small hours that night, when I looked out of my porthole again, I found we were sailing through an endless parade of ships, gloomily illuminated in the darkness: and when at crack of dawn I went on deck to a drizzly morning, still we were passing them, up a scummy river now, lined with ships, thick with ships, barges and tugs, and container ships, and a warship or two, and country craft of shambled wood so fibrous and stringy-looking that it seemed to me the Chinese, who eat anything, might well make a dish of them. Hooting all the way we edged a passage up the Huangpu, narrowly avoiding ferry-boats, sending sampans scurrying for safety, until after thirty miles of ships, and docks, and grimy warehouses, and factories, we saw before us a waterfront façade of high towers and office buildings, red and shabby in the rain. It was my China landfall: it was the city of Shanghai.

'Moonlight Serenade!' demanded the elderly American tourists in the bar of the Peace Hotel, 'Play it again!' The band obliged – half a dozen well-worn Chinese musicians, a lady at the piano, an aged violinist, an excellent trumpeter: Glenn Miller lived again in Shanghai, and the old thump and blare rose to a deafening climax and a smashing roll of drums.

The Americans tapped their feet and shook their hands about, exclaiming things like 'Swing it!' The band's eyes, I noticed, wandered here and there, as though they had played the piece once too often. They have been playing it, after all, since they and the song were young. Their musical memories, like their personal experiences, reached back through Cultural Revolution, and Great Leap Forward, and People's Revolution, and Kuomintang, and Japanese Co-Prosperity Zone, back through all the permutations of Chinese affairs to the days of cosmopolitan Shanghai – those terrible but glamorous times when European merchants lived like princes here, Chinese gangsters fought and thrived, the poor died in their hundreds on the streets and the Great World House of Pleasure offered not only singsong girls and gambling tables, but magicians, fireworks, strip shows, story-tellers, mah-jong schools, marriage brokers, freak shows, massage parlours, porn photographers, a dozen dance platforms and a bureau for the writing of love-letters.

No wonder the musicians looked world-weary. The Great World is the Shanghai Youth Palace now, the past of its former prostitutes being known only, we are primly told, to their Revolutionary Committee leaders. The band plays on all the same, and in many other ways too I was taken aback to find Old Shanghai surviving despite it all. The Race Club building, it is true, has been transformed into the Shanghai Public Library, and the racetrack itself is partly the People's Square, and partly the People's Park, but nearly everything else still stands. The pompous headquarters of the merchant houses still line the Bund, along the waterfront, surveying the tumultuous commerce that once made them rich. The Customs House still rings out the hours with a Westminster chime. The celebrated Long Bar of the Shanghai Club, which used to serve the best martinis at the longest bar in Asia, is propped up now by eaters of noodles with lemonade at the Dongfeng Hotel. The Peace Hotel itself is only the transmogrified Cathay, where Noël Coward wrote *Private Lives*, with its old red carpets still in place, 135 different drinks still on its bar list, and the Big Band sound ringing nightly through the foyer.

Even the streets of Shanghai, where the poor die no longer, seemed unexpectedly like home. There are virtually no private cars in this city of 11 million people, but I scarcely noticed their absence, so vigorously jostled and tooted the taxis, the articulated buses and the myriad bicycles: if there were few bright flowered clothes to be seen along the boulevards, only open-neck shirts and workaday slacks, there were still fewer of the baggy trousers, blue jerkins and Mao caps that I had foreseen. The theme music from *Bonanza* sounded through Department Store No. 10; there were cream cakes at Xilailin, formerly Riesling's Tea Rooms; the Xinya

Restaurant still ushered its foreigners, as it had for a hundred years, into the discreet curtained cubicles of its second floor. On my first morning in Shanghai I ate an ice-cream in the People's Park (admission 2 teng), and what with its shady trees and winding paths, the old men playing checkers at its concrete tables, the students at their books, the health buffs at their callisthenics, the miscellaneous meditators and the tall buildings looking through its leaves above, I thought it, but for an absence of muggers and barouches, remarkably like Central Park.

Mrs Wang had invited me to lunch at her apartment, and this was no culture shock, either. True, we ate eggs-in-aspic, a kind of pickled small turnip, and strips of a glutinous substance which suggested to me jellified seawater, but nevertheless hers was a home that would not seem unduly exotic in, say, Cleveland, Ohio. It was the bourgeois home *par excellence*. It had the statutory upright piano, with music open on the stand, the 16-inch colour TV on the sideboard, a picture of two kittens playing with a ball of wool, a bookshelf of paperbacks and a daily help. It had a daughter who had come over to help cook lunch, and a husband away at the office who sent his regards. 'We are very lucky,' said kind Mrs Wang. 'We have a certain social status.'

So this was *China*? I had to pinch myself. The Dictatorship of the People (Principle of Government No. 3, I remembered) does not visibly discipline Shanghai. Occasionally bespectacled soldiers of the People's Revolutionary Army trundle through town on rattly motor-bikes with sidecars, and outside the Municipal Headquarters (*né* Hong Kong and Shanghai Bank) two fairly weedy-looking troopers stand on sheepish sentry-go. Otherwise Authority is inconspicuous. The traffic flows in cheerful dishevelment over the intersections, ineffectually chivvied along over loudspeakers by policemen smoking cigarettes in their little white kiosks. Jay-walkers proliferate, and in the crinkled back streets of the old quarter there seems no ideological restraint upon the free-enterprise peddlers and stall-holders, with their buckets of peaches, their plastic bags of orange juice, eels squirming in their own froth and compounds of doomed ducks.

Nobody seemed shy of me. Everyone wanted to talk. A factory worker I met in the park took me off without a second thought to his nearby apartment (two dark rooms almost entirely occupied by cooking utensils and bicycles), and the only hazard of the Shanghai street, I discovered, was the student who wished to practise his English. Stand just for a moment on

333

the Bund, watching the ships go by, or counting the flitting sea-bats in the evening, and you are hemmed in, pressed against the balustrade, squeezed out of breath, by young men wanting to know if the word 'intend' can legitimately be followed by a gerund. Go and lick an ice-cream in the park, and like magic there will materialize out of the trees Mr Lu and a troop of elderly friends, all of whom remember with affection their English lessons with Miss Metcalfe at the Mission School, but none of whom has ever been *quite* sure about the propriety of the split infinitive.

Well! So this was the policy of the Open Door, which is bringing modernity to China, and has made foreigners and all their ways respectable. It seemed remarkably liberating. I often talked politics with people I met, and their answers sounded uninhibited enough. The Cultural Revolution, that hideous upheaval of the 1960s? A terrible mistake, a tragedy. The future of China? Nobody knew for sure what kind of country this was going to be. Communism versus capitalism? There was good and bad in both. Would they like to go to America? Of course, but they would probably come home again. What a kind face Zhou Enlai had! Yes, he had a lovely face, he was a good kind man, the father of his people. Did they like the face of Mao Zedong?

Ah, but there was a hush when I asked this question. They thought for a moment. Then – 'We don't know,' was the mumbled answer, and suddenly I realized that they had not been frank with me at all. Not a reply had they given, but was sanctioned by the political orthodoxy of the moment. Did they like the *face* of Chairman Mao? He was a great man they knew, he had fallen into error in his later years, it had been admitted, but nobody it seems had ever told them whether to like his *face*. My perceptions shifted there and then, and where I had fancied frankness, now I began to sense evasions, veils or obliquities everywhere. This was, I reminded myself, the very birthplace and hot-bed of the Gang of Four, that clique of xenophobic zealots – it was from an agreeable half-timbered villa near the zoo, Frenchified in a bowered garden, that their murderous frenzies were first let loose. A decade ago I might have had a very different greeting in Shanghai, and Mrs W. would probably have been banished to one of the remoter onion-growing communes for giving me lunch.

No, perhaps it was not so home-like after all. On the Bund one evening a young man with the droopy shadow of a moustache pushed his way through the crowd and confronted me with a kind of dossier. Would I go through this examination paper for him, and correct his mistakes? But I had done my grammatical duty, I considered, for that afternoon, and I wanted to go and look at the silks in Department Store No. 10. 'No,' said I. 'I won't.'

At that a theatrical scowl crossed the student's face, screwing up his eyes and turning down the corners of his mouth. He looked, with that suggestion of whiskers round his chin, like a Chinese villain in a bad old movie, with a gong to clash him in. I circumvented him nevertheless, and ah yes, I thought in my new-found understanding, if the Gang of Four were still around you would have me up against a wall by now, with a placard around my neck, and a mob there to jeer me, not to consult me about participles!

As it was, I hasten to add, every single soul in Shanghai was kind to me, and as a matter of fact my conscience pricked me, and I went back and corrected his damned papers after all. The Open Door really is open in this city, and Foreign Guests are enthusiastically welcomed, from package tourists shepherded by guides in and out of Friendship Stores to bearded language students scooting about on bicycles. Back-packers labour through town in search of dormitories: peripatetic writers hang over the girders of Waibaidu Bridge watching the barges pass below.

Of these categories, the peripatetic writer seems the hardest for the Chinese mind to accommodate. 'What is your *field*?' Mr Lu asked me. I answered him with a quotation from the Psalms, to the effect that my business was simply to grin like a dog and run about the city. 'You are a veterinary writer?' he inquired. Other people urged me to contact the Writers' Association, or at least to visit the new quarters in the north-east of the city, 'where many intellectuals live', so that we could discuss common literary problems. Just running about the city did not satisfy them. It could not be productive.

One night I went to the acrobats, as every Shanghai visitor must, and realized with a jerk – I choose the word deliberately – what the sense of role means in China. There have been professional acrobats in this country for more than 2,000 years, and in Shanghai they have an air-conditioned circular theatre, elaborately equipped with trapdoors, pulleys and chromium trapezes, for their daily performances of the all-but-incredible. They were astonishing, of course. They leapt and bounced around like chunks of rubber, they hurled plates across the stage faster than the eye could see, they balanced vast pyramids of crockery on tops of poles while standing on one foot on each other's heads, they were yanked to appalling standstills after falling headlong out of the roof.

335

'It is interesting to think,' said my companion, 'that in the Old China acrobats were like gypsies, of very low status. Now they are honoured performers. They have their role in society.' They were slotted, in short, and as I watched them it seemed to me that they not only had acrobats' limbs, and muscles, and eyes, but acrobats' thoughts, too, acrobats' emotions, specifically acrobatic libidos, and I fancied that if you stripped away their masks of acrobat make-up, there would only be other masks below, left behind from previous performances.

And it dawned on me that all those homely shuffling Shanghai crowds could be slotted too, if you had the key, into their inescapable roles. They were not really, as I had thought at first, at all like crowds of Third Avenue or Oxford Street. Every single citizen out there had his allotted place in the order of things, immutable. What is your field? I am a Housewife. I am a Retired Worker. I am a Peasant. I am an Acrobat. I am a Student, and would be much obliged, please, if you would explain to me in simple language the meaning of the following English sentence . . .

I did see one beggar in Shanghai, on the pavement opposite the former Park Hotel. He seemed to have broken his leg, and sat all bowed and bandaged, sobbing, while an associate held up an X-ray of the fracture. I am a Beggar, it seemed to say! The passers-by looked horrified, but whether by the mendicant himself, or by the nature of his illness, I was unable to determine, the Shanghai dialect not being my field.

I went to the Yu Garden from a sense of duty – it is a National Protected Treasure, even though it was built in pure self-indulgence by an official of the Ming dynasty, who caused its Rockery Hill to be constructed out of boulders brought from thousands of miles away and stuck together with rice-glue. I was ensnared there, however, by the children. There must have been a hundred of them outside the Hall for the Viewing of Rockery Hill, all three or four years old, some of them tied together with string to prevent them straying off into the Hall for Watching Swimming Fish, and I wasted a good half-hour playing with them. What adorable merry faces! What speed of mood and response, mock-terror, sham-apprehension, sheer hilarity! I stayed with them until they were led off two by two, a long crocodile of black-haired roly-poly imps, towards the Hall of Jade Magnificence.

There is nowhere like Shanghai for infant-watching, but in the end, among all the increasingly puzzling and deceptive inhabitants of this city, it was the children who baffled me most. They have a particular fondness for foreigners, and will pick one out from miles away, across a crowded square, clean through the Tower of Lasting Clearness, to wiggle an introductory finger. They have no apparent vices. They never cry, they don't know how to suck a thumb, and though their trousers are conveniently supplied with open slits in their seats, I am sure they never dirty themselves anyway.

How I wished I could get inside their little heads, and experience the sensations of a People's Revolutionary childhood! Do they never fret, these infants of the Middle Kingdom? Is that sweet equanimity of theirs force-fed or innate, ethnic or indoctrinated? Could it really be that this society is bringing into being a race that needs no nappies? The children in the Yu Garden waved and made funny faces at me as they stumped away, but they left me uneasy all the same.

So next day I went to one of the notorious Children's Palaces, after-school centres where children can either have fun, or be coached in particular aptitudes. I say notorious, because for years these places have been shown off to visiting foreigners, so that they long ago acquired the taint of propaganda. Certainly through my particular Palace a constant succession of tourist groups was passing, led by the hand by selected infants in somewhat sickly intimacy, and in the course of the afternoon the children presented a musical show, mostly of the Folk-Dance-from-Shanxi-Province kind, which did seem short on innocent spontaneity, and long on ingratiation.

But what disturbed me more than the stage management was the utter oblivion of the children themselves to the peering, staring, bulb-flashing tourists led all among them, room by room, by those minuscule trusties (who have an unnerving habit, by the way, of calling their charges *Auntie*). With an uncanny disregard they continued their ping-pong or their video games, pedalled their stationary bicycles, made their model ships, practised their flutes, repeated once again that last crescendo in the Harvest-Song-of-the-Yugur-Minority, or sat glued to the pages of strip-cartoon books, turning their pages with what seemed to me an unnatural rapidity. Their eyes never once flickered in our direction. Their attention never wavered. They simply pursued their activities with an inexorable concentration, never idle, never squabbling, just turning those pages, batting those balls, pedalling those pedals, twanging those strings or piping those Chinese flutes.

I was bemused by them. Were they really reading at all? Were they even playing, in our sense of the verb? Search me! I can only report one odd

337

little episode, which sent me away from the Children's Palace peculiarly uncomfortable, and came to colour my whole memory of Shanghai. Early in a performance of 'Jingle Bells' by an orchestra of children under the age of five, the virtuoso lead xylophonist happened to get herself a full tone out of key. She never appeared to notice; nor did any of the other performers, all dimples, winsome smiles and bobbing heads up there on the stage. On they went in fearful discord, tinkle-tinkle, clang-clang, simpering smugly to the end.

The airline magazine on CAAC Flight 1502, Shanghai to Beijing, was six months old. It was like flying in a dentist's waiting-room, I thought. Also the seats in the 707 seemed to be a job lot from older, dismembered aircraft, some of them reclining, some of them rigid, while people smoked unrestrictedly in the non-smoking section, and our in-flight refreshment was a mug of lukewarm coffee brought by a less than winning stewardess. I was not surprised by all this. I was lucky, I knew, that there were no wicker chairs in the middle of the aisle, to take care of over-booking, and at least we were not called upon, as passengers on other flights have been, to advance *en masse* upon reactionary hijackers, bombarding them with lemonade bottles.

The enigmas were mounting. Why, I wondered, were the Chinese modernizing themselves with such remarkable ineptitude? Did they not invent the wheelbarrow a thousand years before the West? Had they not, for that matter, split the atom and sent rockets into space? Were they not brilliantly quick on the uptake, acute of observation, subtle of inference? The broad-minded Deng Xiaoping is boss man of China these days, and he is dedicated to technical progress of any derivation – as he once said, in a famous phrase, what does it matter whether a cat is black or white, so long as it catches mice? China simmers all over with innovation and technology from the West: yet still the coffee's cold on Flight 1502.

The brick-laying of contemporary China would shame a backyard amateur in Arkansas. The architecture is ghastly. In the newest and grandest buildings cement is cracked, taps don't work, escalators are out of order. *Respect Hygiene*, proclaim the street posters, but the public lavatories are vile, and they have to put spittoons in the tombs of the Ming emperors. Western architects, I am told, often despair to find air-conditioning connected to heating ducts, or fire-escapes mounted upside-down, and although it is true that the Chinese-made elevators in my Shanghai hotel were the *politest* I have ever used, with buttons marked

Please Open and Please Close, still I felt that all the courtesy in the world would not much avail us if we ever got stuck half-way.

Why? What happened to the skills and sensibilities that built the Great Wall, moulded the exquisite dragon-eaves, dug out the lovely lakes of *chinoiserie*? Feudalism stifled them, the official spokesmen say. Isolation atrophied them, the historians maintain. Maoism suppressed them, say the pragmatists. Communism killed them, that's what, say the tourists knowingly. But perhaps it goes deeper than that: perhaps the Chinese, deprived of their ancient magics, observing that nothing lasts, come Ming come Mao, have no faith in mere materialism, and put no trust in efficiency. Feng shui, the ancient Chinese geomancy which envisaged a mystic meaning to the form of everything, is banned from the People's Republic; and dear God, it shows, it shows.

Never mind: with an incomprehensible splutter over the public address system, and a bit of a struggle among those who could not get their tables to click back into their sockets, we landed safely enough in Beijing.

The first thing that struck me about this prodigious capital, which commands the destinies of a quarter of the earth's inhabitants, was the nature of its light. It was a continental light, a light of steppes or prairies, and it seemed to be tinged with green. At first I thought of it as metallic, but later it seemed to me more like concrete: arched in a vast bowl over the capital, a sky of greenish concrete!

And concrete too was the dominant substance of the city down below: stacks of concrete, yards of concrete, parks paved with concrete, their trees ignominiously sunk in sockets of soil, vast highways like concrete glaciers across the city, and everywhere around the flat skyline the looming shapes of high-rise blocks, their grim squareness broken only by the outlines of cranes lifting final concrete slabs to their summits. No need for rice-glue, I concluded, in Beijing.

I was staying on the outskirts of the city, almost in the country. There the concrete was interrupted often by fields of vegetables, and the traffic that passed in the morning was half-rural – mule-carts all among the buses, juddering tractors sometimes. Most of the drivers looked half-dead with fatigue, so early had they awoken in the communes, I suppose, and the traffic itself seemed to rumble by in monotonous exhaustion. I went one morning to the Lugou Bridge, which used to be the city limit for foreigners, and standing there amongst its 282 sculpted lions, all different, above its green-rushed river, watched those tired reinforcements labouring into the city: on the next bridge upstream, big black puffing freight trains, wailing their whistles and snorting; on the next bridge to the south, bumper to bumper an unbroken line of ugly brown trailer-trucks; across the old structure beside me, past the ancient stele eulogizing Morning Moonlight on Lugou Bridge, half a million bicyclists, half-awake, half-asleep, lifeless on their way to work . . .

Somewhere over there, I knew, was the source and fulcrum of the Chinese presence – the Inner City of Beijing, which used to be Peking, which used to be Peiping, which was Kubla Khan's Dadu – the home of Deng Xiaoping, the home of Chairman Mao, the home of the Manchu emperors, and the Mings and the Hans before them. I approached it warily. Like the supplicants of old China, kept waiting for a year or two before granted audience with the Son of Heaven, I hung around the fringes of the place, waiting for a summons.

I grinned a lot, and ran (but not too energetically, for the temperature was around 95° Fahrenheit). If Shanghai felt at first unexpectedly familiar, Beijing seemed almost unimaginably abroad. Everything was different here. The faces were different, the eyes were different, the manners were colder and more aloof. Nobody wanted help with gerunds. Though as it happened people were more attractively dressed than they had been in Shanghai, far more girls in skirts and blouses, even a few young men in suits and ties, still they were infinitely more alien to me. The children, their heads often shaved or close-clipped, their cheekbones high, did not respond so blithely. A sort of grave and massive contemplation greeted me wherever I went, as though through each pair of thoughtful eyes all the billion Chinese people, Jilin to Yunnan, were inspecting me as I passed.

Beneath that great green sky, treading those interminable concrete pavements, I felt awfully far from home: and when I followed the immemorial tourist route, and took a car to the Great Wall at Badaling, there on the sun-blazed masonry, looking out across those vast northern plains and purpled mountains, I felt I was breaking some strange and lifelong dream. The Wall has been reconstructed around Badaling Gate, and is over-run there by tourists of all nationalities, milling among the cars and buses below, having their pictures taken, riding the resident camel, eating little peaches and drinking Kekou Kele, 'Tasty and Happy' – Coke, that is. It is easy to escape them, though. You make the fearfully steep ascent away from the gate towards the watchtower to the west ('We certainly are thankful to you, Mr Kung,' I heard a sweating American businessman unconvincingly gasp, as he dragged himself, temples pulsing, up these formidable steps, 'for making this trip possible – isn't this a *great* trip, you guys?').

Once at the tower, you find that beyond it the wall is reconstructed no further, but degenerates instantly into crumbled stone and brickwork, rambling away over the undulating ridges with nobody there at all. I walked a long way along it, out into the empty countryside, all silent but for the wind, all lifeless but for the hairy caterpillars which crossed and re-crossed the uneven stonework beneath my feet. But lo, when in the middle of nowhere I sat down upon the parapet to think about my rather lonely situation, out of that wilderness four or five wispy figures emerged, and opening paper bags and wrappings of sackcloth, asked if I wished to buy some antique bells or back-scratchers. Yet again, China had topsy-turvied me. I had fallen among old acquaintances, and when one by one they took turns to look through my binoculars, well, said I to myself, what's so strange about the Great Wall of China, anyway?

Looked at from the east, Beijing is not remote at all – only 100 miles from the sea, only three hours or so by air from Tokyo. It is when you come to it out of the west, or more pertinently out of the Western sensibility, that it remains so romantically distant. On a Monday afternoon I went down to the gigantic railway station, twin-towered and green-roofed (escalator out of order) to see the arrival of the Trans-Siberian Express from Moscow. This was a dramatic occasion. Hundreds of us had come to meet the train. For hours beforehand we waited in the cavernous International Travellers' Waiting Room, and when the bell rang, the great doors were opened and we burst on to the platform, an air of headiest expectancy prevailed. We stood on one leg, so to speak, we stood on the other – we looked at our watches again, we sat down, we got up – we gave the children another bottle of Kekou Kele to keep them quiet – and there, slowly round the curve into the station, very, very grandly appeared the Trans-Siberian.

With a triumphant blast of its whistle it came majestically to Beijing, the three engineers in their cab sitting there like a trio of admirals on a flagship bridge, and the waiting people clapped, and cheered, and waved newspapers, as the doors opened and from Mongolia or Siberia, Omsk or Moscow itself, their travel-worn loved ones fell home into China. One coach was full of a Western travel group; and these voyagers, as they emerged glazed and haggard on the platform, looking wonderingly around them, suggested to me astronauts returning to earth out of a long-lost space-ship.

* * *

341

There is not much left of Old Peking, except for Protected Treasures. The city walls have been torn down, most of the fortress gates have vanished, the clutter of medievalism which so entranced the old travellers has been swept away as though it never were. Across the face of the central city has been laid the cruel thoroughfare called Changan, down which the trolley-buses trundle and the bikes chaotically swarm. Here and there, though, all the same, I felt a powerful tug of organic continuity, in this city of 2,000 years.

I felt it for instance at the Summer Palace of the last of the Manchu empresses, which is now a public park, but is still everyone's idea of a Chinese imperial retreat, with its pagodas and its towering temples, its ornamental bridges among the water-lilies, its myriad boats upon the limpid lake, its covered way, decorated with a thousand scenes of Chinese legend, from which it is said no pair of lovers can emerge unbetrothed, and its ridiculous Marble Paddle-Steamer for ever moored beside the quay (the Empress built the place with money intended for the reconstruction of the Chinese navy, and commissioned this nautical folly, they say, as a slap in the face of the outraged Fleet).

I sensed the constancy of things ominously when, lifting my head unawares as I walked up Qianmen Street, I saw the vast glowering shape of the Qianmen Gate blocking the thoroughfare in front, for all the world as though it were still the portentous gateway, as it used to be, into the Inner City beyond. I sensed it delectably beside the lonely neglected pagoda of Balizhuang, twittered about by martins out on the western outskirts, at whose feet the women of the local commune worked crouching in their straw hats among the beanpoles, chitter-chattering half-hidden like so many swallows themselves. I felt it pungently in the traditional pharmacy called The Shared Benevolence Hall, founded in 1669, which is a treasure-house of arcane specifics, stack upon stack of mysterious powders, brown bottles of roots and seeds, phials of restorative nuts, sea-horses, antlers, extract of deer-tail, heart of monkey . . .

In the early mornings I used to go wandering through the *hutongs*, the crooked quarters of small courtyard houses which survive here and there off the huge new highways. A curious hush pervades these parts. No motor-traffic goes along the alleyways, high walls conceal the jumbled yards. Only by peering through half-open gates can you glimpse the tangled, crowded life within, meshed in laundry and potted plants, here a man in no shirt eating porridge from a tin bowl, there an old woman smoking her first cigarette of the day, or a girl in a spotless white blouse extracting her bicycle from the rubble. A faint haze of smoke hangs in the air, and from the public lavatory, smelling violently of mingled excrement and disinfectant, heavy breathing and a vigorous swishing of brooms show that some unprivileged comrade is fulfilling early-morning labour norms. Nobody ever took much notice of me, wandering these quiet lanes as the sun came up: only a fairly hooded eye focused on me now and then, when a woman emerged to empty her slops down a drain, or a bicycle bell chivvied me out of the way.

And once very early I strayed over a ridge to a leafy path beside a moat. I was led there by a curious cacophony of shouts, singing and twanged instruments, and it turned out to be the most hauntingly timeless place of all. It was a place of self-fulfilment. Resolutely facing a high stone rampart above the moat, like Jews at the Wailing Wall, all along the path men and women were rehearsing their own particular accomplishments privately in the dawn. As we sing in the evening tub, so the people of Beijing go to that wall. Here was a man, his face a few inches from the masonry, declaiming some heroic soliloquy. Here a woman was practising an astonishing range of arpeggios, soprano to resonant baritone. A splendid bass was singing a romantic ballad, a poet seemed to be trying out a lyric, an old man with a bicycle was plucking the strings of an antique lute. I thought of joining in, so universal did these impulses seem, sending To Be or Not To Be reverberating down that wall, or perhaps reciting some of my own purpler passages: but I restrained myself, as a Foreign Guest, and just whistled my way home to breakfast.

I must have walked a hundred miles! And gropingly I circled towards the centre of things – to what the old Chinese would have called the centre of *all* things. The measured and muffled restraint of this city was like a fog in the sunshine. Gentle, un-pushing, polite, its people kept me always wondering, and I missed the flash of underlife that gives most great cities their clarity. I missed scamps, drunks, whores, hagglers, ticket touts offering me seats (which Heaven forfend) for the Chinese opera. I saw no Dostoievsky brooding over his minced shrimps, no tragic rebel sticking up wall posters. All seemed in bland order. I had been told to look out, in the dizzily Westernized new Jianguo Hotel, for Party officials in expensive suits taking luncheon with their mistresses: but all I saw were security guards from the American embassy, eating Weight-Watchers' Salad.

How bored this quarter of the earth must be! Even the procreation of the urban Chinese is limited, if not by law, at least by powerful persuasion.

They must not gamble, there is nowhere to dance, it is miles on a bike to a cinema, and if they turn the TV on, what do they get but improving documentaries, English lessons, historical dramas of suitable import or Chinese opera? Their one emotional release seems to be eating, which they do with a gusto in which all their passions are surely sublimated. The grander restaurants of Beijing generally have two sections, one for bigwigs and foreigners, the other for the masses: but though the downstairs rooms are usually rough and ready, with linoleum tablecloths and creaky old electric fans, an equal riotous festivity attends them all.

No wonder the Chinese are such hypochondriacs. They live so strangely, I was coming to feel, in a condition of such crossed uncertainty and brain-wash, that psychotic illness must be rampant. I went to one restaurant devoted to the cult of Dinetotherapy, sponsored by another 300-year-old herb store, and was not surprised to find it prospering mightily. When I told the waiter I was suffering from headaches and general debility, he prescribed Sautéed Chicken with Fruit of Chinese Wolfberry, followed by Giant Prawns Steamed in Ginger. They worked a treat: I walked out feeling terrific.

But not all the prawns in China can cure the stresses of history, and the real malaise of Beijing, I came to think, was its domination by an ideology so all-pervading, so arbitrary, in many ways so honourable, but apparently so inconstant, which can change the very way the nation thinks from one year to another. Today it is liberal and welcoming, Chinese tradition is honoured, people are free to wear what they like, consort with foreigners if they will, sell their ducks in a free market and even build themselves houses with the profits. Yesterday it was puritanically narrow, the revolutionary condition was permanent, aliens were devils, Mao caps and floppy trousers were *de rigueur*, angry activists with stepladders and paint-brushes went all down that covered way at the Summer Palace, expunging pictures of un-progressive myth. And tomorrow, when another generation succeeds to domination, everything may be different again, and all the values so painstakingly absorbed into the public consciousness may have to be ripped out of mind once more.

There is a blankness to this despotism. What is it? Who is it? Is it the people we see on the TV news, smiling benevolently at visiting delegates, or is it scoundrels out of sight? Is it noble at heart, or rotten? Is it genial Deng Xiaoping, or some up-and-coming tyrant we have never heard of? If you climb to the top of Jingshan, Coal Hill, the ornamental mount on which the last of the Ming emperors hanged himself from a locust tree, you may look down upon a string of pleasure-lakes. Their northern waters, within the Behai Park, are alive with pleasure-craft, and their lakeside walks are always crowded. The southern lakes look dead and sterile. No rowing-boats skim their surfaces. No lovers take each other's photographs. The buildings on their banks, contained within high walls, look rich but tightly shuttered, and only occasionally do you glimpse a big black car snaking its way down to Changan.

This is where that despotism resides. Behind those walls, beside those silent lakes, the condition of the Chinese is decided, whether by cynical opportunists shacked up with girls and Japanese electronics, or by sombre philosophers bent over their calligraphy. The compound is called Zhongnanhai, and if it all looks numb from Jingshan, it must really be full of gigantic thrust and calculation. Its main entrance is to the south, with tilted eaves and two great guardian lions. The red flag flies bravely on a mast outside, and within the gate an inner wall – the 'spirit wall' of old China – is inscribed with the cabalistic text 'Serve The People'. You cannot see past it, though. Two armed sentries stand there, with two more watchful over their shoulders. They look distinctly unwelcoming, even to Foreign Guests, as they stare motionless and expressionless into the street: and sure enough, when I asked them if I could take a stroll inside Zhongnanhai, they seemed to think not.

Dazzled, bewildered, profoundly affected, all at once, I retreated from the Chinese presence. Some of those caterpillars on the Great Wall, I had noticed, never make it to the other side, but settle in crannies among the paving: and from there if all goes well, I suppose, they turn themselves into butterflies, and flutter away into the empyrean from the very substance of China. I felt rather like them when the time came for me to leave, for I took the advice the Bureaucrat had given me, and floated my way out through those humped green mountains of Guangxi, away in the humid south.

My cities of China had left me hazed with conflicting emotions and contradictory conclusions, and like a sleep-walker I wandered back towards the coast. I bicycled down dusty lanes through fecund communes, where labouring girls waved and laughed beneath their comical hats, as in propaganda posters. I clambered precipitous hillocks to take jasmine tea in faery huts. I joined the great daily migration of the tourists down the Li River, stretched out flat in the front of the boat, eating lychees all the way, drifting through a fantasy of bulbous mountains, and green, green paddy-fields, and dragon-flies, and ferry-men, and riverside villages clouded in the song of crickets, and cormorant fishermen squatting on bamboo rafts, and junks punted upstream by women bent agonizingly double at their poles, and geese in the shallows, and peasants high on rock tracks, and water-buffaloes snuffling, and old river steamers panting and thumping, while the lychees got steadily squashier in the sun, and the sad man beside me, erect in the prow, bared his chest in the breeze and sailed through those legendary landscapes singing the proud songs of his revolutionary youth.

And so I came out of the heart of China back to the sea once more. I had found no absolutes after all. I had found nothing immutable. I had met a people as confused as any other. I had seen marvellous things and miserable, I had eaten pickled turnip with Mrs Wang and been sent packing by the sentries of Zhongnanhai. I had been cured of headache by Chinese Wolfberry. I had successfully evaded the Chinese opera. I had bought a bamboo goat, and beaten Mr Lu at checkers in the park. I had visited the grand simplicities of my imagination, and found them grand indeed, but muddled. I had reached that mighty presence at last, and it was smiling nervously.

Out on the Pearl River, surrounded by black sampans, the ship lay waiting.

China has vastly changed since then. The Chinese have come to terms with contemporary technology, Shanghai has been transformed into a metropolis of unrelenting modernity, Beijing is rather less ideologically enigmatic and Tiananmen Square has acquired a different symbolical meaning. The bamboo goat I bought now stands in our house in Wales: it smells evocatively of Chinese adhesive, and I used to encourage children to take a sniff of it, until I heard that glue-sniffing was becoming addictive in Welsh schools.

26

Vienna 1983

I first knew Vienna at the end of the Second World War, but for nearly forty years I never wrote about it. When at last I did, although I gratefully recognized its pleasures, I could not bring myself to like it. It was no place for a Welsh republican.

Nothing so becomes a city as a street-car (or a tram, as we Europeans prefer it), especially if it has a single cyclopean headlamp on its front, and a couple of flags fluttering on its roof, and is connected by sundry pipes and couplings with a trailer-car behind. What weight! What responsibility! What reassurance!

And nowhere does the tram fulfil its municipal functions more staunchly than in the city of Vienna, for here it must trundle its way, day in day out, come war come peace, through a state of affairs utterly alien to the instincts of any self-respecting trolley: fantasy is piled upon fantasy in Wien, Österreich, pretence is compounded by delusion, introspection repeatedly degenerates into complex, and the whole adds up to a baleful parable of the urban condition. In some ways Vienna is the most intensely civic of great cities, the most complete and compact, the most preoccupied with its own civicness – a fifth of the entire Austrian population, after all, lives within this peculiar capital. In other ways it transcends mere city status altogether, and is more a temperament or a sensibility, embodying as it does an inexpungable repertoire of doubts, regrets and ambiguous prides – was it not within living memory the seat of the Habsburgs, the Imperial Capital of Austria-Hungary, the root of all that the word 'Empire' came to mean to the world before the wars?

Steadily notwithstanding, small flags flying, the trams clank their way around town: they are painted in strong and sensible colours, and look rather barge-like, as though they ought to be stirring up bow-waves along the track in front of them.

* * *

Down upon their diligent passings stare the structures of the Ringstrasse, the boulevard which, in the nineteenth century, replaced the ancient ramparts around the inner city of Vienna. Now as then, the Ringstrasse unforgettably dramatizes the false and footling values of this city, and it has given its name to a whole genre of Viennese art and thought – the Ringstrasse genre. Like some mad architect's dream fulfilled, its buildings rise one after another preposterously into view, Gothic or Grecian or baroque, plastered in kitsch or writhing with classical allusion, capped by spires, monstrous domes and silhouetted effigies, clumped with goddesses, chariots, gross escutcheons, caryatids, piles of sculpted trophies – here a titanic opera house, here a refulgently Attic Parliament, a university more utterly academic than Princeton, Padua, Cambridge and the Sorbonne put together, museums as overwhelmingly museumy as museums possibly could be, and dominating the whole ensemble, half-way round the ring, the immense pillared sprawl of the Hofburg, the palace of the Habsburgs until their removal after the First World War, which seems to lie there all but exhausted, as well it might, by the weight of so much consequence.

Vienna is all consequence. It stands at the far end of the Alps like a grandiloquent watchman of history. Its streets lead not just to suburbs or provincial towns, but to ancient satrapies and fields of action: the Ostautobahn strikes grandly out for Budapest and Prague, Triesterstrasse will take you, if you persevere, direct to Dalmatia, and at the end of Landstrasse, as Metternich once observed, Asia itself begins. Everything around here is designed for consequence. The Danube passes a mile or two from the Ringstrasse, crossed by strategic bridges, commanded by castles. Flatlands just made for tanks or cavalry sweep away almost from the suburbs to the marshlands of the east. The spire of St Stephen's Cathedral, plumb in the middle of the inner city, stands as a mighty marker to guide or warn the tribes, the caravans and the warring armies.

God-made then for consequence, long ago the city came to worship it. Under the aegis of the immemorially self-important Habsburgs, the Viennese became the archetypal sychophants of history, and made of their city one vast tribute to the vulgarity of class. How could they help it? For centuries they revered as their models of behaviour men who not only called themselves, in all seriousness, Their Imperial, Royal and Apostolic Majesties, but also claimed to be Kings of Jerusalem, Dalmatia, Bohemia, Transylvania, Croatia and Galicia, Grand Dukes of Tuscany, Princely Counts of Tyrol, dukes of a score of dukedoms and lords of lordships without number. These walking Social Registers, these Grand Panjandrums of Central Europe, were the presiding spirits of this place almost into modern times, and their silly standards and superstitions linger inescapably still.

It reminds me of Beijing. Beijing too has torn down its medieval walls to make way for pompous squares and thoroughfares, it too apparently depends for its self-assurance upon childish charades of grandeur, and it also is haunted by the ghosts of dead autocrats. Franz Josef, the last of the great Habsburgs, was the Mao of nineteenth-century Austria, the Helmsman of Vienna, the Great Father, and like Mao he has left behind him a host of followers who may deny their loyalty to his ideology, but who are subject by hereditary brainwash to his values. Watch now – stand back – here come a couple of Ministers down the steps from the Council Chamber in Parliament, portly important men, deep in portly and important matters of state – and swoosh, like a rocket from his office leaps the porter, buttoning his jacket – out of his door, panting heavily, urgently smoothing his hair, down the steps two at a go, *bitte, bitte!* – just in time, my goodness only just in time to open the door for Their Excellencies, who acknowledge his grovel only with slight inclinations of their heads, so as not to interrupt the flow of the discourse, as they lumber out beneath the figures of Minerva and her attendant sages to their waiting limousine.

Where sundry passers-by look almost inclined to bow and curtsey themselves, to see those dignitaries so lordly! In manners as in symbolisms, Franz Josef's convictions of hierarchy seem to colour everything in Vienna still. Though this is the capital of a republic, and a Second Republic at that, it abounds in princes and archdukes, not to mention mere counts or baronesses, glittering in restaurants with sleek golden hair and predatory half-Magyar faces, elegantly cordial at cocktail parties ('If you're ever in Carinthia, we happen to have a little place down there . . .'), or sometimes to be glimpsed, if young enough, driving around the Ringstrasse in racy Italian cars for all the world as though they should still be dressed in the shakos, plumes and dangling scabbards of White Hussars.

And below the aristocrats, the social order is marshalled still in self-perpetuating gradations of esteem and respectability. The style of the imperial bureaucracy, established to administer a dominion that extended from Switzerland to Albania, now orders the affairs of a powerless neutral republic of 7.5 million souls. People grumble constantly about the size, the slowness, the fussiness, the not unknown corruption, the ornate arcanum of it, but still one feels they are themselves oddly complicit to its survival. It is the last blur of their greatness. It is Franz Josef himself living fuzzily on, honoured still by all Vienna's myriad ranks of social and official import, all its Excellencies and Herr Professors and Frau Doktors and guilds and orders and infinitesimal nuances of protocol – the allegiance symbolized every morning, to this day, by the awe-struck deference that attends the morning exercises of the Imperial Lipizzaner horses, cantering round and round their palatial riding school, and followed obsequiously by a functionary with a shovel to remove their noble defecations.

Vienna feeds upon its past, a fond and sustaining diet, varied with chocolate cake or boiled beef with potatoes (Franz Josef's favourite dish), washed down with the young white wine of the Vienna Woods, digested, and re-digested, and ordered once more, over, and over, and over again . . . If it reminds me sometimes of Beijing, sometimes it suggests to me the sensations of apartheid in South Africa. The city is obsessed, and obsessive. Every conversation returns to its lost greatness, every reference somehow finds its way to questions of rank, or status, or historical influence. Viennese romantics still love to wallow in the tragic story of Crown Prince Rudolf and his eighteen-year-old mistress Marie Vetsera, 'the little Baroness', who died apparently in a suicide pact in the country house of Mayerling in 1889. The tale precisely fits the popular predilections of this city, being snobbish, nostalgic, maudlin and rather cheap. I went out one Sunday to visit the grave of the little Baroness, who was buried obscurely in a village churchyard by command of Franz Josef, and was just in time to hear a Viennese lady of a certain age explaining the affair to her American guests. 'But in any case,' I heard her say without a trace of irony, 'in any case she was only the daughter of a bourgeois . . .'

I often saw that same lady waiting for a tram, for she is a familiar of Vienna. She often wears a brown tweed suit, and is rather tightly clamped around the middle, and pearled very likely, and she never seems to be encumbranced, as most of us sometimes are, with shopping bags, umbrellas or toasters she has just picked up from the electrician's. If you smile at her she responds with a frosty stare, as though she suspects you might put ketchup on your *Tafelspitz*, but if you speak to her she lights up with a flowery charm. Inextricably linked with the social absurdity of Vienna is its famous *Gemütlichkeit*, its ordered cosiness, which is enough to make a Welsh anarchist's flesh creep: the one goes with the other, and just as it made the people of old Vienna one and all the children of their kind father His Imperial, Royal and Apostolic Majesty, still to this day it seems to fix the attitudes of this city as with a scented glue – sweetly if synthetically scented, like the flavours you sometimes taste upon licking the adhesives of American envelopes.

There is nothing *tangy* to this city, except perhaps the dry white wines. There is no leanness to it. Even the slinkiest of those patricians, one feels, is going to run to fat in the end, and the almost complete absence, in the city centre, of any modern architecture means that a swollen sense of inherited amplitude seems to supervise every attitude. Though Vienna is ornamented everywhere with eagles, the double-headed eagle of the Dual Monarchy, the single-headed eagle of the Austrian Republic, nowhere could be much less aquiline. Vienna an eyrie! It is more like a boudoir birdcage, and when one morning I saw a seagull circling over the pool at Schönbrunn Palace it was like seeing a wild free visitor from some other continent.

Wildness, freeness, recklessness – not in Vienna! I went to a minor police court one day, and noticing one of the accused studying a road map between hearings asked him if he was planning an escape. 'No,' he said, 'I am deciding the best route to visit my aunt at Graz.' The famous Big Wheel of the Prater funfair, that beloved image of the Viennese skyline, moves with such a genteel deliberation that I felt like kicking it, or scrawling scurrilous graffiti on its benches: the Vienna Woods which are said to have inspired so many artists in their passion for the Sublime represent Nature about as elementally thrilling as a rectory rock garden.

But who would want it otherwise, in this city of the coffee-house, the white-tie Wholesalers' Ball and the merry tavern evening with accordion accompaniment? Vienna is an elderly, comfortable, old-fashioned city. If you want excitement, a student of my acquaintance told me, you must either go to Munich or work up a peace demonstration. More immediately to hand than in almost any other city, Vienna possesses all the sensations and appurtenances of metropolitan existence, the stream of the sidewalk traffic, the great green parks with ponds and cafés in them, the opulence of long-established stores, the plushy banks and crowded theatres, the consoling lights of restaurants gleaming on wet pavements, the glimpses of opera audiences spilling out for gossip and champagne in the inter-mission, the bookshop after bookshop down the boulevards, the hotels rich in lore and private recipes, the memorials to heroes and historical satisfactions, the newspaper kiosks selling *Le Monde* or *Svenska Dagbladet*, the grand steepled hulk of the cathedral above its square, the buskers in pedestrian precincts, the winking TV tower, the sleepless trams . . . Yet as no other city can, Vienna somehow mutates this glorious distillation of human energy and imagination into something irredeemably domestic and conventional.

351

I walked one day into the Karlskirche, the most spectacular of Vienna's baroque churches, which has a dome like St Peter's, a couple of triumphal columns dressed up as minarets, and two subsidiary towers roofed in the Chinese manner. Inside I found a wedding in progress. It was magnificent. The great church seemed all ablaze with light and gilding, rococo saints floated everywhere, the bride and groom knelt side by side before the high altar, and flooding through the building came the strains of a Haydn string quartet, marvellously played and amplified to a crisp and vibrant splendour. Yet all that glory was subtly plumpened or buttoned by Vienna, for when I looked at the faces of the congregation I saw no exaltation there, only a familial complacency, satisfaction with the decorum of the arrangements only slightly tinged by the thought that dear Father would have played that *adagio* with a little more finesse.

For yes, if there is one art that has the power to make *Gemütlichkinder* of them all, it is the inescapably Viennese art of music. To Beethoven, Mozart, Haydn, Liszt, Schubert, Brahms, Bruckner, Mahler and any number of Strausses the Viennese feel a cousinly and possessive relationship. 'I hate going to concerts,' I rashly announced to a Viennese companion over dinner one evening, and our rapport was never quite the same again: and ah! how I grew to dread the quivering pause in the garden of the Kursalon-conductor with bow and violin raised above his head, orchestra poised expectant over their strings, audience frozen with their spoons half in, half out of their ice-creams – that preceded, twenty or thirty times a day, the fruity melody and relentless beat of the Viennese waltz!

I made a pilgrimage, all the same, to the grave of Beethoven in the Grove of Honour, at the central cemetery, the Zentralfriedhof. Mozart is commemorated there too, if only retrospectively, his body having unfortunately been dumped in an unmarked pauper's grave, and Johann Strauss the Elder is lapped by cherubim near by, and Hugo Wolf the *Lieder* writer, than whom no single human being has ever plunged me into profounder despondency, is among the shrubberies round the corner. Beethoven's tomb was easy enough to find because it had so many wreaths upon it, including one laid that morning, with visiting card attached, by Professor Hisako Kocho, President of the Folk Opera Society of Oita Prefecture (telephone Oita 5386). Yet even this grand sanctuary did not make my heart race, or inspire me to heroic yearnings: for with the gilded lyre upon its headstone, its Old German lettering and its generally metronomic or Edition Peters manner, it reminded me horribly of piano practice.

* * *

At night, however, lights are reflected in the overhead wires of the tram-cars, and seem to slide eerily around the Ringstrasse of their own accord, like beings in a separate field of animation, lighter, faster, airier, more sly, than any No. 2 to Franz-Josefs Kai. Perhaps that well-known Viennese Herr Professor Freud used to contemplate them, as he strode on his long meditative walks: certainly it was from the generic psyche of Vienna that he drew his definition of the subconscious – that part of every human, every city, which lies concealed beneath the personality, or is revealed only by shimmering glints on street-car wires.

The most celebrated contemporary citizen of Vienna is not an analyst of trauma, but a scourer. Policeman lounging feet-up on the stairs outside, files of data stacked macabre around him, Simon Wiesenthal the Nazi-hunter sits in his office above Salztorstrasse, close to the old Jewish quarter and the Gestapo HQ, endlessly considering the darkest categories of angst. Around him are framed testimonials from grateful institutions – he is an award-winning Nazi-hunter – but few of them come from societies in Vienna. Hundreds of the most virulent Nazis, he says, still live unscathed in these parts – one much-respected builder of churches not only constructed the Auschwitz gas chambers, but *repaired* them, too. Dr Wiesenthal is by no means sufficiently *gemütlich* for the Viennese. There was an attempt on his life not long ago, and the city authorities very much wish, he tells me, that he would go somewhere else: in the meantime they put that slovenly policeman on his door, and another one, toting an automatic rifle, stands just in case outside the Synagogue in Seitenstettengasse.

I have to say that for a few hours after visiting Dr Wiesenthal I saw the face of Eichmann all around me – that peaked but ordinary face which I remember so exactly from the courtroom at Jerusalem years ago, and which Hannah Arendt characterized for ever as expressing 'the banality of evil'. Nothing could be more unfair, I know, to the people of Vienna. Half of them are too young to remember Nazidom anyway, and the others, though if we are to believe Dr Wiesenthal they include a far higher proportion of war criminals than survive in any German city, were doubtless the victims above all of their *genii loci*. It was the presence of Vienna, after all, that first incited Adolf Hitler himself to his grandiose dreams of sovereignty – like an enchantment out of the Arabian Nights, he thought the vainglorious horror of the Ringstrasse.

But even if I dismiss from my mind the image of that lady in the brown suit, braided and blonde in those days, greeting the storm troopers with rose petals from the pockets of her dirndl, still I cannot dispel the feeling,

353

as I walk these streets, that I am promenading one great conglomeration of neurosis. The reasons for it are not hard to conjecture – the crippling social legacies of the monarchy, the relentless pressures of *Gemütlichkeit*, historical humiliation, geographical exposure – drive down Metternich's Landstrasse now, and in an hour you are on the frontiers of Czechoslovakia or of Hungary, where the sentinels of the Eastern world, weapons over their shoulders, stand with the great steppes at their backs.

No wonder this is a Freudian city in every sense. Not only is Freud's house in Berggasse maintained as a shrine, where you may buy mounted photographs of his original Couch, or fancy yourself summoning dreams for interpretation in the very room where the Oedipus complex was first isolated. Not only that, but everywhere in the city you feel around you the ideas, the idioms and the subject matter of Freud's vision: Father Figures tower in royal and apostolic statuary, libidos search for discos or Prater prostitutes, repressions wander arm-in-arm on Sunday afternoons down the beckoning avenues of Zentralfriedhof. It is as though at heart this whole famous metropolis, through its bows, smiles and proprieties, would like nothing so much as to flop down on a sofa in tearful revelation – in the presence, of course, of a properly *gemütlich* and well-qualified Herr Dr Professor.

And the last and most marvellous flowering of the Viennese genius, that surge of styles, ideas and mannerisms which orchestrated the decay and collapse of the Habsburgs, was itself a distinctly neurotic blossoming. No lyric joy of liberation seems to have inspired the new artistic forms by which the architects, the painters and the composers of this city rebelled against the old order of things. The temple of their revolution was the art gallery called the Secession House, built by the architect Josef Olbrich in 1898 and still as good as new: but it was officially opened by the Emperor anyway, and with its squat hunched form and its dome of gilded laurel-leaves looks rather like a mausoleum from that Grove of Honour (though I dare say the Secessionists themselves, whose text was Ver Sacrum, Sacred Spring, thought it looked like a pump room). There was not, it seems, much fine careless rapture to this renaissance, to the venomous furies and gold-encased women of its paintings, to the alternate swirls and severities of its ever more loveless architecture.

But it did have a daemonic fire to it, and this strain of tormented or inverted genius lingers today like a reflected glow of the city's inner conflicts. I find it more haunting, if less dazzling, than the excesses of Ringstrasse,

for it shows itself more obliquely, in art as in life: a sudden tangle of decoration, a blank façade of concrete, the sunken eye of a man in the subway,
a woman's twisted face – wrenched by stroke? by bitterness? – as she sits
alone over her coffee. For all its comfort, for all its beauty, for all its wealth
and self-esteem, Vienna does not feel to me a happy city. Its citizens seem
to be still working out, in their various ways, the very same doubts and
frustrations which those artists expressed with such disturbing power in
the last days of the old regime. They often fail. The suicide rate has always
been high in Vienna. 'He died like a tailor', is supposed to have been Franz
Josef's odious comment on the fate of his son and heir at Mayerling, and so
he acknowledged how commonplace, how workaday, was the self-
destructive urge among his children the citizens at large. Death is a born
Viennese, and nowhere is he more *gemütlich*, as it happens, than in the
crypt of the Church of the Capuchins, where the corpses of the Habsburgs
themselves are stored: for there is a small workshop down there too, for
the restoration of imperial sarcophagi, and if you look through its window
you may see a gigantic casket emptied of its contents, having its lid
repaired perhaps, or its supporting angels re-capitated, and looking for all
the world like a car in for its 6,000-mile service, or a lawnmower parked
among the buckets and hose-pipes of the garden shed.

The trams all but killed me once. In some parts of the Ringstrasse they
alone run against the flow of the traffic, and looking to the right to make
sure I was not run down by an archduke in an Alfa, I was all but squashed
by a trolley-car coming up from the left. '*Achtung! Achtung!*' screamed
several ladies in brown tweed suits, but they forgave me my stupidity – had
not Dr Waldheim, they reminded each other, Secretary-General of the
United Nations, almost met his end in the very same way, on that very
same street?
   Inevitably people have seen Freud's Death-Wish exemplified in this city,
so preoccupied with the past, the tomb, and how the mighty fall. It seems
to me though that Vienna is adept at transferring that Wish to others. It is
fateful not so much to itself as to the rest of us. It prospers well enough in
its neuroses – it is we who suffer the traumas! Viennese Modernism hardly
touched the surface of Vienna with its shapes, but everywhere else it was to
cause a tragic alienation between architecture and public taste. Viennese
Atonalism may seldom be heard in Vienna's own *Musikverein*, but
everywhere else it long ago made life's hard pleasures harder still.
Viennese Communalism, expressed in the vast housing estates so dear to

sociologists of the 1930s, turns out to have been a step towards the universal miseries of the Social Security tower block. The anti-Semitism of Vienna pushed us all towards the Final Solution, the Zionism that was born there has left many a young body, Jewish and Gentile too, dead along the path to Israel. Freud himself, though until twenty years ago, I am told, his name was scarcely mentioned at psychiatry seminars in Vienna, long ago left the rest of the world irrevocably addled by his genius.

Is there any city more seminally disturbing? It is as though Vienna has been a laboratory of all our inhibitions, experimenting down the generations in new ways of confusing us. Perhaps rather than all our Death-Wishes it expresses all our schizophrenias? I rather think it may, you know, for as I stepped back from the track that day just in time to avoid extinction – 'Achtung! Stop! Comes the tram!' – I looked up at the passing streetcar and distinctly saw there, just for a moment, my own face in its slightly steamed-up window. We exchanged distant smiles, between Id and Ego, or dream and wake.

27

Y Wladfa: Another Wales

Every Welsh patriot wants, at least once in a lifetime, to visit the most resiliently Welsh of the Welsh communities overseas, in the Argentinian province of Patagonia. It is the only place on earth, now that everyone in Wales itself speaks English too, where the traveller may actually be obliged to speak yr hen iaith – Welsh, or as others put it, the language of God.

A most unlikely statue greets the seafarer at the small port of Puerto Madryn, on Golfo Nuevo in Argentinian Patagonia – if you can call it greeting, because actually the figure stands with its rump to the sea, on a big concrete plinth like a launching ramp. This being Latin America, you might expect the statue to honour Libertad, or Fidelidad, or at least Simon Bolívar. In fact, it honours Welsh Womanhood.

Welsh Womanhood? If you have any doubts, look round that ramp. There, on the front, is a small plaque in that ancient and magically resilient language, Cymraeg – Welsh to the world at large. I come from Wales, and at our great annual festival, the National Eisteddfod, I am always enthralled to see people wandering around who are patently Welsh, but somehow more so, with an extra verve to everything they do. These are the Welsh of Patagonia, whose 163 forebears first went ashore on the site of Puerto Madryn in 1865, and who are commemorated by that image on the waterfront.

They were the original European settlers of Argentinian Patagonia, and they are recognized as the founders of the province of Chubut, which stretches clean across Patagonia from the Atlantic to the Andes. They were not looking for an easy life, or even for profit. They were escaping the oppressive English at home, and hoping to establish here a New Wales of their own, where they could worship as they pleased, order their affairs as they wished and speak their own language. They had chosen a virtually uninhabited destination, ungoverned, no more than technically part of Argentina, and they called it simply Y Wladfa, The Colony.

357

These were not the boozy, bawdy, lyrical Welsh. These were nineteenth-century chapel Welsh, God-fearing and Bible-loving, and it so happened that almost the moment I arrived I found myself at a full-blown Welsh chapel function – a vestry tea-party for a Welsh preacher returning to Wales. This was jumping into Y Wladfa at the deep end. It was Welshness *in excelsis*. The welcome was fervent – 'A visitor from Wales! Come in, come in, have some tea, sit down meet Mrs Williams, meet Mrs Jones!' Not a word was spoken but in Cymraeg, not a face was anything but recognizably Welsh, and among the celebrants was a granddaughter of Lewis Jones, the founding patriarch of The Colony.

Next day a violent wind blew up. Everything banged, everything whistled, dust, paper, bits of trees and tin cans rushed about the streets. Through it all, if I looked through my window, huddled against the blast and half-veiled in dust, I could see Dyffryn Camwy, the valley of the lower Chubut which was the original Y Wladfa. Nowadays the Welsh generally call it just Y Dyffryn, the Valley.

It was not at all what the settlers had been led to expect. It was not a bit like Wales. It was not in the least a land of milk and honey. It was dead flat, it was covered in scrub, it had virtually no trees and the river ran through it muddily, now and then erupting into catastrophic floods. Some of the Welsh understandably returned home again, or went up to Canada, but most of them stuck it out. New migrants arrived from Wales, and in time they made a thriving agricultural colony, forty-odd miles long, irrigated by a complex system of canals, systematically divided among the settler families, and equipped with fourteen thoroughly Welsh chapels. It was a tight-knit, ethnically cohesive society.

By now the original farms of the Valley have mostly been broken up, and its community is largely scattered. The dykes the Welsh built are still at work, but the men you see scything or digging or ploughing by hand are likely to be Bolivian migrants, and in the occasional grocery store, out among the farms, you may find yourself served by wild-looking semi-Indian people.

Here and there, though, all unexpected in little green enclosures, you will come across one of those fourteen chapels. It is probably built of red brick, extremely plain and four-square, but it retains an air of contemplative serenity. Nine chapels are still active in the Valley on and off – when there is a preacher available, or when there is a song festival – and to a Welsh sentimentalist they are almost excruciatingly evocative. Some of them have graveyards, and these are touching too. Whole families of Joneses, Evanses, Williamses and Morgans lie here, sometimes beneath stones of real Welsh slate, carved by masons far away in Wales with the traditional motifs of Welsh mourning.

There are Welsh people in the Valley, still alive, still very Welsh. The first few doors you knock on will bring only regretful responses in Spanish. Then you strike lucky. 'D'you speak Welsh, señor?' you ask for the tenth time, and into a weathered brown face there will come a gleam of welcome. The house will almost certainly be simple. You will be seated at once on a hard-backed chair by the kitchen table, and the kettle will be on the boil for tea. Your conversation will probably be about Roots. Even Patagonian Welsh people who have never been to Wales know its geography well, know which villages their grandparents came from, and very probably know where your own home is on the map. Their Welsh is likely to be slightly rusty and slow, very convenient to somebody like me whose command of the language is at best rough and ready.

It may well be, as legend in Wales habitually has it, that your hosts are living almost exactly as they might be living in Wales today, or at least the day before yesterday: with the same sort of furniture, the same inherited knick-knacks, an upright piano perhaps, a case of books, home-made butter in the refrigerator and a border collie at the door. On the table is likely to be a copy of *Y Drafod*, the Welsh-language journal which has been published in Patagonia for more than a century, and is now less a newspaper than a kind of family circular. Everything is spick-and-span in such a house, very fresh, very clean, very *taclus* – a Welsh word which, meaning 'tidy' in an almost abstract sense, is very popular in Y Wladfa.

But it may be that you hit upon extremely poor Welsh farmers, living in a house of crude brick whose roof may be of mud and wattle, like the houses of medieval Europe. Beneath their bare electric light bulbs these people are living far closer to the soil than ever they would be if their forebears had never left Wales in the first place. The chances are that the family is now half-Hispanic, and that only the father or mother speaks Welsh at all. Another generation, and the language will be lost to this house.

The Valley is hardly an eldorado, anyway, and there were some among the original Welsh who looked further west, into the wide desert plateau that lies beyond. This was the province of the wild beasts and the Tehuelche Indians, and Welshmen from the Dyffryn Camwy were among the first foreigners to cross it. It is some 450 miles from the Valley to the foothills of the Andes, and in every mile of it I felt the mounting exhilaration that must have animated the young men and women of Y Wladfa, striking west out of the valley into the unknown.

Finally, like them, I saw the land of milk and honey. First, distant snow-ridges of the Andes, then rolling foothills, and lakes, and verdant valleys, and thickets of green trees, and wide farmlands, and horses, and on that brilliant summer day, the sort of glow of fulfilment that allegorical artists used to apply to pictures of theological reassurance. It is a marvellous, spectacular country.

The Welsh were the first Europeans to settle it, and they called it Cwm Hyfryd, Lovely Valley. I felt no tristesse here. The culture of the Welsh is slowly fading here too, but I felt it was going out in style. Here the Welsh farms are scattered in space and liberty against the backdrop of the high mountains, and the little metropolis of the Welsh, Trevelin, seemed full of fun and sunshine. I drove from farm to farm in high spirits, buying cheeses here, discussing the future of the Welsh language there, listening to tales of hard winters and economic hazard – for even in a Promised Land, life is seldom easy. There were horses everywhere, and lovely dogs. A young Welsh farmer called up his dad for me in Welsh on his VHF radio. An old Welsh farmer showed me the house he had built himself with the stone he had quarried, the bricks he had baked, the machinery he had made from old Chevrolet parts – 'everything home-made, everything my own!'

And in a farm on the outskirts of Trevelin I found my last archetype of Y Wladfa. He was like the smile, as it were, on the face of the Cheshire Cat. My final Patagonian Welshman cheerfully spoke for history. Not a soul in his household understood a word of Welsh beside himself, but they all clustered eagerly around us as we talked – a jolly Argentinian wife, diverse unidentified children and grandchildren, dogs and chickens and a horse tied to the fence; and with his cloth cap tilted on his head, his hands in his pockets, that Welshman of South America touched my heart not with melancholy at all, but with grateful pride to be Welsh myself.

28

Berlin 1989

The decade ended to universal rejoicing with the abandonment of the Berlin Wall, marking not only a symbolical end to the Cold War, but also the re-uniting of the long-divided city.

I sat over my victuals in the Kurfürstendamm, in a Berlin now all but undivided by its wretched Wall, and to the strains of 'Down By The Riverside' from a street musician with a monotonous guitar. I looked into my mind – and my heart, too, since I am of a certain age – to see what images already loitered there of this infamously ambivalent city.

I found emblems of iconoclastic fun, and comfortable *hausfrau* emblems of flower boxes and sticky cakes, and Le Carré suggestions of the sinister mingled with the seedy, and above all symbols of terrifying power wrestling with tragedy. Berlin has many reputations, but few of them are straightforward. I have been visiting this city intermittently since soon after the Second World War and, realizing that my own perceptions of the place were blurred by time and myth and old emotion, I reluctantly tipped that lugubrious troubadour and set out to wander the city districts, east and west of the crumbling ideological border, to discover which of my mental images were still recognizable on the ground.

I did not have to look far for the fun. The top end of the Kurfürstendamm, the showiest boulevard of West Berlin, offers the liveliest and least inhibited streets scenes in Europe. Beneath the glare of the neon signs, past the crowded pavement cafés, flooding through the tumultuous traffic, an endlessly vivacious young populace laughs, struts, sits around, eats, plays music, kisses, and shows off from the break of afternoon until the end of dawn. It is like a perpetual fair, or perhaps a bazaar, the genteel with the rapscallion, the indigent with the well-heeled: gypsy beggars with babies, bourgeois ladies with dogs on leads, lovers embracing at restaurant tables, unshaven money-changers in dark doorways, an elegant wind trio playing Scarlatti outside a brightly lit shoe shop, a not very skilful acrobat treading a rope between two trees, tireless drummers, tedious mimes, unpredictable skateboarders, portrait sketchers, hang-dog youths with ghetto blasters squatting among their own rubbish, smells of coffee and fresh rolls, double-decker buses sliding by, fountains splashing, sidewalk showcases of leathers and jewels – and presiding over it all, incongruously preserved there as a reminder of old horrors, the ugly tombed hulk of the Kaiser Wilhelm I Memorial Church, defiantly floodlit.

Berliners have always been famous for their irrepressible disrespect and hedonism, maintained through all oppressions and apparent even when I first came here to find a city half in ruins. Even on the east side, where the equivalent of Kurfürstendamm is the loveless Stalinist Alexanderplatz, even there, now that the dictatorship has gone, flashes of high spirit often show through the authoritarian grumps (fostered not only by forty years of communism, but by a decade of National Socialism before that). A waiter winks and bypasses the management ruling that we are too late for a cup of coffee. A young man dashingly V-turns his car, with a glorious screeching of brakes and skidding of tyres, across Karl-Marx Allee to pick up his laughing girl. A stretch of the hitherto sacrosanct Wall – the wrong side of the Wall – has been covered with murals and called the East Side Gallery.

Liberty is in the very air of Berlin now. It is good to be alive here, and to be young must be heaven. Everything is in flux, everything is changing, new horizons open, and nothing demands unqualified respect or allegiance. Although half of Berlin is the theoretical headquarters of the about-to-be-disbanded and thoroughly discredited People's Republic of East Germany, the city is not really the headquarters of anything much, and this gives it a stimulating sense of irresponsibility. Tokens of fun abound, indeed, and none are more endearing than the preposterous little Trabant cars, like goblin cars, that swarm out of East Berlin for a night out or some shopping in the West, with hilarious clankings and wheezings of their primitive engines, and faces smiling from every window.

Walking in the woods beside the Muggelsee, in a corner of East Berlin that would have seemed inexpressibly alarming a year or two ago, I heard through the trees a strain of jovial German music, ho-ho, thump-thump music, with a hearty baritone solo punctuated by jolly choruses. I followed it through the quiet paths, along the reedy edges of the lake (overlooked on its distant eastern shore by the grim black factory chimneys of the former

Workers' Paradise), and although by the time I reached its source the tune had changed to the old Tom Jones favourite 'Green, Green Grass of Home', still the scene I found there was an epitome of *gemütlichkeit* – the snug spirit of domesticity, laced with the sentimental, that was my second Berlin image.

'I'm The Boss' was the first T-shirt slogan I saw, on the ample bosom of a housewife dancing a vigorous disco-jig with her decidedly un-henpecked husband. East Berlin was having a public holiday, and at the hotel beside the lake several thousand citizens, great-grandmothers to babes in arms, were enjoying a family feast in the sunshine. How perfectly they fulfilled my conceptions! How genially they laughed, sang, danced, drank their beer, and ate their pickled pork knuckles! With what indefatigable smiles the two bands alternated, one with the old oom-pah-pah, the other exploring the less raucous fringes of rock! As I watched them there, so hearty, so comradely, I recognized how limitless was the strength of Berlin's *gemütlichkeit*, sustained over tankards and ice-cream cones through war and peace, dictatorship and revolution, hope and disaster, down the generations.

It knows no borders, recognizes no ideologies (Hitler encouraged it in the name of Strength Through Joy, and even the communists were obliged to allow family reunions across the Wall), and for myself I find a faintly disturbing quality to it, so absolutely is it able to disregard history. I distrust its latent tendency to prejudice – against immigrant Turks, for instance, who are ubiquitous in West Berlin. I dislike its silly aspects, evident all over the city in jokey statuary, gimmicky fountains. and fairly ponderous humour.

The Berlin cosiness is an ethos in itself, for better or for worse, and it is inescapable. Here we see it at a modest wedding in Spandau, where the bride in her long white dress, the groom in his high white stock, the priest and amiable altar boys, the intermittently squabbling choir girls, the solitary bespectacled bridesmaid (pink glasses to match her pink dress), the wildly over-accoutred family guests, the casual passers-by and even we ourselves are all embraced within its bonhomie. Here we observe it at an alfresco restaurant in the Grünewald woods in the persons of two middle-aged ladies giggling over their asparagus, smiling and nodding encouragingly at us and balancing their purses carefully on the rims of their glasses to stop the chestnut blossoms falling into their wine.

And it is realized most explicitly at Lübars, at the northern extremity of West Berlin. Lübars is a genuine farming community, surrounded by meadows and marshland within the limits of the great city, It is crystallized *gemütlichkeit*. There is a pretty village church in a sweet village green; there are farmyards and stables and a restaurant with lace tablecloths. Sometimes a plump farmer trundles by in a trap drawn by two horses, and if you walk out of the village centre you may find a kind of pixie settlement, all enveloped in green, where people live in little toylike houses, attended by gooseberry bushes and small lawns exquisitely trimmed, like Germans in a fairy tale.

I looked through a big hole hammered in the Berlin Wall, quite near the site of the old Checkpoint Charlie, and saw into the patch of no-man's-land beyond. It was littered with rolls of discarded barbed wire, surrounded by ruined buildings, and floored with the dismal mixture of sand, gravel and rubble that has resulted from three decades of herbicide – no greenery was allowed to soften the allegory of the Wall, let alone provide cover for escapers. Three East German soldiers were in there, one tilted back on a kitchen chair with his cap over his eyes, the others kicking an old steel helmet about in the dust. It was an epitome of squalor and wasted time.

For yes, the squalor of the Cold War certainly survives in Berlin. Farther along the Wall, Potsdamer Platz, once the busiest intersection in Europe, is now a dingy wilderness of gravel and miscellaneous huts through which the traffic passes as across a patch of desert. Verminous wild rabbits hop around down there, anachronistic hippies with headbands and small children protest against this and that outside grubby tents. Not far away hundreds of Poles run their shambled market of trucks and awnings, selling American cigarettes, crude transistors, some bilious-looking cheese and dismal bric-à-brac; they were guarded, when I was there, by a huge, mastiffy kind of animal, slavering at the jaws, which was not just the most gruesome dog I have ever set eyes on, but the most horrible creature of any species.

Even now, in the centre of Berlin, you know when you are approaching the line of the Wall, whether from the western or eastern side, by an unmistakable air of dubious dereliction: bombed, rubbish-strewn spaces, peeling posters, huddles of men in dark clothes, vestigial street marts with stalls and trailers, apparently abandoned vehicles, faded graffiti like KILL REAGAN or PUNKS UNITE, and, in the more touristically accessible parts, souvenir huts selling Soviet army caps or bits of the Wall encased in plastic. Nobody knows what to do with this dismal swathe, sweeping through the heart of the city in such an unlovely way;

for the moment it is like the pale strip that is left on the human skin when a bandage is ripped off.

Seediness enough, then, from the days when spies were swapped across this false frontier and young people were murdered just for trying to cross it. But the sinister part of my third image? Gone, it seems to me, all gone. Utterly dispersed is the awful fear that used to hang over the Wall like a black cloud, making every crossing from East to West a chill apprehension. The soldiers of the People's Army kick a redundant helmet about a rubble yard, instead of peering over their gun sights from a watch post, and the Democratic Republic's immigration officials, once so terrifyingly robotlike in their zeal, have turned out, to everyone's surprise, to be human after all. The Television Tower above Alexanderplatz, whose bulbous platform used to look like some sleepless, ominous, all-seeing eye, now merely reminds us that if we care to go that way there is a revolving restaurant at the 680-foot level, and an obliging tourist office at the bottom.

All the resonances of the antagonism have gone, too – a whole genre of legend, politics, art, and humour made irrelevant overnight. I had a meeting one day with two German officials, one from each side of the former border, itself an appointment that I would have thought a wild improbability ten years ago. Extracting spontaneous responses from them was rather like unpacking particularly fragile pieces of china, so anxious were they both to appear neither overweening nor apologetic. But I sensed no animosity between them and no resentment, though one was dressed in the sportiest Western fashion and gave me a handsomely printed visiting card with translations in English and Japanese, while the other wore an ill-cut dark suit without a tie, and offered me only a piece of pasteboard with his name typed upon it and a crookedly stamped logo on the back.

And where now is the power of Berlin, which once made the world cringe before Prussian salute and Nazi goose-step, swastika, and rampant eagle? The divided Berlin of our time has possessed no real power, one half having been a mere puppet of Moscow, the other an all-too-obvious advertisement for capitalism. I had to try hard to recognize any symptoms of arrogance in this city.

I did feel a few tremors of it, but only a few, among the relics of the frightful Prussian monarchy, especially in the old royal quarter of the city. There huge triumphal columns still stand on overwhelming façades, supervised by scowling lions, prancing griffins, winged horses, heroes and assorted divinities. The enormous dome of the Cathedral swells over

Marx-Engels Platz (né Lustgarten); helmeted soldiers stamp outside the Memorial to the Victims of Fascism and Militarism (né the New Guardhouse). The Reichstag, rebuilt but still domeless, stands forlorn beyond Potsdamer Platz, and beside the Spree there loom the portentous classical piles of the institutions that proclaimed, in the last half of the nineteenth century, Berlin's resurgent and assertive culture. A battered Brandenburg Gate still dominates the great avenue of Unter den Linden. Between its trees one can almost see, if one really concentrates, the plumed shakos of cavalry colonels, the fierce moustaches of Junkers, or even the open carriage of the All-Highest himself, the Kaiser, the Emperor of all the Germanies, escorted by uhlans from his war ministry to his *schloss* . . .

But only just, and still less remains of Hitler's hubris. There is the brilliantly conceived city-centre airport of Tempelhof, the best thing the Nazis ever built, and there is the unfortunately splendid stadium in which, during the 1936 Olympics, Hitler found himself made a fool of by Jesse Owens (who has a street named after him, just around the corner – more than can be said for the Führer). The rest has mostly gone, and to me it all feels drained of menace. That airport is just a visionary airport, that stadium is just a stadium. I can pass the site of the Gestapo headquarters without a tremor. I can survey without fear the bump where Hitler's bunker used to be. Goering's fat spectre does not show itself upon the steps of his air ministry. The evil has been exorcized.

As for the postwar structures of consequence, they have no sense of command at all. The official buildings of the communist East may be vast and overbearing, but they are essentially sterile, without the sap of true virility. The monumental buildings of the capitalist West feel flimsy, impoverished or contrived: The roof of the Congress Hall collapsed not long ago, the Philharmonic Hall looks as though it has been banged together out of odds and ends, and Mies van der Rohe's design for the New National Gallery was originally used for the Bacardi Building in Cuba.

Few cities on earth, in fact, now feel more dismissive of power for power's sake than Berlin, 1989; all the monuments of Establishment, whether curly-wigged Junker Baroque, Nazi Neo-Classical, steel-and-concrete Stalinist Dogmatic or Capitalist Junk Pile, look a little ridiculous.

Fun, *gemütlichkeit*, malignity, dominance – some of these emblematic qualities I found alive, some mercifully buried. At the end of my stay I searched for another that might represent not my responses to Berlin's past and present, but my intuitions about its future. I spread out before me – in the Café Einstein, pre-eminently the writer's café of contemporary Berlin, where you can write novels until closing time over a single cup of coffee – my 1913 Baedeker's plan of Berlin, and looked for omens in it.

It showed a city of great magnificence, compact and ordered around the ceremonial focus of the Brandenburg Gate, with parklands and residential districts to the west of it, the offices of state and finance to the east. Where now almost everything seems random, ad hoc, or in transition, Baedeker's 1913 plan shows nothing but rational and permanent arrangement. Modern Berlin has no real centre or balance, devastated as it has been by war and fractured by that vile Wall, but the old Berlin was, in its heavy and self-conscious way, almost a model capital.

It is fashionable just now to imagine it as an imperial capital again – as the future capital of Europe, in fact, at the place where the western half of the continent meets the east. In some ways indeed it feels like an international metropolis already, frequented as it is by Westerners of every nationality, and by Turks, Romanians, Poles, Arabs, Africans and gypsies; road signs direct one to Prague and to Warsaw, and at the Zoo railway station you may meet the tired eyes of travellers, peering out of their sleeper windows, who have come direct from Moscow and are going straight on to Paris.

Physically, no doubt, Berlin can be restored to true unity. Already its wonderful profusion of parks, gardens, forests and avenues, lovingly planted and replanted through peace and war, give it a certain sense of organic wholeness. When the wasteland of the Wall is filled in with new building, when the communist pomposities of Karl-Marx Allee and Alexanderplatz have been upstaged by the cheerful detritus of free enterprise, we may see the old municipal logic re-emerging too. The focus of life will return to the old imperial quarter, and the Brandenburg Gate will once more mark the transition between public and private purpose.

But metaphysically, my ancient Baedeker suggests, it will be a different matter. The lost Berlin of its plan was built upon victory – the victory over France, in 1871, which led to the unification of Germany and made this the proudest and most militaristic capital on earth. Everything about it spoke of triumph, Empire, and further victories to come. In today's Berlin the very idea of victory is anomalous, and triumph no longer seems a civic vocation. The world at large may still, at the back of its mind, dread the prospect of German re-unification and the revival of German power, but in my judgement at least, Berlin is no longer a place to be afraid of. I strongly suspect that half a century from now, when this city has finally recovered its united self, it will turn out to be something much less fateful than Europe's capital. It will be a terrific city, beyond all doubt – a city of marvellous orchestras, famous theatres, of scholarship, of research, of all the pleasurable arts – but not, instinct and Baedeker together tell me, the political and economic apex of a continent.

If I had to choose a single abstraction to suggest its future, I thought to myself as I ordered a second coffee after all, it would be something fond and unambitious: relief, perhaps, in this city of interesting times, that the worst is surely over.

Please God.

The 1990s

The last decade of the century seemed to me an indeterminate decade, when nothing was conclusive. There was no world war, but no world reconciliation either, although an abstraction called 'the international community' was much touted. Half the world got richer, but half got poorer too. The Americans continued their apparently inexorable march towards domination of all the continents, fighting a war against Iraq along the way. The communist empire finally disintegrated, a denouement defined by Boris Yeltsin, who presided over it, as 'the end of the twentieth century', but its successor the Russian Federation floundered in corruption and disillusionment. The progress of Europe towards unity was mocked by the terrible War of the Yugoslav Secession. Fundamental brands of Islam became more ominously powerful.

It could have been worse, but it could have been better. For me personally it was a European decade, with intermittent forays elsewhere, and I spent much of it gathering material for a book called Fifty Years of Europe. *I had come to agree with Lord Tennyson's dictum 'better 50 years of Europe than a cycle of Cathay'.*

29

The Flux of Europe

Europe was in a state of flux, as the former states of the Soviet empire tenta-
tively moved into independence, and the old democracies tried to reconcile
their disparate identities with the idea of a continental whole. Contemplating
its continuing uncertainties, and at the same time feeling footloose and
escapist, one day I decided to jump in my car and visit three of those classically
consistent parts of the continent, its famous wine-lands. This slight essay
originally ended with the exclamation 'O, the writer's life for me!', but it
was really a light-hearted prologue to more serious explorations of Europe
in the 1990s.

Vineyards

First I went to Haro, in Spain. I bought a bottle of a 1990 Reserva, from the
Abeica bodega in the nearby village of Albeca, which was recommended to
me as an exceptional example of modern Rioja, and I drank it at a table
outside the Café Madrid, in the main square of the town, with a large plate
of miscellaneous tapas.

Haro stands in the purest Spanish countryside, bare mountains, vine-
sprinkled hillsides, castles, village churches like cathedrals, hilltop her-
mitages, cuckoos and crickets and solitary elderly men hoeing fields. The
pilgrim route to Santiago passes near by, and nobody could ask much
more of Spanishness than the Plaza de la Paz before me, which is built
on a gentle slope around a florid bandstand, and has all the requisite
lamp-posts, pigeons, clocks, cobbles, arcades, benches with old men
asleep on them and mostly inoperative fountains. On a rooftop above my
head a pair of storks is nesting.

Everyone seems to know everyone else in the Plaza de la Paz. Everyone
knows the two ancient ladies who walk up and down, up and down past
the café tables beneath a shared white parasol. Everyone greets the

extremely genteel seller of lottery tickets, and time and again the cry of *Hombre!* rings across the square as stocky *Jarreños* (jug-makers, as they call citizens of Haro) greet one another around the bandstand. Every passer-by peers into the convivial interior of the Café Madrid to see what friends are propping up the bar, and a few look at me curiously as I pour more wine from the bottle I have put under the table to keep it out of the sun.

I must not idealize this scene. A group of suaver Spaniards (from Burgos, they tell me) has just settled at a pair of tables on the pavement, very gold-bangled and silk-scarved and sunglassed, and a terrific pair of thugs whom I take to be Basque terrorists has just swaggered by with an alarming dog. There are a few weirdos about, bikers in leather jackets, babies in ostentatious prams. But in general the citizens do seem people without pose or affectation, a rough but serene kind of people, from a rough but generally serene place.

And the wine? Give me a moment, while I swallow this prawn and think about it. Mmm. More serenity than roughness, I think. It is example number 1,301 of a remarkable vintage of 8,400 bottles that won important prizes in Bordeaux last year, but it is loyal Rioja all the same, well-oaked, honest, strong, straight, an organic-tasting wine; and as is only proper in the new Spain – in the new Europe – its wine-maker was a woman.

Next to constancy of a very different kind – to the Côte de Beaune in Burgundy, France, where the Mercs and Jaguars from Switzerland cruise around looking for rich luncheons and crates of the most expensive white wine in the world.

This is a long way from the storks and homely boulevardiers of Haro. Here, one after another, the wine villages succeed each other in well-heeled complacency, like clichés: their narrow streets are spotless, their charming courtyarded villas all look as though they were steam-cleaned last week. They seem to be mostly deserted, except for meandering gourmands and the odd viniculturist stepping in or out of his Range Rover, but on every other corner a discreetly sculpted sign announces an opportunity of *dégustation*.

Being a crude islander myself, and an iconoclast at that, I decided to cock a snook here. I bought, for the first and probably the last time in my life a Grand Cru Montrachet – Marquis de Laguiche, vintage 1993. I got a kindly waitress in a café to uncork it for me, and picked up a hefty ham and cheese baguette to eat with it. 'Kindly direct me,' I said to a viniculturist who happened to arrive at that moment in his Range Rover, 'to the exact patch of soil that has produced this bottle of wine.'

He raised his eyebrows slightly when he saw its label and the napkin-wrapped sandwich in my hand. It was not much of a day for a picnic, he said, but perhaps the wine would help – and with a wonderfully subtle suggestion of disapproval he pointed the way to Le Montrachet. '*Bon appétit,*' he brought himself to say, for your Burgundy viniculturist is nothing if not charming, and so a few minutes later I found myself sitting on the low stone wall that bounds the celebrated vineyard of Le Montrachet. It might have been made for picnickers. I could reach out and touch the vines, and slowly across the little road in front of me a large grey snail crawled towards the scarcely less illustrious vineyard on the other side.

There I sat and ate my baguette and drank, out of a plastic mug, the most famous dry white on earth. It was very peaceful, rather like picnicking in an extremely up-market cemetery. Not a bird twitched or a lizard flickered. Once or twice people in cars, on the little vineyard road, slowed down to take a look at me, swinging my legs there on the wall, and responded with wary smiles when I raised my mug to them. All around the vineyards extended symmetrically, neat as could be, perfect in their regularity, part of the very contours of the land, as though no human hand had ever tilled or planted them.

The wine was divine, of course. It seemed to me the essence of everything Burgundian: accomplished, fastidious, exquisitely polite, perhaps a bit Range Rovery, a little lofty in the aftertaste. But then, wouldn't you be snooty, to find yourself drunk from a plastic mug with a ham sandwich, there in the very vineyard that had made your name revered among connoisseurs for 400 years?

Four hundred years? That's nothing. My last vineyard was in the Rheingau, the greatest of the German wine-growing areas, and had been in the hands of the same patrician family since the fourteenth century. And the Rhine wine I drank, a 1993 Auslese, was from Schloss Johannisberg, which was granted to Prince Metternich by the Hapsburg emperor after the Congress of Vienna, and is still partly the property of his descendants.

If gentlemanly elegance is the hallmark of Burgundy, power seems to impregnate the soil of the Rheingau: constant, immutable power, impervious to history, sometimes latent, sometimes brazen. I stayed at the spa of Bad Kreuznach, on the west side of the river, which is where the spike-helmeted German General Staff had its headquarters in 1917, and where, thirty years later, Konrad Adenauer and Charles de Gaulle met to lay the first foundations of the European Union. Just over the hill to the north is the awful memorial by which the Germans commemorated their victory over France in 1870, and the foundation of the Second Reich. The vineyards around have always been the fiefs of mighty magnates – Prince Frederick of Prussia, the Landgraf of Hessen, Prince Löwenstein, sundry counts and barons, descendants of Metternich.

Where else to drink my wine this time, then, but on the terrace of Schloss Johannisberg itself, which stands on its proud hill, rather like another triumphant memorial, surveying the Rhine below? The landscape is majestic. The scattered towns lie there like so many tenancies. The Rhine itself is power liquefied, marching down past the Lorelei to Koblenz and away to Rotterdam and the sea, alive with its constant stream of barges – whose chugging reaches me, like a hum of bees, above the calm of the vineyards. And look! There goes as telling a symbol of German continuity as you could ask for – the venerable paddle-steamer *Goethe*, 522 tons, streaming flags and foam, which has been sailing the Rhine in the service of the same owners since before the First World War.

I am looking at one of the Continent's most fateful frontiers, and one of its most profitable conduits. It is the energy of all Europe that is streaming past down there. Beneath the flowering chestnuts on the belvedere of Schloss Johannisberg I pick up my bottle (with its elegant label of the Schloss itself, and its inscription *Fürst von Metternich*) as if I am about to pour an oblation. I have never in my life before tasted a top-class Rhine wine, and it precisely suits this high balcony of history. Rich and golden it flows into the glass, and it is a mighty wine, a noble wine, sweet but not sickly, complicated, a wine of elaborate consequence, such as bishops and margrave might toast Holy Roman Emperors in, or field marshals with big moustaches order to celebrate victories.

A blossom or two floats past me on to the trestle table. The *Goethe* is disappearing round the bend towards Rudesheim. Time to go home. Temporarily reassured by my European certainties, with the beauty of the organic, the elegance of self-esteem, the perverse grace of arrogance all blended in a profound continental aftertaste, I head for Wales, tea and game pie.

Switzerland

I saw Switzerland, although it had not joined what was then the European Community, as epitomizing a profounder constancy of Europe. During the

1990s its reputation was tarnished rather by financial scandals and revelations of wartime misbehaviour, but I wrote this piece in reaction to what I saw as unfair and curmudgeonly foreign attitudes to the republic.

Weggis, said the road sign as I was driving south from Austria towards Geneva, and thinking the name had something amiably Dickensian about it, I turned off the highway and went down there to seek a bed for the night. I found myself in a flawlessly efficient family hotel on the shore of Lake Lucerne. Elderly paddle-steamers eased themselves past its gardens. A convention of insurance agents was taking time off in its lounges. Ladies in greyish cardigans strolled along the neighbouring promenade while waltzes sounded from a bandstand. Swans and ducks loitered, waiting to be fed by plump infants in pushchairs. A sense of sexless charm, kind but condescending, hung on the air like a hygienic perfume.

I found myself, in short, in a very nest, hive or cliché of the Swiss. I decided to give myself a few days there, and sort out the mixed feelings with which, as a member of the Welsh minority nation, I contemplate the matter of Swissness.

In British minds the very word is liable to raise emotions somewhere between sneer and mockery. It was not always so. In the Middle Ages the Swiss were respected as the fiercest and staunchest of soldiers, and in the nineteenth century Britons seem to have regarded the Helvetic Confederation with almost fulsome admiration. There was nothing sneerable about the Swiss then. They had achieved, it seemed, an ideal state. They were sturdy mountaineers and farmers, nature's gentlemen. They could teach even Victorian Britain something when it came to mighty works of engineering, and the idea of an entire nation of citizen-soldiers powerfully appealed to the empire builders.

It was doubtless the two world wars that changed this reputation. To many Englishmen the principle of neutrality has always seemed cowardly, escapist or simply wet, and twice in this century it enabled the Swiss not only to avoid the tragedies that had befallen the rest of Europe, but even to profit from them. To the British, Swissness came to seem a less noble abstraction, and few phrases have more exactly expressed a national resentment than the famous remark about the creativity of the Swiss made in Carol Reed's film *The Third Man*: 'They had 500 years of democracy and peace, and what did that produce? The cuckoo clock.' Our great-grandfathers would have been astonished to hear it said, but Britons quote it even now, and I remembered it often as I walked along the impeccable Weggis waterfront – the sour judgement of a battle-scarred, impoverished imperial kingdom of epic suffering and performance, about a comfortable, well-ordered, chocolaty republic which had not done a damned thing to help save civilization as we know it.

When those ancient tall-funnelled paddle-steamers docked at the Weggis pier, they were navigated by an officer standing all alone on a flying bridge, with a couple of levers and a long, highly polished speaking tube. He may never have sailed with an Arctic convoy, or taken a destroyer into Malta, but there was certainly nothing laughable about him, so coolly bringing his vessel to the quay. He looked proud, fit, competent and stylish. Style is not a word often associated with the Swiss, but for my tastes there is plenty of it around. The Swiss plutocracy does not flaunt its wealth with much flair – you will see more honest swank in half an hour on Sydney harbour than in a week beside Lake Lucerne – and the Swiss bourgeoisie seems determined never to break out of the ordinary. But Swissness in general does have aspects of true splendour.

Consider the Swiss chalet. Nowadays it is linked indissolubly with that miserable cuckoo clock, and it has been so trivialized by developers and speculative builders that it often has about as much dignity as a mullion-windowed executive residence on a housing estate in Dorking. All over Switzerland, though, examples of the real thing remain, and they are not just beautiful, but magnificent: they are stately homes *par excellence*, heroic homes, built for men of stature by master craftsmen, as strong as they are hospitable, given individuality by endless variations of detail and decoration, and sometimes inhabited by the same family as long as any dukely house in England.

Or consider any of the high passes which link Switzerland with the cisalpine world. If they were marvels in Victorian times, they are prodigies today: with their superb roads and brilliantly lit tunnels, their railway lines circling in the hearts of mountains, their crowning forts, their tremendous sense of scale, purpose and infallible calculation, they suggest the constructions of a superpower, not a small land-locked republic of 6.5 million souls.

Even the Swiss are beginning to have doubts about their army, which has been so long the badge of their confederate unity – more than a third of them said in a recent referendum that it ought to be abolished. But I still find something grand and moving in it, especially at the weekend when the citizen soldiery turns out in the mountains, polishing its saddles at cavalry depots among the trees, clambering up hill tracks in pairs with walkie-talkies or reverberating the thunder of its artillery in impossibly inaccessible valleys. It has scarcely fired a shot in anger for 150 years, but then that is what is grand about it.

The Swiss flag is very stylish: clear, simple and distinctive – what a temptation to clutter it up with cantonal devices – and so, to outsiders at least, is the clarity of the Swiss identity. Like it or not, we all know what Swissness is. Although the Swiss speak four languages, their national idioms are far less blurred than most. Franglais, Breutsch and Ameritalian have made relatively few inroads here, Romansch, so far as I know, remains inviolate, and the Swiss postures, manners, apparent outlooks and evident hang-ups are unmistakable still.

Along the lake from Weggis, to be reached only by boat or by precipitous paths from the hills above, is the field of Rutli, the Swiss Runnymede, where (according to pious legend) in 1291 the mountain rebels met to defy the authority of the Habsburgs and bring into being the Swiss Republic. It is a place of pilgrimage still, and on the Sunday I walked there thousands of Swiss patriots were making their way to and from the hallowed site and swarming through the woods. I offered a cheerful good morning to everyone I met, and could not help admiring the utter lack of ingratiation, the courtesy tinged with distinctly suspended judgement, with which most of them responded. That's style, too.

It was scarcely a generous or easy-going response. It was essentially a response *de haut en bas*, and for most of us the most annoying thing about the Swiss is perhaps their unspoken sense of superiority – all the more maddening, of course, to those who feel historically superior themselves. That *Third Man* quip would have no effect on the Swiss at all: they would probably take it as a compliment, so attached do they seem to be to the cuckoo-clock ethos, as it were, and so confident that they are essentially, fundamentally, irrevocably in the right.

This strikes me as a peasant-like characteristic, and in many ways Switzerland is still like a nation of bucolics. I was repeatedly impressed, during my days on Lake Lucerne, by the number of twisted, stooped or withered old people I saw – people of a kind we seldom see nowadays in western Europe. They were one generation removed, I thought, from the goitre, that talismanic ailment of mountain peasantry: and although nowadays the Swiss have a longer life expectancy than any other people in Europe, and the remotest Alpine farm is likely to possess every domestic

377

convenience, still the faces of those crooked ancients, hard-hewn and gaunt, seem to speak of centuries of earthy hardship and isolation.

It is a truism, constantly reiterated by Britons, that Swissness is no recipe for tolerance. It is defensive and inward-looking, and makes for narrow judgements. The parochial is married here to the suburban, and clearly Switzerland is not an easy place for the oddball, the anarchist, the Asian or perhaps even the person who says good morning to strangers too freely. Even Swiss humour seems laboriously contrived, as though it has to force itself out of conformity. So conservative is Switzerland in matters of public liberty, I am told, and so intrusive is authority, that if the republic ever joined the European Community it would probably be in permanent dispute before the Court of Human Rights.

The Swiss know all this. Heaven knows they have been told often enough, and the city radicals are vociferous in their criticisms – one powerful group of intellectuals declined to take part in the anniversary celebrations at all, on the grounds that 700 years were more than enough. Experts say that the Swiss idea is getting out of date. But if you live richly and at peace in a beautifully maintained country, if you have progressed in a few generations from mule-sledge to Mercedes, if your children are extremely well educated and your pension is enough to afford you a spacious balconied hotel room overlooking the lake at Weggis, with a four-course dinner on half-board terms, you are likely to think that on the whole your system is on the right track.

Half-way through my stay at Weggis I cracked my head open entering the lake for a swim, and had to have it stitched up. How glad I was of Swissness then! Calmly and steadily the Herr Doktor worked, assisted by Frau Doktor and by their son, the computer specialist, and delicate was his technique, and state-of-the-art his equipment, and whenever I opened my eyes I saw through the spotless windows of his surgery the glistening lake, streaked with leisurely waves and ringed with green hills, like a visual tranquillizer.

The more I pondered all this, the more I wondered what the British had to sneer about. Are they any freer than the Swiss? I doubt it. Are they any less racist? One wonders. Are their security services any less intrusive? Probably not. Is their power structure more open? Don't make me laugh. Are their schools as good? Is their income as high? Is their unemployment less? Is their production greater? Are their streets as clean? Is their public morality any better? Is their crime rate lower? And are they any happier in their lot? Well, polls seem to show a swing in opinion, but it is still quite likely that when the Swiss come to decide by referendum whether to join the European Community, and thus put an end to the neutral isolation which has made them what they are, the majority will say no – as they said no in 1986 to joining the United Nations. The pundits assure us that this will prove a mistake, and that before long Switzerland will find itself outmoded and dismayed. Want to take a bet?

Besides, as a Welsh republican, and a European federalist, I still find in Switzerland a model and a hope. Citizens of the European nation-states tend to dismiss its example now, but to those of us who see in the new Europe a fresh chance for the minority peoples – the Catalonians, the Corsicans, the Basques, the Bretons, the Scots and the Welsh and all the rest – the Swiss Confederation is by no means an obsolete ideal. Now and then, as I pottered around the lake, I noticed small and unobtrusive boundary markers. Four cantons surround Lake Lucerne, which is indeed called by the indigenes the Lake of the Four Cantons – Lucerne, Uri, Unterwalden and Schwyz (all the names of paddle-steamers, too). To a large degree each canton regulates its own affairs, yet only those modest stones, sometimes far from roads, mark their boundaries.

Switzerland may be backward on human rights, but it is certainly strong on political democracy; not only are the twenty-three cantons of the republic largely autonomous, but the affairs of the federal government, too, are constantly subject to national referendums, on the most profound and essential subjects. Imagine a referendum in Britain about whether to have an army or not! Here the will of the people counts, consulted as fundamentally as it can be, down to the last mountain valley; and it is the will of the Swiss people that has decreed all that we dislike, all that we admire, all that we deplore and envy, all that amuses or rubs us up the wrong way in Switzerland today.

Not for centuries has one of the cantons gone to war with another, or tried to impose itself upon a neighbour. Those simple stones of boundary represent a gentle apotheosis of the nationalist idea, in most other places anything but gentle. I would not at all mind a Europe similarly demar-cated, so that only a block marked 'France' (perhaps with a concrete cock on top) will tell travellers that they have left Germany or Italy, and must swap dictionaries for another language. Hot patriot that I am, I would be perfectly content if the people of Wales, like the people of Unterwalden, governed their domestic affairs under the sovereignty of a multinational, multilingual confederation, with the views of the

Rhymney Valley or the Dwyfor District Council having their statutory if infinitesimal influence upon policies at the centre, and everybody having a direct say in the greatest decisions of state.

Marx wrongly thought communism would prove conclusive: after a week in Weggis I still half-cherish the hope that the end of history is Swissness.

In 1992 the Swiss did hold a referendum to decide whether or not to join the European Union. They decided against, and so far appear to be prospering.

France

The 1990s, before the Channel Tunnel was completed, was the last decade in which Britain was genuinely an island, so that even the 25-mile journey from Dover to Calais still seemed a definitive transition. When I went to France for this tour d'horizon I went by hovercraft, the most truly dramatic vehicle ever to make the crossing.

No mode of transport is more unmistakably engineered for ultimate journeys. This is how we shall cross the Styx at last, with a swoosh of spray and a rattle of bulkhead doors, looming ungainly and amphibious through the night with Charon high in his pilot-house above us. Irrevocable seems the landing upon the soil of France, if one is deposited there by this momentous device, and irrevocable it very often is, for a slight chop in the sea out there, a gusty wind up the Narrows, and Charon is immobilized in the Port d'Aéroglisseur for hours at a time, and is to be seen morosely reminiscing on a high bar stool in the panoramic restaurant.

I like this utterness of landfall, for I am everybody's patriot, responding with almost equal sympathy to lachrymose Welshmen at rugby matches, Americans with hats on their hearts as parades pass by, inexplicable ceremonials of Swaziland or those sad silent sentries who stand, heads bowed and rifles reversed, so still upon the steps of the Vittorio Emanuele memorial in Rome. And most of all, since one associates the emotion of patriotism most expressly with the fact of France, do I respond to the proud Frenchness of the French. I do not wish them to be nice to me. Nor do I want them to adapt in any way to the influences of the world outside, however reasonable or enlightened. I want only to feel, now as always, that when I drive away from the port into those melancholy landscapes of

Pas-de-Calais, I am entering a world not merely separate and different from my own, but perfectly convinced of its superiority to all others, inviting one simply to take or leave it.

These are archaic preferences. Cosmopolitanism, I know, is the contemporary orthodoxy, and while few people nowadays wish to remould foreign countries in their own image, fewer still, it seems to me, wish nations to remain absolutely themselves. To my mind this makes for dullness, and excited though I sporadically am by the prospect of a Europe without frontiers, still I am saddened by the process of bumps smoothed, quirks normalized, anomalies rationalized, contrasts homogenized, which they tell me is sure to be a pan-European concomitant.

So it was with an inner foreboding that I left the hoverport in Boulogne the other day and drove thoughtfully away towards Paris. I had a nagging feeling that France itself might be compromising its style at last; and I did not like the look of things, when at the motorway café they offered me a *Choc-Bar* and *Poulet Far West*, and forbade me wine for safety's sake.

At first, though, I found much to reassure me. People were still walking that special French walk, less loose-limbed than ours, more precise and deliberate, rather as though their legs do not bend at the knee. Traffic cops were still riding their motor-bikes in that particular French posture, hunched far forward over their petrol tanks like so many White Knights and looking as though they too, when discreetly out of sight, might tumble to the ground in a tangle of microphones and report books. Truck drivers, meeting me on the wrong side of the highway with a klaxon cacophony, still melted upon my protestations of self-amused innocence into that cynic half-toss of the head, accompanied by inaudible mutterings, which is an early symptom of French gallantry.

There are still, I found, no mornings like French town mornings, when the bread hangs fragrant upon the awakening air, when the priests converge blackly upon the cathedral for early mass, and the whine of the mopeds about the Place de la Gare incites the first tourist to throw open her shutters and sip her orange juice in the sunshine. There is still nowhere in the world remotely like your French bourgeois country restaurant, at Sunday lunchtime preferably, when the little town outside is echoing and listless, and the Auberge des Gourmets, or Chez Boudin, or Au Relais de la Chanson, is like an island of warmth and gluttony in a sea of empty cobbles.

I went to one such restaurant, on such an apathetic Sunday, in – well, in one of those ancient towns of central France where the streets wind upwards from the railway track, through scowling walls of medievalism, until they debouch in the square outside the cathedral door, surveyed by huge stone animals through the stone latticework of the cathedral tower, and prowled about on Sunday mornings by cats and desultory visitors. Nothing had changed, I discovered, in the corner restaurant, the one with the awnings and the menu in the polished brass frame. It remained quintessential France, as we islanders have loved and loathed it for several centuries. Madame remained the epitome of everything false, narrow-minded and unreliable. One waiter seemed, as ever, to be some sort of a duke, the other was evidently the village idiot. At the table next to mine sat a prosperous local family out for Sunday dinner, well known to the proprietress and esteemed throughout the community – unsmiling, voluminously napkinned, serious and consistent eaters who sometimes, eyeing me out of the corners of their piggy eyes, exchanged in undertones what were doubtless scurrilous sly Anglophobics, before returning sluggishly to their veal.

I do not doubt the bill was wrong. I am sure Madame disliked me as much as I detested her. The veal was, as a matter of fact, rather stringy. But what a contrary delight it all was still! How excellent still the vegetables! How much better the wine in France! How stately that duke! How endearing the idiot! With what real gratitude, evading the final scrutiny of the prefectorial table, and sweetly returning Madame's shifty glittering smile, did I wrap the Frenchness of that café around me like a cloak, and return cherished to the motorway!

In most ways traditional French life seemed to me as robust as ever. The acolytes still swarmed around the celebrant at Chartres like white squires around a champion. The labourers at the Louvre lugged their master-pieces from room to room with the jolly disrespect of furniture removers. The vendeuses in the boutiques of St Honoré remained mistresses of that hardest of hard-selling techniques, the technique disinterested – 'it is *entirely* up to you,' they seemed to be saying, like their mothers before them, 'if you think so sophisticated a fabric is *really* your style . . .' I wandered through the castle at Grimaud in Provence one warm moonlit evening, with the soft lights of the village below the hill, and the Mediterranean a whispering hiss somewhere out of sight, and felt the old velvety magic no less pungent than of old, however frenzied the traffic on the highway far below, or thickened the scummy water on the beaches of St Tropez. The elderly man who helped me park my car in the garage of the Hôtel de la Poste, Corps, Isère, manoeuvred me between its pillars with all the old scrupulous concern – a twitch of the fingers there, a roll of the right arm there, until like a conductor reaching the last chord of fulfilment he dropped both arms with a half-triumphant, half-despairing gesture that told me to turn my ignition off. 'Well, we are still the same in some ways,' said the old friend at Samoëns, where long ago I lived and wrote a book, 'not much richer, still eating the same soup' – just as he would have answered the same question, I do not doubt, in just the same wry inflexion, with just the same crinkling of the face, with an identical toss of the eau-de-vie in its little cut-glass tumbler, if it had been put to him at any time since, say, the turn of the last century.

But as I feared, the more I looked, the more differences I sensed. Even Samoëns, which was much the same on the surface, had deeply changed beneath, for the old alpine culture of Haute-Savoie is almost dead now, most of the mountain farms are weekend retreats for Genevans, and only rarely does one see that dear familiar of the valley roads, the lady knitting on the green grass while her cows, their bells tinkling in the sweet air, lollop and munch behind her. It was not the specifics of France that seemed different: it was far more the generalities, the atmosphere or the climate of life.

First of all France was much younger than it used to be. That lady with the knitting had been, almost by definition, a lady of a certain age, and most of the classic archetypes of France, from the Paris concierge to the Dordogne farmer, were elderly people. Part of the allure of the country was certainly this maturity, which made for the crankiness, the leatheriness, the stubbornness I have always relished there. It used to feel as though the French would never change because by the nature of mortality they would never have time.

Now France feels younger, physically I mean, than any other Western nation I know. Even the bombazine madame at the cash desk, when I looked at her more analytically, seemed half the age she used to be. Those indefatigable wine-breathed farmers are no longer to be seen urging great snorting horses across distant fields. Even the bank manager is likely to be not the foxy and ingratiating bourgeois you are hoping for, but a sleek executive in his early thirties, with a lacquered if plumpish wife, one assumes, and probably a degree in economics. As for the French motorist, who used to chug so endearingly along in a high-rumped corrugated baby Citroën, his cigarette bobbing up and down as he chatted to the companion slumped prickly and expressionless at his side, now he almost invariably travels faster than sound in a futuristic orange blur.

This youngness of France disconcerted me. I had known it was coming, for the French birth rate of the 1940s and 1950s was very high, and I suppose I have unconsciously watched it happening over the years. Even so, when I sat down and considered it, and looked around me at the new faces of the country, I felt taken aback. It was like meeting an elderly aunt in Carnaby Street, shopping around for jeans. It gave me an odd chemical sensation, as though I had touched a new cell formation, artificially achieved in a laboratory.

And yes, with youth has come a new catholicity. There is no denying it. The supermarket, the shopping centre, television, the family car, the deep freezer, Kleenex, all the instruments of universal change have affected France as potently as they have affected all the rest of us. Even the look of the landscape has changed in the past five years or so. France is much better painted nowadays. Its northern villages have thrown off at last that blight of despair which had hung around them like a mist since Verdun and the Marne. Its southern coasts, once so serene and sage-scented, are as gaudily exploited as any Spanish costa. Even Paris, if mostly inviolate in the centre, proliferates on the fringe with high-rise blocks and concrete patios. Le Corbusier is dead, and as if awakening from a long bemusement French architecture is throwing off his drear influence, and building more delicately, more airily, with more sense of pleasure and less of social dogma (for if Corbusier originals at least had grandeur, Corbusier copies were mostly baleful frauds).

Everywhere, too, this new young France greets one in Franglais, that hybrid tongue of the advertising men and the trendy young which Academicians so despise, and which more than anything else, I think, disturbed my emotions in France this time. Franglais is inescapable – in *bungalows* or *hot dogs*, *Play Cottage* and *Garden Centers*, *Choc-Bars* and *Poulets Far West*. People said I was stuffy when I grumbled, but one cannot live in Wales without knowing that language is truly the substance of nationhood, and that each compromise with a foreign idiom, each adaptation of a catchy foreign phrase, is a whittling away of the national identity. I loathed every symptom of Franglais, and thought I had reached its nadir when, strolling down the Rue de la Paix hardly a stone's throw from Opéra, Louvre and Madeleine, I saw a house advertised in an estate agent's window as being only twenty-five miles from 'Paris–France'.

* * *

Especially in Paris, France, I thought I sensed some subduing of the spirit. Young though the French may be, they do not seem greatly daring. By the standards of Chelsea or California they are rather sedate. I missed the legendary spark of Paris. Hardly anybody hooted at me, however abysmally I drove. The café bravos of the Left Bank were slumped in their textbooks. A strange sense of gentlemanly tolerance seemed to grip the capital – even the semblance of phlegm, as the rain slanted viciously across the Tuileries, and the coatless Parisiennes, bent double against the summer wind, doggedly pushed their way back to their offices after meagre slimmers' lunches.

Somehow the city seemed *muffled*. Perhaps it is the zoning restrictions, which have kept from the heart of Paris that fairground ostentation so essential to the new London. *Le Monde* was extraordinarily balanced and restrained, set beside the same day's *Times*, and I searched in vain for scrawled slogans of protest, or Sunday demonstrations. Even the police-men of Paris, dreadfully though they may behave in hidden dungeons of the Sûreté, look disconcertingly nice – their faces set in expressions of kindly repose, as they twiddle their batons benevolently beside the river, or lean obligingly from the waist to help frail old ladies. For one who, like me, habitually thinks of Paris policemen hunched in leather jackets in riot trucks at dawn, this benign new image comes as a deflationary blow. It gives Paris a feeling of premature fulfilment, as though after war and rebellion, bitterness and repression, it has settled into acceptance at last, and left the outrage, the glitter, and the creativity to others.

This is no more than instinct – a sort of metaphysical hearsay. I can only report a sensation of sterility which the country gave me, rather like the deadened feel of a landscape sprayed with insecticides. France was as kind to me as always, and seemed to me as ever one of the grand strongholds of civilization.

But it did not *fire* me. I felt no tingle of excitement there, and when I try to account for this lack of frisson, I put it down chiefly to a fading of *la gloire*. This is not the fault of the French. It is simply that the style of French grandeur is out of date. How bloated and grandiose that black sarcophagus of Napoleon, around whose high vault the pigeons heedlessly flutter, and in whose anti-chambers the Marshals of France lie arrogantly in defeat! How tasteless the immensities of Versailles, corridor upon corridor, battle blurred into battle, the gilt, the ugly mirrors, the superfluity of opulence seeming nowadays less regal than nouveau-riche! The scale of that old France is wrong, and in an age of disposable merit the vast splendours of the French heritage, the acres of pictures and the inexhaustible formality, seem like barren relics of discredited values, not merely pathetic but vulgar too.

Yet they were the true expression of France's patriotism: and as that sense of glorious nationhood weakens, as weaken it must, so France becomes less French. I cannot have it all ways. When I returned to Boulogne at the end of my visit, I told myself that the hovercraft trip would not be so utter after all. Some of the strangeness had gone out of France, and the French were becoming, for better for worse, a little more like everyone else. 'We are all citizens of the world nowadays,' another friend had sententiously observed to me in Paris, hoping I suppose to comfort me, for he did not know my irredentist tendencies. Yet a curious anomaly revived my spirits: for when, with its habitual heavings, seethings and rumblings, the hovercraft opened its jaws to us on the other shore, and I drove into Dover for tea, good gracious, when I thought about it, what an incorrigibly separate country I found myself in then, how queer its habits, how insular its tastes, how droll its public customs, how complacent its leathery Saxon faces, happily sipping their tea-bag tea, and debating whether to embark upon a macaroon or a synthetic cream slice!

Germany

At the core of the new Europe, Germany repeatedly drew me back, but nearly always with the same intention: to compare past and present, and think about future.

Not long before the First World War my mother, in the innocence of her girlhood, arrived at Leipzig to study at the Königliche Conservatorium der Musik, founded by Mendelssohn some seventy years before and by then one of the most celebrated music schools in the world. So happy were the three years she spent in this old Saxon city, and so affectionate her memories of it, that I grew up myself with a vague but indelible reverence for the place that coloured my childhood and was permanently to affect my attitudes.

What a place it always sounded! Leipzig's university was among the most influential in Europe. Its trade fairs had thrived since the twelfth century. Schiller wrote his 'Ode to Joy' in Leipzig, Bach composed the 'St Matthew Passion', Wagner was born there, Goethe and Schumann were students, Mahler conducted the civic theatre orchestra. And there were giants about in my mother's time, too. Arthur Nikisch was *Kapellmeister* of the great Gewandhaus Orchestra, with its world-famous concert hall next door to her Conservatorium, and Robert Teichmüller was her professor of the piano. Hardly had Richard Strauss conducted the first performance of *Salome* along the road in Dresden than he came and conducted it in Leipzig (my mother, forbidden to go to an opera so unsuitable for maidenly minds, climbed out of a window and went anyway).

Oh, she had heard the chimes at midnight! There were glorious parks in Leipzig, she loved to remember, and delightful cafés in ancient squares, and there was music everywhere. Not least, there were the charming Saxon people. Some of the friends she made in Leipzig remained her friends to the end of her life, through two wars against the Germans that killed her only brother and fatally gassed her husband.

Before I came to Leipzig myself, for the first time in my life, reading around the subject made me perceive that my mother's view of the city had been, in its girlish enthusiasm, partial. She had not made it clear to me that in her day, Leipzig – like the rest of the Second Reich – must have been in a ferment of militant pride, as even the charming Saxons progressed towards that clash of vainglories, the Great War. She never told me that the Reichsgericht, the Imperial Supreme Court of all Germany, sat in an immense palace a few hundred yards from her Conservatorium, or that the city was the headquarters of the 13th Army Corps. She never mentioned the War Monument in the market square, with the Emperor Wilhelm I in front of it and Germania triumphant on top.

Perhaps she herself did not realize that Leipzig was a showplace not just of German art, music, literature and scholarship, but of the burgeoning German materialism too. On Blücherplatz they were about to build the biggest railway terminal in Europe, if not in the world, twenty-six parallel tracks beneath a colossal shell of steel and glass. The tram network was a model of efficiency and modernity, and while my mother liked to recall long merry evenings with fellow students in picturesque outdoor eating places, she forgot to tell me about the three Automatik Restaurants, forerunners of Manhattan's Automats, already operating in the city. She had come to Leipzig as a pilgrim to a purely artistic grail. German culture was all the rage among her kind of Britons then; when, half-way through her course, my proud grandfather went out to visit

387

her, he brought a brace of Monmouthshire pheasant as an oblation to Professor Teichmüller.

The great Hauptbahnhof is busier than ever nowadays. The *Heinrich Heine* express from Prague to Paris was just leaving from Platform 16 when my train came in from Berlin, and almost the moment I stepped into Willy Brandt-Platz (né Blücherplatz) a spanking red tram-train swept in to take me to my hotel. Old Leipzig was shattered in the Second World War, and at first sight the genius of the contemporary city seemed to me distinctly more materialist than artistic.

The centre of civil life today is Augustusplatz, mostly wrecked in the war and rebuilt during the years in which Leipzig was the second city of communist East Germany. My mother would have preferred not to notice it. It is brutally dominated by the 34-storey tower of the University, which has emerged from its ignominy as Karl-Marx University but still presents to the world the usual drab pomposity of communist academia. At the north end of the square is a lovelessly restored Opera House. At the other end is the modernistic new Gewandhaus. Gigantic Moscow-style apartment blocks stretch away to the south, and there is the usual parade of nasty curtain walling. It all looked pretty bleak to me that day, but I soon cheered up; only a few steps out of Augustusplatz I was in a Leipzig my mother would instantly have known and loved.

Some of it would have been physically familiar to her, because many relics remain from the bombed and bombarded Altstadt, and have been lovingly restored. The Renaissance Old Town Hall looks as good as new beside the market square; there are lavish burghers' houses here and there; church steeples stand as they always stood above high-pitched roofs and little squares; the Haus zorn Kaffeebaum serves coffee just as it has served it since the sixteenth century. More to my point, within the circuit of the vanished city walls there flourishes still the Saxon *gemütlichkeit* that so seduced my mother long ago.

I took to eating my suppers along there, alfresco at a self-service restaurant in the Naschtmarkt. The baroque Old Bourse looks genially down upon this little piazza, and my evening meal generally consisted of mushrooms, potatoes, strawberries and white wine. The place was full of people to talk to, the wine went down very nicely, I habitually indulged myself with second helpings of strawberries, and what with the music of a busking accordionist around the corner, and the evening sunshine warming the back of my neck, I soon began to feel myself agreeably among friends. (The only unpleasant Leipziger I encountered during my entire stay was a man who brazenly crashed a queue for concert tickets: and him I successfully tripped up, *pro bono publico*, as he swaggered away.)

So despite all that has happened to Leipzig since my mother's time, her rosy half-dreams of the city were confirmed for me. The German Empire had come and gone, the nightmare of the Nazis had passed, the Americans had stormed through with fire and chewing gum, the chilly communists had clamped their dogmas on the place, and only five years ago did liberal standards return to the grand old city. Yet I was unexpectedly at my ease there, even in the bleak Stalinist quarters where skateboarders clattered over concrete paving stones, and graffiti proclaimed 'The Universal Zulu Nation'. Leipzig is a fine place to be, even now. In the 1990s, as in the 1900s, it is a great thing to walk into the Thomaskirche (having knocked off an ice, perhaps, in the café immediately opposite its main door) and to feel oneself instantly in the company of its mighty organist and choirmaster, Johann Sebastian Bach. Bach stands in effigy outside its façade, sternly surveying the ice-creams. Bach sounds tremendously in the music of its organ. Bach lies for ever (we hope – he has been moved once already) beneath his monumental slab in its chancel. And in the Leipzig of today, who could not be moved by the nearby magic of the Nikolaikirche, the very church where the massed will of the Leipzigers, expressed in prayer and candle-lit vigil, led directly to the fall of the communists, the collapse of the whole dread system and the re-unification of Germany?

As to the little cottage where Schiller wrote the 'Ode to Joy' (in Beethoven's setting, the anthem of the European Community), it stands in a particularly joyless quarter of the city, one of the streets that still speaks gloomily of Honecker and the Stasi, surrounded by drear red-brick blocks with bomb sites, broken windows and sagging lintels; but upon it there is a commemorative plaque done in such a gloriously festive baroque, all gilded high spirits, that the house stands there like a defiant declaration of happiness, come what may.

My mother's Leipzig was most particularly the academic Leipzig to the south of the Old City, where every kind of intellectual institution sprang into existence in those heady days of Wilhelmine confidence. I had no idea how much of it had survived the war, but I knew that the Conservatorium still existed somewhere as the Hochschule für Musik Felix Mendelssohn-Bartholdy, so I set off one morning to find it, guided by the splendid maps in my 1913 Baedeker *North Germany* – splendid, but alas now largely useless. In that part of the city, whole areas have been transformed. Where was the Anglo-American Episcopal Church ('Plan 4, B4: Chaplain – Rev JHM Nodder')? What had happened to the König-Albert Park? One of the few things I *could* find was the Schreber-Strasse Swimming and Bath Establishment ('Plan 1, B4'), and there I asked at random, among the sunbathers by the pool, where everything else was. A young man volunteered to guide me to the Conservatorium, where he happened to have been a student himself. I put my Baedeker away, and we set off across my mother's landscapes.

Here was the Johanna Park, very dear to her memories, where she had once seen small frogs (or was it fish?) falling out of the heavens during a sweet Saxon shower. Somewhere over there, across a weedy wasteland, must have been her lodgings, whence she escaped to see *Salome*, and where my grandfather no doubt buttered up her chaperone during his visit of inspection. Over the road was the school house of the Thomaskirche boys' choir, Bach's own choir – frequently in my mother's mind, I do not doubt, when she went home to play her own organ in Monmouth church.

My guide turned out to be one of the Thomaskirche choirmasters, in line of descent to Johann Sebastian himself, and as we walked through the city together I began to feel I had achieved some sort of apotheosis, and really was back in the Leipzig of Nikisch and Teichmüller. My companion, give or take a T-shirt and a pair of trainers, was just how I imagined the students of my mother's nostalgia. No frogs fell from the skies, but the Johanna Park was still green and full of young life. Horn music greeted us faintly from somewhere out of sight, and when we came to a big green space, and my companion announced it to be the site of the old Gewandhaus concert hall, bombed in the 1940s, we stood for a moment in properly reverent silence, thinking of Mendelssohn and my mum.

And here at last was the Königliche Conservatorium itself. It looked to me just as it does in the engraving on my mother's diploma: the very image, acme and epitome of a music conservatoire. In we went, and there were the statutory bearded busts of eminent musicians, and students hurried past with cellos and music cases, and notices of recitals or rehearsals fluttered from noticeboards as they had doubtless been fluttering constantly since my mother's day. 'We shall enter', my guide courteously announced, 'the Piano Department': and there, up a winding staircase, we were back in the Conservatorium of the 1900s. Nothing had changed, so far as I could see or feel; nothing was missing. Beside each door was a list of the Herr Professors, and I would not have been in the least surprised to see the name of Robert Teichmüller among them. And when we went into one of the practice rooms, where a student was hard at it with a Chopin prelude, just for a moment I thought it really was my mother, young and smiling in a lacy dress, looking up at us expectantly from her keyboard.

On the windowsill, I am almost certain, lay a brace of pheasant, wrapped in a copy of the *Monmouthshire Beacon*.

Another centre of old German culture was Weimar in Thuringia. It was full of gracious memories, but like so many German cities, even in the 1990s this sweet town had skeletons in its cupboard.

I am ashamed to admit I had never heard of the composer Benedetto Marcello, although I now know him to have been a seventeenth-century Venetian governor of Pola in Istria, and when I saw his name on the cover of the score on the music-stand for a moment I wondered if he were no more than a student fancy. The whole episode seemed rather hallucinatory. There I was on my first morning in Weimar, walking all alone through the leafy park on the Ilm, when I came across a charmingly unorthodox pair of student buskers. The boy played the trombone, the girl played the cello, and together they were working their way hard, oblivious to me or to any other passer-by, through the Marcello sonata that was propped on their old-fashioned brass stand. What a delightful conceit, I thought to myself! How romantically German! How proper to Weimar, City of Art and Music! The path was dappled. Insects hummed beneath the trees. The river splashed away beside us. The Marcello was melodious. I popped some money in the buskers' collection box, but they didn't seem to notice, so engrossed were they in their performance.

But then Weimar is not an avaricious sort of town. On the contrary, its distinction has traditionally been elegantly cultural. In the late eighteenth century the young Duke Carl August turned his city into a kind of aesthetocracy, an alliance between the aristocratic and the creative. Beauty ruled! Bach and Cranach the Elder had already given the place artistic cachet, and they were to be followed over the years by a regular flood of artistic geniuses – Schiller, Liszt, Richard Strauss, Gropius, Mann, and above all Goethe, who became a kind of wazir to the star-struck duke and did everything from designing public buildings to inspecting the dukely mines. For generations Weimar was a dream of Germany. Madam de Staël reported that it was not so much a small city as one large, liberal and wonderfully enlightened palace.

To this day it is bathed in the light of those great times, when artists and monarchs were equals. Carl August lies in his mausoleum flanked not by his generals, but by his two great poets, Goethe and Schiller, and the names of artists still provide terms of reference for the city. There's a pleasant restaurant, you will be told, behind the Liszthaus. The tourist information centre is next door to the Cranachhaus. Turn right at the Goethehaus to get to the bus station. You want the Schillerhaus? That's easy: just go straight down the Schillerstrasse from the Goethe and Schiller statue – itself, so one local guidebook tells me, 'the world-renowned symbol of Weimar, like the Eiffel Tower for Paris'.

And agreeable indeed it is to amble down the Schillerstrasse and take an ice-cream beneath its avenue. It is a lovely gentle street, as free of motor traffic today as it was when Schiller lived in his unassuming house at No. 12. There is a good antiquarian bookshop. There are pleasant cafés. The tourists are mostly German and greet you with wreathed smiles. A street musician plays agreeable guitar music in the shade. The ice-cream is excellent, and it is easy to imagine the young Carl August promenading past with lyricists on each arm, bowing right and left to his dutiful subjects.

After the Schillerstrasse, a stroll perhaps up the road to the Architectural High School – the original Bauhaus, a little shabby and run-down now, but still a place of fateful importance for the Western world. And after that back to the green park beside the river, where Goethe had his garden house, and the oldest statue of Shakespeare in continental Europe basks upon its terrace, and small boys are wading across the river with fishing-rods, and the music of the cello-trombone combo still echoes diligently among the trees.

Goethe wanted Weimar's visitors to see the little city and its parks as 'a series of aesthetic pictures'. Certainly I know of no city so instinct with the idea of beauty as a political conception, as part of the established order – and not the beauty of pomp and majesty, either, but an amiable, entertaining, chamber-music kind of beauty. It was in the theatre at Weimar, in 1920, that the constitution of the brief Weimar Republic was drawn up, creating for the first time a united Germany that was free and potentially fun.

So I felt on my first morning in Weimar, but after a while things began to curdle. The first rebuff to my euphoria happened in the church of St Peter and St Paul, just off the market square. This fine old church possesses

Lucas Cranach's celebrated altarpiece of the Crucifixion, Weimar's greatest work of visual art, and I eagerly joined the cluster of tourists around it. It is certainly a marvellous thing – vibrant, full of fancy, with Luther and Cranach himself boldly introduced to stand at the foot of the cross. But for my squeamish tastes something distasteful coarsens the scene: a thin stream of blood, emerging from the wound in Christ's right side, arches across the picture to splosh upon the artist's head. Yuk, I could not help thinking: and although I knew it was allegorical blood, the merciful blood of Christ, still I wondered if it perhaps said something unexpected about the sensibilities of sweet Weimar.

It was partly hindsight, I confess. I had already discovered, during my ice-cream reading in the Schillerstrasse, that when Carl August had gone to his mausoleum the enlightenment of Weimar was never quite so absolute again. The dukedom of artists lost some of its delight when Goethe was no longer there to supervise the aesthetics, and it was symbolic that by 1860 a large and showy Russian Orthodox church, built with golden onion domes by a Russian grand duchess, grossly overshadowed the delicate mausoleum of the young duke and his poets.

Besides, the dukely court might be liberal, at least in artistic matters, but the populace was often boorishly Philistine. 'Unbelievably small and narrow,' the dramatist Friedrich Hebbel thought Weimar society when he came here in the 1860s. Poor old Liszt, who became the city's director of music, found himself altogether too avant-garde and patrician for the local petit bourgeoisie, and the cool amateurism of the ducal house became institutionalized, as the nineteenth century passed and the court became more Prussian, in foundations and societies and museums and art schools and all the other heavy expressions of the Wilhelmine Reich. When some nude drawings by Rodin were exhibited in the Museum of Arts and Crafts, the court itself forced its director to resign. As for the Bauhaus, the people of Weimar so despised it and all its works that mothers used to threaten their recalcitrant children with banishment there.

Worse still, as the literary capital of Germany, the repository of its immortal poetic spirit, a retreat of nature-worship and mythic dreams, Weimar became beloved of the Nazis, and it loved the Nazis in return, voting them into local power long before Hitler became chancellor. 'The mixture of Hitlerism and Goethe,' wrote Thomas Mann fastidiously in 1932, 'is particularly disturbing.' In the market square stands the Elephant Hotel, and all the waters of the Ilm cannot wash the taint from this unfortunate

393

hostelry. It is a handsome thirties building, but unfortunately redecorated inside in a glittery, chromy style that irresistibly suggests the imminent arrival of swaggering Gauleiters with blonde floozies out of big black Mercedes. This impression is all too true. Hitler and his crew were particularly fond of the hotel, and more than once the Führer spoke from its balcony to enthusiastic crowds in the square outside.

So enamoured were the Nazis of Weimar, in fact, that they erected there one of their most celebrated and characteristic monuments. The site they chose was on the lovely hill of Ettersberg, just outside the city, which Goethe himself had long before made famous – he loved to sit and meditate beneath an oak tree there. On my last evening in Weimar I paid a hasty and reluctant visit to this place, now a popular tourist site well publicized in the town. My taxi-driver, a gregarious soul, chatted cheerfully to me all the way. Had I enjoyed my stay in Weimar? Did I visit the Goethehaus? What did I think of the food? Did I know that Weimar was to be the European City of Culture in 1999, at the end of the millennium?

Congratulations, I said. Recognition once more for the City of Art and Music. 'Exactly,' said the taxi-driver, and just then we turned off the highway up to Buchenwald.

Italy

Fifty miles only separate the two great cities of Italy that, in my view, most vividly express the great dichotomy of the Italian national character – in Johnny Mercer's analysis, between the immovable and the irresistible. For immobility, of course, where but Rome?

Thinking properly sententious thoughts about the turn of another year, I leant on a balustrade of the Pincio to watch the sunset behind St Peter's. Unfortunately the sun never reached the horizon that evening, instead finding itself glaucously absorbed into the thick pall of smog which lay like a curse over Rome. I could almost hear the noise it made, I thought – not a fizzle, more a kind of glurp – and imagine the sulphurous smell of microwaved exhaust fumes as it disappeared into the murk.

Rome has always been the place for contemplating the passage of time, the rise and decline of certainties, and the departure of a year was no big deal in a city that has triumphed so often and suffered so much. Nevertheless, the symbolism of that sunset struck me as powerful. We had endured a messy year of it, and the corrosive pollution of Rome seemed to me like an allegory of some more general decay. No doubt about it, Rome is in an awful mess. So fearful is the atmosphere, and so appalling the congestion, that they have been allowing cars to circulate in the city only on alternate days. Squalid litter lies everywhere, blown across glorious piazzas, festering in fountains, lining the Appian Way. Loveless and abandoned the poisoned Tiber flows between its concrete quays. Buildings that used to seem picturesque now seem dingy almost beyond redemption, pavements are cracked and potholed, all over the city restorations and excavations are in abeyance for lack of money.

For a time the conclusion I drew, as I wandered the city, was that our civilization, having here once reached so exquisite an epitome, was now running irrevocably down, so that the glittering shops of the Via Condotti, the gorgeous rituals of St Peter's, were no more than cruel anachronisms. Gradually, though, this conviction was replaced by one more invigorating: that if the environment of Rome was invalid, by God, the inhabitants of Rome were robust as ever. Smog or no smog, they remain precisely as they have always been, displaying just the same mixture of swagger and simplicity, cunning and compassion, that visitors have discerned in them down the ages. Recession, pollution, crime and triple parking seem to pass them by; if the whole city were suddenly to be Scandinavianized, I came to think, all its buildings spick and span, all its traffic ordered, all its corruptions cleansed, the Romans would hardly notice.

Several times in the course of my stay I came across a couple of bucolic musicians, dressed in quaint hats and peculiar shoes, tootling on flute and bagpipe in public places. They were like substantial fauns, haunting the city out of its remote rural past. These medieval figures seemed to me wonderfully exotic, until late one night I encountered the pair of them anxiously consulting a bus timetable beneath a streetlight in the Corso. Then I realized that in fact they piquantly illustrated the matter-of-factness of the city. Nobody took the slightest notice of them, as they huddled there; they looked up and asked me for advice about the best way to get home, but when I told them I was a foreigner, '*Ai, ai, ai,*' they said theatrically, like Italians in movies.

Is this what they mean by the Eternal City, this timeless homeliness, which makes one feel that whatever happens to its history, its people remain impervious? Certainly more than ever Rome lives up to its cliché as the most essentially human of the great capitals, more ready than any to muddle through, turn a blind eye, shrug things off, leave well alone. Surely no great historic site on earth is more easy-going than the Roman Forum, the old centre of the world, its paths agreeably overgrown and its ruins left so largely to themselves. The sentries at the Vittorio Emanuele memorial are not above a brief exchange of greetings with passers-by. The gypsy children only giggle when you thwart their transparent efforts to pick your pockets. The taxi driver soon gives in when you decline to pay him half your worldly wealth to drive you from St Peter's to the Spanish Steps. The black boys do nothing worse than laugh and dance when motorists angrily decline to have their windscreens cleaned at traffic lights. OK, OK, *va bene*, this city seems always to say: you win some, you lose some; no harm in trying.

In short, how particularly *real* Rome seems to be! How full of natural character its policewomen, some looking comical in white hats, some caped and capped like U-boat captains! How authentically pudgy its Swiss Guards, especially when bespectacled beneath their plumed and polished helmets! How amused and forgiving the waiter who came running after me in the Piazza del Pòpolo to point out that, owing to a misunderstanding about decimal points, I had left just a tenth of what I ought to have left upon the café table! I happened to enter Santa Maria in Trastevere when there was a charity lunch for the poor, and never did I see faces so unhomogenized – cool patrician faces of charity workers, serving wine along the trestle tables of the nave, spectacularly wrinkled faces of aged and respectable indigents, quick ingenious faces of the gypsy families cautiously segregated near the bottom of the church.

So at the start of another year, I finally decided, Rome's lessons concern not only history's majestic passage, but also the indomitable resilience of humanity, in murky sunsets just as in clear bright mornings. Not only humanity, either. No creature seems more certain to survive than the scrawny Roman cat, now as always living by its wits among the garbage. And one afternoon I noticed motionless upon a buttress of the Ponte Sant'Angelo a very small and curious-looking lizard. I examined it closely, thinking that it might have been mutated in some way by the stinks and chemicals perpetually swirling all about it: but no, it was just immensely old, inconceivably old, and tough.

On the other hand, where but Naples for everything new, noisy and adaptable?

On a spring afternoon we sailed into Naples from Ischia, out of the calm celestial gulf, to find the notorious traffic of the city magnified to the power of hell by a protest march of the unemployed. The whole place seethed and fumed, and although the Hotel Excelsior was almost within sight of the ferry pier, and we never even set eyes on the unemployed, it took us an hour to get there. You might suppose this to have been a dispiriting experience, but in fact after a week of island peace it was a shot in the arm.

Our taxi-driver, an elderly enthusiast for his trade, treated the event as a challenge to his virtuoso skills, and so we progressed through a sequence of short cuts and private diversions, wildly the wrong way up one-way roads, heedlessly squeezing between the stalls of shopping alleys, sometimes obliged to reverse by the sheer pressure of public opinion, sometimes making desperate three-point turns in virtually impassable back streets. We laughed, we shuddered, we shut our eyes. Now and then the driver wiped his brow in a theatrical way, when we momentarily emerged into the relief of a piazza, before putting his foot down again and hurtling us through a line of flapping washing into yet another labyrinth of the slums.

Outside our windows – 'Keep them closed!' cried the driver, 'Bad people here!' – the Neapolitan legend was displayed as in a theme park, or perhaps an aquarium. Suddenly children's faces would appear scowling an inch or two away. Bad people eyed our luggage with predatory sneers. Old ladies gave us what I took to be the evil eye as we scraped against their fruit stalls. On the Via Partenope we stood stagnant for a time in the traffic, but all around us motor scooters shot in and out between the cars, on to the sidewalk and far away, belching exhaust smoke demonically.

Beside the Castel Nuovo an assortment of men and dogs lay apparently dead upon the green, and police officers could sometimes be seen standing in unconcerned impotence amid the maelstrom. At first I saw them as emblems of defeat. In Naples, I thought, the internal combustion engine had won its first great victory in the fight against humanity, and the entire population lived in a condition of perpetual motorized cock-up.

As our journey proceeded, though, I began to doubt if the Neapolitans were beaten after all. It is true that the municipality has launched a series of measures to limit the number of cars at large in the city, but it did not seem to me that the citizenry itself, as it plotted and manoeuvred its way through the nightmare, was in the least despondent. Like our driver, many motorists appeared to be enjoying themselves, in a bitter-sweet Neapolitan way. Tempers did not seem to be fraying. Horns were seldom hooted. Whenever we caught the eye of an adjacent driver, in some evidently terminal gridlock, he seemed more amused than exasperated, and those devilish motor scooters weaved their insouciant way between the traffic for all the world as though they were surfing.

No, if the motor car is going to win a decisive victory anywhere, it will not be here, if only because the Neapolitans are such willing collaborators. Naples would not be Naples without the automobile, and nobody on earth seems more at home behind its wheel than your average Neapolitan – perfectly adjusted to its culture, making the most of it in body and spirit. Besides, here the automobile has powerful friends at court. The endemic corruption of this city is on its side, and so is the brilliant vanity of the people: if the swagger, flattery and condescension of the *passeggiata* was the essential expression of civic self-esteem in previous generations, now its epitome is the dashing display of an Alfa, a Fiat Barchetta or, best of all, one of those lovely prodigies of Italian art and engineering, a Ferrari or a Maserati.

This was not like a traffic jam in London or New York. This had a paradoxical style to it. Experience it day after day, year after year, and it might indeed lose its allure, but to the stranger arriving from the seas it was a revelation of human vigour and adaptability. It seemed natural to the Neapolitans to be in this fix, and all their traditional characteristics of vivacity, opportunism, effrontery and panache, so familiar to travellers down the ages, seemed to qualify them absolutely for life in the age of the motor car. They are the masters of motorized disorder, wiping their brows not in despair, but in dramatic self-satisfaction.

I thought they were wonderful at it – what other city on earth could make a stranger actually enjoy an hour-long crawl through a traffic jam? – and it occurred to me that they were somehow ahead of us sober, sensible northerners in their attitudes. They were readier to accept the inevitable awfulness of modernity, and had already adjusted to it. They were not repelled by litter in the streets. They did not mind noise. They fished and skin-dived contentedly amid the foul pollution of the harbour. They had long been acclimatized to the government fiddle and the extortion of gangsters. They happily went the wrong way up one-way streets. When, losing my nerve for a moment during that manic excursion, I buried my head in the pages of *La Repubblica*, I discovered that the big story of the day concerned several local figures of the Madonna allegedly weeping tears of blood. Surely this easy familiarity with the occult puts the Neapolitans well ahead of the Swedes, say, in the futuristic stakes – where do you suppose a UFO would choose to land, Naples or Gothenburg?

* * *

So that afternoon, in my sentimental way, I was quite seduced by the Neapolitans. Like many a wandering writer before me, I saw in them so much that I would like to see in myself, and in my people. But nobody could really be much less Neapolitan than I am, and when at last we reached the hotel, limp with excitement, amusement and exhaustion, and I had paid our driver his exorbitant but entirely justified fare, I remarked to the hotel receptionist that I wanted to go home. 'Don't say that,' he replied. 'Wait till you get up to your room, and everything will seem different.'

So it did. Dusk was falling by then, the harbour was speckled with small fishing boats, and in the distance Vesuvius loomed hazy in the half-light. The lights were coming up across the city. The docks were full of tall-funnelled white cruise liners, ferries and the light carrier *Vittorio Veneto*, and even as I stood there the *QE2*, on a Mediterranean cruise, slipped away from the quay towards the open sea. For a long time I could see her lights, fainter and fainter to the west – treading her way over Palm Court gins-and-tonics, I liked to imagine, towards the realms of order.

But it did not make me in the least homesick. The receptionist was right. I rang for a bottle of wine, and we sat there on our balcony in perfect contentment, while hell's traffic snarled convivially below.

Bosnia

Hell's traffic snarled in a different way in the Balkans of the 1990s. Formerly a constituent republic of the Yugoslav federation, Bosnia-Herzegovina became the epicentre of the dreadful war between peoples, ideologies, religions and nationalities that followed its dissolution.

I can think of few more suggestive situations than to be lurching through the winter night, half-way through the 1990s, in an inadequately heated minibus from Sarajevo to the Adriatic – the only way we could get out when its airport was closed and the evening plane from the north had flown in, had a look and gone back again.

The snow in Bosnia-Herzegovina was deep that night, the road was unpredictable, every now and then we were stopped at road-blocks in the middle of nowhere and the awful gorges through the mountains loomed around us dark and dangerous. Sometimes we clattered across a temporary iron bridge beside a blown-up original. Sometimes, shadowy in the night, an armoured vehicle stood guard beside a road junction. The only other traffic on the road consisted of huge tanker trucks labouring up to Sarajevo from the coast, their headlights showing far, far away on mountain curves.

Most disturbingly suggestive of all, sometimes I saw through my window scattered ruins passing dismally by – house after house gaping in the darkness, with no sign of life but a single dim light, perhaps, on a ground floor, or a melancholy fire burning in a brazier.

These were not the usual ruins of war. They were not compact villages knocked into general shambles by blanket bombing, street fighting or concentrated artillery bombardment like villages of France, Germany or Italy in the Second World War. They were generally strings of detached houses, well separated, each one of which had lately been individually and deliberately destroyed. In the same way, Sarajevo does not look in the least like those cities of Europe which were bombed in the world war. It is not a wasteland of burnt-out shells and skeletonic blocks. But there is hardly a building in the city centre which has not been specifically targeted, sometimes half-collapsed in a mess of beams and boulders, sometimes just pitted all over with snipers' bullets.

All this gave me an impression of particular and personal hatred. It seemed such a spiteful sort of destruction. Bosnia had been ravaged, it appeared, not by ignorant conscript armies clashing, but by groups of citizens expressing their true emotions – a display of viciousness different in kind from the campaigns of 'Bomber' Harris. A. J. P. Taylor once wrote that the Great War had begun as the most popular of all wars, but I have a feeling that the War of the Yugoslav Secession was undertaken even more genuinely from the human heart. And what did that say, I could not help wondering, about the human heart?

I had spent the previous Sunday in Zagreb, a fervently Christian Croatian city, and was astonished by the congregations that packed its churches, passionately praying, singing, kneeling and receiving the Eucharist. Even market-men at their stalls, I noticed, crossed themselves when the Angelus sounded. In particular I was touched by a young couple I saw praying together before a miraculous Madonna within the stone gate that leads into the Upper Town, and falling into a sweet and grateful embrace when their devotions were done. Outside the gate a pair of beggar children, one on each side of the path, set up a wailful cry of mendicancy whenever somebody emerged from the shrine. When the young lovers walked out, arms entwined, faces shining, they stonily ignored the appeal: and a moment later I caught myself, too, rummaging for a coin insignificant enough to give the brats.

I remembered the moment with a blush, as we lumbered towards the coast, for if we all behave equally shoddily in small things, might we not, if the occasion arose, be just as unpleasant in big?

The week before I had been in Mostar, with a Croatian acquaintance from Dubrovnik, and was taken aback to find the Christian side of the city, on the west bank of the River Neretva, in a condition of lively if dubious prosperity. Scores of cafés flourished. The streets were full of shoppers. Mercedes and BMWs abounded. Nothing seemed to have been damaged by the war, and nothing looked particularly shabby or deprived. But on the Muslim side, the east bank, all was drab misery – buildings toppled, shuttered shops, poorly dressed people scurrying along muddy pock-marked streets. And where the beautiful Turkish bridge over the river had been, the pride of Herzegovina's Muslims, there was only a bouncy temporary suspension span, over which shoppers hurried with their eyes down.

My companion was embarrassed by all this. Many bad people, he murmured, had done quite well out of the Yugoslav war. When I asked him who had destroyed the bridge, one of the supreme treasures of the old Yugoslavia, he prevaricated. It might have been Serbs, he said. It might just have been renegade Muslims, out to get foreign sympathy, perhaps. Could it not have been Croats? Well, yes, it could have been Croats, but not true Croats, not Croats like the Croats of Dubrovnik – not Croats like him, in short.

Later I went with him to Medugorje, the hill-village where, since 1981, the Virgin Mary has been appearing to visionaries, and the sun has danced for hundreds of thousands of pilgrims from all over the world. My Croat was rather embarrassed here, too. He was a devout Catholic, but he could hardly help being slightly repelled by the tinsel opportunism of it all – glittery shops selling sacred souvenirs, pizza stalls, bed-and-breakfast signs everywhere. We went to the Hill of Visions, where a long line of pilgrims plodded beneath their black umbrellas up the track to the holy site, but the rain poured down in torrents, and even for the most credulous the sun did not dance that day. Did he really believe in it as a token of the divine mercy, I asked my friend? He wasn't at all sure, he admitted; but he was frightened of God.

Cynicism laces the air of this country now. The confused condition of the place, with its pockets and enclaves of Serbs, Croats, Bosnian Serbs,

Croatian Bosnians and Muslims, all entangled with the multinational force whose slow convoys crawl this way and that across the shattered land – the condition of Bosnia-Herzegovina, which is virtually inexplicable to the outsider, lends itself to the profitable scams that are spawned by every war, and curdles the milk of human kindness. Would we be very different, I wondered, if it had all happened to us?

At home in Wales we have a bridge not unlike the one at Mostar. It is a single-arch, pack-horse bridge over the Taf at Pontypridd, an old favourite of water-colour artists. We have our ethnic prejudices too, and our mountain villages, and even our religious zealots. I had no difficulty in imagining, as we plodded on through the darkness that night, that the miseries of Yugoslavia had befallen Wales – the lovely old Taf bridge collapsed into the river below, the villages of Gwynedd and Meirionydd wrecked, all our old bigotries, so long suppressed, rampantly in the open. I know plenty of people who would be running BMWs upon the profits of villainy, and probably a few at least who would not have hesitated, if there were English settlers on the other side of the stream, to aim a mortar at them – but not real Welsh people, mind you, not the Welsh of Llanystumdwy, not Welsh like me . . .

There were four other passengers in the mini-bus that night – a Swede, a Finn, a Croat and an Englishman. Behind us a second busload was following us through the darkness. At about two in the morning we stopped, and our driver got out and peered rather helplessly into the black emptiness behind him, up the highway banked with snowdrifts. 'What's happening?' said the Englishman in front of me. 'What have we stopped for?' The driver explained that the other bus seemed to be lost: there was no sign of its lights, and he was worried that it might have got into trouble back there. The Englishman stretched, pulled his coat more tightly around his shoulders, and settled down to sleep again. 'Who cares?' he said. But he may have been joking.

Lithuania

In eastern Europe a process of de-Russification was happening everywhere, as the communist ideology dissolved and the last remnants of the Soviet empire with it. In some countries the process was swifter and more absolute than in others. I was persuaded that an interesting de-Russianifying might

be observed at the Lithuanian city of Siauliai (Schaulen to the Germans),
because in Soviet times it had been forbidden to all foreigners as the site of a
strategically important base of the Red Air Force.

I checked in at the main hotel, a dowdy high-rise that was built in Soviet
times, may well be still Soviet-owned (nobody seemed to know) and has
doggedly stuck to the old ways: which is to say, streaked concrete, no heat,
abandoned telephone booths, dismal food, receptionist muffled in greatcoats, a Moscow chat show on the television and a notice on the wall
quoting different rates for Lithuanian citizens, citizens of the former USSR
and the rest of us. Just what I wanted, said I to myself as the terrifyingly
jerky lift carried me in spasms to my room.

It was almost as though Lithuania had never achieved its independence
and was still in the Soviet Union. I felt quite disorientated when I went out
for a morning walk, and thought I might be in some relatively prosperous
township of the Union of Soviet Socialist Republics ten years ago or so,
except that there were no statues of Stalin or Lenin. Everything else was
there. There were the monumental square office blocks of state overlooking
spacious squares with parks in them. There was the statutorily ornamental
pedestrian highway running through the city centre, with various cultural
institutions on it, and many benches for the well-earned refreshment of
happy workers, and babushkas selling bananas. The crowning church of
St Peter and St Paul, with its tall polygonal steeple, had been handsomely
rebuilt – as a museum of atheism, perhaps? – and there were many manifestations of the whimsical humour that was meant to give a human face
to Soviet communism, like funny statues of rabbits, a stone shoe on a
pillar and a cat museum.

Most of the factories, on the outskirts of town, seemed to be disused,
deprived of their Soviet markets and left to languish. The former air base
was, I was told, being turned into a Free Economic Zone, but it gave me a
shudder nevertheless, as I wandered among its shabby half-dereliction, its
hangars, officers' quarters and abandoned guardhouses, to imagine what
kind of reception I would have had if I had strayed through its barricades
in Stalin's time.

For the communists had been very nasty in Siauliai. They were nasty
throughout the Baltic republics, deporting hundreds of thousands of
Latvians, Lithuanians and Estonians, importing hundreds of thousands of
Russians: but they were symbolically unpleasant here because in the
sweeping countryside just outside the city is the greatest sacred site of all

Lithuania – Kryziu Kalnas, the Hill of Crosses, which they naturally detested.

It is the strangest place. Since the early nineteenth century at least, and probably far longer, people have regarded it as holy. Over the generations they implanted its mound with a tangled forest of crosses, of wood, of iron, of stone, tall carved crosses, crosses made of old pipes, crosses exquisitely sculpted, crosses in rows, crosses in clusters, crosses piled and stacked there in an indistinguishable jumble. Around almost every cross hundreds of lesser crosses are hung, together with tangled masses of rosaries, and between them all little alleys have been trampled by the pilgrims who come here in an endless flow from every corner of Lithuania. The whole hillock looks molten, as if all its myriad symbols have been fused together, leaving jagged protrusions everywhere.

As a pantheist pagan myself I honour this place more for its abstract holiness – it has an overpowering sense of mystic primitivism – than for its Christian meaning. The communists loathed it either way. They rightly saw it as a focus of patriotic as well as religious loyalty, and did their surly best to put an end to it. They bulldozed away some 6,000 of its crosses. They forbade the erection of any more. They put a guard upon the place, like the guards I imagined scowling out at me from their sentry-boxes at the airfield.

Of course it did them no good. Patriots and pietists crept in there at night and planted new crosses anyway, and in the end, at the Hill of Crosses as in Siauliai itself, the Russians gave up and went away. Thousands of new crosses have gone up since they left, spreading out across the meadows about the mound, many of them commemorating the Lithuanian multitudes who were deported into Russia; even as I stood there thinking about it all, on the banks of the little reedy stream which runs near by, I heard on the quiet pastoral air a hammering from somewhere in the thicket of crosses, as yet another was put up.

So it is in Siauliai itself, and throughout the three Balkan republics now accustoming themselves once more to independence. The Soviet presence is there in horrid memory, and sometimes in reality – hundreds of thousands of Russian residents complicate the political scene, many a functionary of the KGB is still in a position of power – but gradually, very gradually, these little states are finding an identity again. They are hammering the crosses in! Here and there along that pedestrian highway in the city, among the resting places for grateful workers of the state, very different institutions are arising.

You can get cappuccinos on the street now. Rock music blares from boutiques. Foreign businessmen eat expense-account lunches at smart new restaurants. You may pay for things with a credit card. Ravishing Baltic girls in mini-skirts will never grow up to be babushkas. There is a bowling alley in the basement of No. 88, and you can get quite a decent hamburger at No. 146. The Universaline department store still looks a bit Stalinist, but as the Business Advisory Centre's *Siauliai at Your Fingertips* indulgently suggests, it is 'a good place to visit for nostalgic reasons'.

At the end of the street looms my hotel. No cappuccino there, no country and western music. It is, as *Siauliai at Your Fingertips* says, 'where most people stay if the other hotels are full'. At breakfast a long, long table covered with a brown velveteen cloth is occupied by twenty young Russian males, like visiting technicians from the old days, while at the end of the dim-lit room there sits alone in silence at her victuals a woman who might be typecast as a lady commissar: severe, spectacled, muscular, her hair in a bun and her skirts long and heavy. A solitary waiter in shirt-sleeves serves us – thick black coffee (they're out of milk), fried eggs with peas, black bread and very good cheese.

Half-way through the meal we are each given a bottle of Coca-Cola. Most of the men drink theirs there and then, in tandem with the coffee: but I notice, as the lady commissar leaves the room, wiping her mouth carefully with her paper napkin and studiously not looking anyone in the eye, she takes hers with her.

Hungary

Further to the east national and social emancipation had gone much further, and memories of communism were fast fading. I had been to Budapest at the very start of the process, and was now able to spend an entirely hedonistic Christmas there.

'How was Budapest? Political situation tricky, isn't it?' So said a card from a friend when I came home from Hungary, and it did not make me feel guilty. Political situation tricky? I had no idea. I had never asked. I gave not a single thought to the political situation during a few days in Budapest that were devoted entirely to the most escapist kind of pleasure.

It was a very different matter when I was last in Budapest, back in the seventies. Then one could hardly help taking an interest in the political situation as a communist Hungary took its first tentative steps into the market economy. Private shops were beginning to open then. Foreign firms were appearing – foreign tourists, too. Merciful Heavens, there was even talk of a Hilton Hotel on Castle Hill, very near the spot where, on summer Sundays, a Red Army band sometimes played for the sceptical indigenes!

Today you must be a resolute visitor indeed to involve yourself in the political situation, for there are few places in Europe that are more fun to do nothing in particular in than Budapest. By the nature of things it was always a fine city to see: situated nobly on both banks of the mighty Danube, Pest so flat, Buda so hilly, with the astonishing parliament ('frantic', Patrick Leigh Fermor called it) dominating one bank, the castle and the spirited Matyas church looking down upon the other, and a series of bridges majestically connecting the two.

Somehow it all used to be muffled, though, by the very presence of communism, and the history of the city itself was blurred and obfuscated. Even the supreme symbol of Hungarian nationhood, the Crown of St Stephen, was notable only by its absence: it had been taken to the United States at the end of the Second World War and was being kept at Fort Knox in Kentucky, along with the gold reserves.

But now come with me. The door in the National Museum opens heavily when we push it, with a theatrical creak, and there in a dim-lit chamber, guarded by a solitary janitor apparently dozing on a chair in the corner – there dazzlingly in a glass cabinet stands the Crown of St Stephen, back where it belongs. It is a Byzantine marvel of gold, gems and enamelled saintly portraits, inscribed with antique letters, like no other crown on earth, and truly proper to the Hungarian spirit is the gold cross jauntily skew-whiff at the top of it.

Nobody knows why it is askew, but not even the dullest civil servant, the most pedantic scholar, would dare suggest that it should be straightened. The joy of Hungary is its heroic convention, the combination of formality and high jinks. Budapest always suggests to me a Vienna with fizz, its heritage of Habsburg hierarchy spiked with sudden flashes of wit or defiance, touches of exaggeration, suggestions of excess.

Hungarians themselves, of course, like to say that this is the Magyar element – the wild originality that the first Kings of Hungary brought galloping out of the Great Plains – and I am myself a sucker for the epic explanation. In the Heroes' Square in Budapest (built for the Hungarian millennial exhibition of 1896) there is a group of equestrian statuary that represents the arrival of King Arpad, the first of all the kings, in the year 896. Arpad himself rides in front, his head high, his eyes firmly fixed down Andrássy Avenue towards the city centre. Around him his fierce bodyguard of chieftains, mounted on splendidly caparisoned horses, look this way and that beneath their feathered helmets with expressions marvellously haughty and sneering – terrifically alarming men, predatory as all hell, the sort you would very much rather have on your side than on the other.

Full of such images, I went one evening to a concert performance of operetta extracts at the Vigadó concert hall. Liszt, Wagner and Mahler all performed there, but our evening was one of sugary pop melodies, all of them as familiar to the Budapest audience as Gilbert and Sullivan used to be to Britons. At first, my mind on St Stephen's Crown and Arpad's bravos, I thought this selection rather unworthy of the city. There was plenty of froth to the old tunes, plenty of gypsy charm, but the young gentlemen of the dancing chorus seemed to me a little weedy as they waltzed around the stage in white ties and tails.

Presently, though, having slipped into something looser, they broke into the violent stamp and strut of the *csárdás*, that old display of everything most dramatically Hungarian; and then as they threw their heads back, drummed the floor, slapped their thighs, flung their arms into the air and sometimes wildly shouted, while the jolly audience clapped to the accelerating rhythm of the piece – then I saw in them, benignly mutated, the cold sneer of the horsemen in Heroes' Square, or for that matter the reckless style of the boys who, swarming over the Red Army's tanks back in 1956, made the first crack in the awful Iron Curtain.

After a few days of Magyar heroizing, anyway, I was content enough to fall back into Habsburgization. There was snow on the ground when I was in Budapest, and this made the snug, fusty, fattening side of the city's life all the more attractive. One cannot sneer and dance the *csárdás* all the time. It was restful to wander the squares and boulevards of Pest, now mostly restored to full capitalist amplitude, thinking about Franz Josef and whistling a tune that you and I know well, I'm sure, but can't quite place – could it be something of Fritz Kreisler's? 'Schön Rosmarin', isn't that it?

There is nowhere better for one of those half-hours in a coffee shop when the coffee goes in the first five minutes, with the sticky cakes, and the rest is a happy aftertaste of observation, jejune philosophizing and making conversation with the people at the next spindly table. No ride could be more *gemütlich* than ten minutes in the funicular up to the Habsburg's royal castle, sitting in a quaint little wooden cabin cosy above the retreating river. There are no better streets for looking at the buildings of the last *fin de siècle*, an eclectic melange apotheosized by that splendid Gothic-Renaissance mongrel, the frantic parliament by the river. And you can hardly feel more comfortably Habsburgian than you can now feel at Gundel's, the famous old restaurant by the zoo. When I was last in Budapest it functioned listlessly under municipal control, but now it has been brought to plush life again by enterprising American-Hungarians. I did not eat the soup described as Franz Josef's Favourite, but I did indulge myself in a sufficiently courtly dish called Count Széchenyi's Roast Breast of Pheasant, which is stuffed with goose liver and has baked apple on the side.

I have never enjoyed a city more. When I got home I telephoned some Hungarian friends in Australia to tell them I had been in Budapest. 'Ah,' said they, 'but didn't you detect *disconcerting undercurrents*?' I did not blush, even to myself: just tilted my crown a little more rakishly and took another bite of *Sachertorte*.

Bulgaria

Bulgaria too was becoming known as a pleasant place to visit – very different from its reputation during the days of the Cold War, when it was thought to be the most dangerously militant of the Soviet satellites.

Quite suddenly, when you drive into the mountains south of the capital, Sofia, high in a narrow wooded pass you find the monastery of St John at Rila, a multi-domed church in a wide slabbed courtyard, surrounded by tall galleried blocks like a medieval inn. It is one of the most satisfying architectural ensembles I know, and is far more than just a monastery: for besides being a patently holy place, and a sort of fortress, and a familiar picture-postcard spectacle, it is the prime national talisman of Bulgaria. It is Bulgaria emblemised. It is the Eiffel Tower, the Sydney Opera House, the Nelson's Column, the Washington Monument, the Brandenburg Gate or the Red Square of the contemporary Bulgars.

God knows they need a national talisman or two, because their more recent history has been, by and large, one long record of difficulty and frustration. Geography placed this unlucky people between two of the most uncomfortable neighbours on earth. Russia has traditionally been Bulgaria's protector, finally bestowing upon it a particularly distasteful Stalinist regime; Turkey has traditionally been its oppressor, occupying the country for several centuries and intermittently indulging in massacres. It is only during the past decade that the Bulgarians, charming people that nearly everyone likes, have really been free to be themselves.

Only natural, then, that a journey around Bulgaria seems to become a journey from one national shrine to another, through rings of pride radiating out from Rila. Such monuments of fortitude and National Revival! Such museums of sacrifice and revolution! Such cenotaphs, mausolea and tombs of poets and soldiers! Such statues of heroes and churches of thanksgiving and sites of constituent assemblies! No patriot on earth is more patriotic than a patriotic Bulgar, and nothing is more symbolical than a Bulgarian symbol.

The central triumph of Bulgarian history was the 1876 rising against the Turks, which eventually won the nation its independence, and its memory has risen above many a subsequent discomfort – the slaughter that followed it, despotisms of one kind and another, defeat in the Balkan War of 1913, humiliation in the First World War, the unfortunate alliance with the Nazis in the Second, the Russian 'liberation' of 1945, the long years of communist autocracy. More than a century on, you cannot escape the trophies of 1876.

On the Danube riverfront at Ruse is the house of the formidable grandmother Baba Tonka, who led the patriotic women of Ruse in an armed attack on the Turkish town prison, and whose five sons all fought in the cause. At Kozloduy upstream a monument honours the impetuous poet Hristo Botev, who led 200 Bulgarian émigrés from Romania in the hijacking of an Austrian river steamer, and stormed ashore here to join the rising beneath the banner Liberty or Death. In Sofia a memorial marks the execution site of poor Vasil Levsky, 'the Apostle of Freedom', who had roamed the country in disguise recruiting revolutionaries. And crowning all is the Freedom Memorial at Shipka, where the Bulgarians won the most famous of their victories ('supported', so my Bulgarian history bravely says, 'by not very many Russians'). An almost constant stream of schoolchildren climbs the 894 steps to this enormous hill-top cenotaph, which is guarded by the mightiest and best-fed of all commemorative lions.

Having developed a most decided weakness for the Bulgarians, I heartily sympathize with these emotions, and am as stirred as any schoolchild by

409

the Freedom Memorial, the tales of Levsky and Baba Tonka, the seizure of the steamer *Retsb* by the wild lyricist and his comrades. Every people needs its moments of success to make up for its miseries, and Bulgaria's troubles do not seem to be over yet. The countryside looks lovely, the wine is delicious, flowers are everywhere, waiters smile, geese, goats and donkeys roam the purlieus of picturesque villages, truckers' halts serve nourishing soups, the package-tour resorts on the Black Sea thrive; but most people are extremely poor still, politics sound murky, and when I pick up a copy of the *Bulgarian Economic News* I find it full of anxieties. Base interest rate stands at 108 per cent. Volume of business is down 33 per cent. Fruit production has plummeted. The Minister of Internal Affairs has resigned, having been filmed celebrating with models at a beauty contest the day after three of his policemen were murdered by gunmen.

Poor Bulgaria! Will life never be easy here? Will the world never leave it alone? The Turks are quite friendly these days, but up at Ruse, the chief point of entry from the north, I still feel a nagging sense of alien interference. A mile or two downstream from the city a great iron bridge crosses the river, and here it is easy to fancy all the new skulduggery of eastern Europe flooding down from the north, to fan out across the little country in stolen Mercedes cars – Romanian rogues, opportunists from Moldavia, gypsy thieves, Hungarian conmen, Russian crooks (as a Bulgarian lady said to me the other day, 'Russians are not ordinary people; they are merchants and robbers.') Bulgaria stands on its own facing these new hazards: not yet a member of Europe, no longer a member of an Eastern bloc, only a small, delightful republic of 9 million souls, trying to sort itself out.

Of course the Bulgarians want symbols! Who wouldn't? Often enough they go far back into their history to find them – beyond Rila itself, into the rich hazy world of proto-Bulgars, Thracians and Bogomils. The most apposite of all their patriotic icons, to my mind, is one of these. Above the village of Madara, with a railway station that suggests to me something to be blown up by Lawrence of Arabia on the Hejaz Railway, in the cliffs above the dusty hamlet there is carved an antique figure. So old is it, and so eroded, that you can discern it only when the setting sun catches its outline, and no more than vaguely even then. But in photographs you can see more clearly the Horseman of Madara, and realize how relevant he is to the condition of his country.

There he rides, indomitable but only just recognizable. He has a jolly greyhound at his heels, and seems to have lately slaughtered a lion. With

THE FLUX OF EUROPE

his right hand he grasps the reins of his prancing horse, but his left hand is raised exuberantly high above his head: and in it he is holding a wine cup. '*Nazdrave!*' the Madara Horseman cries to history – 'Cheers!' And '*Nazdrave!*', down the centuries, this country of wine, pride and suffering has loyally cried back.

Romania

Romania was a different matter, because its Communist experience had been of a different kind. For twenty-five years it had been ruled by a pair of psychotics, Nicolai Ceausescu and his all-but-illiterate wife, who had both been put to death in 1989.

They seem to talk a lot about tunnels in Bucharest – tunnels through which licentious aristocrats gained access to their mistresses, tunnels offering escape to dictators, webs of tunnels beneath the lost Jewish quarter – and after a few days in the city I felt as though I was groping through a surrealist labyrinth myself.

Physically there are certainly holes and burrows enough in this capital, much of which feels like one vast building or demolition site. There are the mole-like fetid staircases to the Metro, the gloomy corridors which run Piranesi-like through the Supreme Court, compelling their anxious multitudes towards the dim-lit chambers of their fate, or the narrow lanes of the Lipskani quarter, like Turkish bazaars, where the traffic is squeezed between stalls of jeans, paperbacks and anoraks and the air is opaque with a blend of rock and quavering folk music. And metaphysically there is the maze of puzzle and paradox through which all Bucharest speculations seem to stray. Which is Moldova and which Moldavia? What is the difference between Iron Guardists and Legionnaires? What is the trans-Dneister issue? Who were the Szekels? What used to be called Kronstadt?

When there is light at the end of a Romanian tunnel, it often turns out to be a will-o'-the-wisp. Ask why a building appears to be half-abandoned, and you will be told almost indiscriminately that it has fallen into neglect, was damaged in an earthquake, was knocked about during the revolution or has never been finished. The other day I was given six reasons why I might not enter a particular museum: (1) it was being rebuilt; (2) there had been a robbery in it; (3) an inventory was being conducted; (4) it was about to be visited by President Mubarak of Egypt; (5) it had lately been visited by President Niazov of Turkmenistan; (6) it was closed.

Raffish but devout, crumbled but still stately, with women tram-drivers smoking on the job and elderly ladies crossing themselves as they brave the downtown maelstrom; with sellers of medicinal roots and peasants in high fur hats; with filmic rogues disappearing conspiratorially down hotel corridors; with sweet small churches to visit and the megalomaniac monuments of Ceausescu to marvel or shudder at; with head-scarved babushkas sweeping leaves, and the cabs of railway locomotives prettied up with lace curtains: exotic despite everything, Bucharest is an everyday performance of everything most headily Balkan, with Latin overtones all its own.

Sometimes the municipal allusions seem to come from another age altogether. One hears of just such unacceptable frontiers and discontented minorities as Chamberlain once discussed with Hitler. Romanian schools have been attacked, somebody assures us in the pages of *Romania Libera*, by Russian-speakers in Tighina. The fate of all Europe, says somebody else, depends upon the solution of the trans-Dneister issue – 'the territory east of the Dneister is the ultimate frontier of Latinity!' One can be a European, we are told by somebody else again, 'only in the tradition established by Christianity'. I would hardly have been surprised to learn that, rather than an impending President Mubarak or a retreating President Niazov, it was the Sultan of Turkey who was keeping me out of the museum.

On the other hand, here I sit at the dinner table with a jolly crew of acquaintances, eating pike-perch from the Danube and drinking a happy Moldavian Riesling (as against Moldovan, I think), to the deafeningly amplified thump of a band in the chandeliered dining room of the Central House of the Army (1912, architect D. Maimarolu). I have poked my nose with impunity into several such unpromising-sounding bastions of the Bucharest Establishment. At the Writers' Union, for instance, which I assume to have been for several decades a tribunal of communist orthodoxy, I wandered bemused and unhindered through the accumulated cigar smoke of a thousand ideological debates, amiably nodded at now and then by marvellously literary-looking confreres. And at the Military Hotel, strolling in, I was befriended without question by a most formidable captain of the Romanian Navy, wearing over his gilded uniform a leather coat like a U-boat commander.

It is a queer mixture of sensations. On the one hand, nearly everybody is welcoming. On the other hand, few seem altogether frank. An insidious suggestion of caution hangs over conversations here, even among bold sea captains, to remind one that many of Ceausescu's apparatchiks are still running this country and that the conviction of liberty is tentative still. It could hardly be otherwise. Bucharest's communist despotism was different in kind from those in Warsaw, Budapest, Sofia, Prague or East Berlin. It was a Latin despotism. It was often at odds with the Soviet Union. And its rulers were more like crazed tyrants of the Orient than normal Stalinists.

Even more than historical grievances, Ottoman complexities or the awful example of Yugoslavia down the road, the ghosts of this appalling couple still muffle and muddle the affairs of Bucharest. It is only five years since they were executed; a whole generation grew up under their aegis, and it shows. Time and again young people have said to me: 'We are learners, we are only beginning.' They mean, I suppose, that they are only now setting out on the path to join the ordinary world, and I never have the heart to wonder aloud how soon they will get there. This is the city where Ionesco learnt his trade, and I see now that in his plays he was reflecting not only the irrational tragi-comedy of life in general, but the particular topsy-turviness of his native land.

At the time I assumed the fall of the Ceausescus to be something definitive in Romanian history, like the collapse of the Berlin Wall – the end of dreams and nightmares, the opening of the road to the prosaic. After a few days here I am not so sure. An immense boulevard, still unfurnished (and its myriad fountains dry) forms the central axis of Ceausescu's notorious new Bucharest. Visually, at least, its architecture seems to me not much worse than the sillier examples of post-modernism in the West, and parts of it are already being humanized by the general bric-à-brac and commotion of city life, so that I can imagine it in another twenty years being essential to the flavour of Bucharest.

Even the vast palace which crowns it is becoming familiar, if hardly homely. Its scale and ugliness are inexpungible. If you can imagine the impact of the Victor Emmanuel monument in Rome magnified twenty or thirty times, you can have some idea of the clout of the Parliament Palace (né Palace of the People, *i.e.* Palace of the Ceausescus). In living space it is surpassed in size only by the Pentagon; in sheer volume only by a rocket assembly hangar at Cape Canaveral.

It isn't finished either, yet tourists go there, conferences are held in its immense salons, and both houses of parliament are expected to move in one day. In 1990 the revengeful mob burst in here and slashed the very carpets in their hate and triumph: yesterday what most seemed to interest my cicerone was the fact that the curtains had been made by nuns. When I left the building I noticed, curled up outside the ceremonial doors, an elderly dog snoozing in the chill sunshine.

So to the stranger's eye, at least, Ceausescu's follies have become organic to the place. Perhaps it is the nature of Bucharest to absorb everything, simply adding even the wildest excess to its historical repertoire. I walked directly from the Parliament Palace to the Patriarchal Cathedral, a lovely little building on a hill near by, shimmering with the silver and lamplight of Orthodox Christianity. In it I found a long stream of pilgrims standing in line to kiss the sacred icons. At the head of this patient queue a tall twitchy priest sprinkled the faithful with holy water, and erratically among them a mad-woman straight from the Bible paraplegically staggered, occasionally patted on the shoulder by sympathetic Christians.

Was I really in twentieth-century Europe, I marvelled as I emerged from the holy half-light? It will be a long time, I fear, before the young people of Bucharest join the rest of us, before the curtain goes down on this civic theatre of the absurd.

Albania

Even crazier than the Ceausescus, if anything, had been Enver Hoxha, maverick communist dictator of Albania – 'Friend Hoxha', as his subjects were encouraged to call him. He could cause the rain to come! Flowers blossomed in his footsteps! He died in 1990, leaving behind him an appalling legacy of decay and 800,000 concrete pill-boxes scattered across the country. Who were they to defend Albania against? I once asked. 'Everyone,' was the reply.

In 1992, when the communist regime came to an end, there were only fifty cars in the capital, Tirana, and pictures of Skanderbeg Square, the heart of the city, showed it all but empty, with only a few disciplined pedestrians crossing its enormous ceremonial space. By the time I got there in 1996 40,000 cars swarmed the Tirana streets (a third of them Mercedes, almost all of them second-hand, most of them stolen in Germany) and Skanderbeg Square was a sort of maelstrom. It contained a mosque, a clock-tower, a museum, a cultural centre, a functional-modernist hotel, a national bank, a fountain or two, sundry Italianate government offices, dozens of street stalls, an equestrian statue of the eponymous fifteenth-century hero Skanderbeg and two extremely noisy funfairs. Countless men of all ages wandered around offering black-market exchange rates. Innumerable children rode the funfair rides. Around the edges of the place scores of cafés were in a perpetual kind of frenzy, and round the back an immense street market pullulated in a welter of fish-stalls, butcheries, vegetable carts and stacks of old bicycles. It was rather as though the great square of Marrakesh had been worked over successively by Ataturk, Mussolini and Stalin, and then handed over to the management of the Tivoli gardens at Copenhagen.

In the evening the entire population of Tirana seemed to emerge for the twilight *passeggiata*, strolling up and down the main avenue, sitting on the edges of fountains, milling about the funfairs, wandering haphazardly across the highways apparently under the impression that there were still only fifty cars in the city. The noise then seemed to me a supremely Albanian noise – the hooting horns of a thousand newly acquired and uncertainly driven automobiles, the whistles of distraught traffic cops and the deafening beat of mingled rap, rock and Balkan folk-music. I loved the louche insouciance of it all, ever-ready smiles from the citizenry, inescapable suggestions of roguery, the immense hum over everything, the quirks and surprises. Sometimes I felt a small dry kiss on my arm and turned to find a gypsy child irresistibly importuning me for cash. When I testily shooed off a young man in T-shirt and jeans, supposing him to be yet another currency tout, he shyly introduced himself as one of the President's bodyguards, trying to warn me away from the Presidential front gate.

I walked one night into the huge pyramidical structure which had been designed to be a museum of Enver Hoxha – in his own lifetime! – and was now converted to more secular uses. It was strikingly lit up after dark, and swarmed all around by crowds of idlers, up and down its ceremonial steps, in and out of its basement café, eating ice-creams and loudly talking. Irrepressible urchins climbed its smooth concrete buttresses in order to slide down again. What should I find in the main hall of this tumultuous building, this hilariously discredited monument of egotism, but four young people exquisitely performing Ravel's string quartet?

Poor old Hoxha! What would he think? Ogre though he was, I rather regretted his posthumous elimination from Tirana. For most foreigners, after all, he was Albanian No. 1. I did visit his house, in the formerly sealed-off official quarter known as The Block – a respectable suburban-style part of town from which, in Hoxha's day, ordinary citizens had been entirely banned. Even in 1996, as I wandered the tyrant's garden paths I was followed always by an armed guard, and when I stooped to pick a flower from a bed of Michaelmas daisies I thought I heard behind me (although perhaps I was fantasizing) the click of a safety-catch. Was it OK for me to take a flower? I asked the young man over my shoulder, just in case; but instead of shooting me he had an expansive gesture of permission. Take the lot, he seemed to be saying. They were only Friend Enver's.

I wished Hoxha's museum were still his museum, and in particular I wished that his immense bronze statue still stood in Skanderbeg Square (where its plinth did remain, beside one of those funfairs, and was tottered over by enterprising infants in need of parental guidance). So I was excited when somebody told me that the statue still existed in Tirana, preserved in the Monuments Factory where it had originally been cast. In a flash I was there, accompanied by a young Albanian engineer of my acquaintance. Like most Albanian factories the Monuments Factory had gone out of business, but a watchman directed us to a windowless warehouse apparently sealed off for ever. 'Enver's in there,' he said.

We circled this gloomy mausoleum searching for keyholes to look through or doors to peer under, and in the end I found a spyhole between the bricks. There Enver was, recumbent in the shadows, just his bronze thigh to be glimpsed like something not very interesting in Tutankhamun's tomb. It was enough. My engineer positively identified the old monster, and he should know. As a student he had been in the forefront of the rejoicing crowd when the statue was pulled down in Skanderbeg Square. 'I pissed on it,' he complacently recalled, and you can't get more positive than that.

Ireland

Throughout the 1990s a running sore of Europe was Northern Ireland, which still formed part of the United Kingdom nearly half-a-century after the establishment of the Irish Republic in the south.

* * *

Ever and again in this haunted country one comes across monuments to the dead, of one side or the other: here ten Protestants gunned down by the IRA at Kingsmills in County Armagh, remembered now in gold lettering on black shiny marble; there three young Catholics ambushed and killed by British undercover agents at Strabane in County Tyrone, commemorated by wooden crosses in the field where they died. In the churchyard at Scotstown, in County Monaghan, I stood before the grave of Seamus McElwain, a young IRA man whose whole life had been a succession of bloodshed and imprisonments, until he was killed by British soldiers in a nearby meadow. His epitaph was in Irish, and on the cross, together with the relief of a bird escaping through a mesh of barbed wire, was affixed a coloured photograph of him, a good-looking dark-haired boy in a dinner jacket. The tears came to my eyes as I stood there: (the wind rustling the hedges all around), and a gardener working near by asked me if perhaps I was a McElwain myself? But I said I was crying for them all, whatever side they were on. 'That's the truth,' he said, 'that's the truth.'

In some places the fact of the contemporary Troubles is so much a part of life that the people continue their daily affairs apparently impervious to the bizarre and awful things happening all around them. In Belfast hardly anybody seems to notice the weirdly screened and armoured trucks that trundle around the city, or the infantry patrols that wander ever and again down perfectly ordinary city streets – I saw a patrolling soldier one evening, in Donegal Square, which is the very heart of Belfast, tuck his gun under his arm for a moment in order to draw some money out of a cash-card machine. In the country many villages seem able to close their eyes to the army installations hideously embedded in their midst, shut off from the community by barbed wire or high walls, their radio aerials protruding high above the rooftops. Eerie tall watchposts stand in the middle of the countryside, and on back roads along the frontier you may see white crosses painted on the tarmac – location signs for the army helicopters which perpetually prowl around.

The unhappiest place of all seemed to me the village of Crossmaglen, in south Armagh, made notorious over the decades by the many killings and bombings there. It stands in the heart of what the tabloids like to call the Bandit Country, or the Killing Fields, where the Irish Republican nationalists, though within British territory, are in generally unchallenged control, and on my way there I saw a large hand-written notice attached ominously to a telegraph pole, warning that somebody or other was an informer.

I would not like to be that man in Crossmaglen, for the whole village felt privy to conspiracy. It was very silent, very empty, and people seemed to talk to each other generally in undertones. They tell me known Protestants, let alone members of the armed forces, are distinctly unwelcome in the town pubs, and even in the coffee shop where I stopped for a hamburger people responded to my bright enquiries kindly enough, but warily, avoiding my eye, I thought.

Poor Crossmaglen! A pleasant enough village, like many another, it ought to be a place of convivial merriment, and perhaps one day it will be, but for the moment it is terribly depressing. The large central square (in which at least seventeen British soldiers have been killed) is surveyed from one side by an indescribably sinister army post, thirty or forty feet high, surrounded by barbed wire and made of brownish concrete, through whose narrow slits silent figures, vaguely to be discerned, stare down upon the village – over their gun barrels, one assumes. It is like some monster of space fiction, or perhaps a robot. Immediately below this fort is a memorial erected by the populace to their own patriots, in Irish and in English:

Glory to you all, praised and humble heroes,
who have willingly suffered for your unselfish
and passionate love of Irish freedom.

I stood in the silence and copied the inscription in my notebook, and when I walked away I saw a hand forlornly waving me goodbye from one of those fortress slits.

30

Light and Shade in the USA

I made repeated visits to the United States in the 1990s, and was often saddened to find that its old public character, which had so captivated me in earlier decades, seemed less stalwart every year under the impact of militarism, unbridled capitalism, national ambition and plain hubris. But I often loved it, too.

Portland, Oregon

I went to Portland to give a lecture – it is the only place where I have seen my own name go up in lights! – and having a day to kill set out from my hotel to saunter around the city. Downtown Portland seemed to me delightfully civilized.

It is one of the few big American cities that never succumbed to the high-rise epidemic, and although the Portland Building, Michael Graves' original exercise in post-modernism, cast a chill through me as an awful portent of what was going to follow it, for the most part meandering through the streets was very agreeable. The blocks are unusually short in Portland, making for pleasant serendipity, the architecture is mostly genial, there are plenty of coffee-shops, not all of them insisting that you drink their cappuccino out of plastic cups, and the gloriously rambling Powell's City of Books must be one of the best bookshops on earth.

Travel is free on the downtown public transport system, and what with the cleanness and sensibleness of everything, the evident prosperity and the prospect of a late lunch at the Heathman Hotel (red snapper, perhaps, with a glass of one of the excellent local whites), I thought what a lesson in civility Portland, Oregon, offered the world at large.

* * *

But following the tourist signs towards the Old Town District and Chinatown, and expecting the usual harmless flummery of restored gas-lamps and dragon-gates, I crossed Burnside Street and found myself in a corner of hell. Suddenly all around me were the people of Outer America, flat out on the sidewalk, propped against walls, sitting on steps, some apparently drugged, some evidently about to vomit and nearly all of them, it occurred to me, idly wondering whether it was worth while mugging me as I passed. They were of all ages and several colours. They did not look exactly hostile, or even despairing, but simply stupefied, as though life and history had condemned them to permanent poverty-stricken sedation.

Every city has its seamy underside, and American cities more than most. The moment came as a shock to me in Portland because here the well-off and the poor, the hopeful and the hopeless, not to mention the whites and the coloureds, are more than usually separated. A languid stranger could spend a week at the Heathman, with intermissions at the City of Books, almost without realizing that poverty, crime or crack existed here at all, or any un-Caucasians except exquisitely urbane Asiatics. Portland has repeatedly been voted one of the most Liveable Cities in the United States, and if you choose the right part to live in, it undoubtedly is.

When I withdrew across Burnside again to a restorative coffee in a more soothing part of town, I found myself paradoxically reminded of another country altogether. In India, within the scrambled millions of the poor, there exists a complete modern nation, rich, sophisticated, worldly, which if it could be isolated and moved somewhere else, would constitute a formidably capable state of the middle rank. This thought led me on to some uncomfortable conjectures: while educated India forms a small minority, civilized America is presumably a majority – but for how long, I wondered as I looked around me over my coffee cup at the kindly, comfortable faces of the American centre? And how civilized?

The gods have loved America, but I sometimes think they are already making it mad. One expects insanity among those poor huddled masses of the sidewalk, but every time I come to this country I feel that the neuroses and paranoias are spreading, across all the Burnside Streets of the nation, into the amiable neighbourhoods over the way. Suburban nerves twitch ceaselessly, downtown eyes flicker, as the monstrous contrasts and energies of capitalism unalloyed tear away at the communal composure.

The Americans, even those civilized Americans of the centre, have gone half-crazy already with legalism, feminism and political correctness. They are well on the way to the asylum with sexual obsessions. They are moonstruck by matters grotesque and macabre, from clowns to vampires. They are so addled by the allure of violence that in America now there are more federally licensed gun dealers than there are gas stations, and one of their incessant self-lacerating polls recently showed that half their school-children knew how to get hold of a firearm.

On the front of the Portland Building there is a truly colossal female figure, whom I now know to be Portlandia herself. I asked three passers-by, two men and a woman, who she was. The woman said that, although she found the figure 'pretty', she had no idea of its identity. Both the men seemed never to have given the matter a thought. This struck me as odd, since the image is the second largest hammered copper sculpture in the world, beaten only by the Statue of Liberty, but I later reached the conclusion that it was only a symptom of the general alienation. If Portlandia were dripping blood, or in the process of being mutated into a dinosaur, everyone would know all about her: as it is, she is robustly healthy and well-balanced, and so hardly worth noticing.

I pick up a newspaper, and here is a plastic surgeon assuring potential male clients that for $10,000-odd they can have chest implants, abdominal liposuction and calf implants which will ensure 'a fine looking physique for the busy executive without spending endless hours in the gym'. Buried away on an inside page is the news that a man who was about to be executed for a murder in Oklahoma has been temporarily reprieved because he first has to serve twenty years for a murder in New York. Almost every agony column displays self-questionings, religious ravings, breakdowns of trust, preposterous grievances of age, gender, race or condition; even some of the comic cartoons have moved into a disoriented kind of surrealism.

You can be sure that at any hour of any day, one television channel or another will be showing scenes of appalling bloodshed, cases live from a criminal court, chat shows concerning child abuse, marital disharmony, sexual misbehaviour, predatory law-suits. No self-respecting best-seller is without its detailed evocations of couplings, masturbations, dismemberments or disembowellings, and nobody seems particularly surprised that an Oregon Senator presently stands accused of sexual malpractice (whatever that may mean in PC-speak) towards a sizeable number of his employees.

Mad! Yet this is the Great Republic whose founding principles were nothing if not rational, and whose purposes were all harmonious. From the very beginning the United States has satisfied many of the universal

421

human yearnings, and shared with all of us the recipes of its success. Declaration of Independence to Bob Dylan, Hollywood and John Cheever and the dry martini and the Freedom of Information Act – the list of American blessings is endless, and their adoption and imitation around the world has brought us infinite good.

They have been, though, the gifts of a culture supremely confident and logical, recognizably the culture in fact that Jefferson and his colleagues created. What is emerging in America now, still to be exported willy-nilly around the globe, is a jumble of philosophies so distracted, so uncertain, that they seem to lack any cohesion at all, and are more like the nervous responses of hostages than any body of ruling values. The centre, it seems to me, is only just holding, and is patently showing the strain: yet still it stands as exemplar to most of the world, copied in blind faith everywhere, and especially among peoples like the English and the Canadians who share a language with the Americans, and whose own sense of identity is weakened or uncertain.

And waiting just over the street there is the other culture, America Ulteria, or perhaps America Ultima, the inchoate slouching presence which is giving the nation these disturbing jitters. It has no standards of its own. It has little to lose, and not much hope of winning. Its language is half-comprehensible, its reasoning is obscure, but one day America and the world may wake up to find that like the destitute masses of India, it is less the exception than the norm.

That evening I gave a reading in the Arlene Schnitzer Hall – the Schnitz for short, I believe – a splendid concert hall next door to the Heathman. I never enjoyed an occasion more. The audience was immensely quick, generous and entertaining, and at the reception afterwards people raised many penetrating points about the influence of travel upon the work of Virginia Woolf, and the proper place of the imagination in non-fiction.

On the Zephyr

The trains of America, which I had loved from the start, still cheered me up.

'Jesus Christ!' were the very first words the sleeper attendant said to me, when I boarded Amtrak's California Zephyr at Emeryville, Calif., on my way to Chicago. They seemed the *mots justes*, for the boarding process was an awful shambles – we had to walk through another train to get to ours, with a fearful confusion of bags and mystified passengers. 'Is it always like this?' I asked the attendant. 'It don't always start like this,' he replied, 'but it don't take them but a minute to *get* it like this.'

I didn't mind. I was boarding the famous train just for the romance of it – for a taste of an older America. I had lately been dazzled by the futuristic virtuosity of young California, Internet, the information super-highway and all that. I had marvelled at its enthusiasm and inventiveness, but now I felt like taking a restful step backwards. I would be experiencing, so the brochure assured me, the utmost in train travel, 'Enjoying On-board Accommodations That Pamper and Please!' It is 2,420 miles from Emeryville to Chicago, a journey of three days and two nights, and I wasn't a bit put out by that kerfuffle at the start (which was due, it was later explained to me, to the fact that the Coast Starlight had arrived from Seattle two hours late).

The romance was certainly there. Our ten double-decker blue, red and silver coaches, with their two locomotives and four baggage cars, thundered through desert, prairie and mountain gorge just like in the movies, occasionally rounding so spectacular a bend that from my window I could see both ends at the same time, and half-expected to find goodies and baddies struggling on the roof. We glimpsed the mothball fleet of Suisun Bay. We went through Reno, The Biggest Little City in the World. We skirted Donner Lake where, in 1846, a party of stranded immigrants cast lots and ate each other. We passed Verdi and Elko and the headquarters of the Strategic Air Command. For 238 miles we followed the banks of the Rio Grande, 'the longest' (said a train announcement) 'any major railroad follows any major river in the world'. Unfortunately it was dark when we passed the water tower at Stanton, Nebraska, which is shaped like a coffee-pot, but we saw the Mississippi all right as we clanked over the bridge at Burlington.

Sometimes our whistle authentically wailed. Sometimes, the Zephyr being a no-smoking environment, we made a smoking stop and a handful of tense-looking addicts climbed down to puff their cigarettes at some more or less deserted halt where they could do no harm. We spent an hour at the funereal railway station at Denver, which is monumental but which nowadays handles only two passenger trains a day. We bought fruit and bananas on the platform at Grand Junction, the farm-wives awaiting us at their stalls for all the world like babushkas on the Trans-Siberian. We paused briefly at small towns of the Middle West, Osceola

423

and Mount Pleasant and Ottumwa (famous, so the brochure told me, as the hometown of Radar O'Reilly in M*A*S*H), where families waiting to board, with bags and excited children against a backdrop of clapboard houses and corner drugstores, made even the towering Zephyr feel like a local.

However I cannot claim that the old America seemed to be working as well as it used to. The California Zephyr appeared to be run in a mood of elderly, but on the whole genial, resignation. 'Jesus Christ,' said my sleeper attendant once more, when I reported to him that my bed had collapsed beneath me, and he had to prop it up with an egg crate borrowed from the dining car. The loudspeaker in my compartment was not audible, so I was obliged to go into the corridor to hear the announcements. But I still did not mind. Stuffing a pillow in the lavatory door soon stopped it rattling and the shower never did flood the compartment, as I had been warned it sometimes did. The maximum legal speed of the Zephyr is 79 mph, only sporadically achieved, and I realized that the motion I had thought of as 'pounding' was really more like 'plodding'; but hell, what was the hurry?

And in any case my fellow-passengers were all I could ask for. Not a computer evangelist, hardly a cellular phone among the lot of them. 'Oh, how I wish those trees would get out of my way, so I could photograph a real Iowa farmhouse!' said my companion at breakfast one morning: she had never been on a train in her life before, she had seldom left Fresno, California, and she came straight out of a fifties movie. She couldn't wait to see Chicago! She couldn't wait to see her best friend in Akron, Ohio! She couldn't wait to – and oh, look, there's a Little League baseball diamond! 'Isn't that real *neat*? Don't you guys think that's real neat?'

A former professional footballer (Green Bay Packers) taught me all I needed to know about pro football. Several passionate railroad buffs kept me informed about the state of the track. One woman engaged me in a challenging discourse about evolution, another had strong views on capital punishment. I commiserated with some of those pallid smokers – I thought they should have had a coach to themselves. I told an elderly lady that on the whole I thought I would *not* join her, as she kindly suggested, in her retirement home in Omaha. I loved them all. They were all one wants America to be: long- winded, opinionated and essentially good.

But just as the Zephyr, labouring heavily eastward, seemed a quaint anachronism in the world of e-mail and TGV, so those dear people seemed left over from some different society altogether. Each morning my attendant slipped the morning paper under my door (I could have helped myself to morning tea, too, but the machine at the end of the corridor was defective). Every day it was full of anxieties and uncertainties almost inconceivable in that pleasant company: not just the horror of everyday violence that we have learnt to accept as part of the American way, but a vast broiling stew of distrust, foreboding and ethnic hostility through which the great nation passes, like the Zephyr, with incessant rattling and unexplained delays.

Even as we sat so convivially over our plastic plates of salad in the dining car, we felt these toxicities intruding. Our conversation faltered as we found ourselves heading for some ethnic or feminist quicksand, the footballer being black, the lady from Omaha politically immaculate. We skirted them, of course, as the nice people we all were, but those moments were like jets of hot, unhealthy air suddenly penetrating the Zephyr's cool air-conditioning.

Outside our windows, as we all knew, beyond the splendid landscapes, things were by no means so genteel. Out there it was a battleground: rich v. poor, women v. men, the drugged v. the sober, black v. white v. Hispanic v. American Indian v. Korean v. Jew. The nation that used to think of itself as a melting-pot of all the peoples is more fissiparous than I have ever known it, with no grand leader or even common loyalty to unify it. A people preoccupied with role models looks no higher than rock stars, athletes, actors, miscellaneous two-bit celebrities and even criminals for its shots of charisma. Yet that other America is in turn a role model for the world.

I travel in a different spirit from Paul Theroux, the prince of railroad passengers. He assumes, for professional purposes, the character of a curmudgeon. I am ingratiating almost to a fault – a literary Mary Poppins, as one of those damned Australian critics recently suggested. However, I did have one altercation on the Zephyr. My ticket, I had been told, entitled me to anything I liked on the menu, but when I asked for cornflakes and scrambled eggs for breakfast I was told that I was entitled to one or the other, but not both. I called for the supervisor to expostulate, as I thought Theroux would, but I did not get far. This was the old America after all, and the talk was straight. I had got it wrong, the functionary said, not unkindly, and I quote him word for word: 'You're not from this country. You don't speak the lingo.'

But the girl from Fresno said she thought that man had been rather rude, and one of the train buffs offered to share his scrambled eggs with me –

only fair, really, because I had already urged upon him some of my Cooper's Oxford Marmalade.

West Point

Once I found myself so dispirited by the state of America that I picked up a car in Manhattan and drove up the Hudson River, intending to wander for a few days in search of consolation. In the event I got no further than West Point, and this essay explains why.

After dark I went down alone to the Plain, the great playing-field and parade ground of the US Military Academy at West Point. This was like an American fiction. A moon was rising, the Hudson lay dark and velvety below, and across the grass a solitary skunk came snuffling through the dusk. Now and then aircraft winked their way overhead. A train wailed somewhere. A tug and its barges laboured upstream towards Albany. A military police car coasted inquisitively by. There was not another soul about, down there above the river, but in the great monastic buildings of the Academy, dimly crowned by their chapel tower, myriad lights steadily and silently burnt.

Four thousand four hundred young American men and women, I knew, were hard at work in there: steadfast before computer screens, deep into ballistic theories, economic principles, translations from the Russian, comparative equations or historical relevances. They were being prepared as an elite, an officer corps to lead the armies of the Republic into a world subject more than ever to American power and decision – the world of the Pax Americana. My few minutes alone there seemed to me an almost transcendental experience: one of those moments of travel when history, place and circumstance all seem in collusion to proclaim some truth or other, if we can only discover what it is. The police car came back again. 'You OK, ma'am?' Sure, I said, quite OK: just watching the skunk.

It was true that I had never seen a skunk in the wild before, but in fact I was contemplating the moment. I cannot deny that I was greatly depressed just then by the condition of the United States, which seemed more than usually sunk in crime, corruption and hypocrisy, bewildered by racialism and enervated by crackpot introspections. West Point was like a world of its own, a place where the old American values counted still, honour and duty were watchwords and to tell a lie was to betray one's heritage: a place too, so it appeared that evening, where purpose was so exactly matched by appearance that the whole scene became an allegory.

Next day I went back in daylight, and saw the future elite for myself – classes of '92 to '95. Every day at noon the entire Corps of Cadets parades in its grey working uniform between the statues of Eisenhower and MacArthur, with Washington on his high plinth in the middle. Some of the West Point mystique, accumulated since the Academy's foundation in 1802, is then on display for any passer-by to see. Ensigns flutter. A band plays. Swords flash. Tradition's Long Grey Line is regimentally massed. And one of the place's better-known peculiarities is publicly demonstrated.

The quizzing of the 'plebes', or freshmen (freshpersons, as the world outside West Point would probably call them) is a demanding ritual. There in the open air, on the parade ground, first-year cadets are orally examined by their seniors in anything from the dates of presidents to the contents of that morning's *New York Times*. I watched it all through my binoculars, and alarming indeed were the attitudes of the examining seniors, testing the responses of the apparently terrified freshmen, as with military severity snap questions were put and answers offered. Sometimes lists of names were demanded. Sometimes they seemed to be reciting poems, or perhaps military regulations. Sometimes songs were compulsorily sung.

'Is that some patriotic ballad?' I asked of a senior cadet, as a not very musical salvo of melody reached me from the other end of the ground. 'Ma'am,' he replied (courtesy is endemic at West Point), 'Ma'am, I believe that is the national anthem' – and hardly had he spoken than the band struck up, orders were barked, swords were shouldered, and the whole grey seething mass swarmed up the steps into Washington Hall, where a plain but nourishing lunch awaited it.

Actually they were bellowing, so I later learnt, the *second verse* of the National Anthem. Everyone knows the first verse, after all, and almost nothing about West Point is easy, or exactly simple. Hanging around the place another time, when the cadets were coming out of class, I noticed that whenever juniors passed badged seniors, they uttered a kind of mantra. What they were saying was this: 'Beat Louisville, Sir' – 'Beat Louisville, Sir' – 'Beat Louisville, Sir'. Louisville was West Point's next football opponent, and having to remember the fact, and mouth this esoteric spell time and time again as they walked across the campus, was one of the subtle ways in which the Academy brainwashes its recruits. Brainwashing it undoubtedly is. The West Point System, as it is constantly called (reminding me uncomfortably of the names they used to give especially horrid Victorian methods of penal discipline) – the West Point System presupposes that the new recruit has to be recreated from scratch. All the high-school swank has to be scoured, all childish pride expunged, and since this is achieved not by members of the staff, but by the endless harassing and criticism of cadets only a few years senior, the whole nature of military discipline and hierarchy is experienced. Now you are the unfortunate underdog, now you are in command: you know the bitter trade from both sides.

At the same time the pressure of daily life is merciless, the pace terrific, the standard of everything frighteningly high. A cadet graduates from West Point not only with a science degree, but with a military education both theoretical and practical, and a physique transformed by endless exercise. There is no slouching about on this campus. Everybody moves at a spanking pace, left right, left right, head up, eyes often a bit glazed, generally sunk in thought – trying to remember differential calculi, perhaps, or what the *Times* said that morning about economic conditions in Sumatra.

It is a hard, calculated regime, and some of those plebes look tired enough to wring a mother's heart. Observe though some of their seniors, as they prepare for the afternoons' exercise! Handsome and amiable young giants jog down to the football field. Astonishingly energetic girls do violent aerobics. Sweating toughs lift enormous weights, throw themselves around exercise bars, or do so many press-ups, with such enthusiasm, that it exhausts me just to watch them. 'Let's go!' cry the coaches, 'Lift those knees!' 'Carry that ball!' – breaking off sometimes to offer me a polite 'Hi' as I meander flabbily past.

I was seeing it only from the outside, but nevertheless I was greatly cheered up by all this. A quarter of West Point's cadets drop out, and I don't blame them, but the ones who survive seem to me just fine. I tried hard to detect symptoms of fraud, hypocrisy or Rambo arrogance in the ones I met, but they seemed to me, to resurrect a phrase, ladies and gentlemen every one. If it is an elite that West Point produces, it is a very attractive elite, and hardly homogeneous: there are cadets black, brown and yellow, Jewish cadets, many bespectacled cadets, cadets short and even cadets who look to me a little plump for press-ups. They come from all backgrounds, posh to poor, and the one thing they have in common, so West Point likes to think (me, too) is the devotion instilled to them, during their four years in the place, to principles that the Founding Fathers would have approved of.

I am anything but a militarist – more of a pacifist-anarchist, actually – and I was surprised to find myself, as I pottered around West Point, so attracted by its atmosphere. Partly, of course, it was the contrast between this place of old-school values and the contemporary squalors outside. Partly perhaps it was the aesthetic appeal of order and tradition, set against the glorious landscape of the Hudson valley. But perhaps it was chiefly a sense of nostalgic *déjà vu*. In the days when we British were masters of the world we too consciously produced an elite to keep it straight, and West Point has a lot in common with the schools that educated the English governing classes. *Mens sana in corpore sana*, a healthy mind in a healthy body – that was their ideal, as it is the Academy's now, and they too liked to suppose that they were educating a band of brothers, united in trust and loyalty, to organize a New World Order, in those days called the Pax Britannica.

Hyped up as I was by these conjectures, West Point never let me relax, just as it never lets the Long Grey Line drop its guard. Everywhere I went trophies and symbolisms prodded me: rows of captured artillery, benches inscribed with 'Dignity', 'Perseverance', 'Responsibility', eagles and crossed swords, the flag on a flagpole forty feet high, the Cadets' Prayer ('guard us against flippancy and irreverence') the Academy motto ('Duty, Honor, Country'), the sundial presented by the Class of '33 ('From its Time and Place in the Long Grey Line'), the vulgar gold and ivory baton surrendered by Reich-Marshal Goering, the very antithesis of a West Pointer, to the forces of Truth in 1945. 'Beat Louisville, Sir,' mumbled the plebes. 'Duty, Honor, Country', thundered the text around General McArthur's statue. 'To be good officers, you must be good men', said the shade of General Sherman. 'If you admit you're wrong,' I heard a coach assure his perspiring footballers, 'you're already right, and you don't get yelled at.'

Best of all, most genuinely inspiring, was a little cameo I saw on my last afternoon at West Point. It was a Saturday, and many of the cadets were preparing to receive visitors, or go out. I saw one vigorous plebe emerging from her barracks in what I took to be her semi-dress uniform – not the famous ceremonial one that we always see in West Point photographs, with the cross-belting and the plumed hat, but a trim grey trouser suit with a shiny-peaked cap, very smart and very flattering (if one may dare say such a thing, in such a context) , to her lithe figure.

429

I followed her down the path towards the Eisenhower statue – left right, left right, head up, arms swinging, brisk as could be to where her father was waiting to meet her: and then – talk about symbolisms! He was your very image of a kindly homespun countryman, a figure from an old magazine cover, wearing boots and a floppy brown hat, his face shining with pride and happiness. She broke into a run, her cap went skew-whiff for a moment, and into his strong American arms she fell.

Manhattan

And there was always Manhattan . . .

It's been rough weather in Manhattan, but I haven't cared. I've wrapped up warm and enjoyed myself. In the Colombian seaport of Cartagena there is, or used to be, a big bronze sculpture of a pair of well-worn boots, recalling the remark of a local poet that he loved the city in the way he loved some old familiar footwear. After four decades of knowing Manhattan I have come to feel the same about this legendary sink and summit of the world.

Old boots as a metaphor of Manhattan! You may well laugh. They are not very smart boots either. They need soleing and heeling. They leak a bit. They creak. They could do with a polish. I've got used to them, though; and in the winter especially, when the city is so often snarled up in catastrophe, I can almost see them standing there, scrawled about with graffiti, beloved and familiar among the snows of Central Park. Manhattan in the cold has always been a sentimental sort of place. Miracles happen on 34th Street. The other day I saw a young man at the Rockefeller Center ice-rink actually fall on his knees before his partner to press his ring upon her finger: the girl performed an ecstatic pirouette of acceptance, and the crowd fondly applauded.

One evening I was taken to a venerable mid-town club, and was persuaded by a mature and most courtly waiter to sample its celebrated in-house cocktail, which seemed to be something to do with rum and was served in a silver tankard. 'When I was a little boy,' said my host, 'I used to be brought here by my father, and he always let me have one.' How touchingly Old New York, I thought: the kindly Exeter-and-Harvard Daddy, the eager boy in his best suit, the smiling avuncular servants, the happy sense of continuity and complicity – for the boy's mother, I'm sure, would not have approved. Draining my tankard, and unwisely accepting a second, I presently staggered out into 49th Street feeling decidedly sentimental myself (and realizing that, as usual, Mother had been right).

Scarf-wrapped, woolly-hatted, gloved and ear-muffed, all mid-Manhattan becomes rather Old New York at this time of the year – and not least when some appalling weather-front storms out of the ocean. Then the inhabitants of the place become almost Norman Rockwellian in their manners. Of course behind the rosy cheeks and frosted whiskers all the usual malice lies dormant. The pickpocket, we need not doubt, wistfully eyes our handbags. The rapist reluctantly stifles his passions. The intolerable dogmatist harbours her political correctness. The serial killer takes a hold of himself. The racialist smiles companionably enough at the laughing ethnic family, as they all slither together across the frozen intersection, but still secretly wishes the motherfuckers would all go back where they came from. But for the moment the villainies are suppressed. In this Manhattan, I assure you, evil-looking youths really do come to the help of elderly ladies, murmuring improbable mantras like, 'It's a pleasure, ma'am, now you watch how you go . . .'

I have been helping to make a television film here, and those old boots have often been in my mind. As we have stumbled here and there through the snow, lugging our damned equipment from site to site, climbing over frozen fences, explaining ourselves to inquisitive cops, Manhattan has often seemed a homely kind of place – in the English sense of the word. We filmed on a tug in the harbour one bitter squally dawn. The coffee was always on the boil, the assistant engineer was the son of an African king, the deckhand was very entertaining, the captain was infinitely relaxed, and as we nudged the *QE2* into her moorings, apparently almost without thinking about it, I felt myself in the amiable company of all the hundreds of tug-men and pilots who have nudged ships into these quays since Manhattan was born.

We filmed from a helicopter, too, after the pilot had excused himself for a moment to fly off and find some gasoline. We filmed the annual meet of the Central Park Hunt, scrupulously red-coated ladies and gentlemen taking a stirrup-cup at the Inn on the Park ('What do you hunt?' I asked one amiable old cove. 'People, of course,' he cried). We would have filmed in the foyer of the Seagram Building, if it had not been for the cheerful choir of office-workers who were giving a lunchtime concert there.

431

And we filmed in a bus. What homely fun that was! What bonhomie! Only two passengers were unwilling to say something into the camera: the tiny old lady in front of me, who was busy reading the poems of Terence in Latin, and the chalk-faced youth behind, in shades and a woolly cap, who gave me the strong impression that he might be the serial killer I mentioned a few paragraphs back.

There is no affectation to all this. It is true, if temporary. Long ago in New York a friend of mine expounded on American and European varieties of sincerity. The European kind, he theorized, was spontaneous, but did not always run deep. The American kind was embedded under layers of calculation and opportunism, but lay there true and profound beneath. As everyone knows, New Yorkers are Americans only more so, and at desperate moments of winter they cast off the national veneers to reveal the real kindness below. Anyway, even at the worst of times they are spared a particular pretence which has seized most of the rest of the Western world: they do not have to pretend to be Americans. It does not look silly when a New Yorker, white, black, brown or yellow, wears his baseball cap back to front. The New York rock singer sings his lyrics in his own dialect, not in a pastiche of somebody else's, and the slang of the streets is home-grown, fresh from local sources. The mass culture of this city, as of America as a whole, is altogether indigenous.

God knows the Americans have never evolved a single racial identity, as the old melting-pot idea used to envisage, but as to national identity, no problem. Occasionally I do come across a Lebanese, a Haitian or a Jamaican who wants to go home to die, but for the most part, melting-pot or no melting-pot, nearly all the immigrants I meet in New York are very happy to be American. They are eager to adopt all the traditional American attitudes, from working immensely long hours to exploiting the social security system or wearing their baseball caps back to front.

They are not pretending to be Americans. If not in actual citizenship, or even all too often in legal residence, in true Jeffersonian essentials they *are* Americans. No doubt this organic confidence is partly multi-ethnical. America, and especially its dazzling epitome New York, has a hundred different traditions to draw upon, absorbs them all, and makes nearly everyone feel at home. England, Germany, or even perhaps Australia, have not had much time to adjust to the idea of a nation-of-all-the-races; not only are they uncomfortable with their newcomers, they are uncomfortable with themselves. America has been welcoming its tired, poor and huddled masses for centuries and, however awful its racial problems, at least offers a sense of national membership to all.

But it has another great advantage, when it comes to a sense of assurance: the advantage of being a superpower. Power is not only an aphrodisiac, it can be a tranquillizer too. It makes people easy with themselves. Manhattan, the greatest of American cities – the *only* American city for me – does not need to ape any place else or reject any place either. It is altogether itself. It speaks a dozen languages, and they are all its own. In the bounty of its self-esteem, as the snow comes down, it can even make a stranger from a small and distant country feel that this most opulent, terrible, magnificent, demanding, alarming, squalid and spectacular metropolis has all the allure of a pair of old boots.

31

Sydney 1995

My book on Sydney was published in 1992, and later in the decade I returned cautiously to the city, for I had not forgotten its original reactions to my journalism . . .

An acquaintance of mine down here, overhearing an exchange I was enjoying with one of the most formidable of the Sydney media bosses, said it reminded her of a confrontation between a Christian and a gladiator. Which of us was the Christian she did not say, but I can guess – Sydneysiders can be a tough bunch, and none come much tougher than your high-powered, high-tech young business people, well-travelled, highly educated, clever, rich, whose steel so often glints a warning beneath a not very velvet glove.

I tread warily in the presence of these people, suspecting that an argument with one of them might be only a step less perilous than actually being thrown to the lions. Not that they are ever discourteous. They have no need to be. Their strength is of the coiled kind, like a whip held in reserve; just when you think it is about to lash out, it is pre-empted by a smile of wolfish charm, deceiving nobody but undeniably disarming. In fact I know of no city whose people, even the most rapacious of them, are more exuberantly welcoming. They may despise your guts, but they seldom let it sour the panache of their hospitality. Foreigners often say that Sydney reminds them of an older America, before the innocence faded. I think this a misinterpretation. The lost American innocence was founded upon a profoundly simple sense of rightness and permanence, supported by lofty ideals and by a conviction of power. The Sydney attitude, I think, reflects a national identity altogether more fragile.

All the more delightful that even in times of economic difficulty Australia, which has so long liked to think of itself as The Lucky Country, still feels the happiest place of all. Every morning I leave the Regent Hotel before breakfast and take my exercise in the Botanic Gardens, beyond the

434

Opera House gleaming there in the early sun, along the edge of the harbour where the ferries are already foaming past Pinchgut Island to Manly. I speak to nearly everyone I meet. 'What a marvellous day', I throw at them in passing, or more often 'What a marvellous country!' And everyone seems to answer 'Yes!' Not only the stalwart joggers sweating by, and the anglers at the waterfront with their tangles of lines and buckets, and the occasional eccentrics ambling around in comical hats or gum-boots, and the man who practises his trumpet there before the day's work begins, but the very egrets themselves, foraging spindlily under the foliage of the gardens. It is hard to find a Sydneysider who is not fond of his city, and glad to be an Australian.

In this way it *is* like an older America. Your new immigrant here generally seems enviably laid-back and optimistic, as though he has fallen among friends. It is true that he may complain about racism among old-school Australians, but he can generally afford to ignore it, and may indeed indulge in a little racism himself, concerning Abos or Poms. The chances are that he has a thriving ethnic community of his own to support him, speaking his language, sharing his heritage and bolstering in him the conviction that he has chosen the right place to come – no problems, take it easy, sit back and enjoy yourself, as Sydney taxi-drivers sometimes say to me.

During my present stay I have employed taxis six times, and I have kept a record of my drivers. One was born in Beirut, and showed me with pride the long row of Lebanese restaurants we passed. One was a Welshman from Bangor. One defied me to identify his origins, and turned out to be from Ecuador. One I rightly guessed to be from Lahore. One came out here on a £10 subsidized fare from England, and one was a Sydney-born financier, temporarily incommoded by the recession. All were helpful, merry and inquisitive (this is a very inquisitive city), offering me no grumbles and not much caring whether I tipped them or not; while the ex-financier, dropping me off for dinner at a private house, sent his kind regards to my hostess, an old acquaintance of his.

I sense a certain unreality about all this, as though Sydney from the very start has been able to ignore unpalatable truths about itself. Even the earliest settlers, dumped on this inconceivably remote and awful shore in the most cheerless of circumstances, seem somehow to have been jolly enough, when they were not being flogged. Perhaps it is the Cockney strain that makes the citizenry so incorrigibly blithe, or perhaps the inherent improbability of the whole situation, the mere survival of this glittering city on the underside of the globe, makes for a kind of illusory existentialism.

I find myself that after only a few days I am perfectly used to Sydney's unlikely ambience – those recondite birds pecking and squawking about the gardens, the big black fruit-bats that flap out at night, trees which seem to be growing upside-down, bits of wild bush-land which penetrate the genteel suburbs, and are perfectly likely to have koalas and duck-billed platypuses in them. In no time everything seems perfectly normal, all co-existing easily with the life of a modern European city.

I say 'European' advisedly, because the cosmopolitanism of contemporary Sydney is of a decidedly European kind. A century ago James Bryce called Manhattan 'a European city, but of no particular country', and the description now fits Sydney just as well. Of course its sub-stratum is aboriginal, its structure is still British, and like all English-speaking cities it has American overtones. More and more of its citizens are Asians. However, for the moment anyway its superficial flavour seems to me vaguely Mediterranean, Italianate, Greekish, Portuguesy, Lebanese-like – cappuccino after its oysters, street cafés, the lights of fishing boats passing beneath the Harbour Bridge in the dark – tinged, though, with the Irishness that has been so potent a part of it since the beginning.

Sydney never strikes me as a very religious city, but largely because of the Irish, Catholicism is resilient here, and now and then, on a day that might be in the Aegean, to a Neapolitan smell of coffee, over a Provençal kind of meal, one is suddenly jerked back to Dublin or even to Knock. I had such a moment only yesterday, crossing the harbour on the elderly ferry-launch that runs between Blues Point and Circular Quay. A very Irish lady, sitting beside me as the boat chugged crab-like across the water, told me sadly that her car had just been stolen, and deliberately driven over a bluff. Never mind, I said, it was only a thing. 'Only a thing!' Her eyes misted. 'Only a thing! Sure that's the way to look at it. Only a thing! I must look at it that way. God bless you, God bless you for that!' 'God bless you too,' I responded lamely, not knowing, as so often happens in discourse with the Irish, anything better to say.

But that gladiatorial media executive offered me no blessings, nor did I want any from him. It was his hardness I relished, the touch of malevolence behind the charm. Nearly everybody likes modern Sydney, but nobody could call it nice. It is no place for the loser, even now, and if I were a stranger in trouble I would feel more sure of compassion in downtown Manhattan than I would in this fortunate city. Gossip in Sydney is by no means forgiving, still less discreet. Sometimes making dinner conversation can be like riding a roller-coaster, so dizzy are the revelations, and expressed with such ruthless and hilarious gusto.

It is a city that brings out the reckless in me, and this is partly because I always feel it to be in some sense transitory. It never feels built to last. That gossip is particularly ephemeral and kaleidoscopic, and each time I come here the colours have changed, names in the news have shifted, and I am presented with a new cast of 'identities' – Sydney's word for 'personalities'.

Identities! Doesn't it sound like a police-station word? Sydneysiders, once so testily sensitive about the original purpose of their city, are now rather proud of its beginnings, and they will not be resentful when I say that for me one of the fascinations of the place is the feeling I sometimes get – in discourse with one of its more predatory brokers, say, or across the table from some appallingly overpaid and brilliant lawyer – that I am in touch with the irrepressible ebullience of the convicts.

32

Hong Kong: The End

In June 1997 the British relinquished their sovereignty over Hong Kong, and after 150 years handed the colony to the communist People's Republic of China, of which it would in future form a Special Administrative Region. This was in effect the end of the British Empire, and I was invited by the London Evening Standard *to describe the concluding imperial ceremonial. It was my final exercise in reportage.*

The very moment they struck up 'God Save The Queen' at the British farewell ceremony in Hong Kong last night, the heavens opened and we all got soaked through. It did not matter. Soothsayers may say it was a bad omen, but the British took it on the chin. Down came the rain, the stands were a mass of umbrellas, water trickled down our necks, but the soldiers marched bravely on, the pipers piped, the singers sang, and Prince Charles, in his admiral's white uniform, made his speech without a flinch as the rain poured all over him.

The farewell programme was a mixture of show-biz and Aldershot, predictably offering Andrew Lloyd Webber, 'The Last Rose Of Summer', 'Scotland The Brave', a bit of Elgar and 'I'll See You Again'. As a Welsh nationalist republican I thought I had grown out of such flummery but I cannot deny an atavistic tug of the heart when, in the gathering dusk and the relentless rain, the Union Jack came gently down from its high flagpole to the grand old strain of 'The Day Thou Gavest, Lord, Is Ended'. Grant it them – nobody does it quite like the British. Nobody else has the swagger of the gloriously gilded drum-major who led last night's parade. Nobody can play a lament quite like the lone piper who ended the ceremony. I would have had to wipe away a tear were it not that my face was awash with rain.

For me the best and bravest part of the whole evening, all the same, was a noble performance by the massed bands of Beethoven's 'Ode to Joy'. I doubt if they all knew they were playing the national anthem of the European Union, but I accepted it anyway as a gesture of liberation. Freed at last from their historical burdens of imperial tradition, the British must surely now move towards the next fulfilment of their astonishing historical destiny – final reconciliation with the rest of Europe.

For them as for the Chinese, their departure from Hong Kong represents both an end and a fresh start. When the Union Jack came down the dignitaries moved on to the Convention Centre along the harbour shore, where the Chinese were about to assume authority over the Special Administrative Region. I, on the other hand, squelched back through the streets to my hotel on the opposite shore of the harbour. As I struggled through the immense excited crowds, illuminated by neon signs, noisy, laughing, merry, very wet and universally good-tempered, £325,000-worth of British-sponsored fireworks thundered into the sky. Up to my hotel bedroom then, open the curtains, and there before me was the harbour of Hong Kong, and at its heart the great glassy Convention Centre where at that moment diplomats and dignitaries from half the world were finishing a banquet, toasting the Queen and the President of China and preparing to move on at midnight to the official conclusion of British sovereignty in Hong Kong.

This city is one great television set, and every screen in town was showing the scene. Every now and then I looked at mine, and it was a bewildering experience. Now we saw the yacht *Britannia*, waiting to take Prince Charles away when the ceremony was done. Now we saw the banqueters raising their champagne glasses. Faces strange and familiar succeeded one another in flashes – Deng Xiaoping's widow, the Foreign Minister of Indonesia, the President of Colombia, Kofi Annan, Lady Thatcher, Richard Branson, Ted Heath, the Argentinian Foreign Minister, Chris Patten, Prince Charlie and all.

A cut between cameras, and here was the advance guard of the People's Liberation Army, crossing the border from China rigid as automatons in their buses and open trucks. Another cut, and it was Martin Lee the chief Democrat promising loyal opposition from the balcony of the Legislative Council building. Protests, troops, diplomats, champagne, Deng Xiaoping's widow; all Hong Kong life was there, flickering on one or another of the thirty-two channels. But I spent most of the time till midnight drinking red wine, playing Wagner on the stereo and looking out of my window. There lay the marvellous city, awaiting the moment. Interminable crowds milled about the streets below. The incomparable skyline was ablaze. The sky was angry with storm clouds, reddened by the city lights, and all about the harbour the lights of police boats were winking, keeping the water-traffic away from the Convention building. What were the people of Hong Kong really thinking down there? Were they as happy as they appeared to be? Should we have doubts, in these last few minutes between the British goodbyes and the Chinese acceptance?

It seemed to me, as I thought about it then, that the Hong Kong the British were leaving behind them was neither quite as good as the place might be, nor quite as bad. Economically, re-unification seemed to be, if anything, a shot in the arm. Socially the territory was free and mostly fair. But it was the political condition of the place that history would chiefly remember, and this was rather better than we feared it might be when Hong Kong was handed over, but rather worse than we hoped. On the one hand in a few moments the democratic structure so carefully put together during the last years of British rule was to be rudely dismantled in a few minutes. On the other hand there would remain a seed-core of libertarian instinct and purpose, a practised political society which will still form an able and determined opposition.

And then, I thought – but hang on, it was very nearly midnight, and Hans Sachs of *Der Meistersinger* was on his last triumphant aria – empires might dissolve in mist, holy art would remain! Across the harbour the Convention Centre now seemed to be glowing rather than blazing, like a reactor. On the television screens, more speeches, more bands, more stamping honour guards until, on the stroke of midnight, we saw the Union Jack come down in Hong Kong for the very last time, and the flag of China go up for the very first.

Car horns sounded through my windows, and a great cheering too, and down below the people still meandered in their thousands here and there. And presently, out there in the night, I saw the yacht *Britannia*, with its guardship HMS *Chatham* and the last three small warships of the Royal Navy's Hong Kong flotilla, steal away from the quayside and sail slowly off to sea, slipping away beneath the skyscrapers with a certain glory after all.

The British had gone.

Whether the Special Administrative Region of Hong Kong will preserve its liberties is still, as I write, open to question, but anyway that night's vision of departing grandeur represented for me not only my final exercise in reportage, and the end of a lifetime's preoccupation, but the conclusion of my own half-century.

It signalled the end too of the incessant wanderings around the world that have provided the material for this book. I enjoyed almost every minute of these journeys – to be travelling alone on a job, all my antennae out, thinking about nothing but the work in hand, seemed to me one of life's greatest pleasures. It did not always appear so to others. Visiting the Isle of Man, in the Irish Sea, to write an essay about it, I sat down at a café table beside a glistening bay with a plate of prawns, half a pint of Guinness and a book I had just bought about Manx folklore. I was in very heaven! Presently a lady handed me a pamphlet. Oh thank you, said I, what's it about? 'It is only to reassure you, my dear,' she emolliently told me, 'that God is always with the lonely . . .'

Epilogue: Fulfilling a Long-Needed Want

So my half-century came to an end. It took me far from home for the greater part of my life, treading 'the shiny track', as Robert Musil once put it, 'that is left by the snail of history'; so it is perhaps only proper that its epilogue should concern a small happening in my own minute corner of the world.

One drizzly morning in the summer of 2001, not long before my 75th birthday, I went to a political meeting at a village in the Llŷn Peninsula, at the top left corner of Wales, which is a legendary stronghold of Welshness. Several hundred people had assembled there to express their dismay at the whittling away of the Welsh culture and language by the influx of English settlers into their country.

This was not a new anxiety. For a thousand years Welsh patriots had been resenting the intrusion of the English, sometimes violently. It seemed to me, though, that this meeting expressed something more profound. They were not hell-for-leather young nationalists who packed the village hall, and crowded outside listening to the speeches over loudspeakers. They were sober, courteous Welsh country people, of all ages, who sensed that their ancient way of life was in terminal crisis. Sadly and seriously they listened, and I felt they instinctively knew that their heritage was threatened not just by the flood of English retirees and second-homers, but by infinitely greater alien influences looming behind: huge, inchoate, almost unimaginable forces of finance, technology, globalization, homogenization, which were pressing down on them and beginning to make them no longer themselves.

It seemed to me that this infinitesimal event, away up there on the fringe of Europe, concerning a language and a culture that most of the world has never heard of, marked more by disturbed foreboding than by any vehemence, was a symptom of a hazy malaise that was shadowing the new world of the twenty-first century. I had known where I was in my world, my fifty years of the century before. Heaven knows there had been

442

horrors, squalors and miseries enough, from Cold War to Aids – when aren't there? – but on the whole it had seemed to me a relatively straight-forward time, a time of some promise. In fact I used to like to fancy, as I wandered the planet in my twentieth-century prime, that there was coming into existence a sort of Fourth World, a nation beyond frontiers, a diaspora and freemasonry of the decent whose values would one day emerge supreme.

Those villagers of Llŷn were certainly potential citizens of any such nation of goodwill, but it did not seem, that damp July summer morning in 2001, that they were about to inherit the earth. On the contrary, their anxious arguments, their intimations of despair, made me feel that at the start of the new century my own hopeful zeitgeist had faded, as spirits do: and accordingly soon afterwards I set out to circumnavigate the world one last time in search of its successor.

Almost at once, in St Petersburg in Russia, I met a former colonel of the Red Air Force living alone in a comfortless flat (bed unmade, crockery unwashed) in an apparently deserted and half-derelict tenement block. He seemed to me like a man floundering. The lost Soviet empire of the twentieth century, he told me, had been the rock of his life. He had come up the hard way, from the red bandanas of the Young Pioneers to the ridiculous floppy caps and huge epaulettes of the Red Air Force, and he had gone down the hard way too, abruptly from the absolute conviction of national mastery and privilege to the unmade bed high above the desolate courtyard. He was left wondering what it had all been about.

He was an archetype, I presently realized. Everywhere people were similarly disturbed, with the same sense of rudderless betrayal. There was something febrile in the air of the world, like the start of a fever. There was something threatening and unwholesome about the emergence of the United States as a power that could do anything it liked. There was some-thing ominous about science, which seemed to be tinkering with matters almost occult in their significance – it would not be long, an Egyptian student seriously assured me, before mankind mastered the creation of life itself. There was something creepy to the Internet, an ectoplasmic presence seeping into private homes.

'What are men for?' a man said to me in Trieste. 'Tell me that – what are we for?' He was bewildered by the mighty changes in relationship between men and women, leaving him as unsure about his new status as many women were about theirs. 'Sure I'm a Christian,' a woman at a café table in

443

San Francisco assured me, 'but, I don't know, I can't believe in all that Jesus stuff any more.' She was recognizing in herself, half-way through life, the desolating loss of innocence. 'What's happened to the frogs?' a child asked me in England. She was already observing, so early in life, the universal degradation of nature.

The intermingling of peoples around the world, which had once seemed so happy a portent, was beginning to feel an oppression. In Hawaii I was told that you could park a canoe on a beach only if you could prove that your ancestors had lived in the island for more than a century, and when I arrived in Australia they had just turned away 450 Asian refugees who had been rescued from a sinking ship – 'the people have had enough', wrote Mr A. Prizibilla (*sic*) to the *Sydney Daily Telegraph*, 'Australia is not a dumping ground for depressed citizens of the world.' And disorienting the spirit of the new age most elementally was the baffling gulf, growing every minute of every day, between the rich and the poor, the well-fed and the hungry – between those who had plenty, and expected to have more, and those who had almost nothing, and could expect nothing better.

We were all mixed up, I came to think as I travelled on, all unsure, and it sometimes occurred to me that the condition was even blurring our thought at the edges, and making our very speech more imprecise. Somebody in America told me of a recent review he had read of a television series. 'This series', it said, 'fulfils a long needed want' – and it took me several moments, I confess, before I realized that while the syntax was OK, the sense was decidedly uncertain.

The lingering reproaches of imperialism, the mysteries of technology, the antipathies of race, shifts of balance, bewilderments of progress, corrosions of money and power – all, it seemed to me, were reaching some kind of dark climax. For years I had sneered at the old stiffs and farts who had been assuring us, down the generations, that the world was going to pot. Now at last I began to fear that they might have been right all along. It was not a rush towards apocalypse that I sensed, more a welter of discrete and contradictory forces throwing us about, tossing us here and there, rather as we are sometimes told the universe itself was whirled into existence out of a bouillabaisse of floating gases.

As I get old I realize more clearly than ever that to the ultimate question – what's it all about? – there is not, and never will be, an answer. The truest and most brilliant brains down the centuries have fudged the issue with their various species of mumbo-jumbo, from High Mass at St Peter's to witch-doctors' prancing spells. The best we can do, I have come to think, is to ignore the conundrum, as we move from one age to another, and to my mind there need be only one commandment to help us cope: *Be Kind*. This plain injunction embraces the highest teachings of all the religions. Flexible enough to allow for free will and human frailty, it is, at the core of it, solid as granite – firm as St Peter's rock, mysterious as the Black Stone of the Kaaba, simple as Stonehenge, organic as the Buddha's Bodhi Tree, authoritative as any Mosaic law.

Yes, I thought to myself as I ended my journey and boarded the last flight home, kindness is the one principle that can see us through, a rule of life so straightforward that we all know what it means, and need no theologians to explain it for us. Contemplating this simple discipline, I remembered the confused colonel of St Petersburg, the Cairo student, the canoe-owners of Hawaii, Mr Prizibilla, the disillusioned Triestino, the vanished frogs, the lost faiths and the worried villagers of Llŷn so close to home; and imagining how a universal devotion to kindness might have comforted all their anxieties, thoughtfully I returned to Wales on 10 September 2001.

The very next day, far away in dear old Manhattan, the next zeitgeist declared itself.

TREFAN MORYS, 2003

Index